Cultural Struggles

Cultural Struggles

Performance, Ethnography, Praxis

Dwight Conquergood

Edited and with a critical introduction by E. Patrick Johnson

THE UNIVERSITY OF MICHIGAN PRESS
Ann Arbor

Published in the United States of America by
The University of Michigan Press
Manufactured in the United States of America
♾ Printed on acid-free paper

2016 2015 2014 2013 4 3 2 1

A CIP catalog record for this book is available from the British Library.

All royalties from this publication are being donated to the Dwight Conquergood Award for Teaching Excellence Fund at Northwestern University.

ISBN 978-0-472-07195-1 (cloth : alk. paper)
ISBN 978-0-472-05195-3 (pbk. : alk. paper)
ISBN 978-0-472-02929-7 (e-book)

Acknowledgments

This book has been a long time in the making. Dwight had actually been working on two manuscripts and charged me with making sure that at least one of them saw the light of day after his passing. I could not have made that happen, however, without the commitment from LeAnn Fields at the University of Michigan Press. LeAnn's gentle persistence over the years to get me to cull Dwight's essays into a manuscript made all of the difference in the world and kept enough pressure on me to make sure it happened.

I want to thank my two wonderful research assistants, Jasmine Mahmoud, who worked tirelessly to convert the essays from one format to another and helped me in so many other ways to prepare the manuscript, and Margaret Lebron, who helped to prepare the index. To my colleagues Micaela di Leonardo, Judith Hamera, Shannon Jackson, D. Soyini Madison, Lisa Merrill, Della Pollock, and Joseph Roach—thank you for not hesitating to write essays for the volume. Your love and respect for Dwight shines through every word of your contributions.

Thanks to the Northwestern University Library archives for organizing all of Dwight's papers. It is an invaluable resource to scholars around the world and made this book possible.

Finally, thank you, Dwight, for leaving us the wonderful gift of your work.

Some of the essays in this book have appeared in other publications: "Performing Cultures: Ethnography, Epistemology, and Ethics" originally appeared in *Miteinander Sprechen und Handeln: Festschrift fur Hellmut Geissner*, ed. Edith Slembek (Scriptor, 1986); "Of Caravans and Carnivals: Performance Studies in Motion" originally appeared in *TDR*, Winter 39.4 (1995); "Beyond the Text: Toward a Performative Cultural Politics" originally appeared in *The Future of Performance Studies: Visions and Revisions*, ed. Sheron J. Dailey (National Communication Association, 1998); "Performance Studies: Interventions and Radical Research" originally appeared in *TDR*, Summer 46.2 (2002); "Performing as a Moral Act: Ethical Dimensions of the Ethnography of Performance" originally appeared in *Literature in Performance* 5 (April 1985); "Rethinking Ethnography: Towards a Critical Cultural Politics" originally appeared in *Communication Monographs* 58 (June 1985); "Rethinking Elocution: The Trope of the Talking Book and Other Figures of Speech" originally appeared in *Text and Performance Quarterly* 20.4 (October 2000); "Health Theatre in a Hmong Refugee Camp: Performance, Communication and Culture" originally appeared in *TDR* 32.3 (Fall 1988); "Life in Big Red: Struggles and Accommodations in a Chicago Polyethnic Tenement" originally appeared in *Structuring Diversity: Ethnographic Perspectives on the New Immigration*, ed. Louise Lamphere (University of Chicago Press, 1992); "Homeboys and Hoods: Gang Communication and Cultural Space" originally appeared in *Group Communication in Context: Studies of Natural Group*, ed. Lawrence R. Frey (Erlbaum, 1994); "Lethal Theatre: Performance, Punishment and the Death Penalty" originally appeared in *Theatre Journal* 54.3.17 (Fall 2002); "Caravans Continued" by Shannon Jackson originally appeared in *TDR* 50:1 (Spring 2006), and is reprinted here with permission of *TDR* and MIT Press; a portion of "Dwight Conquergood and Performative Political Economy," by Micaela di Leonardo originally appeared in *Cultural Studies* 21:6 (November 2007), and is reprinted here with permission of *Cultural Studies* and Taylor and Francis.

Contents

IV Critical Responses

Introduction
"Opening and Interpreting Lives"

E. Patrick Johnson

Most institutions of higher learning prioritize three areas in which its faculty must excel: research, teaching, and service. These three areas are often the sites where administrations make faculty accountable at the time of tenure and promotion. Rarely, however, do any of us excel in all three without making some kind of personal sacrifice or succumbing to burnout. Before tenure, teaching might suffer so that we can work on a book manuscript or produce a string of "paradigm shifting" articles. After tenure, the research may wane due to being overextended on committees. The road to full professor may take yet another toll on our teaching as we work on the second or third book manuscript. Whatever the case, ours is a constant negotiation of priorities and balancing acts in which we aspire to be good citizens of the academy. I know of no other person who excelled at all three as adeptly and gracefully as Dwight Conquergood. His life and his legacy stand as academic benchmarks.

Lorne Dwight Conquergood was born in 1949, one of five children, to the late Daniel Conquergood and Dorothea Conquergood in Thunder Bay, Ontario. At a very early age his family moved to rural Indiana and lived on a farm. It was during his formative years as a farmhand alongside his father, with whom he was very close, that Dwight's sense of social responsibility and the valuation of life began to emerge. "I hated when it was time to kill the animals," he once told me. "I became very attached to them and I would be depressed for days after they were slaughtered. I was inconsolable." Thus, from an early age he was committed to the conditions of the disenfranchised and dedicated himself to a life of advocacy. Undoubtedly, his working-class background and modest upbringing impacted his intellectual interests as well.

Not wanting to travel too far from his family for college, Dwight attended Indiana State University in Terre Haute. There he double-majored in Speech Communication and English, which not only would prove to be instrumental in his effectiveness as a skilled rhetorician but also helped him become an adept writer who cared almost as much about how a message was communicated as about the message itself. He went on to receive a master's degree in Communication in 1972 at the University of Utah where he worked under the tutelage of Mary Strine, a fierce theorist in her own right who encouraged Dwight to pursue a PhD. After looking at several programs, he decided to apply to and was accepted into Northwestern's Department of Interpretation (now Performance Studies) and worked with Wallace Bacon, a Shakespeare scholar trained at the University of Michigan who founded that department at Northwestern in the early 1940s. Landing at Northwestern was a boon for Dwight. The department was a part of the School of Speech, which housed four other departments—Radio, Television, and Film; Theater; Communication Studies; and Communication Sciences and Disorders. This unique combination of related disciplines proved instrumental in Dwight's own intellectual development as an interdisciplinary thinker. His work in the departments of Communication Studies, renowned for producing some of the best scholarship in historical rhetoric and oratory, and Radio, Television, and Film, which had a very strong production emphasis, provided Dwight the skills to hone his rhetorical chops and gave him the basic tools for film production.

Undoubtedly, it will come as a surprise to many to know that Conquergood's dissertation topic was the use of the boast in *Beowulf*. But, as Joseph Roach notes in his essay in this volume, for those who read his later published work his beginnings as a medievalist was critical to Dwight's careful attention to the "voice" of others—and his own. It was also in the graduate program at Northwestern that he began to understand more fully the triumvirate of theory, method, and practice because it was fully a part of the departmental culture. Indeed, it was during this period that Robert Breen developed "Chamber Theater," a theory of how to adapt narrative for the stage, and also that Wallace Bacon published articles about the "sense of the other" through the performance of literature. Intellectual promiscuity was Dwight's trademark, and this hotbed of creative and theoretical energy was just the kind of environment for him to forge his own critical voice—and he did so with abandon.

After graduating from Northwestern in 1977, his first job was as an assistant professor of English at SUNY-Binghamton, where he stayed for just a year before being hired back at Northwestern in the department where he was trained. It was a fortuitous move—for him and for the department—because it is where he would launch a career that would change the department and the field forever.

I met Dwight Conquergood in the spring of 1990 during my first year of graduate school at the University of North Carolina at Chapel Hill. My thesis adviser, D. Soyini Madison, one of Dwight's advisees, invited him to campus to screen his documentary, "The Heart Broken in Half," an ethnographic film about the life of the Latin King street gang in Chicago. Soyini designated me as Dwight's host until she was done teaching that day and asked me to pick him up at the airport. I remember being so excited to meet *the* Dwight Conquergood, the scholar who had done all of this courageous work with street gangs and who had become an advocate on their behalf. As I peered through the crowd at baggage claim, I did not expect to find the short, salt-and-pepper-headed, timid-looking man that was Dwight. "How on earth," I thought, "did *this* man befriend street gangs?" After a long and engaging lunch with him, I came to understand how. Behind that mild-mannered smile, easygoing demeanor, and gentle spirit was a fierce intellectual and an even fiercer ethnographer and activist.

Some nine years after our first face-to-face encounter, Dwight chaired the search committee that hired me as an assistant professor of performance studies at Northwestern. As a junior scholar it was an honor and a privilege to be mentored by such a giant in the field. While I, like so many others outside Northwestern, knew his work, I had never been afforded the opportunity to experience Dwight up close to do some "deep hanging out," as he often called field research. Up close, I became aware of just how committed he was to integrating theory and practice, and of the high ethical, political, intellectual, and moral standards to which he held not only others but also himself. Indeed, Dwight was his own worst critic and spent hours and hours poring over every single word of anything he published or any presentation he was about to make. He also had a penchant for working himself to exhaustion, often spending the night in his office or risking his life in the service of others. His hard work was matched by serious play, especially if it involved gossip—which he often referred to as "the poor man's truth"—or food because he loved to cook for and break bread with people as a part of community building.

In the summer of 2002 Dwight was diagnosed with stage-four colon and liver cancer and was told he had a few months to live at most. As expected by those who knew him, Dwight defied the doctors' prognosis and continued to teach and conduct research for another fourteen months. Indeed, just two months after undergoing surgery he delivered the Carrol C. Arnold Distinguished Lecture at the annual meeting of the National Communication Association in New Orleans to a standing-room-only audience. The topic of his lecture was the death penalty, to which he was adamantly opposed and about which he had just published an award-winning essay, collected in this volume.

Outside the academy he demonstrated his commitment to breaking the theory/practice binary by becoming active on boards and in institutions that served the communities in which he did research. From his extensive ethnographic research in refugee camps in Thailand and the Gaza Strip, as well as in new immigrant neighborhoods in Chicago, emerged a sense of social obligation to serve as ambassador for human rights. For example, he acted as consultant on intercultural projects for the International Rescue Committee; the Office of the Illinois Appellate Defender; the State of Minnesota, Department of Human Services, Refugee Program; the State of Wisconsin, Department of Health and Social Services; the Indiana Public Defenders Council; and the Chicago Human Relations Foundation. He also taught at the Bryan Schachmeister Death Penalty College, School of Law, Santa Clara University, cosponsored by the American Bar Association, and served as consultant for the Institute on the Arts and Civic Dialogue at Harvard University.

Conquergood the fierce theorist, ethnographer, and performer did not overshadow Conquergood the exemplary teacher. Students across generations have testified that his teaching changed their lives and that his gentle and gracious spirit was matched only by his high standards of excellence. It was often a treat for colleagues from other departments who sat on performance studies students' qualifying exams and dissertation committees—and for me—to watch him in action at the oral defense meetings. In the midst of "tempering justice with mercy," as he often said, his engagement with the students always stretched their thinking and pushed them to reflect more critically on their projects. My colleagues and I often took as many notes as the students and were often spellbound by his encyclopedic and bibliographic brilliance. Even during his final days in hospice care, he was advising students, lecturing one of his advisees about the politics of footnoting! Unsurprisingly, he won several teaching awards, including the 1993 State of Illinois Professor of the Year, awarded by the Council for the Advancement and Support of Education (CASE), Washington, DC, and the Charles Deering McCormick Professorship of Teaching Excellence at Northwestern, the highest award bestowed upon a faculty member for teaching at the university.

In his teaching statement for the McCormick Professorship nomination, Conquergood articulates how he infused his commitment to theory and practice in his teaching.

> The overarching goal in all my classes is to promote a vigorous exchange between critical reflection and creative practice.

> Whereas analytical interpretation and artistic creativity often are segregated in the academy (liberal arts/fine arts), I try to unpin these thinking/doing, interpreting/making, theory/practice oppositions and help students appreciate the productive dialectical tension between ideas and action. Theory is enlivened and most vigorously tested when it hits the ground in practice. Likewise, artistic practice can be deepened, complicated, and challenged in meaningful ways by engaging critical theory.
>
> Although my courses have a reputation for being demanding and intense, I try to mitigate the pressure by giving careful attention to the creation of a classroom community. I find that students can be challenged to their highest potential if the classroom is a safe and supportive space. Both performance and field research are public, embodied, vulnerable, and risky ventures; therefore, it is all the more imperative for the teacher to set the tone and create a classroom environment that is more communal than competitive. I signal on all my syllabi the importance and value of creating "a performance community," "a community of fellow fieldworkers," and I follow up with exercises/workshops that simultaneously facilitate group interaction and advance one of the issues of the course. And, I do simple things like arranging for the class to share food together.

From his own teaching philosophy we gain insight into how important training students to break down false binaries in their own critical and creative work was to him and, like the work he did in the various field sites, how he worked to make his classroom a collaborative community. It is no wonder, then, that many of his advisees, of which there were over forty, have gone on to become influential in the field, often picking up where Conquergood left off in terms of arguing for and demonstrating the connections among theory, method, and practice.

Before his untimely death in November 2004, Dwight Conquergood had amassed an enormous body of scholarly and artistic work. In addition to a series of paradigm-shifting essays, he created two documentaries and curated several performance events. His one remaining goal, however, was to publish a monograph. Knowing that he would not likely meet that goal before he made his transition, he summoned me to his bedside while in hospice care and informed me—*he did not ask*—that I would be his literary executor and that I should make sure his work was brought together in a book. Like an obedient student I promised him that I would.

Cultural Struggles: Performance, Ethnography, Praxis is a collection of

Dwight Conquergood's essays authored over a twenty-year period. The title reflects not only what he saw as the contested site of culture but also the disciplinary and methodological debates that arose during the "culture wars" of the 1980s and that his own publications were partly responsible for generating. The subtitle stems from Conquergood's interests in generating theories about performance studies and its relationship to ethnography; critiquing and developing methodologies to enact these theories; and, actually deploying theory and method in field research. Thus, the essays not only reflect his thinking about these disciplinary and methodological concerns but also provide foundational examples of how theory and method work in tandem within field research. Below, I outline three nodes of Conquergood's writing: performance ethnography as theory, performance as method, and performance ethnography as praxis.

Performance Ethnography as Theory

From the early years of his career, Dwight Conquergood was invested in legitimating performance studies as an intellectually rigorous, morally sound, and ethically engaged field of study. Alongside his commitment to legitimating performance studies to naysayers outside the field, he was also committed to changing the field from within. In fact, some of his early essays theorizing performance developed from conference papers he delivered at the American Theatre for Higher Education (ATHE), National Communication Association (NCA), and Performance Studies international (PSi) conferences. His craft as an orator coupled with his precise and often arresting critiques of conservative and positivist scholarship drew standing-room-only crowds to his presentations. Indeed, his scholarship was integral to the gradual paradigm shift from "Interpretation Studies" to "Performance Studies," in the early 1980s within the National Communication Association (formerly Speech Communication Association). He advocated envisioning performance as a "border" discipline that rigorously challenges positivism, expands the meaning of texts, and privileges embodied research. In his last publication in *The Drama Review* (*TDR*), "Performance Studies: Interventions and Radical Research," he solidified his critique of the theory/practice split, arguing that performance studies "struggles to open the space between analysis and action, and to pull the pin on the binary opposition between theory and practice" (145). Ultimately, Conquergood was committed to holding all stakeholders accountable: academic disciplines in the hard and social sciences whose empirical methods often led to the dismissal of performance as unscientific, anti-intellectual or invalid as a discipline altogether; and, performance and theater scholars who focused too narrowly on written texts as source material for performance in lieu of validating and considering oral culture as performance to be an alternative site of knowledge. These theoretical interventions were important to Conquergood because they laid the groundwork for him to discuss methodology.

Performance as Method

Heavily influenced by theories and methods in cultural anthropology, especially the work of Victor Turner, Conquergood believed the best way to understand how people made meaning of their lives and how they resisted oppression was to study how they performed their identities and how those performances spoke back to structural forms of power. In this regard, there are three interrelated themes that work their way through Conquergood's writing on methodology. First, he is interested in macro-structures of political economy. More specifically, he is invested in how macro-structures impinge on micro-textures of subjugated peoples' experience and how individuals caught within forbidding structures struggle for agency and resist. Second, he is invested in performance as a lens for examining culture, particularly the communication practices of subaltern groups—the power of symbols and imagination in both consolidating and contesting oppression and how cultural creativity and human agency are both inscribed and incited by domination. Finally, he is invested in the politics of location. For Conquergood location does not refer to a circumscribed site, but rather how bodies and meanings travel through various routes, diaspora, and displacement. Performance, then, is the most apt method for accounting for location as an itinerary as opposed to a prescribed place. His thinking here is in keeping with his commitment to the interplay between grand theory and grounded theory. The quotidian, everyday practices from a *body* below rather than from an abstract theory above guides his theorization of performative ethnographic methods.

Conquergood's work was more than appropriative of anthropological theories and methods, however, and became a corrective of them through his employment of performance. Framing ethnographic field research as performance, according to Conquergood, has everything to do with conceptual frameworks and methodological commitments, and vice versa. His intervention in how anthropologists employ ethnographic methods, then, centers on how the ethnographer herself is implicated in the research on the Other and how the Others' performances of self for the researcher complicate how the researched are represented. He believed, and rightly so, that cultural groups do not wait for outside ethnographers to come along and document and write them into existence. They are quite capable of preserving their histories in the performance of memory, story, and ritual.

Out of this line of reasoning came Conquergood's concept of "dialogic performance," which draws on Russian literary theorist Mikhail Bakhtin's notion of dialogue in which texts mutually inform each other over time and space. Conquergood used dialogic performance to focus on issues of embodiment and the body itself as sources and sites of meaning in ethnographic field research and as a way to privilege performance as a legitimate and *ethical* method. A part of dialogic performance as a method is the recognition of the ethnographic encounter as unavoidably entrenched in the politics of representation. Both the researcher and the researched are implicated in the meaning-making process. Within this frame Conquergood stresses the importance of self-reflexivity on the part of the ethnographer such that he or she accounts for the circumstances under which the research is conducted, the knowledge produced, and the influence he or she has on the Other in the ethnographic moment.

With his 1990 documentary film on Chicago street gangs, *Heart Broken in Half,* Conquergood practices his dialogic/reflexive approach as he turns the camera over to his informants in the making of the film to allow them to focus on what's important about their culture and how to interpret their signs and symbols; he also shares the filmic frame and narration alongside them. Ever careful not to romanticize any of his theoretical concepts, Conquergood in this film demonstrates his constant search for a politically responsible reflexivity, to not "disappear" from the ethnographic frame—rhetorically or corporeally. But he also strives to be reflexive in ways that are political rather than narcissistic, such that the personal poetics don't replace the political and moral ethics of personal accountability. He first theorizes the notion of dialogic performance in his essay "Performing as a Moral Act: Ethical Dimensions of the Ethnography of Performance," an essay that is required reading not only in performance studies and theater, but also in communication methods courses around the country. Published in 1985 in what was then the journal *Literature in Performance* (now *Text and Performance Quarterly*), a quarter of a century later this essay has stood the test of time, representing a watershed moment in legitimating performance as an important method of analysis for human behavior.

As is the case with most influential thinkers, Conquergood began to rethink his own theorizations over time and moved from the concept of "dialogue" to that of "co-performative witnessing" to better encapsulate the power differential between the researcher and the researched. For Conquergood, "dialogue" was ultimately too thin a trope to consider the complicated and contested dynamic between the performance ethnographer and the ethnographic subject. In his essay "Rethinking Ethnography: Towards a Critical Cultural Politics," Conquergood's shift away from dialogue to co-performance emerges for the first time in his writing: "The power dynamic of the research situation changes when the ethnographer moves from the gaze of the distanced and detached observer to the intimate involvement and engagement of 'co-activity' or co-performance with historically situated, named, 'unique individuals'" (187–88). He would continue to develop the notion of co-performative witnessing over the next decade, but not crystallize it until 2002 with the publication of "Lethal Theatre: Performance, Punishment, and the Death Penalty," an essay that represents his ongoing interest in performance, criminality, and the death penalty. This particular essay, like "Performing as a Moral Act," has become a classic because it brings to the field for the first time—much in the same way that Foucault's elaboration of Bentham's concept of the panopticon changed the way we theorize the hegemony of surveillance—a way to discuss the *dramaturgical* aspects of state-sanctioned punishment.

Performance Ethnography as Praxis

All of Conquergood's theorizing about performance and method culminates in his ethnographic case studies. The notion of the armchair theorist was anathema to who he was as a scholar and an activist. Indeed, critical praxis was the ultimate goal of his research, for more than anything, the liberation of people on the margins of society was forever in the forefront of his agenda. Co-performing with Laotian refugees in Thailand and in the Asian diaspora, Palestinian refugees in the Gaza Strip, Chicago street gangs, and convicted felons on death row, Conquergood's studies explicitly engage subjugated knowledges, as he considered the performative practices of non-whites, the working class, immigrants, refugees, exiles, outcasts, women, and street youth worthy of scholarly attention. Conducting research on and with these groups was his way of "studying up," allowing the on-the-ground embodied practices of subaltern groups to generate their own theories of selfhood and resistance. The dispersed locations of these studies—a Chicago tenement building, Thailand refugee camp, the Gaza Strip, prisons—are situated at the intersection of geopolitics and local development, and demonstrate that where one lives shapes perception and the discourse that one inhabits. Conquergood does a careful ethnographic examination of each of these contested and contesting sites and how each is caught in the crosscurrent of conflictual communications. Each site produces and is produced by contentious interpretations and is entangled in a web of contested representation, knowledges, and meanings.

Emblematic of these case studies is his research in a Chicago tenement nicknamed "Big Red" by longtime residents of the Albany Park neighborhood in northwest Chicago. The apartment building was the home of members of street gangs, ethnic immigrants, refugees, and the working poor. For Conquergood, Albany Park in general and "Big Red" in particular were symptomatic of systemic and structural issucs around local redevelopment, geopolitics, the criminal justice system, and the cleavages among working-class and ethnic minorities. While local media and government representation undergirded the portrayal of this Chicago neighborhood as "Little Beirut," Conquergood understood that below the surface of such characterizations was a much more complex dynamic at work that could only be understood from the perspective of those who lived in and felt the consequences of the existence of Big Red. He also understood that to capture this dynamic would require more than a journalistic account. Performance ethnography was key to grappling with these questions that would link material conditions and metaphorical meanings. Following in the steps of Zora Neale Hurston, whom he considered to be the foremother of performance ethnography, Conquergood knew that in order to *know* there, he had to *go* there to do some "deep hanging out." As Judith Hamera's essay in this volume implies about the body in ethnographic research, Conquergood moved into Big Red not merely to make the residents the objects of academic study but to understand through his own body the pressures of living under siege. In his field notes on Big Red he writes, "From inside my apartment I hear gunfire on the average of three nights a week—every weekend, and usually at least one of the weeknights. That is not counting what I sleep through and neighbors tell me about the following morning. 'Did you hear those shots last night?' functions as conversational currency among neighbors." His riveting account of life in Big Red is not that of a sensationalist academic or liberal martyr pandering to other well-intentioned academics who are nonetheless implicated in neoliberal discourses and policies. On the contrary, his motivations for moving into Big Red had to do with his life's work of using his academic credentials as a *tactic* to undermine structures of power and advocate for those who did not have access to the same kind of power to employ in their own defense.

At the same time, as co-performer, standing shoulder to shoulder in the hallway discussing the gunshots heard throughout the night, the lack of hot water in the building, the cockroach infestation, and the host of other less than ideal living conditions in the community, he wanted to understand these residents' everyday symbols, communication practices, and performances that were simultaneously in collusion with and resistant to power. Aligned with the feminist approach of Margery Wolf, Conquergood knew that "the field experience does not produce a mysterious empowerment, but without it, the ethnographer would not encounter the context—the smells, sounds, sights, emotional tensions, feel—of the culture she will attempt to evoke in a written text."[1] Making Big Red his personal home was a way to inhabit the felt-sensing context of the other's personal space. He reconceptualized fieldwork as "homework" to connect the "being there" (field research) with "being here" (homework), to collapse the two sites, or at least bring them together into productive tension. He also made a home in the academy, which afforded him privileges not experienced by the residents of Big Red. His "homeplace" then, was betwixt and between material and symbolic power, concrete place and cultural space, socioeconomic forces and symbols, the stoop and the podium, a liminal space that allowed him to empathize and advocate from below and from above.

As co-performer in his home/field site he gave assistance to his neighbors and received it from them: he loaned them money and daily supplies while "two Latin King neighbors (Mexican) actually cornered and killed a mouse for [him] in [his] apartment. An Assyrian man who saw mice running up and down [his] living room curtains offered to give [him] a cat" (field notes). He wrote about these people's plight in academic venues like articles and conferences and in academic discourse, but he also used their own words and analyses to allow them to speak for themselves. Research as *doing*—performance—was the vehicle that he used to bridge the ethnographic divide between doing fieldwork and writing ethnography, the tension between fieldnotes and footnotes. He understood "how ragged the line between our community and the communities we study [had] become."[2] Ultimately, like anthropologist Lila

Abu-Lughod he was invested in ethnography as an "instrument of a tactical humanism"[3] where the researcher's own humanity, vulnerability, and power are deployed in the service of the story that must be told and in concert with the stories told by the informants.

Like few before or after him Dwight Conquergood took the relationships among theory, method, and praxis to a new level within the academy and provided a way for humanists and social scientists to have impact in venues that affected social policies. One way that he did this was through his attention to the rhetorical efficacy of writing itself. Though he critiqued the fetishization of written forms over oral ones, Conquergood understood the value of persuasive writing because of the written word's rhetorical weight within structures of power. Nonetheless, his writings are "speakerly" texts in their reliance on poetic forms such as alliteration, consonance, and assonance. Take, for example, this sentence from his essay "Rethinking Ethnography": "The radical empiricist's response to the vulnerabilities and vicissitudes of fieldwork is honesty, humility, self-reflexivity, and an acknowledgement of the interdependence and reciprocal role-playing between knower and known" (85). Or, the example of what has perhaps become one of his most oft-cited triplets of alliteration taken from his essay "Performance Studies: Interventions and Radical Research": "Speaking from my home department at Northwestern, we often refer to the three a's of performance studies: artistry, analysis, activism. Or to change the alliteration a commitment to the three c's of performance studies: creativity, critique, citizenship (civic struggle for social justice)" (41–42). Conquergood's poetics are not merely playful explorations with words for their own sake but rather examples of performative writing whose effectiveness, as Della Pollock suggests, depends "on how well it performs within a system animated not only by democratic conflict but by conflict over the nature and aims of democracy."[4] In other words, the rhetorical strategies within Conquergood's writing were his way of addressing the Realpolitik of the academy and the world.

The essays in *Cultural Struggles* reflect the various ways in which Conquergood enacted theory, developed and theorized methodologies of performance ethnographies, and demonstrated how the two come together through embodied research in the field. Along the way, the reader witnesses Conquergood's own growth as a theorist and ethnographer. The essays reflect his zeal not only for teaching but also for learning. A ravenous reader who inscribed every inch of white space of every page of his books and articles in a call-and-response fashion, Conquergood was forever on the pulse of scholarship, seeking out new ways to theorize and practice his own work to make it better. In turn, his work made those of us in the field who dared to follow in his footsteps better ethnographers, scholars, teachers, activists—human beings.

Cultural Struggles is the first collection of its kind to bring together theory, method, and *complete* case studies. It also shows the evolution of one scholar's thinking across a career of scholarship, teaching, and activism. Indeed, what the field has not had is access to the breadth of Conquergood's work in one volume. Some of his essays appear in obscure books (e.g., *Miteinander Sprechen und Handlen: Festschrift für Hellmut Geissner*) and/or those that circulate only within the field of communication (e.g., *The Future of Performance Studies*). Much of the impact of Conquergood's work, therefore, has been fostered by its employment by his own students and his students' students (I include myself in this category), and so on.

These essays stand on their own, but to contexualize the impact of Conquergood's work on the field, I have invited other scholars—some of whom are his former students and/or colleagues—to contribute short essays that engage various aspects of his work. While still tributory, inclusion of these essays provides further insight into how Conquergood's work has withstood the test of time long after his passing, as scholars still draw on his work to inform their current research interests and methods. Chief among these is Joseph Roach who collaborated with Conquergood at Northwestern in the late eighties to build the interdisciplinary theater graduate program. Roach's essay provides a biographical sketch of Conquergood as a medievalist to reflect on the depth and intensity of his "eloquence and vocation" as a scholar. Lisa Merrill's essay complements Roach's by also focusing on the many valences of "voice" in Conquergood's work, especially as it relates to the voiceless. Pivoting toward a less discussed aspect of Conquergood's work, longtime colleague and friend Micaela di Leonardo highlights the abiding political-economic aspects of Conquergood's oeuvre across his writing, filmmaking, and political work.

The final four essays are by alums of the department and Conquergood's former students who have gone on to have quite distinguished careers themselves and who have headed major performance studies programs across the country. The first of these is Shannon Jackson. Jackson uses the occasion of Conquergood's memorial service as a place to demonstrate his disciplinary legacy beyond what is erroneously referred to as the "Northwestern strain of performance studies." Drawing on her work on movement and dance, Judith Hamera examines Conquergood's ethics as they derive from the embodied practices of his fieldwork and his representations of others' bodies in his research. Della Pollock takes up the politics of place and space as they relate to Conquergood's notion of co-performance in order to imagine how those politics redound to actual policy. Finally, D. Soyini Madison interrogates Conquergood's racial politics as they relate to his raced body in relation to research on and advocacy for racial others.

Many continue to mourn the loss of the great colleague, mentor, teacher, friend, scholar, and activist that was Dwight Conquergood. And yet, his spirit and legacy live on in the lives that he touched and saved, and through his work—collected here between these book covers. In one of his most poignant lines, Dwight assures us that "opening and interpreting lives is very different from opening and closing books." It is my hope that *Cultural Struggles* will be the exception to Conquergood's own rule by providing readers who open and close this book with the tools to understand how to open and interpret lives with courage, ethics, and integrity—all things that Conquergood, by example, accomplished.

NOTES

1. Margery Wolf, *A Thrice-Told Tale: Feminism: Postmodernism & Ethnographic Responsibility* (Stanford: Stanford University Press, 1992), 128–29.
2. Ibid., 137.
3. See Lila Abu-Lughod, "Writing Against Culture," in *Anthropology in Theory: Issues in Epistemology*, ed. Henrietta L. Moore and Todd Sanders (Malden, MA: Blackwell, 2006), 466–79.
4. Della Pollock, "Performing Writing," in *The Ends of Performance*, ed. Peggy Phelan and Jill Lane (New York: New York University Press, 1998), 78.

I
Performance

Performing Cultures
Ethnography, Epistemology, and Ethics

At last there is a species of anthropology that is processual and participatory, it has the candor to view its fieldwork as dialogue. The conversation between investigator and investigated is not a 'means to an end' or a 'necessary evil,' but the Object itself in the process of projection. Such science grows accurate through self-study. It belongs to a larger and unnamed area of investigation, which *could* be called the History of Conscious Discourse or the Archaeology of Conversation.

—GEORGE QUASHA

With the "interpretive turn"[1] in the human sciences, researchers have begun restoring and unpacking the ancient *theatrum mundi* topos for fresh ways of thinking and talking about social life. Victor Turner summarizes this current shift in his field:

> Anthropology itself is shifting from a stress on concepts such as structure, equilibrium, system, and regularity to process, indeterminacy, reflexivity, resilience . . . There is also a renewed interest in "performance," partly stemming from sociolinguists such as Dell Hymes, partly from modern folklorists . . . , and partly from the fundamental work of Gregory Bateson and Erving Goffman. (Turner 1983, 337)

With the importance of Kenneth Burke to American communication studies, the dramaturgical perspective has been influential since mid-twentieth century, but recently there has been rekindled interest (see Fine and Speer 1977, Gronbeck 1980, Conquergood 1983a, Pacanowsky and O'Donnell-Trujillo 1983). The danger with analogies and concepts that seem so apt *prima facie* is that they produce a satisfying sense of closure before all the comparative complexities can be opened and drawn out. To prevent foreclosure on a potentially rich concept—e.g., "Yes, life is like theatre, isn't it?"—I would like to discuss dimensions of performance within two intersecting planes of "ethnography of performance research"[2]: (1) performance as cultural process, and (2) performance as ethnographic praxis.[3]

Performance as Cultural Process

The concept of culture an ethnographer takes into the field will determine his or her "positionality"[4] within the field, thus shaping how the data are collected, or construed, and represented. Nonetheless, ethnographers are least reflective about the concept of culture. Surveying anthropological scholarship, Mary Douglas concludes, "Culture is a blank space, a highly respected, empty pigeonhole" (Douglas 1982a, 183). The social theorist Zygmunt Bauman opens his book on concepts of culture with this statement, "The unyielding ambiguity of the concept of culture is notorious" (Bauman 1973, 1). Is culture a system, a cross-hatch of rules, a pattern of meanings, a deep storage vault, a set of distorting filters or blinders, a worldview, or so on?

Instead of entering into an idealist-metaphysical debate about the essence of culture, its "true" nature and ontological status, I shall take the philosophical stance of pragmatism and put forth the view of culture as performance. This view of culture commends its use not according to presumed correspondence with reality criteria, but with a simple criterion of usefulness (Rorty 1983). To paraphrase Rorty, what kind of stories does it enable us to tell about fields of experience and how do they fit with the other kinds of stories we want to tell about these and other local fields?

Construing culture as performance is useful to the interpretive researcher because it will help her withstand cognitive reductionism. What Jonathan Culler urged his literary-critical cohorts to confess—"We are all New Critics" and therefore must strenuously resist the notion of the autonomy of a text (Culler 1982)—can be transposed for all the human sciences—"We are all naive empiricists." Rabinow points to one of the ironies of contemporary scholarship: whereas on the one hand "the bankruptcy of the mere observer position today manifests" through the "vast array of theoretical arguments brought into play against it," on the other hand, "the scientistic paradigm still holds sway in the everyday practices of the discipline" (Rabinow 1982, 174).

It will require struggle for interpretive researchers to escape the domination of our positivistic past. Rabinow points to the depth of the ideological struggle: "The sustained hold which the model of science for anthropology maintains is a tribute to the deep embeddedness of these assumptions in our culture and how much interest there is in protecting them" (Rabinow 1982, 174). Construing culture as performance can be a radically discomposing idea, profoundly threatening to positivist scientists because the concept of culture is rendered solvent. A performance paradigm prevents the reification of culture into variables to be isolated, measured, and manipulated. Moreover, it dissolves hard-edged distinctions between observer/observed, self/other, subject/object, "the almost de rigueur opposition of subjectivity and objectivity" (Rabinow and Sullivan 1979, 5). The performance paradigm desacralizes the cherished assumptions of logical positivism and enables us to critique "without pity the illusions which surround the supposed autonomy and substantial firmness of the subject" (Rabinow 1982, 173).

From a performance perspective, culture is more like a vortex than a variable. It is not one of Rorty's "lumps" that can be found by turning over stones. Culture possesses us as much as we possess it; culture performs and articulates us as much as we enact and embody its evanescent qualities. Instead of using visual metaphors,[5] we might play with the idea of culture as a felt flow of enabling energies swirling around an axis. These volatile energies sweep and pull in opposite directions, simultaneously exerting centripetal and centrifugal forces. The centripetal force is the power of culture to draw everything in its ambit towards the center, which is always a moral center, a cosmology. Cosmologies, Mary Douglas makes clear, are coercive (Douglas 1982a, 205). They are also alchemic, they mediate all perceptions, endow meaningfullness, and saturate with significance. In this way Clifford Geertz can take a "fleck of culture" as the starting point for "thick description," and wrest worlds from winks (Geertz 1973).

Before pursuing this discussion in the other direction—tracing the centrifugal force of this double spiralling helix, the pull of extroversion, the tendency of cultures to express themselves—we should question the source of these enabling and constraining energies. From where do they spring, and how are they sustained? There is no need to valorize culture as a metaphysical or immanent entity, something prior to, above, and privileged from social performance. What keeps the performative nature of culture as enlivening energies in perpetual motion is that people continuously enact—perhaps it is more fitting to say "transact"—culture. In everyday communication, people reconstitute culture as they articulate or imply the premises upon which they predicate, and the values by which they assess, their own social performances as well as those of their co-actors. Douglas has a vivid image for how social action constitutively feeds back into its own constituting frame: "In his very negotiating activity, each is forcing culture down the throats of his fellow-men. When individuals transact, their medium of exchange is in units of culture" (Douglas 1982, 189). This "clash of will which gives rise to society" (Douglas 1982, 3) has been discussed at length by Turner, who refers to it as "social drama" (Turner 1974). The energies of cultural process derive from the dramas of social life: human attempts to contain or widen breach of a cherished norm, dampen or foment crisis, redress conflicts and grievances, achieve resolution and consensus, or recognize schism. Cultures are not organic; they cannot exist where there is no human life and strife.

This view of culture as a swirling constellation of energies with crossdrafts, wind pressures, and choppy air currents, can help blast researchers free from positivistic moorings because culture can no longer be grasped so much as it needs to be felt and engaged. With this notion of culture, knowledge derived from systematic investigation is displaced by understanding that comes from experience—from getting caught up, or plunging into, the hurly burly of social life.

The question arises that once we shake up hypostatizing concepts of culture to this extent, have we not made culture so dynamic and evanescent as to prevent analysis? What would be the unit of analysis? Pacanowsky and O'Donnell-Trujillo sensibly recognize the same difficulty with conceptualizing cultural structures as coming into being through processes of communication. The concept of communication becomes "so thick and ubiquitous as to be analytically inaccessable" (Pacanowsky and O'Donnell-Trujillo 1983, 129). The way out of this cul-de-sac for performance as cultural process is opened up by the notion of centrifugal force as part of the energy field. Cultural processes both pull towards a moral center as social dramas are enacted while they simultaneously express themselves outward from the depths of that symbolizing, synthesizing core. That is, cultures throw off forms of themselves—literally, "expressions"—that are publicly accessible. These formal expressions of culture collect, set, heighten, frame, stylize, regulate, reproduce, refract, contain, and fix amorphous energies, drives, impulses, tensions. These heightened surfacing forms throw into bold relief the core values, virtues, and visions of a culture. Turner calls these formal expressions "cultural performances" and refers to them as "peaks" of social experience, "precipitates" from the eventful social flow that function as prismatic lenses through which one can glimpse the inner dynamics and depths of culture (Turner 1982, 11–12).

These displays of culture are eminently available to the researcher because they function as social meta-commentaries for the participants within a culture. Cultural performances remain at mirror distance from ongoing social processes and are important monitoring mechanisms, scanning devices whereby a people can interpret themselves to themselves as well as to others. Turner reminds us that even for natives, culture is never wholly "given, but gropingly discovered, and some parts of it quite late in life" (Turner 1981, 144). Cultural performances, such as rituals, ceremonies, celebrations, myths, stories, songs, jokes, carnivals, contests, games, parties, politesse, and other expressive traditions, are culturally reflexive events that focus, interpret, punctuate, and endow meaningfulness to experience. Clifford Geertz's now classic essay, "Deep Play: Notes on the Balinese Cockfight," is a luminous exegesis of the epistemological functions of cultural performance (Geertz 1972; reprinted in Rabinow and Sullivan 1979, 181–223).

These formal expressions of culture are not simply static or passive reflectors of the status quo. As Michel Foucault reminds us, knowledge is power (Foucault 1980). It is the capacity of cultural performance to induce self-knowledge, self-awareness, plural reflexivity, that makes it political. Turner explains that the various genres of cultural performance collectively produce "a set of meta-languages whereby a group or community not merely expresses itself but, more actively, tries to understand itself *in order to change itself*" (Turner 1983, 338; emphasis added). Cultural performance must be understood "as social *product*ivity" no less than "as social *product*" (Strine 1983, 150). Cultural performance holds the potential for negation, as well as affirmation. Even as the conservative, centripetal energies of culture are set in motion through ongoing social dramas wherein factions are consolidated and coherence achieved in the crucible of crisis, the revisionary, centrifugal energies of culture are liberated in cultural performance. Turner uses the following image to capture the dialectical tensions between social drama and cultural performance: "All the genres [of cultural performance] have to circle, as it were, around the earth of the social drama, and some, like satellites, may exert tidal effects on its inner structure" (Turner 1981, 159).

Cultural performance is the appropriate unit of analysis—perhaps we should say "focus of reflection"—for the interpretive researcher because it is self-consciously available for plumbing insights into cultural process, for natives primarily, for ethnographers incidentally. It is an indigenous form of native epistemology. By construing performance as constitutive of culture, not simply one of its compartments or excrescences, the interpretative researcher has an heuristically rich but at the same time precise point of entry for cultural studies. Positivism can be resisted without sacrificing precision. Cultural performances are dynamic, ephemeral, volatile, but nonetheless framed, repeated, and recognizable events.

Ethnographic Praxis as Performance[6]

At a second level of analysis, the conduct of fieldwork can be viewed as a delicately balanced performance between ethnographer and native consultants. The standard situation of fieldwork involves a concrete encounter between the participant-observer and members of another culture. The everyday praxis of fieldwork involves dialogue, conversation, and participation as the ethnographer endeavors to understand the Other "from the native's point of view" (Geertz 1977). The relationship between ethnographer and native is not a natural one: it is absolutely constructed and contingent upon a willing suspension of disbelief by both parties in the encounter. Fieldwork rests on mutually sustained fictions, and resembles the denial of perceived reality that we associate with playacting, rather than enactment.

Geertz labels this fabricated quality of fieldwork "anthropological irony" (Geertz 1968, 147). He characterizes the relationship between ethnographer and native, Self and Other, as contingent upon "the implicit agreement to regard one another, in the face of some very serious indications to the contrary, as members of the same cultural universe" (Geertz 1968, 152). The illusions that enable fieldwork are meaningfully sustained as long as both parties confirm each other's performance:

> . . . usually the sense of being members, however temporarily, insecurely and incompletely, of a single moral community can be maintained even in the face of the wider social realities which press in at almost every moment to deny it. It is this fiction—fiction, not falsehood—that lies at the heart of successful anthropological field research; and because it is never completely convincing for any of the participants, it renders such research, considered as a form of conduct, continuously ironic (Geertz 1968, 154; see also Rabinow 1977, 153, 162).

The "truth" of ethnographic praxis rests, paradoxically, in acknowledgment of the fictions of fieldwork. Falsehood in fieldwork would follow from the assumption of easy identification with the Other. Not only would this assumption ring false, it would be morally problematical because it would deny the profound distinctiveness of the Other. Further, it would block self-consciousness that might lead to self-critique (Conquergood 1985).

A practicing ethnographer is one who is performing at many levels, and aware that she is performing. Since her enterprise is to produce actor-oriented descriptions of culture, she must attempt to take the perspective of the other by participating in unfamiliar tradition while maintaining her own integrity as self. Like a good actor playing Hamlet, she must paradoxically immerse herself in the role of the other while simultaneously maintaining distance from the role through awareness of the performance. Otherwise, she might actually slay Polonius, or caught up in the frenzy of chasing Ophelia, fall off the stage. Performance, both for the fieldworker and stage actor, requires a special doubling of consciousness, an ironic awareness. One must take oneself simultaneously as both subject and object.

Authentic fieldwork depends on acknowledgment of its mutual constructedness through performance, fiction, intersubjective dialogue between Self and Other (Webster 1982). The Other is never pristinely encountered or experienced apart from the historical conditions and mediating paradoxes of fieldwork. Thinking about ethnographic praxis as a disciplinary performance will help displace positivist claims for objectivity by which knowledge of the other is abstracted from its historical and dialogical conditions. Not only are metaphysical pretensions of scientific objectivity epistemologically suspect in a fieldwork setting, they are ethically shaky as well. Positivist claims have the moral consequences of fixing people in subject-object categories in an alignment of power relations where the fieldworker observes from a privileged distance the Other who becomes the field studied. The performative view brings ethnographer and native together as co-actors, mutually engaged collaborators in a fragile fiction. There is an interdependence between Self and Other in the performative view, both are vulnerable. Instead of the researcher presented as detached and controlling, the performative view admits the fragile situation of the fieldworker.

Geertz talks about the "humbling" nature of fieldwork experience and says that one of the "benefits" of fieldwork research is that it teaches you how it feels to be thought of as a fool and used as an object, and how to endure it (Geertz 1968, 148). I do not want to imply that fieldwork predicated on performance principles is above and beyond ethical pitfalls, or more removed from moral difficulties than fieldwork derived from positivist premises. The performance paradigm makes no claims for moral purity. The ethical difference between the two fieldwork premises is that whereas positivism denies its moral entailments, the performance approach recognizes and struggles agonizingly with the inescapable moral tensions of ethnographic praxis:

> To recognize the moral tension, the ethical ambiguity, implicit in the encounter of anthropologist and informant, and to still be able to dissipate it through one's actions and one's attitudes, is what encounter demands of both parties if it is to be authentic, if it is to actually happen. And to discover that is to discover also something very complicated and not altogether clear about the nature of sincerity and insincerity, genuineness and hypocracy and self-deception. Fieldwork is an educational experience all around (Geertz 1968, 155).

It is this self-consciousness of moral implications that makes the performance paradigm ethically more sensitive than positivism. The difference between the two remains one of moral sensitivity, not moral superiority. In the same paradoxical fashion, it is the acknowledgment of its fictionality that makes performance more epistemologically sound than positivism. The performance paradigm struggles for epistemological authenticity instead of accuracy, moral honesty instead of innocence.

NOTES

1. See Paul Rabinow and William M. Sullivan, "The Interpretive Turn: Emergence of an Approach" for a helpful discussion of this movement in the human sciences (1979, 1–21). For examples of the influence of the interpretive approach in communication studies, see Mary S. Strine and Michael E. Pacanowsky, "How to Read Interpretive Accounts of Organizational Life: Narrative Bases of Textual Authority," 1985; and Linda L. Putnam and Michael E. Pacanowsky, *Communication and Organizations: An Interpretive Approach,* 1983.

2. Jill Taft-Kaufman sets forth the disciplinary context for the emergence of "ethnography of performance" within the field of speech communication. "Oral Interpretation: Twentieth-Century Theory and Practice" (Benson 1985, 172–75).

3. While there is only space in this paper to deal with these first two levels of conceptualization, I believe there are at least two more interlocking levels of analysis: (3) performance as ethnographic hermeneutics, and (4) performance as mode of ethnographic representation. Elsewhere I have discussed performance as ethnographic hermeneutics, a way of deeply sensing the Other (Conquergood 1983b, 1984). The fourth part of the project, discussion of performance as a mode of representation, a mode of "publishing" ethnographic knowledge, is in progress. While I have not yet developed fully all the philosophical, rhetorical, and political

ramifications of performance as a mode of disciplinary discourse, I have experimented with the form (Conquergood 1985a, 1985b).

4. For an incisive discussion of the "positionality of the researcher" see Mary S. Strine, "The Cultural Relevance of Speech Communication: Approaching the Field from a Humanistic-Artistic Perspective" (1983b, 17).

5. Stanley Deetz provocatively links the everyday use of visual metaphors with political acts of suppression: " . . . the greatest acts of suppression in Western cultural development have come primarily . . . from acts like the everyday translation of the experience of sound and feelings into visual metaphors where understanding and engagement in the world are all reduced to sight, and, consequently, where action-at-a-distance and objectivity rule. Technology and control thus become the organizing principles for all understanding" (Deetz 1983, 61). Johannes Fabian makes a similar argument in "The Other and the Eye: Time and the Rhetoric of Vision" (Fabian 1983, 105–41).

6. Although I refer to the higher authority of Clifford Geertz throughout this discussion of ethnographic praxis, his introspective and courageous statements about the moral tensions and ethical ambiguities implicit in the fieldwork situation resonate deeply with my own recent fieldwork experience. From February through July, 1985, I conducted fieldwork in Thailand, and spent most of that time living in a hilltribe refugee camp. That experience was the impetus for dealing with the ethical issues in this paper. I gratefully acknowledge the grant from the Northwestern University Research Council that facilitated my research. My work was also supported by the International Rescue Committee.

REFERENCES

Bauman, Zygmunt. 1973. *Culture as Praxis.* London: Routledge & Kegan Paul.

Benson, Thomas, ed. 1985. *Speech Communication in the 20th Century.* Carbondale: Southern Illinois University Press.

Conquergood, Dwight. 1983a. "Communication as Performance: Dramaturgical Dimensions of Everyday Life." In *The Jensen Lectures: Contemporary Communication Studies,* edited by John Sisco, 24–43. Tampa: Department of Communication, University of South Florida.

Conquergood, Dwight. 1983b. "A Sense of the Other: Interpretation and Ethnographic Research," Proceedings of the Southwest Conference on Oral Traditions," edited by Isabel Crouch, 148–455. Las Cruces: New Mexico State University.

Conquergood, Dwight. 1984. "Performance and Dialogical Understanding: In Quest of the Other," *Proceedings of the Ninth International Colloquium on Communication,* edited by Janet Larsen McHughes. Tempe: Arizona State University.

Conquergood, Dwight. 1985a. "Performing as a Moral Act: Ethical Dimensions of the Ethnography of Performance." *Literature in Performance* 5: 1–13.

Conquergood, Dwight, co-producer. 1985b. *Between Two Worlds: The Hmong Shaman in America,* video-documentary, 28 minutes. Chicago: Siegel Productions.

Culler, Jonathan. 1982. *On Deconstruction: Theory and Criticism after Structuralism.* Ithaca: Cornell University Press.

Deetz, Stanley. 1983. "The Politics of the Oral Interpretation of Literature." *Literature in Performance* 4: 60–64.

Douglas, Mary. 1982a. *In the Active Voice.* London: Routledge & Kegan Paul.

Douglas, Mary. 1982b. *Essays in the Sociology of Perception.* London: Routledge & Kegan Paul.

Fabian, Johannes. 1983. *Time and the Other: How Anthropology Makes Its Object.* New York: Columbia University Press.

Fine, Elizabeth C., and Speer, Jean H. 1977. "A New Look at Performance." *Communication Monographs* 44: 374–89.

Foucault, Michel. 1980. *Power/Knowledge: Selected Interviews and Other Writings 1972–1977.* Edited by Colin Gordon. New York: Pantheon Books.

Geertz, Clifford. 1968. "Thinking as a Moral Act: Ethical Dimensions of Anthropological Fieldwork in the New States." *Antioch Review* 28: 139–58.

Geertz, Clifford. 1972. "Deep Play: Notes on the Balinese Cockfight." *Daedalus* 101: 1–37.

Geertz, Clifford. 1973. *Interpretation of Cultures.* New York: Basic Books.

Geertz, Clifford. 1977. "'From the Native's Point of View': On the Nature of Anthropological Understandings." In *Symbolic Anthropology,* edited by Janet L. Dolgin, David S. Kemnitzer, and David M. Schneider, 480–92. New York: Columbia University Press.

Gronbeck, Bruce. 1980. "Dramaturgical Theory and Criticism: The State of the Art (or Science?)." *Western Journal of Speech Communication* 44: 315–30.

Pacanowsky, Michael E., and O'Donnell-Trujillo, Nick. 1983. "Organizational Communication as Cultural Performance." *Communication Monographs* 50: 126–47.

Putnam, Linda L., and Pacanowsky, Michael E., eds. 1983. *Communication and Organizations: An Interpretive Approach.* Beverly Hills: Sage Publications.

Rabinow, Paul. 1977. *Reflections on Fieldwork in Morocco.* Berkeley: University of California Press.

Rabinow, Paul. 1982. "Masked I Go Forward: Reflections on the Modern Subject." *A Crack in the Mirror: Reflexive Perspectives in Anthropology,* edited by Ruby and Barbara Myerhoff, 173–86. Philadelphia: University of Pennsylvania Press.

Rabinow, Paul, and Sullivan, William M., eds. 1979. *Interpretive Social Science.* Berkeley: University of California Press.

Rorty, Richard. 1983. "Lumps and Texts," manuscript circulated at the School of Criticism and Theory, Northwestern University, summer institute.

Strine, Mary S. 1983a. "Performance Theory as Science: The Formative Impact of Dr. James Rush's *The Philosophy of the Human Voice.*" In *Performance of Literature in Historical Perspectives,* edited by David W. Thompson, 509–28. Lanham: University Press of America.

Strine, Mary S. 1983b. "The Cultural Relevance of Speech Communication: Approaching the Field from a Humanistic-Artistic Perspective." *ACA Bulletin* 46: 15–17.

Strine, Mary S., and Michael E. Pacanowsky. 1985. "How to Read Interpretive Accounts of Organizational Life: Narrative Bases of Textual Authority." *Southern Speech Communication Journal* 50: 283–97.

Taft-Kaufman, Jill. 1985. "Oral Interpretation: Twentieth-Century Theory and Practice." In *Speech Communication in the 20th Century,* edited Thomas W. Benson, 157–83. Carbondale: Southern Illinois University Press.

Turner, Victor. 1974. *Dramas, Fields, and Metaphors.* Ithaca: Cornell University Press.

Turner, Victor. 1981. "Social Dramas and Stories About Them." In *On Narrative,* edited by W. J. T. Mitchell, 141–68. Chicago: University of Chicago Press.

Turner, Victor. 1982. *Celebration: Studies in Festivity and Ritual.* Washington, D.C.: Smithsonian Institution Press.

Turner, Victor. 1983. Review of *Ethnopoetics.* In *Symposium of the Whole: A Range of Discourse Toward an Ethnopoetics,* edited by Jerome Rothenberg and Diane Rothenberg, 337–42. Berkeley: University of California Press.

Webster, Steven. 1982. "Dialogue and Fiction in Ethnography." *Dialectical Anthropology* 7: 91–114.

Of Caravans and Carnivals

Performance Studies in Motion

Peggy Phelan has presented us with a challenging exercise: to identify a key issue, a pressing point of intersection between our local institution and the more expansive future of the field—and, she has enjoined us to be brief.

I offer the following principle more as a catalyst for opening conversation than a proposition for closing down controversy. The starting point for discussion that I affirm is this: Performance is an essentially contested concept. I borrow this idea from Strine, Long, and Hopkins' fine metadisciplinary essay, "Research in Interpretation and Performance Studies: Trends, Issues, Priorities" (1990).[1] Thinking about performance as an "essentially contested concept" locates disagreement and difference as generative points of departure and coalition for its unfolding meanings and affiliations. Any attempt to define and stabilize performance will be bound up in disagreement, and this disagreement is itself part of its meaning:

> Thus, we understand not just that others disagree, but that this disagreement is inevitable and healthy. [. . .] Factions in the controversy do not expect to defeat or silence opposing positions, but rather through continuing dialogue to attain a sharper articulation of all positions and therefore a fuller understanding of the conceptual richness of performance. (Strine, Long, and Hopkins 1990, 183)

The idea that performance is a contested and contesting practice rings true for me in my dual role as an ethnographer of cultural performance and as an administrator of an academic department of performance studies. What I have learned from both fields—ethnographic "fieldwork" as well as the disciplinary "field" of performance studies—is that performance flourishes within a zone of contest and struggle. That observation is as true for the everyday resisting performance practices of subaltern groups as it is for performance studies programs. Life on the margins can be a source of creativity as well as constraint, what Michel de Certeau described as "makeshift creativity" and a mobile art of "making do" (de Certeau 1984, xiv, 29). Performance studies is a border discipline, an interdiscipline, that cultivates the capacity to move between structures, to forge connections, to see together, to speak with instead of simply speaking about or for others. Performance privileges threshold-crossing, shape-shifting, and boundary-violating figures, such as shamans, tricksters, and jokers, who value the carnivalesque over the canonical, the transformative over the normative, the mobile over the monumental.

Victor Turner, inspired by his performance ethnography collaborations with Richard Schechner, coined the epigrammatic view of "performance as making, not faking" (Turner 1982, 93). His constructional theory foregrounded the culture-creating capacities of performance and functioned as a challenge and counterproject to the "antitheatrical prejudice" that, since Plato, has aligned performance with fakery and falsehood (Barish 1981). After his sustained work on social drama, cultural performance, liminality, and, of course, definition of humankind as *homo performans,* it would be hard for anyone to hold a "mere sham and show" view of performance. Turner shifted thinking about performance from mimesis to poiesis.

Now, the current thinking about performance constitutes a shift from poiesis to kinesis. Turner's important work on the productive capacities of performance set the stage for a more poststructuralist and political emphasis on performance as kinesis, as movement, motion, fluidity, fluctuation, all those restless energies that transgress boundaries and trouble closure. Thus, postcolonial critic Homi K. Bhabha deployed the term "performative" to refer to action that incessantly insinuates, interrupts, interrogates, antagonizes, and decenters powerful master discourses, which he dubbed "pedagogical" (Bhabha 1994, 46–49). From Turner's emphatic view of performance as making not faking, we move to Bhabha's politically urgent view of performance as breaking and remaking.[2]

Donna Haraway argues for a performance-friendly worldview, a "reinvention of nature," in which "objects" of study are actively engaged and seen as dynamic "agents": "we must rethink the world as witty actor and agent of transformation, a coding trickster with whom we must learn to converse" (Haraway 1991, 201). Performance studies, in Haraway's view, would be the search for trickster figures "that might turn a stacked deck into a potent set of wild cards, jokers, for refiguring possible worlds" (4).

Kinesis unleashes centrifugal forces that keep culture in motion, ideas in play, hierarchies unsettled, and academic disciplines alert and on the edge: "the guerilla tactics of multiple, uneasily jostling theories and stories can at least disrupt the smug assumptions of comfortably settled monologics" (Tsing 1993, 33).[3]

And now I turn to the second part of Phelan's challenge: to sketch the local institutional context where performance issues and ideas take shape. Anna Tsing's rethinking of "the local" is relevant for my sketch of a particular institutional configuration of performance studies: "By 'local,' I do not mean to invoke tiny bounded communities, but rather acts of positioning within particular contexts" (Tsing 1993, 31). I chair the Department of Performance Studies at Northwestern University. Housed within the School of Speech, Performance Studies attracts a robust mix of faculty, graduate students, and undergraduate majors. They are an unruly and rambunctious group. I tremble before the task of summarizing them. They give new meaning to the idea of performance as a creative and contentious space—and I say that with the utmost respect and affection. However, my task in representing them is made less daunting by the fact that many of my Northwestern colleagues, graduate students, alumnae, and undergraduate majors are attending and participating in this conference. They are quite able to speak for themselves. Collectively, their presentations at this conference reflect the diverse array of performance perspectives and projects that defines our program. Having said all that, still it might be possible to set forth some shared commitments that provide common ground, meeting places, in the midst of all the eclecticism.

Here goes: Most of us at Northwestern are committed to a bracing dialectic between performance theory and practice. We believe that theory is enlivened and most rigorously tested when it hits the ground in practice. Likewise, we believe that artistic practice can be deepened, complicated, and challenged in meaningful ways by engaging critical theory. What all this means is that our curriculum, from freshman gateway course to advanced doctoral seminar, embraces courses in which students perform as an embodied way of knowing, as a supplement to (not a substitute for) the more conventional epistemologies and pedagogies of reading and discussing texts, writing research papers, conducting fieldwork, and so forth. Stated succinctly: at Northwestern we take performance as both subject and method of research. And I should make it clear for newcomers to performance studies that our students by and large are not performing plays: the study of dramatic texts at Northwestern is handled most excellently by our neighbors in the Department of Theatre. Because the study of canonical plays and their production processes and histories by no means exhausts the range of performance genres and practices, the performance studies department picks up where the theatre department stops: the study of nondramatic texts and nonelite performance practices. We have faculty in our department who specialize in the adaptation and staging of fictional and nonfictional texts alongside scholars of Yoruba ritual performance. Because of the division of labor, we have an excellent relationship with the theatre department, remarkably free of border disputes and turf struggles. We also are in intellectual and institutional solidarity with anthropologists, literary critics, and ethnomusicologists, as well as other interdisciplinary programs such as cultural studies, women's studies, African studies, diaspora studies, and queer studies. The distinctive contribution we bring to the table is the heuristic potential of performance as concept, practice, and epistemology.

Another way to express our departmental commitment to a theory-practice dialectic is to say that many of us endeavor, not so much to position as to pivot our work on a turning point among analytical, artistic, and activist perspectives. We believe in the replenishing coarticulation of analytical insights, artistic energies, and activist struggles—approaches to problems that all too often are segregated, polarized, or pitted against one another. I think that our departmental commitment to praxis, to multiple ways of knowing that engage embodied experience with critical reflection is strengthened structurally by the fact that we have both an undergraduate major and a PhD program. Our undergraduates are unusually bright but, like most undergraduates, they have little taste for jargon or tolerance for undue abstraction; certainly they hold our feet close to the ground of experience. On the other hand, our doctoral students keep pushing the limits and advancing the conceptual frontier of what counts as performance studies. Many of them work on dissertation projects for which they have something at stake, both personally and politically. The interaction between undergraduate majors and PhD students in performance studies is complex and mutually invigorating. Certainly it would be simpler to devote all our energy and resources either to an undergraduate or a PhD program, but, ultimately, I think it would be less interesting. There are important and lively points of intersection and exchange between the undergraduate and PhD programs, but even their different and sometimes competing concerns, demands, and agendas all help to keep things stirred up and moving.

I will leave you with a resonant quotation from Gloria Anzaldúa: "the future depends on the breaking down of paradigms, it depends on the straddling of two or more cultures" (Anzaldúa 1987, 80). Anzaldúa was speaking about the future of the planet, but this insight is just as relevant for "the future of the field" of performance studies. Instead of a stable, monolithic paradigm of performance studies, I prefer to think in terms of a caravan: a heterogeneous ensemble of ideas and methods on the move.

NOTES

1. Strine, Long, and Hopkins' discussion of performance as an essentially contested concept builds on the work of W.B. Gallie (1964).
2. I first traced the performance as mimesis-poiesis-kinesis trajectory in 1992 (Conquergood 1992a).
3. Even the imagery of kinesis needs to be questioned and located. It can be invoked for repressive as well as progressive ends. Emily Martin (1994) has analyzed how late 20th-century capitalism has appropriated the postmodern imagery of motion, mobility, and flexibility in the service of capital accumulation and consolidation. Elsewhere, I have documented ethnographically how dominant powers deploy the imagery of flux and motion to stigmatize subordinate groups, e.g., "transients," "floaters," an "influx" of poor people, "transitional" neighborhoods, demographic "turnover," etc. (Conquergood 1992b).

REFERENCES

Anzaldúa, Gloria. 1987. *Borderlands/La Frontera: The New Mestiza.* San Francisco: Spinsters/Aunt Lute.
Barish, Jonas. 1981. *The Antitheatrical Prejudice.* Berkeley: University of California Press.
Bhabha, Homi K. 1994. *The Location of Culture.* New York: Routledge.
Conquergood, Dwight. 1992a. "Ethnography, Rhetoric, and Performance." *Quarterly Journal of Speech* 78: 80–91.
Conquergood, Dwight. 1992b. "Life in Big Red: Struggles and Accommodations in a Chicago Polyethnic Tenement," in *Structuring Diversity: Ethnographic Perspectives on the New Immigration,* edited by Louise Lamphere, 95–144. Chicago: University of Chicago Press.
de Certeau, Michel. 1984. *The Practice of Everyday Life.* Translated by S. Randall. Berkeley: University of California Press.
Gallie, W.B. 1964. *Philosophy and the Historical Understanding.* New York: Schocken Books.
Haraway, Donna. 1991. *Simians, Cyborgs, and Women: The Reinvention of Nature.* New York: Routledge.
Martin, Emily. 1994. *Flexible Bodies: Tracking Immunity in American Culture from the Days of Polio to the Age of AIDS.* Boston: Beacon.
Strine, Mary, Beverly Long, and Mary Frances Hopkins. 1990. "Research in Interpretation and Performance Studies: Trends, Issues, Priorities." In *Speech*

Communication: Essays to Commemorate the Seventy-fifth Anniversary of the Speech Communication Association, edited by Gerald Phillips and Julia Wood, 181–204. Carbondale: Southern Illinois University Press.

Tsing, Anna Lowenhaupt. 1993. *In the Realm of the Diamond Queen: Marginality in an Out-of-the-Way Place.* Princeton, NJ: Princeton University Press.

Turner, Victor. 1982. *From Ritual to Theatre.* New York: PAJ Publications.

Performance Studies

Interventions and Radical Research

According to Michel de Certeau, "what the map cuts up, the story cuts across" (de Certeau 1984, 129). This pithy phrase evokes a postcolonial world crisscrossed by transnational narratives, diaspora affiliations, and, especially, the movement and multiple migrations of people, sometimes voluntary, but often economically propelled and politically coerced. In order to keep pace with such a world, we now think of "place" as a heavily trafficked intersection, a port of call and exchange, instead of a circumscribed territory. A boundary is more like a membrane than a wall. In current cultural theory, "location" is imagined as an itinerary instead of a fixed point. Our understanding of "local context" expands to encompass the historical, dynamic, often traumatic, movements of people, ideas, images, commodities, and capital. It is no longer easy to sort out the local from the global: transnational circulations of images get reworked on the ground and redeployed for local, tactical struggles. And global flows simultaneously are encumbered and energized by these local makeovers. We now are keenly aware that the "local" is a leaky, contingent construction, and that global forces are taken up, struggled over, and refracted for site-specific purposes. The best of the new cultural theory distinguishes itself from apolitical celebrations of mobility, flow, and easy border crossings by carefully tracking the transitive circuits of power and the political economic pressure points that monitor the migrations of people, channel the circulations of meanings, and stratify access to resources (see Gilroy 1994; Appadurai 1996; Lavie and Swedenburg 1996; Clifford 1997; di Leonardo 1998; Joseph 1999; Ong 1999). We now ask: For whom is the border a friction-free zone of entitled access, a frontier of possibility? Who travels confidently across borders, and who gets questioned, detained, interrogated, and strip-searched at the border (see Taylor 1999)?

But de Certeau's aphorism, "what the map cuts up, the story cuts across," also points to transgressive travel between two different domains of knowledge: one official, objective, and abstract—"the map"; the other one practical, embodied, and popular—"the story." This promiscuous traffic between different ways of knowing carries the most radical promise of performance studies research. Performance studies struggles to open the space between analysis and action, and to pull the pin on the binary opposition between theory and practice. This embrace of different ways of knowing is radical because it cuts to the root of how knowledge is organized in the academy.

The dominant way of knowing in the academy is that of empirical observation and critical analysis from a distanced perspective: "knowing that," and "knowing about." This is a view from above the object of inquiry: knowledge that is anchored in paradigm and secured in print. This propositional knowledge is shadowed by another way of knowing that is grounded in active, intimate, hands-on participation and personal connection: "knowing how," and "knowing who." This is a view from ground level, in the thick of things. This is knowledge that is anchored in practice and circulated within a performance community, but is ephemeral. Donna Haraway locates this homely and vulnerable "view from a body" in contrast to the abstract and authoritative "view from above," universal knowledge that pretends to transcend location (Haraway 1991, 196).

Since the enlightenment project of modernity, the first way of knowing has been preeminent. Marching under the banner of science and reason, it has disqualified and repressed other ways of knowing that are rooted in embodied experience, orality, and local contingencies. Between objective knowledge that is consolidated in texts, and local know-how that circulates on the ground within a community of memory and practice, there is no contest. It is the choice between science and "old wives' tales" (note how the disqualified knowledge is gendered as feminine).

Michel Foucault coined the term "subjugated knowledges" to include all the local, regional, vernacular, naïve knowledges at the bottom of the hierarchy—the low Other of science (Foucault 1980, 81–84). These are the nonserious ways of knowing that dominant culture neglects, excludes, represses, or simply fails to recognize. Subjugated knowledges have been erased because they are illegible; they exist, by and large, as active bodies of meaning, outside of books, eluding the forces of inscription that would make them legible, and thereby legitimate (see de Certeau 1998; Scott 1998).

What gets squeezed out by this epistemic violence is the whole realm of complex, finely nuanced meaning that is embodied, tacit, intoned, gestured, improvised, coexperienced, covert—and all the more deeply meaningful because of its refusal to be spelled out. Dominant epistemologies that link knowing with seeing are not attuned to meanings that are masked, camouflaged, indirect, embedded, or hidden in context. The visual/verbal bias of Western regimes of knowledge blinds researchers to meanings that are expressed forcefully through intonation, silence, body tension, arched eyebrows, blank stares, and other protective arts of disguise and secrecy—what de Certeau called "the elocutionary experience of a fugitive communication" (de Certeau 2000, 133; see Conquergood 2000). Subordinate people do not have the privilege of explicitness, the luxury of transparency, the presumptive norm of clear and direct communication, free and open debate on a level playing field that the privileged classes take for granted.

In his critique of the limitations of literacy, Kenneth Burke argued that print-based scholarship has built-in blind spots and a conditioned deafness:

> The [written] record is usually but a fragment of the expression (as the written word omits all telltale record of gesture and tonality; and not only may our "literacy" keep us from missing the omissions, it may blunt us to the appreciation of tone and gesture, so that even when we witness the full expression, we note only those aspects of it that can be written down). (Burke 1969, 185)

In even stronger terms, Raymond Williams challenged the class-based arrogance of scriptocentrism, pointing to the "error" and "delusion" of "highly educated" people who are "so driven in on their reading" that "they fail to notice that there are other forms of skilled, intelligent, creative activity" such as "theatre" and "active politics." This error "resembles that of the narrow reformer who supposes that farm labourers and village craftsmen were once uneducated, merely because they could not read." He argued that "the contempt" for performance and practical activity, "which is always latent in the highly literate, is a mark of the observer's limits, not those of the activities themselves" (Williams 1983, 309). Williams critiqued scholars for limiting their sources to written materials; I agree with Burke that scholarship is so skewed toward texts that even when researchers do attend to extralinguistic human action and embodied events they construe them as texts to be read. According to de Certeau, this scriptocentrism is a hallmark of Western imperialism. Posted above the gates of modernity, this sign: "'Here only what is written is understood.' Such is the internal law of that which has constituted itself as 'Western' [and 'white']" (de Certeau 1984, 161).

Only middle-class academics could blithely assume that all the world is a text because reading and writing are central to their everyday lives and occupational security. For many people throughout the world, however, particularly subaltern groups, texts are often inaccessible, or threatening, charged with the regulatory powers of the state. More often than not, subordinate people experience texts and the bureaucracy of literacy as instruments of control and displacement, e.g., green cards, passports, arrest warrants, deportation orders—what de Certeau calls "intextuation": "Every power, including the power of law, is written first of all on the backs of its subjects" (1984:140). Among the most oppressed people in the United States today are the "undocumented" immigrants, the so-called "illegal aliens," known in the vernacular as the people "sin papeles," the people without papers, *indocumentado/as.* They are illegal because they are not legible, they trouble "the writing machine of the law" (de Certeau 1984, 141).

The hegemony of textualism needs to be exposed and undermined. Transcription is not a transparent or politically innocent model for conceptualizing or engaging the world. The root metaphor of the text underpins the supremacy of Western knowledge systems by erasing the vast realm of human knowledge and meaningful action that is unlettered, "a history of the tacit and the habitual" (Jackson 2000:29). In their multivolume historical ethnography of colonialism/evangelism in South Africa, John and Jean Comaroff pay careful attention to the way Tswana people argued with their white interlocutors "both verbally and nonverbally" (Comaroff 1997, 47; see also Comaroff 1991). They excavate spaces of agency and struggle from everyday performance practices—clothing, gardening, healing, trading, worshipping, architecture, and homemaking—to reveal an impressive repertoire of conscious, creative, critical, contrapuntal responses to the imperialist project that exceeded the verbal. The Comaroffs intervene in an academically fashionable textual fundamentalism and fetish of the (verbal) archive where "text—a sad proxy for life—becomes all" (Comaroff and Comaroff 1992, 26). "In this day and age," they ask, "do we still have to remind ourselves that many of the players on any historical stage cannot speak at all? Or, under greater or lesser duress, opt not to do so?" (Comaroff and Comaroff 1997, 48; see also Scott 1990).

There are many ethnographic examples of how nonelite people recognize the opacity of the text and critique its dense occlusions and implications in historical processes of political economic privilege and systematic exclusion. In Belize, for example, Garifuna people, an African-descended minority group, use the word *gapencillitin,* which means "people with pencil," to refer to middle- and upper-class members of the professional-managerial class, elites who approach life from an intellectual perspective. They use the word *mapencillitin,* literally "people without pencil," to refer to rural and working-class people, "real folks" who approach life from a practitioner's point of view.[1] What is interesting about the Garifuna example is that class stratification, related to differential knowledges, is articulated in terms of access to literacy. The pencil draws the line between the haves and the have-nots. For Garifuna people, the pencil is not a neutral instrument; it functions metonymically as the operative technology of a complex political economy of knowledge, power, and the exclusions upon which privilege is based.

In his study of the oppositional politics of black musical performance, Paul Gilroy argues that critical scholars need to move beyond this "idea and ideology of the text and of textuality as a mode of communicative practice which provides a model for all other forms of cognitive exchange and social interaction" (Gilroy 1994, 77). Oppressed people everywhere must watch their backs, cover their tracks, suck up their feelings, and veil their meanings. The state of emergency under which many people live demands that we pay attention to messages that are coded and encrypted; to indirect, nonverbal, and extralinguistic modes of communication where subversive meanings and utopian yearnings can be sheltered and shielded from surveillance.

Gilroy's point is illustrated vividly by Frederick Douglass in a remarkable passage from his life narrative in which he discussed the improvisatory performance politics expressed in the singing of enslaved people. It is worth quoting at length:[2]

> But, on allowance day, those who visited the great house farm were peculiarly excited and noisy. While on their way, they would make the dense old woods, for miles around, reverberate with their wild notes. These were not always merry because they were wild. On the contrary, they were mostly of a plaintive cast, and told a tale of grief and sorrow. In the most boisterous outbursts of rapturous sentiment, there was ever a tinge of deep melancholy [. . .]. I have sometimes thought that the mere hearing of those songs would do more to impress truly spiritual-minded men and women with the soul-crushing and death-dealing character of slavery, than the reading of whole volumes [. . .]. Every tone was a testimony against slavery [. . .]. The hearing of those wild notes always [. . .] filled my heart with ineffable sadness [. . .]. To those songs I trace my first glimmering conceptions of the dehumanizing character

> of slavery [. . .]. Those songs still follow me, to deepen my hatred of slavery, and quicken my sympathies for my brethren in bonds. (Douglass 1969, 97–99)

Enslaved people were forbidden by law in 19th-century America to acquire literacy. No wonder, then, that Douglass, a former enslaved person, still acknowledged the deeply felt insights and revelatory power that come through the embodied experience of listening to communal singing, the tones, cadence, vocal nuances, all the sensuous specificities of performance that overflow verbal content: "they were tones loud, long, and deep" (Douglass 1969, 99).

In order to know the deep meaning of slavery, Douglass recommended an experiential, participatory epistemology as superior to the armchair "reading of whole volumes." Douglass advised meeting enslaved people on the ground of their experience by exposing oneself to their expressive performances. In this way, Douglass anticipated and extended Johannes Fabian's call for a turn "from informative to performative ethnography" (Fabian 1990, 3), an ethnography of the ears and heart that reimagines participant-observation as coperformative witnessing:

> If any one wishes to be impressed with a sense of the soul-killing power of slavery, let him go to Colonel Lloyd's plantation, and, on allowance day, place himself in the deep pine woods, and there let him, in silence, thoughtfully analyze the sounds that shall pass through the chambers of his soul, and if he is not thus impressed, it will only be because "there is no flesh in his obdurate heart." (Douglass 1969, 99)

Instead of reading textual accounts of slavery, Douglass recommended a riskier hermeneutics of experience, relocation, copresence, humility, and vulnerability: *listening to and being touched by* the protest performances of enslaved people. He understood that knowledge is *located,* not transcendent ("let him go" and "place himself in the deep pine woods, and there [. . .]"); that it must be *engaged,* not abstracted ("let him [. . .] analyze the sounds that shall pass through the chambers of his soul"); and that it is forged from *solidarity with,* not separation from, the people ("quicken my sympathies for my brethren in bonds"). In this way, Douglass's epistemology prefigured Antonio Gramsci's call for engaged knowledge: "The intellectual's error consists in believing that one can know without understanding and even more without feeling and being impassioned [. . .] that is, without feeling the elementary passions of the people" (Douglass 1971, 418). Proximity, not objectivity, becomes an epistemological point of departure and return.

Douglass recommended placing oneself quietly, respectfully, humbly, in the space of others so that one could be surrounded and "impressed" by the expressive meanings of their music. It is subtle but significant that he instructed the outsider to listen "in silence." I interpret this admonition as an acknowledgment and subversion of the soundscapes of power within which the ruling classes typically are listened to while the subordinate classes listen in silence. Anyone who had the liberty to travel freely would be, of course, on the privileged side of domination and silencing that these songs evoked and contested. In effect, Douglass encouraged a participatory understanding of these performances, but one that muffled white privilege. Further, because overseers often commanded enslaved people to sing in the fields as a way of auditing their labor, and plantation rulers even appropriated after-work performances for their own amusement, Douglass was keenly sensitive to *how* one approached and entered subjugated spaces of performance.

The mise-en-scène of feeling-understanding-knowing for Douglass is radically different from the interpretive scene set forth by Clifford Geertz in what is now a foundational and frequently cited quotation for the world-as-text model in ethnography and cultural studies: "The culture of a people is an ensemble of texts, themselves ensembles, which the anthropologist strains to read over the shoulders of those to whom they properly belong" (Geertz 1973, 452). Whereas Douglass featured cultural performances that register and radiate dynamic "structures of feeling" and pull us into alternative ways of knowing that exceed cognitive control (Williams 1977), Geertz figures culture as a stiff, awkward reading room. The ethnocentrism of this textualist metaphor is thrown into stark relief when applied to the countercultures of enslaved and other dispossessed people. Forcibly excluded from acquiring literacy, enslaved people nonetheless created a culture of resistance. Instead of an "ensemble of texts," however, a repertoire of performance practices became the backbone of this counterculture where politics was "played, danced, and acted, as well as sung and sung about, because words [. . .] will never be enough to communicate its unsayable claims to truth" (Gilroy 1994, 37).

In addition to the ethnocentrism of the culture-as-text metaphor, Geertz's theory needs to be critiqued for its particular fieldwork-as-reading model: "Doing ethnography is like trying to read [. . .] a manuscript" (10). Instead of listening, absorbing, and standing in solidarity with the protest performances of the people, as Douglass recommended, the ethnographer, in Geertz's scene, stands above and behind the people and, uninvited, peers over their shoulders to read their texts, like an overseer or a spy. There is more than a hint of the improper in this scene: the asymmetrical power relations secure both the anthropologist's privilege to intrude and the people's silent acquiescence (although one can imagine what they would say about the anthropologist's manners and motives when they are outside his reading gaze). The strain and tension of this scene are not mediated by talk or interaction; both the researcher and the researched face the page as silent readers instead of turning to face one another and, perhaps, open a conversation.

Geertz's now classic depiction of the turn toward texts in ethnography and cultural studies needs to be juxtaposed with Zora Neale Hurston's much earlier and more complex rendering of a researcher reading the texts of subordinate others:

> The theory behind our tactics: "The white man is always trying to know into somebody else's business. All right, I'll set something outside the door of my mind for him to play with and handle. He can read my writing but he sho' can't read my mind. I'll put this play toy in his hand, and he will seize it and go away. Then I'll say my say and sing my song." (Hurston 1990, 3)

Hurston foregrounds the terrain of struggle, the field of power relations on which texts are written, exchanged, and read. Whereas Geertz does not problematize the ethnographer's will-to-know or access to the texts of others, Hurston is sensitive to the reluctance of the subordinate classes "to reveal that which the soul lives by" (Hurston, 2) because they understand from experience the ocular politics that links the powers to see, to search, and to seize. Aware of the white man's drive to objectify, control, and grasp as a way of knowing, subordinate people cunningly set a text, a decoy, outside the door to lure him away from "homeplace" where subjugated but empowering truths and survival secrets are sheltered (hooks 1990). In Hurston's brilliant example, vulnerable people actually redeploy the written text as a tactic of evasion and camouflage, performatively turning and tripping the textual fetish against the white person's will-to-know. "So driven in on his reading," as Williams would say, he is blinded by the texts he compulsively seizes: "knowing so little about us, he doesn't know what he is missing" (Hurston [1935] 1990, 2). Once provided with something that he can "handle," "seize," in a word, *apprehend*, he will go away and then space can be cleared for performed truths that remain beyond his reach: "then I'll say my say and sing my song." By mimicking the reifying textualism of dominant knowledge regimes, subordinate people can deflect its invasive power. This mimicry of textualism is a complex example of "mimetic excess" in which the susceptibility of dominant images, forms, and technologies of power to subversive doublings holds the potential for undermining the power of that which is mimed (Taussig 1993, 254–55).

Note that in Hurston's account, subordinate people read and write, as well as perform. With her beautiful example of how a text can perform subversive work, she disrupts any simplistic dichotomy that would align texts with domination and performance with liberation. In Hurston's example, the white man researcher is a fool not because he values literacy, but because he valorized it to the exclusion of other media, other modes of knowing. I want to be very clear about this point: textocentrism—not texts—is the problem.

From her ethnographic fieldwork in the coal camps and "hollers" of West Virginia, Kathleen Stewart documents an especially vivid example of text-performance entanglements: how official signs and local performances play off and with each other in surprising and delightful ways. After a dog bit a neighbor's child, there was much talk and worry throughout the camp about liability and lawsuits:

> Finally Lacy Forest announced that he had heard that "by law" if you had a NO TRESPASSING sign on your porch you couldn't be sued. So everyone went to the store in Beckley to get the official kind of sign. Neighbors brought back multiple copies and put them up for those too old or sick or poor to get out and get their own. Then everyone called everyone else to explain that the sign did not mean them. In the end, every porch and fence (except for those of the isolated shameless who don't care) had a bright NO TRESPASSING, KEEP OFF sign, and people visited together, sitting underneath the NO TRESPASSING signs, looking out. (Stewart 1996, 141; see also Conquergood 1997)[3]

Through the power of reframing, social performances reclaim, short-circuit, and resignify the citational force of the signed imperatives. Moreover, Ngũgĩ wa Thiong'o's concept of "orature" complicates any easy separation between speech and writing, performance and print, and reminds us how these channels of communication constantly overlap, penetrate, and mutually produce one another (Thiong'o 1998).

The performance studies project makes its most radical intervention, I believe, by embracing *both* written scholarship *and* creative work, papers and performances. We challenge the hegemony of the text best by reconfiguring texts and performances in horizontal, metonymic tension, not by replacing one hierarchy with another, the romance of performance for the authority of the text. The "liminal-norm" that Jon McKenzie identifies as the calling card of performance studies (McKenzie 2001, 41) manifests itself most powerfully in the struggle to live betwixt and between theory and theatricality, paradigms and practices, critical reflection and creative accomplishment. Performance studies brings this rare hybridity into the academy, a commingling of analytical and artistic ways of knowing that unsettles the institutional organization of knowledge and disciplines. The constitutive liminality of performance studies lies in its capacity to bridge segregated and differently valued knowledges, drawing together legitimated as well as subjugated modes of inquiry.

There is an emergent genre of performance studies scholarship that epitomizes this text-performance hybridity. A number of performance studies–allied scholars create performances as a supplement to, not substitute for, their written research. These performance pieces stand alongside and in metonymic tension with published research. The creative works are developed for multiple professional reasons: they deepen experiential and participatory engagement with materials both for the researcher and her audience; they provide a dynamic and rhetorically compelling alternative to conference papers; they offer a more accessible and engaging format for sharing research and reaching communities outside academia; they are a strategy for staging interventions. To borrow Amanda Kemp's apt phrase, they use "performance both as a way of knowing and as a way of showing" (Kemp 1998, 116). To add another layer to the enfolding convolutions of text and performance, several of these performance pieces have now been written up and published in scholarly journals and books (see Conquergood 1988; Becker, McCall, and Morris 1989; McCall and Becker 1990; Paget 1990; Pollock 1990; Jackson 1993, 1998; Allen and Garner 1995; Laughlin 1995; Wellin 1996; Jones 1997; Kemp 1998).

Performance studies is uniquely suited for the challenge of braiding together disparate and stratified ways of knowing. We can think through performance along three crisscrossing lines of activity and analysis. We can think of performance (1) as a work of *imagination*, as an object of study; (2) as a pragmatics of *inquiry* (both as model and method), as an optic and operator of research; (3) as a tactics of *intervention*, an alternative space of struggle. Speaking from my home department at Northwestern, we often refer to the three *a*'s of performance studies: artistry, analysis, activism. Or to change the alliteration, a commitment to the three *c*'s of performance studies: creativity, critique, citizenship (civic struggles for social justice). We struggle to forge a unique and unifying mission around the triangulations of these three pivot points:

1. *Accomplishment*—the making of art and remaking of culture; creativity; embodiment; artistic process and form; knowledge that comes from doing, participatory understanding, practical consciousness, performing as a way of knowing.
2. *Analysis*—the interpretation of art and culture; critical reflection; thinking about, through, and with performance; performance as a lens that illuminates the constructed creative, contingent, collaborative dimensions of human communication; knowledge that comes from contemplation and comparison; concentrated attention and contextualization as a way of knowing.
3. *Articulation*—activism, outreach, connection to community; applications and interventions; action research; projects that reach outside the academy and are rooted in an ethic of reciprocity and exchange; knowledge that is tested by practice within a community; social commitment, collaboration, and contribution/intervention as a way of knowing: praxis.

Notwithstanding the many calls for embracing theory and practice, universities typically institutionalize a hierarchical division of labor between scholars/researchers and artists/practitioners. For example, the creative artists in the Department of Fine Arts are separated from the "serious" scholars in the Department of Art History. Even when scholars and practitioners are housed within the same department, there often is internal differentiation and tracking, e.g., the literary theorists and critics are marked off from those who teach creative and expository writing. This configuration mirrors an entrenched social hierarchy of value based on the fundamental division between intellectual labor and manual labor. In the academy, the position of the artist/practitioner is comparable to people in the larger society who work with their hands, who make things, and who are valued less than the scholars/theorists who work with their minds and are comparable to the more privileged professional-managerial class. Indeed, sometimes one of the reasons for forming schools of fine and performing arts is to protect artists/ practitioners from tenure and promotion committees dominated by the more institutionally powerful scholar/researchers who do not know how to appraise a record of artistic accomplishment as commensurate with traditional criteria of scholarly research and publication. The segregation of faculty and students who make art and perform from those who think about and study art and performance is based on a false dichotomy that represses the critical-intellectual component of any artistic work, and the imaginative-creative dimension of scholarship that makes a difference. A spurious, counterproductive, and mutually denigrating opposition is put into play that pits so-called "mere technique, studio skills, know-how" against so-called "arid knowledge, abstract theory, sterile scholarship." This unfortunate schism is based on gross reductionism and ignorance of "how the other half lives." Students are cheated and disciplines diminished by this academic apartheid.

A performance studies agenda should collapse this divide and revitalize the connections between artistic accomplishment, analysis, and articulations with communities; between practical knowledge (knowing how), propositional knowledge (knowing that), and political savvy (knowing who, when, and where). This epistemological connection between creativity, critique, and civic engagement is mutually replenishing, and pedagogically powerful. Very bright, talented students are attracted to programs that combine intellectual rigor with artistic excellence that is critically engaged, where they do not have to banish their artistic spirit in order to become a critical thinker, or repress their intellectual self or political passion to explore their artistic side. Particularly at the PhD level, original scholarship in culture and the arts is enhanced, complemented, and complicated in deeply meaningful ways by the participatory understanding and community involvement of the researcher. This experiential and engaged model of inquiry is coextensive with the participant-observation methods of ethnographic research.

The ongoing challenge of performance studies is to refuse and supercede this deeply entrenched division of labor, apartheid of knowledges, that plays out inside the academy as the difference between thinking and doing, interpreting and making, conceptualizing and creating. The division of labor between theory and practice, abstraction and embodiment, is an arbitrary and rigged choice, and, like all binarisms, it is booby-trapped. It's a Faustian bargain. If we go the one-way street of abstraction, then we cut ourselves off from the nourishing ground of participatory experience. If we go the one-way street of practice, then we drive ourselves into an isolated cul-de-sac, a practitioner's workshop or artist's colony. Our radical move is to turn, and return, insistently, to the crossroads.

NOTES

A shorter version of this paper was presented at the "Cultural Intersections" conference at Northwestern University, 9 October 1999. "Cultural Intersections" was the inaugural conference for Northwestern's Doctoral Studies in Culture: Performance, Theatre, Media, a new interdisciplinary PhD program.

1. I thank my Belizean colleague, Dr. Barbara Flores, for sharing this Garifuna material with me. I had the privilege of working with Dr. Flores when she was a graduate student at Northwestern.

2. An earlier version of the Frederick Douglass–Zora Neale Hurston discussion appeared in 1998 (Conquergood 1998).

3. Stewart's experimental ethnography is remarkably performance-sensitive and performance-saturated. Her text is replete with voices, sometimes explicitly quoted, but often evoked through literary techniques of indirect and double-voiced discourse so that the reader is simultaneously aware of the ethnographer's voice and the voices from the field, their interaction and gaps. The students in my critical ethnography seminar adapted and performed passages from the ethnography as a way of testing Stewart's stylistic innovations and textual evocations of performance.

REFERENCES

Allen, Catherine J., and Nathan Garner. 1995. "Condor Qatay: Anthropology in Performance." *American Anthropologist* 97 1 (March): 69–82.

Appadurai, Arjun. 1996. *Modernity At Large: Cultural Dimensions of Globalization.* Minneapolis: University of Minnesota Press.

Becker, Howard S., Michal M. McCall, and Lori V. Morris. 1989. "Theatres and Communities: Three Scenes." *Social Problems* 36, 2 (April): 93–116.

Burke, Kenneth. 1969. *A Rhetoric of Motives.* Berkeley: University of California Press, [1950].

Certeau, Michel de. 1984. *The Practice of Everyday Life.* Translated by Steven Rendall. Berkeley: University of California Press.

Certeau, Michel de. 1998. *The Capture of Speech and Other Political Writings.* Edited by Luce Giard. Translated by Tom Conley. Minneapolis: University of Minnesota Press, 1998.

Certeau, Michel de. 2000. *The Certeau Reader.* Edited by Graham Ward. Oxford: Blackwell.

Clifford, James. 1997. *Routes: Travel and Translation in the Late Twentieth Century.* Cambridge: Harvard University Press.

Comaroff, Jean, and John Comaroff. 1991. *Of Revelation and Revolution: Christianity, Colonialism, and Consciousness in South Africa,* Volume 1. Chicago: University of Chicago Press.

Comaroff, Jean, and John Comaroff. 1992. *Ethnography and the Historical Imagination.* Boulder, CO: Westview.

Comaroff, Jean, and John Comaroff. 1997. *Of Revelation and Revolution: The Dialectics of Modernity on a South African Frontier,* Volume 2. Chicago: University of Chicago Press.

Conquergood, Dwight. 1988. "Health Theatre in a Hmong Refugee Camp: Performance, Communication, Culture." *TDR* 32.3: 174–208.
Conquergood, Dwight. 1997. "Street Literacy." In *Handbook of Research on Teaching Literacy through the Communicative and Visual Arts,* edited by James Flood, Shirley Brice Heath, and Diane Lapp, 354–75. New York: Macmillan.
Conquergood, Dwight. 1998. "Beyond the Text: Toward a Performative Cultural Politics." In *The Future of Performance Studies: Visions and Revisions,* edited by Sheron J. Dailey, 25–36. Washington, DC: National Communication Association.
Conquergood, Dwight. 2000. "Rethinking Elocution: The Trope of the Talking Book and Other Figures of Speech." *Text and Performance Quarterly* 20.4: 325–41.
Douglass, Frederick. 1969 [1855]. *My Bondage and My Freedom.* Introduction by Philip Foner. New York: Dover.
Fabian, Johannes. 1990. *Power and Performance: Ethnographic Explorations through Proverbial Wisdom and Theater in Shaba, Zaire.* Madison: University of Wisconsin Press.
Foucault, Michel. 1980. *Power/Knowledge.* Edited by Colin Gordon. Translated by Colin Gordon, Leo Marshall, John Mepham, and Kate Soper. New York: Pantheon.
Geertz, Clifford. 1973. *The Interpretation of Cultures.* New York: Basic Books.
Gilroy, Paul. 1994. *The Black Atlantic.* Cambridge: Harvard University Press.
Gramsci, Antonio. 1971. *Selections from the Prison Notebooks.* Edited and translated by Quintin Hoare and Geoffrey Smith. New York: International.
Haraway, Donna. 1991. *Simians, Cyborgs, and Women: The Reinvention of Nature.* New York: Routledge.
hooks, bell. 1990. "Homeplace: A Site of Resistance." In *Yearning: Race, Gender, and Cultural Politics,* 41–49. Boston: South End Press.
Hurston, Zora Neale. 1990 [1935]. *Mules and Men.* New York: Harper.
Jackson, Shannon. 1991. "Ethnography and the Audition: Performance As Ideological Critique." *Text and Performance Quarterly* 13, 1 (January):21–43.
Jackson, Shannon. 1998. "White Noises: On Performing White, On Writing Performance." *TDR* 42.1:49–64.
Jackson, Shannon. 2000. *Lines of Activity: Performance, Historiography, Hull-House Domesticity.* Ann Arbor: University of Michigan Press.
Jones, Joni L. 1997. "sista docta: Performance as Critique of the Academy." *TDR* 41.2:51–67.
Joseph, May. 1999. *Nomadic Identities: The Performance of Citizenship.* Minneapolis: University of Minnesota Press.
Kemp, Amanda. 1998. "This Black Body in Question." In *The Ends of Performance,* edited by Peggy Phelan and Jill Lane, 116–29. New York: New York University Press.
Laughlin, Robert. 1995. "From All for All: A Tzotzil-Tzeltal Tragicomedy." *American Anthropologist* 97.3: 528–42.
Lavie, Smadar, and Ted Swedenburg, eds. 1996. *Displacement, Diaspora, and Geographies of Identity.* Durham: Duke University Press.
Leonardo, Micaela di. 1998. *Exotics At Home: Anthropologies, Others, American Modernity.* Chicago: University of Chicago Press.

McCall, Michal M., and Howard S. Becker. 1990. "Performance Science." *Social Problems* 37.1:117–32.

McKenzie, Jon. 2001 *Perform or Else: From Discipline to Performance.* London: Routledge.

Ong, Aihwa. 1999 *Flexible Citizenship: The Cultural Logics of Transnationality.* Durham: Duke University Press.

Paget, Marianne A. 1990. "Performing the Text." *Journal of Contemporary Ethnography* 19.1:136–55.

Pollock, Della. 1990. "Telling the Told: Performing *Like a Family.*" *Oral History Review* 18.2:1–36.

Scott, James C. 1990. *Domination and the Arts of Resistance.* New Haven: Yale University Press.

Scott, James C. 1998. *Seeing Like a State.* New Haven: Yale University Press.

Stewart, Kathleen. 1996. *A Space on the Side of the Road: Cultural Poetics in an "Other" America.* Princeton, NJ: Princeton University Press.

Taussig, Michael. 1993. *Mimesis and Alterity.* New York: Routledge.

Taylor, Diana. 1999. "Dancing with Diana: A Study in Hauntology." *TDR* 43, 1 (T161):59–78.

Thiong'o, Ngũgĩ wa. 1998. "Oral Power and Europhone Glory: Orature, Literature, and Stolen Legacies." In *Penpoints, Gunpoints, and Dreams: Towards a Critical Theory of the Arts and the State in Africa.* Oxford: Oxford University Press.

Wellin, Christopher. 1996. "'Life at Lake Home': An Ethnographic Performance in Six Voices; An Essay on Method, in Two." *Qualitative Sociology* 19, 4:497–516.

Williams, Raymond. 1977. *Marxism and Literary Study.* Oxford: Oxford University Press. 1983 [1958] *Culture and Society.* New York: Columbia University Press.

Beyond the Text
Toward a Performative Cultural Politics

The good news is that in recent decades there has been a remarkable constellation of thinking around performance. The "antitheatrical prejudice" notwithstanding, performance is now a powerful locus for research in the human sciences, a rallying point for scholars who want to privilege action, agency, and transformation (Barish 1981). The bad news is that the almost total domination of textualism in the academy makes it difficult to rethink performance in non-eurocentric ways. Edward Said coined the term "textual attitude" to describe the widespread tendency "to prefer the schematic authority of a text to the disorientations of direct encounters with the human" (Said 1979, 93). Further, he declared "that it is a fallacy to assume that the swarming, unpredictable, and problematic mess in which human beings live can be understood on the basis of what books—texts—say" (Said 1979, 93). It is ironic that progressive intellectual movements, such as cultural studies, are still dominated by a "largely 'white on white' textual orientation" (Giroux & McLaren 1994, x).

Even a performance theorist as astute as Jill Dolan does not question the hegemony of the text in her recent metadisciplinary essay: "Perhaps the most distinctive contribution of performance studies is to expand even further the scope of *the textual object,* opening its purview into folklore and festivals, rituals and rites," and so on (Dolan 1993, 430 [emphasis mine]). Because the conceptual deck is stacked in favor of text-based disciplines, methods, and epistemologies, we need to ask whose interests are served by the textualization of performance practices? What are the consequences of thinking about performance and textuality as fluid, exchangeable, and assimilable terms? What is at stake in the desire to blur the edges, dissolve the boundary, dismantle the opposition, and close the space between text and performance? What are the costs of dematerializing texts as textuality, and disembodying performance as *performativity,* and then making these abstractions interchangeable concepts? What gets lost in the exchange, in the "reworking of performativity as citationality" (Butler 1993, 14)? Because knowledge in the West is scriptocentric, we need to recuperate from performance some oppositional force, some resistance to the textual fundamentalism of the academy.

Performance studies scholars must continue to engage critically the visualist/textualist bias of western intellectual systems by deploying performance as a lever to decenter, not necessarily discard, the textualism that pervades dominant regimes of knowledge (Olson 1994). It is important to take up this challenge for at least two related reasons: (1) performance-sensitive ways of knowing hold forth the promise of contributing to an epistemological pluralism that will unsettle valorized paradigms and thereby extend understanding of multiple dimensions and a wider range of meaningful action; (2) performance is a more conceptually astute and inclusionary way of thinking about many subaltern cultural practices and intellectual-philosophical activities. Whereas a textual paradigm privileges distance, detachment, and disclosure as ways of knowing, e.g., "knowledge means rising above immediacy," a performance paradigm insists upon immediacy, involvement, and intimacy as modes of understanding, e.g., "the primordial meaning of knowledge as a mode of being-together-with" (Said 1979, 36; M. Jackson 1989, 8).

The textual paradigm is not a sensitive register for the nonverbal dimensions and embodied dynamics that constitute meaningful human interaction, what Mikhail Bakhtin calls bodies of meaning (6). Jackson notes a contradiction and cultural bias in the widespread influence of the world-as-text model in ethnography and cultural studies:

> The idea that "there is nothing outside the text" may be congenial to someone whose life is confined to academe, but it sounds absurd in the village worlds when anthropologists carry out their work, when people negotiate meaning in face-to-face interactions, not as individual minds but as embodied social beings. In other words, textualism tends to ignore the flux of human interrelationships, the ways meanings are created intersubjectively as well as "intertextually" embodied in gestures as well as in words, and connected to political, moral and aesthetic interests. Quite simply, people cannot be reduced to texts any more than they can be reduced to objects. (M. Jackson 1989, 184)

I am not reassured by the much celebrated expansion of meaning from text to textuality and intertextuality because I believe that the wider, more expansive meanings too often slide back and get compacted into the narrow meaning of text as readable words on a page (Worthen 1995).

In his study of the oppositional politics of black musical performance, Paul Gilroy also argues for the need to move beyond "the idea and ideology of the text and of textuality as a mode of communicative practice which provides a model for all other forms of cognitive exchange and social interaction" (Gilroy 1994, 77). The extreme surveillance and silencing of slaves demand that we give attention to messages that are not spelled out, to indirect, nonverbal, and extralinguistic modes of communication where utopian desires and subversive meanings could be nurtured and hidden from the sight of overseers. The textual model blocks understanding of black musical performances

> in which identity is fleetingly experienced in the most intensive ways and sometimes socially reproduced by means of neglected modes of signifying practice like mimesis, gesture, kinesis, and costume. Antiphony (call and response) is the principal formal feature of these musical traditions. It has come to be seen as a bridge from music into other modes of cultural expression, supplying, along with improvisation, montage, and dramaturgy, the hermeneutic keys to the full medley of black artistic practices. (Gilroy 1994, 78)

Gilroy's point is illustrated vividly by Frederick Douglass in a remarkable passage from his life narrative in which he discusses the improvisatory performance politics of slaves singing. It is worth quoting at length:

> But, on allowance day, those [slaves] who visited the great house farm were peculiarly excited. . . . While on their way, they would make the dense old woods, for miles around, reverberate with their wild notes. These were not always merry because they were wild. On the contrary, they were mostly of a plaintive cast, and told a tale of grief and sorrow. In the most boisterous outbursts of rapturous sentiment, there was ever a tinge of deep melancholy. . . . I have sometimes thought, that the men hearing of these songs would do more to impress truly spiritual-minded men and women with the soul-crushing and death-dealing character of slavery, than the reading of whole volumes of its mere physical cruelties. . . . Even, tone was a testimony against slavery, and a prayer to God for deliverance from chains. The hearing of those wild notes always depressed my spirit, and filled me with inef-

> fable sadness. The mere recurrence, even now, afflicts my spirit, and while I am writing these lines, my tears are falling. To those songs I trace my first glimmering conception of the dehumanizing character of slavery. I can never get rid of that conception. Those songs still follow me, to deepen my hatred of slavery, and quicken my sympathies for my brethren in bonds. (Douglass 1969, 97–99)

Slaves were forbidden by law to acquire literacy, a historical fact that underscores the exclusionary politics of textuality where even today in many parts of the world a writing elite is separated from peasants and proletarians who have restricted access to literacy (Gates 1986, 6). No wonder, then, that Douglass, a former slave, still acknowledged the deeply felt insights and revelatory power that come through the embodied experience of listening to song performance, the tones, cadence, and vocal nuances of meaning as much as the verbal content: "they were tones loud, long, and deep" (Douglass 1969, 99).

In order to know the deep meaning of slavery he recommends an experiential, participatory epistemology. Superior to the armchair "reading of whole volumes," Douglass advises meeting slaves on the ground of their experience by exposing oneself to their expressive performances. In this way, Douglass anticipates Johannes Fabian's call for a turn "from informative to performative ethnography" (Fabian 1990, 3):

> If an one wishes to be impressed with the soul-killing diets of slavery, let him go to Colonel Lloyd's plantation, and, on allowance-day, place himself in the deep pine woods, and there let him, in silence, thoughtfully analyze the sounds that shall pass through the chambers of his soul, and if he it not thus impressed, it will only be because "there is no flesh in his obdurate heart." (Douglass 1969, 99)

Douglass displaces textual authority, *reading about* the subject of slavery, with a hermeneutics of experience, copresence, humility, and vulnerability: *listening to and being touched by* the protest performances of slaves. He understands that knowledge is *located,* not transcendent ("let him go" and "place himself in the deep pine woods, and there . . ."), that it must be *engaged,* not abstracted ("let him . . . analyze the sounds that shall pass through the chambers of his soul"), and that it is derived from *solidarity with,* not separation from the people ("quicken my sympathies for my brethren in bonds"). In this way, Douglass' epistemology prefigures Antonio Gramsci's approach to knowledge:

> The intellectual's error consists in believing that one can know without understanding and even more without feeling and being impassioned (not only for the knowledge in itself but also for the object of knowledge): in other words that the intellectual can be an intellectual (and not a pure pedant) if distinct and separate from the people-nation, that is, without feeling the elementary passions of the people. (Gramsci 1971, 418)

Proximity, instead of purity, becomes the epistemological point of departure and return.

Douglass recommended placing oneself quietly, respectfully, humbly, in the space of the other so that one could be surrounded and "impressed" by the expressive meanings of their music. It is subtle but very significant that he instructed the outsider to listen "in silence." I interpret this admonition as an acknowledgment and subversion of the acoustical environment of power within which the ruling classes typically are listened to while the subordinate classes listen in silence (see Baker 1993; Slim and Thompson 1993). Anyone who had the liberty to travel at will would be, of course, on the privileged side of the structure of domination and silencing that these songs resisted. In effect, Douglass encourages a participatory understanding of these performances, but one that muffles white privilege. Further, because the performances of slaves often were commanded or appropriated as festive entertainments for the plantation rulers, Douglass is keenly sensitive to how one approaches and enters subjugated spaces of performance (see Abrahams 1992).

The *mise-en-scene* of feeling-understanding-knowing for Douglass is radically different from the interpretive scene set forth by Clifford Geertz in what is now a foundational and frequently cited quotation for the world-as-text model in ethnography and cultural studies: "The culture of a people is an ensemble of texts, themselves ensembles, which the anthropologist strains to read over the shoulders of those to whom they properly belong" (Geertz 1973, 452). The ethnocentrism of this textualist metaphor is thrown into stark relief when applied to slave culture and other disenfranchised people. Forcibly excluded from acquiring literacy, slaves nonetheless created a culture of resistance. However, instead of an "ensemble of texts," a repertoire of performance practices became the backbone of this counterculture where politics was "played, danced, and acted, as well as sung and sung about, because words, even words stretched by melisma and supplemented or mutated by the screams which still index the conspicuous power of the slave sublime, will never be enough to communicate its unsayable claims to truth" (Gilroy 1994, 37).

Instead of holding texts that properly belonged to them, slaves were themselves objects of "intextuation," held in subordinate place by an array of legal statutes, commercial auction posters, bills of sale, broadside advertisements for runaways, and so forth: "Every power, including the power of law, is written first of all on the backs of its subjects" (de Certeau 1984, 140). Moreover, the slaves' performances described by Douglass were not authorized by an originary text, nor were they sites for the reproduction of authority. They were collective upsurgings of pain and protest, "they breathed the prayer and complaint of souls boiling over with the bitterest anguish" (Douglass 1969, 37). These performances contested and subverted the soul-numbing oppression that was authorized by an entire apparatus of legal-juridical and commercial texts, as well as the dominant performative spectacles of slave auctions, that transformed human beings into property (see Roach). They created "a counterculture that defiantly reconstructs its own critical, intellectual, and moral genealogy in a partially hidden public sphere" that was directly opposed to the representations of them in public discourse (Gilroy 1994, 37–38).

Bernice Johnson Reagon provides another compelling example of counterhegemonic performance that can empower displaced people to reclaim a space of identity and resistance, and, in effect, reterritorialize dominant space. In a documentary interview with Bill Moyers, she describes the spatial-sonic politics of singing in place that was a key strategy in the struggle to end segregation in public places and secure civil rights for African-Americans:

> Sound is a way to extend the territory you can effect.
> People can walk into you way before they can get close to your body. . . .
> And certainly the communal singing that people do together
> is a way of announcing that we are here,
> that this is real
> And, so anybody who comes into that space,
> As long as you're singing,
> they cannot change the air in that space.
> The song will maintain the air
> as your territory.
> And I've seen meetings
> where a sheriff has walked into a mass meeting
> and established the air. . . .
> The only way people could take the space back

was by starting a song. And inevitably
when police would walk into a mass meeting,
somebody would start a song,
and then people would, like, join in,
and, like, as people joined in
The air would change.[1]

The power of these performances, like those Douglass recounted, is not certified by an antecedent, authorizing text. They are connected to texts, to be sure—sheriffs' arrest warrants, police reports, zoning laws, Jim Crow statutes—but these performances derive their meaning in opposition to the textuality of apartheid. At ground-level, the textualism of racial oppression does authorize performances, e.g., the sheriff's swagger, the police officer's command-the-space walk into a room, but these dominance displays get sabotaged by the counterperformances Reagon describes.

In addition to the ethnocentrism of the culture-is-text metaphor, Geertz's theory needs to be interrogated for its particular fieldwork-as-reading model: "Doing ethnography is like trying to read . . . a manuscript" (Geertz 1973, 10). Instead of listening, absorbing, and standing in solidarity with the protest performances of the people, as Douglass recommends, the ethnographer, in Geertz's scene, stands above and behind the people and, uninvited, peers over their shoulders to read their texts, like an overseer or a spy. There is more than a hint of the improper in this scene: the asymmetrical power relations secure both the anthropologist's privilege to intrude and the people's acquiescence (although one can imagine what they would say about the anthropologist's manners and motives when they are outside his reading gaze). The strain and tension of this scene are not mediated by talk or interaction; both the researcher and the researched face the page as silent readers instead of turning to face one another and, perhaps, open a conversation.

Geertz's now classic depiction of the turn towards texts in ethnography and cultural studies needs to be juxtaposed with Zora Neale Hurston's much earlier and more complex rendering of a researcher reading the texts of subordinate Others: "The theory behind our tactics: The white man is always trying to know into somebody else's business. All right, I'll set something outside the door of my mind for him to play with and handle. *He can read writing but he sho' can't read my mind.* I'll put this play toy in his hand, and he will seize it and go away. Then I'll say my say and sing my song" (Hurston 1990, 3 [emphasis mine]). Hurston foregrounds the terrain of struggle, the field of power relations on which texts are written, exchanged, and read. Whereas Geertz does not problematize the ethnographer's will-to-know or access to the texts of the Other, Hurston is sensitive to the reluctance of the subordinate classes "to reveal that which the soul lives by" (2) because they understand from experience the ocular politics that links the powers to see, to search, and to seize. Oppressed people everywhere must watch their backs, cover their tracks, hide their feelings, and veil their meanings. "The frenzy of knowing and the pleasure of looking," de Certeau argues, "reach into the darkest regions and unfold the interiority of bodies as surfaces laid out before our eyes," surfaces "which are transformed into legible spaces" (de Certeau 1984, 232, 234). Aware of the white man's drive to objectivize, control, and grasp as a way of knowing, subordinate people cunningly set a text, a decoy, outside the door to lure him away from "homeplace" where subjugated but empowering truths and survival secrets are sheltered (see hooks 1990). In this instance, the writing of texts actually is deployed by vulnerable people as a tactic of evasion and camouflage (see Scott 1990). Hurston explains how vulnerable people turn the fetishizing of texts against the white person's will-to-know. He is blinded by the texts he compulsively seizes: "—knowing so little about us, he doesn't know what he is missing" (2). Once provided something he can "handle," "seize," in a word, *apprehend,* he will go away and then space will be cleared for performed truths that remain beyond his reach: "Then I'll say my say and sing my song." By mimicking the reifying textualism of dominant knowledge regimes, subordinate people can deflect its invasive power. This mimicry of textualism is a complex example of "mimetic excess" in which the susceptibility of dominant images, forms, and technologies of power to subversive doublings holds forth the potential of undermining the power of that which is mimed (Taussig 1993, 254–55).

Hurston incisively features the manual dimension of text-interpretation: "play with and *handle* . . . in his *hand* . . . he will *seize it*. . . . "(3 [emphasis mine]). Text-reading depends on a special kind of eye-hand coordination. Beholding something in a text means holding it down, fixing it in place. It is interesting to note that the word *apprehend* has the dual meanings of grasping with the mind, "to understand," and grasping with the hand, "to arrest," "to take into custody" (see *Oxford English Dictionary* 1989). Geertz makes clear that the "inscription" of meaning is tantamount to "the fixation of meaning"—and this drive to pin down meaning, to privilege "the said, not the saying," is the defining agenda of the textual paradigm (Geertz 1983, 31). Indeed, meaningfulness is constructed as stasis, the antithesis of motion, the flux and flow of events.

This anti-motion ideology is spelled out forcefully in the preeminent articulation of the textual paradigm, Paul Ricoeur's enormously influential "The Model of the Text: Meaningful Action Considered as a Text"[2]: "Meaningful action is an object for science only under the condition of a kind of objectification which is equivalent to the fixation of a discourse by writing . . . . In the same way that interlocution is overcome in writing, interaction is overcome in numerous situations in which we treat action as a fixed text" (Ricoeur 1971, 537–538). In order for discourse to be meaningful, according to Ricoeur, *it must hold still,* or, more to the point, it must be held still: "In living speech, the instance of discourse has the character of a fleeting event. It appears and disappears. This is why there is a problem of fixation, of inscription" (Ricoeur 1971, 531).

Ricoeur values "sedimentation" over "something which flees," and sets up distance and detachment as superior to the "limits of being face-to-face" (Ricoeur 1971, 543; 442; 537). He writes in masculinist metaphors of heroic conquest and rescue that insidiously engender writing as masculine, aligned with strength, permanence, closure, objectivity, and engender performance as feminine, associated with weakness, mobility, open-endedness, and the protean: "Writing was given to men to 'come to the rescue' of the 'weakness of discourse,' a weakness which was that of the event . . . [T]he *sagen*—the saying—wants to become *Aus-sage*—the enunciation, *the* enunciated. . . . It is the meaning of the speech event, not the event as event" (Ricoeur 1971, 532). He writes as if performance process ("the saying") had fixation envy, that it yearns to be settled. Textual inscription aims to rescue meaning from perishable events, make it a perusable, inspectable, (and therefore respectable) form of knowledge, distilled from situational contingencies: "knowing that" as opposed to "knowing how," which is "knowledge without observation" (Ricoeur 1971, 538).

Instead of endeavoring to rescue the *said* from the *saying,* a performance paradigm struggles to recuperate the *saying* from the *said,* to put mobility, action, and agency back into play. Michel de Certeau set forth a performative theory of everyday life that celebrates the restless energies and subversive powers of *kinesis,* "this challenging mobility that does not respect places" (de Certeau 1984, 130). He argued that "the foundation of a textual space carries with it a series of distortions" (de Certeau 1988, 86). Chief among these distortions is fixation, the freeze-frame of action, the pinning down of practice, the *rigor mortis* of writing. Inscription, "intextuation," enables the knower to grasp without feeling, to grip without touching. He privileged timing, tuning, touching, and rupture over Ricoeur's containment, inscription, abstraction, and closure: "Whereas the object beheld can be written—made homogenous with the linearities of stated meaning and constructed space—the *voice* can create an *aparte,* opening a breach in the text and restoring a contact of body to body . . . the locus where the rupture of an excess will expand in the urgency of a 'saying,' of an act of speech which will be neither docile to a spoken truth nor subject to a statement" (de Certeau 1988, 235). Unlike Ricoeur, de Certeau thought of meaning in terms of active verbs instead of nouns, unfinalizable processes instead of enduring propositions.

De Certeau encouraged a kinetic turn toward process and event in ethnography and cultural studies that Renato Rosaldo aptly termed: "putting culture into motion" (Rosaldo 1989, 91). From structure, stasis, continuity, and pattern, ethnographers and cultural critics have turned their attention toward process, change, improvisation, and struggle. Particularly struggle. By focusing on power, ethnographers avoid apolitical theories of motion as free play, floating ironic detachments, and the endless deferral of political commitment—the hollow luxury of never having to take a stand.

The contours of this new analytic emphasis on process over product can be seen in the shifting meanings of the key word *performance* as it has emerged with increasing prominence in cultural studies. This semantic genealogy can be summarized as the movement from performance as *mimesis* to *poiesis* to *kinesis,* performance as imitation, construction, dynamism.[3] Erving Goffman was an early and influential exponent of the mimetic view of performance in the social sciences. He studied the parts of social life that are staged, clearly demarcated frontstage and backstage boundaries, and gave currency to notions of frames, role-playing, impression management, and benign fabrications. Although his work is valuable and still useful—particularly his emphasis on detailed ethnographic analysis of taken-for-granted social interactions—the ultimate effect of his dramaturgical theory was to reproduce the Platonic dichotomy between reality and appearance, and thus reinforce an antiperformance prejudice.

Victor Turner was the pivotal figure in moving performance from mimesis to poiesis with his constructional theory of performance, epigrammatically stated as "making, not faking" (Turner 1982, 93). After his sustained work on social drama, cultural performance, liminality, and, of course, definition of humankind as *homo performans,* it would be difficult for anyone to hold a "mere sham and show" view of performance. Further, the philosophy of language gave an enormous assist to the constructional theory of performance, notably the speech act theory of J. L. Austin in which the term "performative" designated the kind of utterance that actually does something in the world, e.g., promising, forgiving, apologizing, as opposed to "constative" utterances that merely report a state of affairs in the world independent of the act of enunciation (Austin 1962; Searle 1969).

Turner's influential work on the productive capacities of performance set the stage for a more post-structuralist and political emphasis on performance as kinesis, as a decentering agency of movement, struggle, disruption, and centrifugal force. Thus postcolonial critic Bhabha uses the term "performative" to refer to action that incessantly insinuates, interrupts, interrogates, and antagonizes powerful master discourses, which he dubs "pedagogical" (Bhabha 1994, 146–149). Drawing on kinetic imagery, he associates the performative with fluctuation, that which is in perpetual motion, and the pedagogical with sedimentation, that which is settled in a proper place. From Turner's emphatic view of performance as making, not faking we move to Bhabha's politically urgent view of performance as *breaking and remaking.* This is a move from cultural *invention* to *intervention.* Performance flourishes in the liminal, contested, and recreative space between deconstruction and reconstruction, crisis and redress, the breaking down and the building up of the workshop-rehearsal process, the Not Me and the Not Not Me (see Turner; Schechner).

Michael Taussig's recent work on *mimesis* makes a full circle connection with *kinesis.* He helps us understand that the subversive movement and liberating mobility can be in the miming, and that imitation can be an intervention. His view of the "make-believe" foundations of reality resonates with Donna Haraway's performative rethinking of the world as Coyote, "witty actor and agent" of transformation, the "coding trickster with whom we must learn to converse" (Taussig 255; Haraway 201).

Performance as *kinesis,* breaking and remaking, gives an altogether new and radical meaning to Dell Hymes' discussion of "performance breakthrough" in his landmark essay, "Breakthrough into Performance." Performance, according to Hymes, is a heightened, stylized mode of communication through which a speaker assumes responsibility for presentation of tradition: "performance is full, authentic or authoritative performance, when the standards intrinsic to the tradition are accepted and realized" (Hymes 1975, 84). Hymes emphasizes performance as an achievement, not a process, that an inspired communicator "breaks into," and that is keyed and set off as a distinctive moment. Richard Bauman builds on Hymes' theory and defines the "essence" of performance as "the assumption of responsibility to an audience for a display of communicative skill, highlighting the way in which communication is carried out, above and beyond its referential content" (Bauman 1986, 3). Both

Hymes and Bauman construe the performer as a conservative exemplar of audience expectations and tradition: "to responsibility for knowledge of tradition the speaker joins willingness to assume the identity of tradition's authentic performer" (Hymes 1975, 85–8). Although both performance theorists gesture towards the socio-political, their view ultimately enlists performance in the service of stabilizing status quo norms and expectations. There is little room in their theory for "a contentious, performative space" that aims to subvert, not sustain, tradition (Bhabha 1994, 157). Tradition needs to be problematized, particularly in a postcolonial world characterized by dislocation, discontinuity, and diaspora communities: "the difference of space returns as the Sameness of time, turning Territory into Tradition, turning the People into One" (Bhabha 1994, 149). Instead of construing performance as *transcendence,* a higher plane that one breaks into, I prefer to think of it as *transgression,* that force which crashes and breaks through sedimented meanings and normative traditions and plunges us back into the vortices of political struggle—in the language of bell hooks as "movement beyond boundaries" (Bhabha 1994, 207).

I have argued against the elision and absorption of performance by disciplines of the text. Although I very much appreciate contributions made by the world-as-text paradigm, particularly the way it has functioned as a counterproject to positivism, its limits need to be acknowledged and presuppositions critiqued. I hasten to emphasize, however, that there is nothing innately liberatory about performance, as several ethnographers and cultural critics have noted. Based on careful and long-term fieldwork among the Meratus of Indonesia, Anna Tsing documented how shamanic performance traditions contributed to the marginalization of women, and how women shamans used writing and picture drawing to enhance their power. In this essay, I have emphasized performance as a counterbalance to the weight and prestige given texts in the academy—both text as a metaphor for conceptualizing social reality, and actual texts (books, monographs, articles, essays, archives) as representations of knowledge. I have provided this emphasis because I believe that the hegemony of inscribed texts is insufficiently challenged even in performance-based ethnographies because, after all is said and done, the final word is on paper. Furthermore, it is interesting to note that even the most radical deconstructions still take place on the page, thus consolidating the textbound structure of the academy. The move from scholarship about performance to scholarship as, *scholarship by means of,* performance strikes at the heart of academic politics and issues of scholarly authority. Talal Asad pointed in this direction:

> If Benjamin was right in proposing that translation may require not a mechanical reproduction of the original but a harmonization with its intentio, it follows that there is no reason why this should be done only in the same mode. Indeed, it could be argued that "translating" an alien form of life, another culture, is not always done best through the representational discourse of ethnography, that under certain conditions a dramatic performance, the execution of a dance, or the playing of a piece of music might be more apt. (Asad 1986, 159)

If post-structuralist thought and the postmodern moment continue to open up received categories and established canons, more of this experimentation with scholarly form and resistance to the domination of textualism might take place. Several lines of inquiry come to mind: What are the epistemological underpinnings that would legitimate performance as a supplementary, complementary, or alternative form of research publication? What are the institutional practices that would open space for performance as scholarship? What are the rhetorical challenges and strategies for framing performance as scholarship?

For philosophical as well as pragmatic reasons, I believe that we will make the most headway on this front by juxtaposing performed scholarship with written scholarship, instead of jettisoning the text. If a performance-grounded approach to scholarship simply is pitted against the Textual Paradigm, then its radical force will be coopted by yet another either/or binary construction that ultimately reproduces modernist thinking. Performance as both an object and method of research will be most useful if it interrogates and decenters, without discarding, the text. I do not imagine the world, particularly the university world, without texts, nor do I have any wish to stop writing myself. But I do want to keep thinking about what gets lost and muted in texts. I want to take up the challenge posed by Peggy Phelan: "The challenge raised by the ontological claims of performance for writing is to re-mark again the performative possibilities of writing itself" (Phelan 1993, 148).[4] And I want to think about performance as a complement, supplement, alternative, and critique of inscribed texts. Elizabeth Enslin argued: "a concern for academic writing and the politics of the text should not marginalize other actual or potential forms of practice, such as teaching, activist research, solidarity work, writing in other languages, journalism, or communicating with audiences through drama, dance, and song" (Enslin 1994, 559). There is a growing body of research in which the published text exists in metonymic tension with embodied performance: Conquergood ("Performing as Moral Act"; "Health Theatre"), Crow, Ford-Smith, S. Jackson, McCall & Becker, Paget, Pollock, Sistren Theatre Collective, Turner & Turner.[5] Gloria Anzaldúa reminds us that "the future depends on the breaking down of paradigms, it depends on the straddling of two or more cultures" (Anzaldúa 1987, 80). This insight is as relevant for politically engaged academics as it is for "the new mestiza." Instead of a performance paradigm, I prefer to think in terms of a caravan—a heterogeneous ensemble of ideas and methods on the move.

NOTES

1. In order to evoke the cadence and rhythms of performed speech I have used the poetic transcription methods discussed and practiced by Fine (1984), Glassie (1982), Smith (1993, 1994), and Tedlock (1983); see also Conquergood & Thao (1989).

2. Geertz's culture-as-text model is derived explicitly from Ricoeur.

3. I first discussed the mimesis-poiesis-kinesis trajectory in "Ethnography, Rhetoric and Performance."

4. Feminist ethnographers recently have experimented with performance-sensitive writing styles and strategies. See particularly Abu-Lughod, Brown, Tsing, and Visweswaran. See also legal scholar Williams.

5. For a discussion of performance-text relations as metonymic, instead of metaphoric, see Strine, Long, & Hopkins (1990).

REFERENCES

Abrahams, Roger. 1992. *Singing the Master: The Emergence of African American Culture in the Plantation South.* New York: Pantheon.

Abu-Lughod, Lila. 1993. *Writing Women's Worlds: Bedouin Stories.* Berkeley: University of California Press.

Anzaldúa, Gloria. 1987. *Borderlands/La Frontera: The New Mestiza.* San Francisco: Spinsters/Aunt Lute.

Asad, Talal. 1986. "The Concept of Cultural Translation in British Social Anthropology." *Writing Culture; The Poetics and Politics of Ethnography.* Ed. James Clifford and George Marcus. Berkeley: University of California Press.

Austin, J.L. 1962. *How To Do Things With Words.* London: Oxford University Press.

Baker, Houston. 1993. "Scene . . . Not Heard." *Reading Rodney King Reading Urban Uprising,* ed. Robert Gooding-Williams. New York: Routledge.

Bakhtin, M.M. 1986. *Speech Genres.* Trans. Vern W. McGee. Austin, TX: University of Texas Press.

Barish, Jonas. 1981. *The Antitheatrical Prejudice.* Berkeley: University of California Press.

Bauman, Richard. 1986. *Slog, Performance and Event: Contextual Studies in Oral Narrative.* New York: Cambridge University Press.

Berliner, Paul. 1994. *Thinking in Jazz: The Infinite Art of Improvisation.* Chicago: University of Chicago Press.
Bhabha, Homi K. 1994. *The Location of Culture.* New York: Routledge.
Brown, Karen McCarthy. 1991. *Mama Lola: Vodou Priestess in Brooklyn.* Berkeley: University of California Press.
Butler, Judith. 1993. *Bodies That Matter: On the Discursive Limits of Sex.* New York: Routledge.
Conquergood, Dwight. 1985. "Performing as a Moral Act; Ethical Dimensions of the Ethnography of Performance." *Literature in Performance* 5: 1–13.
Conquergood, Dwight. 1988. "Health Theatre in a Hmong Refugee Camp." *The Drama Review* 32: 171–208.
Conquergood, Dwight. 1992. "Ethnography, Rhetoric, and Performance." *Quarterly Journal of Speech* 78: 80–97.
Conquergood, Dwight and Paja Thao. 1989. *I Am a Shaman: A Hmong Life Story with Ethnographic Commentary.* Trans. Xa Thao. Minneapolis: University of Minneapolis, Center for Urban and Regional Affairs.
Crow, Bryan. 1988. "Conversational Performance and the Performance of Conversation." *The Drama Review* 32: 23–54.
de Certeau, Michel. 1984. *The Practice of Everyday Life.* Trans. S. Randall. Berkeley: University of California Press.
de Certeau, Michel. 1988. *The Writing of History.* Trans. Tom Conley. New York: Columbia University Press.
Dolan, Jill. 1993. "Geographies of Learning: Theatre Studies, Performance, and the 'Performative.'" *Theatre Journal* 45: 417–41.
Douglass, Frederick. 1969. *My Bondage and Freedom.* Unabridged and unaltered republication. New York: Miller, Orton and Mulligan, 1855. Introd. Philip S. Foner. New York: Dover Publications.
Enslin, Elizabeth. 1994. "Beyond Writing: Feminist Practice and the Limitations of Ethnography." *Cultural Anthropology* 9.4: 537–58.
Fabian, Johannes. 1990. *Power and Performance.* Madison: University of Wisconsin Press.
Fine, Elizabeth. 1984. *The Folklore Text; From Performance to Print.* Bloomington, IN: Indiana University Press, 1984.
Ford-Smith, Honor. 1986. "Sistren: Exploring Women's Problems Through Drama." *Jamaica Journal,* 19: 2–12.
Fraser, Nancy. 1990. "Rethinking the Public Sphere." *Social Text* 25/26: 56–80.
Gates, Henry Louis. 1986. "Writing Race and the Difference It Makes." *Race, Writing and Difference,* ed. Henry Louis Gates. Chicago: University of Chicago Press.
Geertz, Clifford. 1973. *Interpretation of Cultures.* New York: Basic, 1973.
Geertz, Clifford. 1983. *Local Knowledge: Further Essays in Interpretive Anthropology.* New York: Basic.
Gilroy, Paul. 1991. *There Ain't No Black In the Union Jack; The Cultural Politics of Rate and Nation.* Chicago: University of Chicago Press.
Gilroy, Paul. 1994. *The Black Atlantic.* Cambridge: Harvard University Press.
Giroux, Henry and Peter McLaren, eds. 1994. *Between Borders: Pedagogy and the Politics of Cultural Studies.* New York: Routledge.
Glassie, Henry. 1982. *Passing the Time in Ballymenone: Culture and History of an Ulster Community.* Philadelphia: University of Pennsylvania Press.

Gramsci, Antonio. 1971. *Selections from the Prison Notebooks.* Ed. and Trans. Quintin Hoare and Geoffrey Smith. New York: International.

Haraway, Donna. 1991. *Simians, Cyborgs and Women: The Reinvention of Nature.* New York: Routledge.

hooks, bell. 1990. "Homeplace: A Site of Resistance." *Yearning: Race, Gender and Cultural Politics.* Boston: South End Press.

hooks, bell. 1994. *Teaching to Transgress.* New York: Routledge.

Hurston, Zora Neal. 1990. *Mules and Men.* New York: Harper.

Hymes, Dell. 1975. "Breakthrough Into Performance." *Folklore: Performance and Communication,* ed. Dan Ben-Amos and Kenneth Goldstein. The Hague: Mouton.

Hymes, Dell. 1981. *In Vain I Tried to Tell You: Essays in Native American Ethnopoetics.* Philadelphia: University of Pennsylvania Press.

Jackson, Michael. 1989. *Paths Toward a Clearing: Radical Empiricism and Ethnographic Inquiry.* Bloomington, IN: Indiana University Press.

Jackson, Shannon. 1993. "Ethnography and the Audition: Performance as Ideological Critique." *Text and Performance Quarterly* 13: 21–43.

McCall, M.M. & Howard Becker. 1990. "Performance Science." *Social Problems* 37: 117–32.

Olson, David. 1994. *The World on Paper: The Conceptual and Cognitive Implications of Writing and Reading.* New York: Cambridge University Press.

Paget, Marianne. 1993. "Performing the Text." *Journal of Contemporary Ethnography* 19 (1990): 136–55.

Phelan, Peggy. 1993. *Unmarked: The Politics of Performance.* London and New York: Routledge.

Pollock, Della. 1990. "Telling the Told: Performing *Like a Family.*" *Oral History Review* 18: 136.

Reagon, Bernice Johnson. 1991. *The Songs Are Free: Bernier Johnson Reagon with Bill Myers.* Public Affairs Television. Produced and Directed by Gail Pellett. South Burlington, VT: Mystic Fire Video.

Ricoeur, Paul. 1971. "The Model of the Text: Meaningful Action Considered as a Text." *Social Research* 38: 529–62.

Roach, Joseph. 1996. *Cities of the Dead: Circum-Atlantic Performance.* New York: Columbia University Press.

Rosaldo, Renato. 1989. *Culture and the Truth: The Remaking of Social Analysis.* Boston: Beacon.Said, Edward. 1979. *Orientalism.* New York: Vintage.

Schechner, Richard. 1985. *Between Theater and Anthropology.* Philadelphia: University of Pennsylvania Press.

Scott, James C. 1990. *Domination and the Arts of Resistance.* New Haven, CT: Yale University Press.

Searle, John R. 1969. *Speech Acts: An Essay in the Philosophy of Language.* Cambridge: Cambridge University Press.

Stare, John. 1969. *Speech Acts.* New York: Cambridge University Press.

Sistern Theatre Collective. 1987. *Lionhead Gal: Life Stories of Jamaican Women.* Toronto: Sister Vision: Black Women and Women of Colour Press.

Slim, Hugo and Paul Thompson. 1993. *Listening For a Change: Oral Testimony and Development.* London: Panos.

Smith, Anna Deavere. 1993. *Fires in the Mirror: Crown Heights, Brooklyn and Other Identities.* New York: Doubleday, 1993.

Smith, Anna Deavere. 1994. *Twilight: Los Angeles, 1992.* New York: Doubleday.

Strine, Mary, Beverly Long, and Mary Frances Hopkins. 1990. "Research in Interpretation and Performance Studies." In *Speech Communication: Essays to Commemorate the Seventy-fifth Anniversary of the Speech Communication Association.* Ed. Gerald Phillips and Julia Wood. Carbondale, IL: Southern Illinois University Press.

Taussig, Michael. 1993. *Mimesis and Alterity.* New York: Routledge.

Tedlock, Dennis. 1983. *The Spoken Word and the Work of Interpretation.* Philadelphia: University of Pennsylvania Press.

Tsing, Anna Lowenhaupt. 1993. *In the Realm of the Diamond Queen: Marginality is an Out-of-the-Way Place.* Princeton: Princeton University Press.

Turner, Victor. 1974. *Dramas, Fields and Metaphors: Symbolic Action in Human Society.* Ithaca, NY: Cornell University Press, 1974.

Turner, Victor. 1982. *From Ritual to Theatre.* New York: PAJ Publications.

Turner, Victor and Edith Turner. 1982. "Performing Ethnography." *The Drama Review* 26: 33–50.

Visweswaran, Kamala. 1994. *Fictions of Feminist Ethnography.* Minneapolis: University of Minnesota Press.

Williams, Patricia. 1991. *The Alchemy of Race and Rights: Diary of a Law Professor.* Cambridge: Harvard University Press.

Worthen, William. 1995. "Disciplines of the Text, Sites of Performance." *The Drama Review* 39: 13–28.

II
Ethnography

Performing as a Moral Act
Ethical Dimensions of the Ethnography of Performance

For the story of my life is always embedded in the story of those communities from which I derive my identity. . . . The self has to find its moral identity in and through its membership in communities such as those of the family, the neighborhood, the city, and the tribe . . . . Without those moral particularities to begin from there would never be anywhere to begin; but it is in moving forward from such particularity that the search for the good, for the universal, consists.

—ALASDAIR MACINTYRE (1984, 221)

During the crucial days of 1954, when the Senate was pushing for termination of all Indian rights, not one single scholar, anthropologist, sociologist, historian, or economist came forward to support the tribes against the detrimental policy.

—VINE DELORIA, JR. (1969, 98)

Ethnographers study the diversity and unity of cultural performance as a universal human resource for deepening and clarifying the meaningfulness of life. They help us see performance with all its moral entailments, not as a flight from lived responsibilities. Henry Glassie represents the contemporary ethnographer's interest in the interanimation between expressive art and daily life, texts, and contexts:

> I begin study with sturdy, fecund totalities created by the people themselves, whole statements, whole songs or houses or events, away from which life expands, toward which life orients in seek-

> ing maturity. I begin with texts, then weave contexts around them to make them meaningful, to make life comprehensible. (Glassie 1982, xvi)

Joining other humanists who celebrate the necessary and indissoluble link between art and life, ethnographers present performance as vulnerable and open to dialogue with the world.

The repercussions for "thinking," which Clifford Geertz attributes to Dewey, can be transposed to a socially committed and humanistic understanding of "performing":

> Since Dewey, it has been much more difficult to regard thinking as an abstention from action, theorizing as an alternative to commitment, and the intellectual life as a kind of secular monasticism, excused from accountability by its sensitivity to the Good. (Geertz 1968, 140)

This view cuts off the safe retreat into aestheticism, art for art's sake, and brings performance "out into the public world where ethical judgment can get at it" (Geertz 1968, 139).

Moral and ethical questions get stirred to the surface because ethnographers of performance explode the notion of aesthetic distance.[1] In their fieldwork efforts to grasp the native's point of view, to understand the human complexities displayed in even the most humble folk performance, ethnographers try to surrender themselves to the centripetal pulls of culture, to get close to the face of humanity where life is not always pretty. Sir Edward Evans-Pritchard wrote that fieldwork "requires a certain kind of character and temperament. . . . To succeed in it a man must be able to abandon himself to native life without reserve" (Geertz 1983, 72–73). Instead of worrying about maintaining aesthetic distance, ethnographers try to bring "the enormously distant enormously close without becoming any less far away" (Geertz 1983, 48).

Moreover, ethnographers work with expressivity, which is inextricable from its human creators. They must work with real people, humankind alive, instead of printed texts. Opening and interpreting lives is very different from opening and closing books. Perhaps that is why ethnographers worry more about acquiring experiential insight than maintaining aesthetic distance. Indeed, they are calling for empathic performance as a way of intensifying the participative nature of fieldwork, and as a corrective to foreshorten the textual distance that results from writing monographs about the people with whom one lives and studies (Turner

1982). When one keeps intellectual, aesthetic, or any other kind of distance from the other, ethnographers worry that other people will be held at an ethical and moral remove as well.

Whatever else one may say about ethnographic fieldwork, Geertz reminds us, "one can hardly claim that it is focused on trivial issues or abstracted from human concerns" (Geertz 1968, 139). This kind of research "involves direct, intimate and more or less disturbing encounters with the immediate details of contemporary life" (Geertz 1968, 141). When ethnographers of performance complement their participant observation fieldwork by actually performing for different audiences the verbal art they have studied *in situ,* they expose themselves to double jeopardy. They become keenly aware that performance does not proceed in ideological innocence and axiological purity.

Most researchers who have extended ethnographic fieldwork into public performance will experience resistance and hostility from audiences from time to time.[2] This disquieting antagonism, however, more than the audience approval, signals most clearly that ethnographic performance is a form of conduct deeply enmeshed in moral matters. I believe that all performance has ethical dimensions, but have found that moral issues of performance are more transparent when the performer attempts to engage ethnic and intercultural texts, particularly those texts outside the canon and derived from fieldwork research.

For three and a half years I have conducted ethnographic fieldwork among Lao and Hmong refugees in Chicago. The performance of their oral narratives is an integral part of my research project and a natural extension of the role of the ethnographer as participant to that of advocate. When working with minority peoples and disenfranchised subcultures, such as refugees, one is frequently propelled into the role of advocate. The ethnographer, an uninvited stranger who depends upon the patient courtesies and openhearted hospitality of the community, is compelled by the laws of reciprocity and human decency to intervene, if he can, in a crisis. Further, the stories my Laotian friends tell make claims on me. For example, what do you do when the coroner orders an autopsy on a Hmong friend and the family comes to you numb with horror because according to Hmong belief if you cut the skin of a dead person the soul is lost forever, there can be no hope of reincarnation? Moreover, that disembodied soul consigned to perpetual limbo will no doubt come back to haunt and terrorize the family.

I have performed the stories of the refugees for dozens of audiences. In addition to academic audiences, where the performance usually complements a theoretical argument I want to make about the epistemological potential of performance as a way of deeply sensing the other, I have performed them before many and varied non-academic audiences. I have tried to bring the stories of the Lao and Hmong before social service agencies, high schools where there have been outbreaks of violence against refugee students, businessmen, lawyers, welfare case workers, public school teachers and administrators, religious groups, wealthy women's clubs, and so forth. Often I have been gratified to see the way the performance of a story can pull an audience into a sense of the other in a rhetorically compelling way. Many times, however, the nonacademic audiences are deeply disturbed by these performances. I have been attacked, not just in the sessions of discussion and response immediately following these performances. One time the anger and hostility was so heated that I was invited back to face the same group two weeks later for a three-hour session that began with attack and abuse but moved gradually, and painfully, to heightened self-reflexivity (for me, as well as them). The last hour we spent talking about ourselves instead of the refugees.

Here is a partial list of the offenses for which I am most frequently condemned. Members of certain religious groups indict me for collaborating in the "work of the devil." My refugee friends are not Christian, and their stories enunciate a cosmology radically different from Judeo-Christian traditions. Fundamentalist Christians perceptively point out that by the very act of collecting, preserving, and performing these stories, I am legitimizing them, offering them as worthy of contemplation for Christians, and encouraging the Lao and Hmong to hold fast to their "heathenism." Welfare workers despise me for retarding the refugees' assimilation into mainstream America and thereby making the case-worker's job more difficult. From their point of view, these people must be Americanized as quickly as possible. They simply must drop their old ways of thinking, "superstitions," and become American. Developing resettlement programs that involve careful adjustments and blends between the old and new would require too much time or energy or money. Some social workers and administrators clearly emphasize that videotaping ancient rituals, recording and performing oral history are not morally neutral activities. Some public school educators interrogate me for performing in a respectful tone a Lao legend that explains the lunar eclipse as a frog in the sky who swallows the moon. After one performance I was asked, "How do the Lao react when you tell them they are wrong?" When I replied that I do not "correct" my Lao friends about their understanding of the lunar eclipse, the audience was aghast. Some stormed out, but some stayed to chastise me. I've been faulted for not correcting the grammar and pronunciation of the narrative texts I've collected and thus making the people "sound stupid and backward." Weeks after a performance I've received letters from people telling me how angry they were, that they "couldn't sleep" when thinking about the performance, and that it had given them "bad dreams."

In another vein, from audiences who are moved by the performance, I am sometimes challenged in an accusing tone, "How can you go back to being a professor at a rich university? Why don't you spend full time trying to help these people learn English, get jobs, find lost relatives?" In comparison to nonacademic audiences, the criticism from academic audiences pales. Nevertheless, remarks get back to me about how I'm "moving the field off-center." The ostensibly neutral question, "What does this have to do with oral interpretation of literature?" thinly veils deep misgivings. One specialist in eighteenth-century literature was more direct, and I respect him for that. At a Danforth conference, this senior gentleman rose to his feet after my presentation and in authoritative and measured tones declared: "You have confused art and nature, and *that* is an abomination!"

The one question I almost never get, however, is the "white guilt" accusation, "What right do you, a middle-class white man, have to perform these narratives?" Usually whoever introduces me gives some background information about my participant observation research. One time some audience members came in late, after the introduction, and sure enough, one of them was the first to raise his hand after the performance and accuse me of white man's presumptuousness. However, other audience members came to my defense before I had a chance to respond. They explained to him that I had lived with the people for more than three years, that I was not a weekend commuter from a comfortable suburban house. This information seemed to subdue him.

Even though my ego is probably as vulnerable as the next person's, I take courage in knowing that negative response, more than approving applause, testifies to the moral implications of this kind of work. I can be grateful to my detractors for forcing into my awareness the complex ethical tensions, tacit political commitments, and moral ambiguities inextricably caught up in the act of performing ethnographic materials. Indeed, I began doing this kind of work focused on performance as a way of knowing and deeply sensing the other. Hostile audiences have helped me see performance as the enactment of a moral stance. Now I have become deeply interested in the ethical dimensions of performing the expressive art that springs from other lives, other sensibilities, other cultures.

I agree with Wallace Bacon that the validity of an intercultural performance is "an ethical concern no less than a performance problem"

(Bacon 1984). Good will and an open heart are not enough when one "seeks to express cultural experiences which are clearly separate from his or her lived world" (Bacon 1984, 95). I would like to sketch four ethical pitfalls, performative stances towards the other that are morally problematic. I name these performative stances "The Custodian's Rip-Off," "The Enthusiast's Infatuation," "The Curator's Exhibitionism," and "The Skeptic's Cop-Out." These four problem areas can be graphically represented as the extreme corners of a moral map articulated by intersecting axes of ethnographic tensions. The vertical axis is the tensive counterpull between Identity and Difference, the horizontal axis between Detachment and Commitment (see Figure 1). The extreme points of both sets of continua represent "dangerous shores" to be navigated, binary oppositions to be transcended. The center of the map represents the moral center that transcends and reconciles the spin-off extremes. I call this dynamic center, which holds in tensive equipoise the four contrarities, "Dialogical Performance."[3] After mapping the five performative stances in order to see their alignments, I will discuss each one in more detail.[4]

The Custodian's Rip-Off

The sin of this performative stance is Selfishness. A strong attraction toward the other coupled with extreme detachment results in acquisitiveness instead of genuine inquiry, plunder more than performance. Bacon provided a striking example of this performative stance when he cited the case of the Prescott Smoki cultural preservation group who continued to perform the Hopi Snake Dance over the vigorous objections of Hopi elders. This group appropriated cherished traditions, reframed them in a way that was sacrilegious to the Hopi, and added insult to injury by selling trinkets for $7.50, all in the name of preserving "dying cultures" (Bacon 1984, 94–95). The immorality of such performances is unambiguous and can be compared to theft and rape.

Potential performers of ethnographic materials should not enter the field with the overriding motive of "finding some good performance material." An analogy from my fieldwork situation would be my performance of some of the stunningly theatrical shaman chants of Hmong healers replete with black veil over face and sacred costume. Not even a Hmong man or woman may perform these sacred traditions at will. You must be called to shamanic performance, which typically is signaled by a life-threatening illness, during which you have tremors, "shake" (*oy nang*, the Hmong word for "shaman," is the same word for "shake").

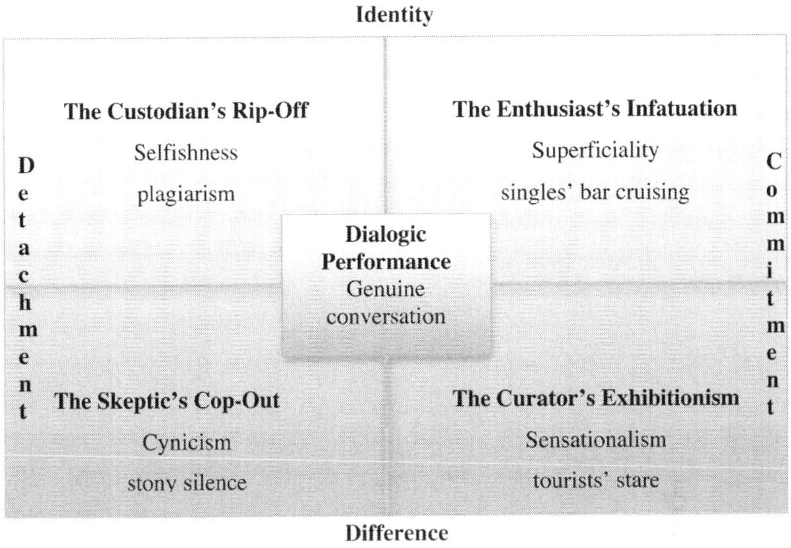

Figure 1: Moral Mapping of Performative Stances Toward the Other

When the shaman shakes and chants, he or she is talking and pleading with the spirits that control the world. These ecstatic performances are extraordinarily delicate and dangerous affairs. A Hmong shaman risks his or her life each time the soul leaves the body and ascends the tree of life on the ecstatic journey to the spirit kingdom. I had worked with the Hmong for about three years before I was privileged to witness one of these ecstatic trance performances. Now I am not only permitted, but encouraged to videotape them. I have even participated in one of these rituals of affliction as the victim. An elderly shaman "shook"—went into ecstatic performance—for my blind eye. However, I would never try to simulate one of these powerful performances because not only would that be a desecration, it would be perceived by the Hmong as having catastrophic consequences.

The Enthusiast's Infatuation

Too facile identification with the other coupled with enthusiastic commitment produces naive and glib performances marked by superficiality. This is the quadrant of the quick-fix, pick-up artist, where performance runs aground in the shallows. Eager performers get sucked into the quicksand belief, "Aren't all people really just alike?" Although not as transparently immoral as "The Custodian's Rip-Off," this performative stance is unethical because it trivializes the other. The distinctiveness of the other is glossed over by a glaze of generalities.

Tzvetan Todorov unmasks the moral consequences of too easy and eager an identification with the other:

> Can we really love someone if we know little or nothing of his identity, if we see, in place of that identity, a projection of ourselves or ideals? We know that such a thing is quite possible, even frequent, in personal relations; but what happens in cultural confrontations? Doesn't one culture risk trying to transform the other in its own name, and therefore risk subjugating it as well? How much is such love worth? (Todorov 1984, 168)[5]

"The Enthusiast's Infatuation," which is also the quadrant where "fools rush in where angels fear to tread," is neither innocent nor benign.

Fredric Jameson, to whom we are indebted for naming the Identity-Difference interpretive dilemma, (Jameson 1979) complements Todorov by showing how too easy affirming of identity not only banalizes the other, but seals off the self from any moral engagement:

> . . . if we choose to affirm the identity of the alien object with ourselves—if, in other words, we decide that Chaucer, say . . . or the narratives of nineteenth-century Russian gentry, are more or less directly or intuitively accessible to us . . . then we have presupposed in advance what was to have been demonstrated, and our apparent comprehension of these alien texts must be haunted by the nagging suspicion that we have all the while remained locked in our own present with its television sets and superhighways . . . and that we have never really left home at all, that our feeling of *Verstehen* is little better than mere psychological projection, that we have somehow failed to touch the strangeness and the resistance of a reality genuinely different from our own. (Jameson 1979)

Secure in our protective solipsism, those of us in this performative stance will never permit the other "to come before us as a radically different life form that rises up to call our own form of life into question and to pass judgment on us, and through us, on the social formation in which we live" (Jameson 1979, 70). Superficiality suffocates self as well as other.

The Curator's Exhibitionism

Whereas the enthusiast assumed too easy an Identity with the other, the curator is committed to the Difference of the other. This is the "Wild Kingdom" approach to performance that grows out of fascination with the exotic, primitive, culturally remote. The performer wants to astonish rather than understand. This quadrant is suffused with sentimentality and romantic notions about the "Noble Savage." Performances from this corner of the map resemble curio postcards, souvenirs, trophies brought back from the tour for display cases. Instead of bringing us into genuine contact (and risk) with the lives of strangers, performances in this mode bring back museum exhibits, mute and staring.

Jameson explains that when one affirms "from the outset, the radical Difference of the alien object from ourselves, then at once the doors of comprehension begin to swing closed . . ." (Jameson 1979, 43). The manifest sin of this quadrant is Sensationalism, and it is an immoral stance because it dehumanizes the other. Todorov makes strikingly clear the moral consequences of exoticizing the other in his brilliant case study of the most dramatic encounter with the other in our history, the discovery and conquest of America.[6] He clarifies how the snap-shot perspectives of "Noble Savage" and "dirty dog" can come from the same view-finder:

> How can Columbus be associated with these two apparently contradictory myths, one whereby the other is a 'noble savage' (when perceived at a distance) and one whereby he is a "dirty dog," a potential slave? It is because both rest on a common basis, which is the failure to recognize the Indians, and the refusal to admit them as a subject having the same rights as oneself, but different. Columbus has discovered America but not the Americans. (Jameson 1979, 49)

Too great a distance—aesthetic, romantic, political—denies to the other membership in the same moral community as ourselves.

The Skeptic's Cop-Out

The fourth corner of the map is the prison-house of Detachment and Difference in which, according to Jameson, "we find ourselves separated by the whole density of our own culture from objects or cultures thus initially defined as other from ourselves and thus as irremediably inaccessible" (Jameson 1979, 43–44). Instead of a performative stance, it is an easy bail-out into the no man's land of paralyzing skepticism. This corner of the map is the refuge of cowards and cynics. Instead of facing up to and struggling with the ethical tensions and moral ambiguities of performing culturally sensitive materials, the skeptic, with chilling aloofness, flatly declares, "I am neither black nor female: I will not perform from *The Color Purple.*"

When this strange coupling of naive empiricism and sociobiology—only blacks can understand and perform black literature, only white males John Cheever's short stories—is deconstructed to expose the absurdity of the major premise, then the "No Trespassing" disclaimer is unmasked as cowardice or imperialism of the most arrogant kind. It is only the members of the dominant culture who can hold to this high purity argument regarding cultural intercourse. It is a fact of life of being a member of a minority or disenfranchised subculture that one must and can learn how to perform cultural scripts and play roles that do not arise out of one's own culture. As a matter of sheer survival refugees must learn how to play American ways of thinking and social conduct. "Code-switching" is a commonplace ethnographic term used to describe the complex shifts minority peoples deftly and continuously negotiate between the communication styles of dominant culture and subculture. Todorov, who refers to his own "simultaneous participation in two cultures," (Todorov 1984, 69) offers a strong rebuttal to the skeptic's position:

> Ultimately, understanding between representatives of different cultures (or between parts of my own being which derive from one culture or the other) is possible, if the will-to-understand is present: there is something beyond "points of view," and it is characteristic of human beings that they can transcend their partiality and their local determinations. (Todorov 1984, 70)

There is no null hypothesis in the moral universe. Refusal to take a moral stand is itself a powerful statement of one's moral position. That is why I have placed squarely on the moral map the skeptic's refusal to risk encounter to show that nihilism is as much a moral position as its diagonal counterpart, naive enthusiasm. In my view, "The Skeptic's Cop-Out" is the most morally reprehensible corner of the map because it forecloses dialogue. The enthusiast, one can always hope, may move beyond infatuation to love. Relationships that begin superficially can sometimes deepen and grow. Many of my students begin in the enthusiast's corner of the map. It is the work of teaching to try to pull them toward the center. The skeptic, however, shuts down the very idea of entering into conversation with the other before the attempt, however problematic, begins. Bacon, who is keenly aware of the "deep and difficult and enduring problems," (Bacon 1984, 96) rejects the skeptic's cop-out when facing up to the alternatives for action in the world:

> What, then, do we do? Do we give up performing ethnic materials? Do we say. with Anaya, that to the Hispanics belong Hispanic treasures? Surely not, because our world has never before cried out so needfully for understanding among us all. Never has a sense of the other seemed more crucial for our own humanity. The embodiment of texts of all kinds is . . . one real path to the understanding of others. (Bacon 1984, 97)

The skeptic, detached and estranged, with no sense of the other, sits alone in an echo-chamber of his own making, with only the sound of his own scoffing laughter ringing in his ears.

Dialogical Performance

One path to genuine understanding of others, and out of this moral morass and ethical minefield of performative plunder, superficial silliness, curiosity-seeking, and nihilism, is dialogical performance.[7] This performative stance struggles to bring together different voices, world views, value systems, and beliefs so that they can have a conversation with one another. The aim of dialogical performance is to bring self and other together so that they can question, debate, and challenge one another. It is a kind of performance that resists conclusions, it is intensely committed to keeping the dialogue between performer and text open and ongoing. Dialogical understanding does not end with empathy. There is always enough appreciation for difference so that the text can interrogate, rather than dissolve into, the performer. That is why I have charted this performative stance at the center of the moral map. More than a definite position, the dialogical stance is situated in the space *between* competing ideologies. It brings self and other together even while it holds them apart. It is more like a hyphen than a period.

The strength of the center is that it pulls together mutually opposed energies that become destructive only when they are vented without the counterbalancing pull of their opposite. For example, good performative ethnographers must continuously play the oppositions between Identity and Difference. Their stance toward this heuristically rich paradox of fieldwork (and performance) is both/and, yes/but, instead of either/or. They affirm cross-cultural accessibility without glossing very real differences. Moreover, they respect the Difference of the other enough to question and make vulnerable her own *a priori* assumptions. When we have true respect for the Difference of other cultures, then we grant them the potential for challenging our own culture. Genuine dialogical engagement is at least a two-way thoroughfare. Glassie insists that the ethnographer's home culture should be as open to interpretation, questioning, weighing of alternatives, as the host culture.

> Old societies alienated from us by chronology become but academic curios, no challenge at all to the status quo. The outward search for alternatives can likewise die into thrills and souvenirs, but when the traveler is serious, the quest through space leads through confrontation into culture, into fear, and it can prove trying, convincing, profoundly fruitful. The reason to study people, to order experience into ethnography, is not to produce more en tries for the central file or more trinkets for milord's cabinet of curiosities. It is to stimulate thought, to assure us there are things we do not know, things we must know, things capable of unsettling the world we inhabit. (Glassie 1982, 12–13)

In order to keep fieldwork dialogically alive, Glassie construes it as "intimate conversation," a description that resonates both literally and metaphorically with the praxis of ethnography:

> Ethnography is interaction, collaboration. What it demands is not hypotheses, which may unnaturally close study down, obscuring the integrity of the other, but the ability to converse intimately. (Glassie 1982, 14)

Todorov makes the same point about the dialogical stance towards textual criticism:

> Dialogic criticism speaks not *of* works but *to* works, rather *with* works. It refuses to eliminate either of the two voices present. . . . The author is a "thou," not a "he," an interlocutor with whom one discusses and even debates human values. (Todorov 1984, 72)

He argues that the honesty of dialogic criticism lies in two voices that can speak simultaneously and interactively. Like good conversation, the event is a cooperative enterprise between two voices, neither of which succumbs to monologue: " . . . as in personal relations, the illusion of fusion is sweet, but it is an illusion, and its end is bitter, to recognize others as others permits loving them better" (Todorov 1984, 73).

Dialogical performance is a way of having intimate conversation with other people and cultures. Instead of speaking about them, one speaks to and with them. The sensuous immediacy and empathic leap demanded by performance is an occasion for orchestrating two voices, for bringing together two sensibilities. At the same time, the conspicuous artifice of performance is a vivid reminder that each voice has its own integrity. The performer of a Laotian cosmological legend stands before an audience in all his Scots-German facticity. Dialogical performance celebrates the paradox of "how the deeply different can be deeply known without becoming any less different" (Geertz 1983, 48). Bacon quoted Auden, who evocatively etched the moral lineaments of dialogical performance: "When truly brothers/men don't sing in unison/but in harmony" (Bacon 1984, 94).

Dialogical performance is a way of finding the moral center as much as it is an indicator that one is ethically grounded. One does not have to delay entering the conversation until self and other have become old friends. Indeed, as the metaphor makes clear, one cannot build a friendship without beginning a conversation. Dialogical performance is the means as much as the end of honest intercultural understanding. But what are the qualities one absolutely needs before joining the conversation? Three indispensables, according to Glassie: energy, imagination, and courage.

> Scholars need energy to gather enough information to create full portraits. They need imagination to enter between facts, to feel what it is like to be, to think and act as another person. They need courage to face alternatives, comparing different experiences to help their fellows locate themselves. (Glassie 1982, 12)

If we bring to our work energy, imagination, and courage—qualities that can be exercised and strengthened through dialogical performance—then we can hope not to trample on "the sweet, terrible wholeness of life" (Glassie 1982, xiv).

Finally, you don't have to do years of fieldwork with a people before you can perform their verbal art. Fieldwork is enormously time-consuming and labor-intensive; it appeals to a certain kind of person and temperament, but certainly it's not for everyone. Ethnographers would be selfish and arrogant to set themselves up as cultural game wardens, insisting that you have to have "been there" before you understand. Geertz is quite insistent that good ethnography is not dependent on the fieldworker's being possessed of some mystical powers that enable her to "commune with natives"; good ethnography can be done "without recourse to pretensions to more-than-normal capacities for ego-effacement and fellow-feeling" (Geertz 1977, 492). He argues that ethnographic understanding "is more like grasping a proverb, catching an allusion, seeing a joke—or, as I have suggested, reading a poem—than it is like achieving communion" (Geertz 1977, 492).

It is the responsibility of the ethnographer of performance to make performance texts derived from fieldwork that are accessible—and that means performable—for responsible interpreters of texts who have callings other than fieldwork.[8] The ethnographic movement in performance studies will die if it does not reach out to share the human dignity of the other, the other-wise, with audiences larger than a coteric of specialists. If it turns in upon itself, then, quite appropriately, it will become an "inside joke" that only fieldworkers can "get." The ethnographic movement is dependent on the existence of traditional interpreters and teachers of literature, who continue to deepen in new generations of students sensitivity to the other of a Renaissance text, or a contemporary poem, so that when performance texts from nonliterate cultures are produced and made available, it will be possible for more voices to join the human dialogue.

NOTES

1. For an incisive historical explanation of this concept, see Beverly Whitaker Long, "A 'Distanced' Art: Interpretation at Mid-Century," *Performance of Literature in Historical Perspectives,* ed. David Thompson (Lanham, MD: University Press of America, 1983), pp. 567–88. See also the provocative discussion of "moral distance" in Mary Frances HopKins, "From Page to Stage: The Burden of Proof," *The Southern Speech Communication Journal,* 47 (Fall 1981), 1–9.

2. See Jean Speer and Elizabeth Fine, "What Does a Dog Have to do with Humanity?: The Politics of Humanities Public Programming," paper presented at the Eastern Communication Association Convention, Ocean City, Md., 1983.

3. I have discussed "dialogical performance" in the philosophical context of the theories of Martin Buber, Mikhail Bakhtin, and Wallace Bacon in "Performance and Dialogical Understanding: In Quest of the Other," *Proceedings of the Ninth International Colloquium on Communication,* ed. Janet McHughes (Tempe: Arizona State University, 1984).

4. This graphic representation is derived from Mary Douglas' method of grid/group analysis. See *Cultural Bias* (1978) and *In the Active Voice* (1982).

5. *The Conquest of America: The Question of the Other,* trans. Richard Howard (New York: Harper and Row, 1984), p. 168. It is noteworthy that two other books have appeared recently that deal centrally with the concept of "the other": Johannes Fabian, *Time and the Other: How Anthropology Makes its Object* (New York: Columbia Univ. Press, 1983); Michael Theunissen, *The Other: Studies in the Social Ontology of Husserl, Heidegger, Sartre, and Buber,* trans. Christopher Macann (Cambridge, Mass.: MIT Press, 1984).

6. Todorov writes, "My main interest is less a historian's than a moralist's, the present is more important to me than the past," 4.

7. The recent explosion of interest in the works of Mikhail Bakhtin now being translated from the original Russian and made accessible to western readers has given widespread currency to the idea of "dialogue" as a way of being in the world. Two of Bakhtin's works now available in translation are useful starting points for engaging the complexities of his thinking: *The Dialogic Imagination,* trans. Caryl Emerson and Michael Holquist, ed. Michael Holquist (Austin: Univ. of Texas Press, 1981), and *Problems of Dostoevsky's Poetics,* ed. and trans. Caryl Emerson (Minneapolis: Univ. of Minnesota Press, 1984). I recommend also two invaluable scholarly tools for anyone working with Bakhtin: the intellectual biography by Katerina Clark and Michael Holquist, *Mikhail Bakhtin* (Cambridge: Harvard Univ. Press, 1984), and the critical assessment of his ideas in their programmatic context by Tzvetan Todorov, *Mikhail Bakhtin: The Dialogical Principle,* trans. Wlad Godzich (Minneapolis: Univ. of Minnesota Press, 1984). Clark and Holquist point out in their biography that Bakhtin had a lifelong involvement with performance and theatre ranging from the German governess who organized the young Bakhtin brothers in dramatic renderings of the *Iliad* to his dramatic performances in the Nevel theatre groups long after his university days (21). Todorov concludes his assessment of Bakhtin's lifelong career by arguing that the term that most richly encompasses the scope and depth of his intellectual project is "philosophical anthropology": "I have reserved for this last chapter those ideas of Bakhtin that I value most and that, I believe, hold the key to his whole work: they constitute, in his own terms, his 'philosophical anthropology.'" (94).

8. See Elizabeth C. Fine, *The Folklore Text From Performance to Print* (Bloomington: Indiana Univ. Press, 1984), and Dennis Tedlock, *The Spoken Word and the Work of Interpretation* (Philadelphia: Univ. of Pennsylvania Press, 1983).

REFERENCES

Bacon, Wallace. 1984. "The Interpretation of Oral and Ethnic Materials: The Ethical Dimension." *Literature in Performance* 4: 94–97.

Bakhtin, Mikhail. 1981. *The Dialogic Imagination.* Translated by Caryl Emerson and Michael Holquist, edited by Michael Holquist. Austin: University of Texas Press.

Bakhtin, Mikhail. 1984. *Problems of Dostoevsky's Poetics.* Edited and translated by Caryl Emerson. Minneapolis: University of Minnesota Press.

Clark, Katerina and Michael Holquist. 1984. *Mikhail Bakhtin.* Cambridge: Harvard University Press.

Conquergood, Dwight. 1984. "Performance and Dialogical Understanding: In Quest of the Other." *Proceedings of the Ninth International Colloquium on Communication,* edited by Janet McHughes. Tempe: Arizona State University.

Deloria, Vine. 1969. *Custer Died for Your Sins: An Indian Manifesto.* New York: Avon.

Fabian, Johannes. 1983. *Time and the Other: How Anthropology Makes its Object.* New York: Columbia University Press.

Fine, Elizabeth C. 1984. *The Folklore Text From Performance to Print.* Bloomington: Indiana University Press.

Geertz, Clifford. 1977. "From the Native's Point of View: On the Nature of Anthropological Understanding." In *Symbolic Anthropology,* edited by Janet L. Dolgin, David S. Kemnitzer, and David M. Schneider. New York: Columbia Univ. Press.

Geertz, Clifford. 1983. *Local Knowledge: Further Essays in Interpretive Anthropology.* New York: Basic Books.

Geertz, Clifford. 1983. "Slide Show: Evans-Pritchard's African Transparencies." *Raritan* 3: 62–80.

Geertz, Clifford. 1968. "Thinking as a Moral Act: Ethical Dimensions of Anthropological Fieldwork in the New States." *Antioch Review* 28: 139–58.

Glassie, Henry. 1982. *Passing the Time in Ballymenone: Culture and History of an Ulster Community.* Philadelphia: Univ. of Pennsylvania Press.

HopKins, Mary Frances. 1981. "From Page to Stage: The Burden of Proof." *The Southern Speech Communication Journal* 47: 1–9.

Jameson, Frederic. 1979. "Marxism and Historicism." *New Literary History* 11: 41–73.

Long, Beverly Whitaker. 1983. "A 'Distanced' Art: Interpretation at Mid-Century." *Performance of Literature in Historical Perspectives,* edited by David Thompson, 567–88. Lanham, MD: University Press of America.

MacIntyre, Alasdair. 1984. *After Virtue: A Study in Moral Theory,* 2nd edition. Notre Dame: Univ. of Notre Dame Press.

Speer, Jean and Elizabeth Fine. 1983. "What Does a Dog Have to Do with Humanity?: The Politics of Humanities Public Programming." Paper presented at the Eastern Communication Association Convention, Ocean City, Md.

Tedlock, Dennis. 1983. *The Spoken Word and the Work of Interpretation.* Philadelphia: University of Pennsylvania Press.

Theunissen, Michael. 1984. *The Other: Studies in the Social Ontology of Husserl, Heidegger, Sartre, and Buber.* Translated by Christopher Macann. Cambridge, Mass.: MIT Press.

Todorov, Tzvetan. 1984. *The Conquest of America: The Question of the Other.* Translated by Richard Howard. New York: Harper and Row.

Todorov, Tzvetan. 1984. "A Dialogic Criticism?" *Raritan* 4: 64–76.

Todorov, Tzvetan. 1984. *Mikhail Bakhtin: The Dialogical Principle.* Translated by Wlad Godzich. Minneapolis: University of Minnesota Press.

Turner, Victor. 1982. *From Ritual to Theatre: The Human Seriousness of Play.* New York: Performing Arts Journal Publications.

Rethinking Ethnography
Towards a Critical Cultural Politics

Critical theory is not a unitary concept. It resembles a loose coalition of interests more than a united front. But whatever it is or is not, one thing seems clear: Critical theory is committed to unveiling the political stakes that anchor cultural practices—research and scholarly practices no less than the everyday. On this point the participants in this forum agree. Yes, critical theory politicizes science and knowledge. Our disagreements arise from how we view (and value) the tension between science/knowledge and politics. Logical empiricists are dedicated to the *eviction* of politics from science. Critical theorists, on the other hand, are committed to the *excavation* of the political underpinnings of all modes of representation, including the scientific.

Ethnography, with its ambivalent meanings as both a method of social science research and a genre of social science text (see Clifford and Marcus 1986; Van Maanen 1988), has been the most amenable of the social sciences to post-structuralist critique. It presents a particularly sensitive site for registering the aftershocks of critical theory. No group of scholars is struggling more acutely and productively with the political tensions of research than ethnographers. For ethnography, the undermining of objectivist science came roughly at the same time as the collapse of colonialism. Since then, post-colonial critics have set about unmasking the imperialist underpinnings of anthropology (Mad 1973; Ashcroft, Griffiths, and Tiffin 1989; Miller 1990), the discipline with which ethnography has been closely but not exclusively associated. Clifford Geertz explains:

> The end of colonialism altered radically the nature of the social relationship between those who ask and look and those who are asked and looked at. The decline of faith in brute fact, set procedures, and unsituated knowledge in the human sciences, and

> indeed in scholarship generally, altered no less radically the askers' and lookers' conception of what it was they were trying to do. Imperialism in its classical form, metropoles and possessions, and Scientism in its impulsions and billiard balls, fell at more or less the same time. (Geertz 1988, 131–132)

The double fall of scientism and imperialism has been, for progressive ethnographers, a *felix culpa,* a fortunate fall. The ensuing "crisis of representation" (Marcus and Fischer 1986, 7) has induced deep epistemological, methodological, and ethical self-questioning.

Though some assume defensive or nostalgic postures, most ethnographers would agree with Renato Rosaldo's current assessment of the field (Rosaldo 1989, 37): "The once dominant ideal of a detached observer using neutral language to explain 'raw' data has been displaced by an alternative project that attempts to understand human conduct as it unfolds through time and in relation to its meanings for the actors." Moreover, a vanguard of critical and socially committed ethnographers argues that there is no way out short of a radical rethinking of the research enterprise. I will chart four intersecting themes in the critical rethinking of ethnography: (1) The Return of the Body, (2) Boundaries and Borderlands, (3) The Rise of Performance, and (4) Rhetorical Reflexivity.

Return of the Body

Ethnography's distinctive research method, participant-observation fieldwork, privileges the body as a site of knowing. In contrast, most academic disciplines, following Augustine and the Church Fathers, have constructed a Mind/Body hierarchy of knowledge corresponding to the Spirit/Flesh opposition so that mental abstractions and rational thought are taken as both epistemologically and morally superior to sensual experience, bodily sensations, and the passions. Indeed, the body and the flesh are linked with the irrational, unruly, and dangerous—certainly an inferior realm of experience to be controlled by the higher powers of reason and logic. Further, patriarchal constructions that align women with the body, and men with mental faculties, help keep the mind-body, reason-emotion, objective-subjective, as well as masculine-feminine hierarchies stable.

Nevertheless, the obligatory rite-of-passage for all ethnographers—doing fieldwork—requires getting one's body immersed in the field for a period of time sufficient to enable one to participate inside that culture.

Ethnography is an *embodied practice;* it is an intensely sensuous way of knowing. The embodied researcher is the instrument. James Clifford acknowledges (Clifford 1988, 24): "Participant-observation obliges its practitioners to experience, at a bodily as well as an intellectual level, the vicissitudes of translation." In a posthumously published essay, "On Fieldwork," the late Erving Goffman emphasized the corporeal nature of fieldwork:

> It's one of getting data, it seems to me, by subjecting yourself, your own body and your own personality, and your own social situation, to the set of contingencies that play upon a set of individuals, . . . so that you are close to them while they are responding to what life does to them. (Goffman 1989, 125)

This active, participatory nature of fieldwork is celebrated by ethnographers when they contrast their "open air" research with the "arm chair" research of more sedentary and cerebral methods.

Ethnographic rigor, disciplinary authority, and professional reputation are established by the length of time, depth of commitment, and risks (bodily, physical, emotional) taken in order to acquire cultural understanding. Letters of recommendation often refer approvingly to bodily hardships suffered by the dedicated ethnographer—malarial fevers, scarcity of food, long periods of isolation, material discomforts, and so forth, endured in the field.

Bronislaw Malinowski, credited with establishing modern standards of ethnographic fieldwork—whose own practice remains unsurpassed—recommended bodily participation, in addition to observation, as a mode of intensifying cultural understanding:

> [I]t is good for the Ethnographer sometimes to put aside camera, note book and pencil, and to join in himself in what is going on. He can take part in the natives' games, he can follow them on their visits and walks, sit down and listen and share in their conversations. (Malinowski 1961, 21–22)

Fifty years later, Geertz still affirms the corporeal nature and necessity of fieldwork:

> It is with the kind of material produced by long-term, mainly (though not exclusively) qualitative, highly participative, and almost obsessively fine-comb field study in confined contexts that

> the mega-concepts with which contemporary social science is afflicted . . . can be given the sort of sensible actuality that makes it possible to think not only realistically and concretely *about* them, but, what is more important, creatively and imaginatively *with* them. (Geertz 1973, 23)

Although ethnographic fieldwork privileges the body, published ethnographies typically have repressed bodily experience in favor of abstracted theory and analysis. In the shift from ethnographic method (fieldwork) to ethnographic rhetoric (published monograph), named individuals with distinct personalities and complex life histories are inscribed as "the Bororo" or "the Tikopia." Finely detailed speech and nuanced gesture are summarized flatly: "All the voices of the field have been smoothed into the expository prose of more-or-less interchangeable 'informants'" (Clifford 1988, 49). The interpersonal contingencies and experiential give-and-take of fieldwork process congeal on the page into authoritative statement, table, and graph. According to post-colonial feminist critic Trinh T. Minh-ha (Trinh 1989, 56): "It is as if, unvaryingly, every single look, gesture, or utterance has been stained with anthropological discourse . . ."

Recognition of the bodily nature of fieldwork privileges the processes of communication that constitute the "doing" of ethnography: speaking, listening, and acting together. According to Stephen Tyler the postmodern recovery of the body in fieldwork means the return of speaking, communicating bodies, a "return to the commonsense, plurivocal world of the speaking subject" (Tyler 1987, 172). He pushes this point: "Postmodern anthropology is the study of [wo]man—'talking.' Discourse is its object and means" (Tyler 1987, 171). Trinh reminds us that interpersonal communication is grounded in sensual experience: "[S]peaking and listening refer to realities that do not involve just the imagination. The speech is seen, heard, smelled, tasted, and touched" (Trinh 1989, 121). When modernist ethnographers systematically record their *observations,* they forget that "seeing is mediated by saying" (Tyler 1987, 171).

Michael Jackson wants to recuperate the body in ethnographic discourse to reestablish "the intimate connection between our bodily experience in the everyday world and our conceptual life" (Jackson 1989, 18). He argues, "If we are to find common ground with them [the people we study], we have to open ourselves to modes of sensory and bodily life which, while meaningful to us in our personal lives, tend to get suppressed in our academic discourse" (Jackson 1989, 11). Jackson wants to restore the epistemological and methodological, as well as etymological, connection between experience and empiricism. He names his project "radical empiricism" and positions it within and against "traditional empiricism." What traditional empiricism attempts to control, suspend, or bracket out—"the empirical reality of our personal engagement with and attitude to those others" (Jackson 1989, 34)—radical empiricism privileges as "the intersubjective grounds on which our understanding is constituted" (Jackson 1989, 34):

> The importance of this view for anthropology is that it stresses the ethnographer's *interactions* with those he or she lives with and studies, while urging us to clarify the ways in which our knowledge is grounded in our practical, personal, and participatory experience in the field as much as our detached observations. Unlike traditional empiricism, which draws a definite boundary between observer and observed, between method and object, radical empiricism denies the validity of such cuts and makes the *interplay* between these domains the focus of its interest. (Jackson 1989, 3)

The project of radical empiricism changes ethnography's traditional approach from Other-as-theme to Other-as-interlocutor (Theunissen 1984), and represents a shift from monologue to dialogue, from information to communication.

Jackson provocatively argues that traditional ethnographic "pretenses" about detached observation and scientific method reveal anxiety about the uncontrollable messiness of any truly interesting fieldwork situation:

> Indeed, given the arduous conditions of fieldwork, the ambiguity of conversations in a foreign tongue, differences of temperament, age, and gender between ourselves and our informants, and the changing theoretical models we are heir to, it is likely that 'objectivity' serves more as a magical token, bolstering our sense of self in disorienting situations, than as a scientific method for describing those situations as they really are. (Jackson 1989, 3)

The radical empiricist's response to the vulnerabilities and vicissitudes of fieldwork is honesty, humility, self-reflexivity, and an acknowledgement of the interdependence and reciprocal role-playing between knower and known:

> In this process we put ourselves on the line; we run the risk of having our sense of ourselves as different and distanced from the people we study dissolve, and with it all our pretensions to a supraempirical position, a knowledge that gets us above and beyond the temporality of human existence. (Jackson 1989, 4)

Johannes Fabian focuses on temporality as a strategy for bringing back the body-in-time in ethnographic discourse, and with it the body politic. In a trenchant rhetorical critique of ethnographic texts he identifies the "denial of coevalness" as a strategy for "keeping Anthropology's Other in another time" and thereby keeping "others" in their marginal place (Fabian 1983, 148). Coevalness is the experience of cotemporality, the recognition of actively sharing the same time, the acknowledgement of others as contemporaries. Fabian argues forcefully that ethnography manifests "schizochronic tendencies" (Fabian 1983, 37). On the one hand, the discipline insists on the coeval experience of fieldwork as the source of ethnographic knowledge, and on the other hand, this coevalness is denied in professional discourse that temporally distances others through labels such as "tribal," "traditional," "ancient," "animistic," "primitive," "preliterate," "neolithic," "underdeveloped," or the slightly more polite "developing," and so forth. Clifford calls this tactic a "temporal setup" (Clifford 1988, 16). In a deeply contradictory way, ethnographers go to great lengths to become cotemporal with others during fieldwork but then deny in writing that these others with whom they lived are their contemporaries. Fabian warns, "These disjunctions between experience and science, research and writing, will continue to be a festering epistemological sore" (Fabian 1983, 33).

More problematically, he reveals how the expansionist campaigns of colonialist-imperialist policies "required Time to accommodate the schemes of a one-way history: progress, development, modernity (and their negative mirror images: stagnation, underdevelopment, tradition). In short, *geopolitics* has its ideological foundations in *chronopolitics*" (Fabian 1983, 144). Anthropology is complicit with imperialism and the ideology of progress when it rhetorically distances the Other in Time.

For Fabian, the way to prevent temporal reifications of other cultures is for ethnographers to rethink themselves as communicators, not scientists. He states this fundamental point in strong terms, "Only as communicative praxis does ethnography carry the promise of yielding new knowledge about another culture" (Fabian 1983, 71). Ethnographers must recognize "that fieldwork is a form of communicative interaction with an Other, one that must be carried out coevally, on the basis of shared intersubjective Time and intersocietal contemporaneity" (Fabian 1983, 148). He privileges communication because "for human communication to occur, coevalness has to be *created*. Communication is, ultimately, about creating shared Time" (Fabian 1983, 30–31). Whereas Paul Ricoeur (1971) wanted to fix the temporal flow and leakage of speaking, to rescue "the said" from "the saying," contemporary ethnographers struggle to recuperate "the saying from the said," to shift their enterprise from nouns to verbs, from mimesis to kinesis, from textualized space to co-experienced time.

This rethinking of ethnography as primarily about speaking and listening, instead of observing, has challenged the visualist bias of positivism with talk about voices, utterances, intonations, multivocality. Sight and observation go with space, and the spatial practices of division, separation, compartmentalization, and surveillance. According to Rosaldo "the eye of ethnography" is connected to "the I of imperialism" (Rosado 1989, 41). Sight and surveillance depend on detachment and distance. Getting perspective on something entails withdrawal from intimacy. Everyday parlance equates objectivity with aloofness. Being "too close" is akin to losing perspective and lacking judgment.

Metaphors of sound, on the other hand, privilege temporal process, proximity, and incorporation. Listening is an interiorizing experience, a gathering together, a drawing in, whereas observation sizes up exteriors. The communicative praxis of speaking and listening, conversation, demands copresence even as it decenters the categories of knower and known. Vulnerability and self-disclosure are enabled through conversations. Closure, on the other hand, is constituted by the gaze. The return of the body as a recognized method for attaining "vividly felt insight into the life of other people" (Trinh 1989, 123) shifts the emphasis from space to time, from sight and vision to sound and voice, from text to performance, from authority to vulnerability.

Boundaries and Borderlands

Geertz's well-known "Blurred Genres" essay charts ethnography's ambivalent participation in the postmodern redistribution of analytical foci from center to periphery, delimitation to dispersal, whole to fragment, metropole to margin (Geertz 1983, 19–35). To be sure, ethnographers for a long time have been situated more characteristically in the peripheral village than in the metropolitan center. They have been predisposed professionally to seek out the frontier and hinterlands, the colony rather than the capital. But this preoccupation with marginal cultures that obliged them figuratively and literally to live on the boundary did not prevent them from still seeing identity and culture, self and other, as discrete, singular, integral, and stable concepts. Once they crossed the border and pitched their tent on the edge of the encampment, they confidently set about describing "the Trobrianders," or "the Nuer," or "the ghetto," interpreting these cultures as distinct, coherent, whole ways of life. In so doing, they centralized the peripheral instead of de-centering the "metropolitan typifications" that they carried inside their heads (Rosaldo 1989, 207).

All that confidence in continuous traditions and innocent encounters with pristine cultures has been shattered in our post-colonial epoch. Borders bleed, as much as they contain. Instead of dividing lines to be patrolled or transgressed, boundaries are now understood as crisscrossing sites inside the postmodern subject. Difference is resituated within, instead of beyond, the self. Inside and outside distinctions, like genres, blur and wobble. Nothing seems truer now than Trinh's pithy insight "Despite our desperate, eternal attempt to separate, contain, and mend, categories always leak" (Trinh 1989, 94).

Rosaldo believes that contemporary geo-politics, including decolonization and multinational corporations, requires thinking about boundaries not simply as barriers but as bridges and membranes, "All of us inhabit an interdependent late-twentieth-century world marked by borrowing and lending across porous national and cultural boundaries that are saturated with inequality, power, and domination" (Rosaldo 1989, 217). Further, the border-crossings emblematic of our postmodern world challenge ethnography to rethink its project: "If ethnography once imagined it could describe discrete cultures, it now contends with boundaries that crisscross over a field at once fluid and saturated with power. In a world where 'open borders' appear more salient than 'closed communities,' one wonders how to define a project for cultural studies" (Rosaldo 1989, 45). Rosaldo argues that the research agenda needs to move from centers to "borderlands," "zones of difference," and "busy intersections" where many identities and interests articulate with multiple others (Rosaldo 1989, 17, 28).

The major epistemological consequence of displacing the idea of solid centers and unified wholes with borderlands and zones of contest is a rethinking of identity and culture as constructed and relational, instead of ontologically given and essential. This rethinking privileges metonym, "reasoning part-to-part" over synecdoche, "reasoning part-to-whole" (Tyler 1987, 151); it features syntax over semantics. Meaning is contested and struggled for in the interstices, *in between* structures. Identity is invented and contingent, not autonomous: "'I' is, therefore, not a unified subject, a fixed identity, or that solid mass covered with layers of superficialities one has gradually to peel off before one can see its true face. 'I' is, itself, *infinite layers*" (Trinh 1989, 94).

Clifford argues that much of non-western historical experience has been "hemmed in by concepts of continuous tradition and the unified self" (Clifford 1988, 10). The presuppositions of pattern, continuity, coherence, and unity characteristic of classic ethnography may have had more to do with the West's ideological commitment to individualism than with on-the-ground cultural practices. "I argue," says Clifford, "that identity, ethnographically considered, must always be mixed, relational, and inventive" (Clifford 1988, 10). The idea of the person shifts from that of a fixed, autonomous self to a polysemic site of articulation for multiple identities and voices.

From the boundary perspective, identity is more like a performance in process than a postulate, premise, or originary principle. From his historical study of the "colonial assault" on Melanesia, and his 1977 fieldwork study of a courtroom trial in Massachusetts where land ownership by Mashpee Native Americans was contingent upon "proof" of tribal identity, Clifford came to understand identity as provisional, "not as an archaic survival but as an ongoing process, politically contested and historically unfinished" (Clifford 1988, 9). In our postmodern world the refugee, exile, has become an increasingly visible sign of geopolitical turbulence as well as the emblematic figure for a more general feeling of displacement, dispersal, what Clifford describes as "a pervasive condition of off-centeredness . . ." (Clifford 1988, 9).

Betwixt and between worlds, suspended between a shattered past and insecure future, refugees and other displaced people must create an "inventive poetics of reality" for recollecting, recontextualizing, and refashioning their identities (Clifford 1988, 6). The refugee condition epitomizes a postmodern existence of border-crossings and life on the margins. With displacement, upheaval, unmooring, come the terror and potentiality of flux, improvisation, and creative recombinations. Refugees, exiles, homeless people, and other nomads enact the poststructuralist idea of "putting culture into motion" through experiences that are both violent and regenerative (Rosaldo 1989, 91). Taking the Caribbean as an illuminating example, Clifford notes that its history is one of "degradation, mimicry, violence, and blocked possibilities," but it is also "rebellious, syncretic, and creative" (Clifford 1988, 15).

In *The Practice of Everyday Life,* Michel de Certeau celebrates the interventions of marginal people whose creativity, "the art of making do," gets finely honed from living on the edge, a borderlands life:

> Thus a North African living in Paris or Boubaix (France) insinuates *into* the system imposed on him by the construction of a low-income housing development or of the French language the ways of 'dwelling' (in a house or a language) peculiar to his native Kabylia. He superimposes them and, by that combination, creates for himself a space in which he can find *ways of using* the constraining order of the place or of the language. Without leaving the place where he has no choice but to live and which lays down its law for him, he establishes within it a degree of *plurality* and creativity. By an art of being in between, he draws unexpected results from his situation. (de Certeau 1984, 30)

My own fieldwork with refugees and migrants in Thailand, the Gaza Strip, and inner-city Chicago resonates deeply with Clifford's observations. "Many traditions, languages, cosmologies, and values are lost, some literally murdered; but much has simultaneously been invented and revived in complex, oppositional contexts. If the victims of progress and empire are weak, they are seldom passive" (Clifford 1988, 16).

There are implications for rhetoric and communication studies from ethnography's current interest in boundary phenomena and border negotiations. Communication becomes even more urgent and necessary in situations of displacement, exile, and erasure. Trinh, a Vietnamese-American woman, speaking as an exile to other exiles, articulates the difficulty and urgency of expression for all refugees and displaced people:

> You who understand the dehumanization of forced removal-relocation-reeducation-redefinition, the humiliation of having to falsify your own reality, your voice—you know. And often cannot *say* it. You try and keep on trying to unsay it, for if you don't, they will not fail to fill in the blanks on your behalf, and you will be said (Trinh 1989, 80).

The *discourse of displacement* is a project that beckons rhetorical and communication scholars.

And if the increasingly pervasive feeling of discontinuity and finding oneself "off center among scattered traditions" (Clifford 1988, 3) incites us to speak, then we must draw on *topoi* from among multiple discursive styles and traditions. Jackson notes the intertextual and heteroglossic nature of discourse. "Reviewing the historical mutability of discourse,

I am also mindful that no one episteme ever completely supercedes another. The historical matrix in which our present discourse is embedded contains other discursive styles and strategies, and makes use of them" (Clifford 1989, 176). Never has the rhetorical canon of *inventio* taken on more emphatic meaning than in the current rethinking of culture and ethos (see Wagner 1980).

Cities throughout the United States have become sites of extraordinary diversity as refugees and immigrants, increasingly from the hemispheres of the South and the East, pour into inner-city neighborhoods. Rosaldo makes the point that one does not have to go to the "Third World" to encounter culture in the borderlands. "Cities throughout the world today increasingly include minorities defined by race, ethnicity, language, class, religion, and sexual orientation. Encounters with 'difference' now pervade modern everyday life in urban settings" (Rosaldo 1989, 28). For more than three years I have been conducting ethnographic research in one of these polyglot immigrant neighborhoods in inner-city Chicago. More than 50 languages and dialects are spoken by students at the local high school. The "Bilingual Student Roster" displays an exotic array of languages that in addition to Spanish, Korean, and Arabic, includes Assyrian, Tagalog, Vietnamese, Khmer, Hmong, Malayalam, Gujarati, Lao, Urdu, Cantonese, Greek, Pashto, Thai, Punjabi, Italian, Armenian, Dutch, Turkish, lbo, Amharic, Slovenian, Farsi, and others. For the first 20 months of fieldwork I lived in an apartment alongside refugee and immigrant neighbors from Mexico, Puerto Rico, Iraq, Laos, Cambodia, Poland, Lebanon, as well as African-American, Appalachian White, and elderly Jew all living cheek-by-jowl in the same crowded, dilapidated tenement building. The local street gang with which I work reflects the same polyglot texture of the neighborhood. It is called the Latin Kings, originally a Puerto Rican gang, but the current members include Assyrian, African-American, Puerto Rican, Guatemalan, Salvadoran, Vietnamese, Lao, Korean, Palestinian, Filipino, Mexican, White, and others (Conquergood, Friesma, Hunter and Mansbridge, 1990).

Few phrases have more resonance in contemporary ethnography—and with my own fieldwork—than Bakhtin's powerful affirmation that "the most intense and productive life of culture takes place on the boundaries. . . ." (Bakhtin 1986, 2).

The Rise of Performance

With renewed appreciation for boundaries, border-crossings, process, improvisation, contingency, multiplex identities, and the embodied nature of fieldwork practice, many ethnographers have turned to a performance-inflected vocabulary. "In the social sciences," Geertz observes, "the analogies are coming more and more from the contrivances of cultural performance than from those of physical manipulation" (Geertz 1983, 22). No one has done more than Victor Turner to open up space in ethnography for performance, to move the field away from preoccupations with universal system, structure, form, and towards particular practices, people, and performances. A dedicated ethnographer, Turner wanted the professional discourse of cultural studies to capture the struggle, passion, and praxis of village life that he so relished in the field. The language of drama and performance gave him a way of thinking and talking about people as actors who creatively play, improvise, interpret, and re-present roles and scripts. In a rhetorical masterstroke, Turner subversively redefined the fundamental terms of discussion in ethnography by defining humankind as *homo performans,* humanity as performer, a culture-inventing, social-performing, self-making and self-transforming creature (Turner 1986, 81). Turner was drawn to the conceptual lens of performance because it focused on humankind alive, the creative, playful, provisional, imaginative, articulate expressions of ordinary people grounded in the challenge of making a life in this village, that valley, and inspired by the struggle for meaning.

Distinguishing characteristics of performance-sensitive research emerge from Turner's detailed and elaborated work on social drama and cultural performance. The performance paradigm privileges particular, participatory, dynamic, intimate, precarious, embodied experience grounded in historical process, contingency, and ideology. Another way of saying it is that performance-centered research takes as both its subject matter and method the experiencing body situated in time, place, and history. The performance paradigm insists on face-to-face encounters instead of abstractions and reductions. It situates ethnographers within the delicately negotiated and fragile "face-work" that is part of the intricate and nuanced dramaturgy of everyday life (see Goffman, 1967).

Turner appreciated the heuristics of embodied experience because he understood how social dramas must be acted out and rituals performed in order to be meaningful, *and* he realized how the ethnographer must be a co-performer in order to understand those embodied meanings. In one of his earlier works he enunciated the role of the performing body as a hermeneutical agency both for the researcher as well as the researched:

> The religious ideas and processes I have just mentioned belong to the domain of performance, their power derived from the par-

> ticipation of the living people who use them. My counsel, therefore, to investigators of ritual processes would be to learn them in the first place "on their pulses," in coactivity with their enactors, having beforehand shared for a considerable time much of the people's daily life and gotten to know them not only as players of social roles, but as unique individuals, each with a style and a soul of his or her own. Only by these means will the investigator become aware. . . . (Turner 1975, 28–29)

The bodily image of learning something "on their pulses" captures the distinctive method of performance-sensitive ethnography. The power dynamic of the research situation changes when the ethnographer moves from the gaze of the distanced and detached observer to the intimate involvement and engagement of "coactivity" or co-performance with historically situated, named, "unique individuals."

The performance paradigm can help ethnographers recognize "the limitations of literacy" and critique the textualist bias of western civilization (Jackson, 1989). Geertz enunciates the textual paradigm in his famous phrase: "The culture of a people is an ensemble of texts, themselves ensembles, which the anthropologist strains to read over the shoulders of those to whom they properly belong" (Geertz 1973, 452). In other words, the ethnographer is construed as a displaced, somewhat awkward reader of texts. Jackson vigorously critiques this ethnographic textualism:

> By fetishizing texts, it divides—as the advent of literacy itself did—readers from authors, and separates both from the world. The idea that "there is nothing outside the text" may be congenial to someone whose life is confined to academe, but it sounds absurd in the village worlds where anthropologists carry out their work, where people negotiate meaning in face-to-face interactions, not as individual minds but as embodied social beings. In other words, textualism tends to ignore the flux of human relationships, the ways meanings are created intersubjectively as well as "intertextually," embodied in gestures as well as in words, and connected to political, moral, and aesthetic interests. (Jackson 1989, 184)

Though possessed of a long historical commitment to the spoken word, rhetoric and communication suffer from this same valorizing of inscribed texts. A recent essay in the *Quarterly Journal of Speech* provides a stunning example of the field's extreme textualism: "Such a [disciplinary] grounding can only come about in the moment of methodological commitment *when someone sits down with a transcript of discourse* and attempts to explain it to students or colleagues—in *that moment we become scholars of communication*" (Brummett 1990, 71; emphasis mine). In the quest for intellectual respectability through disciplinary rigor, some communication and rhetorical scholars have narrowed their focus to language, particularly those aspects of language that can be spatialized on the page, or measured and counted, to the exclusion of embodied meanings that are accessible through ethnographic methods of "radical empiricism" (Jackson 1989).

The linguistic and textualist bias of speech communication has blinded many scholars to the preeminently rhetorical nature of cultural performance—ritual, ceremony, celebration, festival, parade, pageant, feast, and so forth. It is not just in non-western cultures, but in many so-called "modern" communities that cultural performance functions as a special form of public address, rhetorical agency:

> [C]ultural performances are not simple reflectors or expressions of culture or even of changing culture but may themselves be active agencies of change, representing the eye by which culture sees itself and the drawing board on which creative actors sketch out what they believe to be more apt or interesting "designs for living." . . . Performative reflexivity is a condition in which a sociocultural group, or its most perceptive members acting representatively, turn, bend or reflect back upon themselves, upon the relations, actions, symbols, meanings, codes, roles, statuses, social structures, ethical and legal rules, and other sociocultural components which make up their public "selves." (Turner 1986, 24)

Through cultural performances many people both construct and participate in "public" life. Particularly for poor and marginalized people denied access to middle-class "public" forums, cultural performance becomes the venue for "public discussion" of vital issues central to their communities, as well as an arena for gaining visibility and staging their identity. Nancy Fraser's concept of "subaltern counterpublics" is very useful: " . . . arenas where members of subordinated social groups invent and circulate counterdiscourses, which in turn permit them to formulate oppositional interpretations of their identities, interests, and needs" (Fraser 1990, 67).

What every ethnographer understands, however, is that the mode of "discussion," the discourse, is not always and exclusively verbal: Issues and attitudes are expressed and contested in dance, music, gesture, food, ritual artifact, symbolic action, as well as words. Cultural performances are not simply epideictic spectacles: Investigated historically within their political contexts, they are profoundly deliberative occasions (see Fernandez 1986).

Although cultural performances often frame a great deal of speech-making—formal oratory, stylized recitation and chant, as well as backstage talk and informal conversation—it would be a great mistake for a communication researcher simply "to sit down with a transcript of discourse" and privilege words over other channels of meaning. Turner emphatically resists valorizing language or studying any of the multiple codes of performed meaning extricated from their complex interactions: "This is an important point—rituals, dramas, and other performative genres are often orchestrations of media, not expressions in a single medium" (Turner 1986, 23). There is a complex interplay, for example, between song, gesture, facial expressions, and the burning of incense, and even incense has different meanings when it is burned at different times, and there are different kinds of incense. "The master-of-ceremonies, priest, producer, director creates art from the ensemble of media and codes, just as a conductor in the single genre of classical music blends and opposes the sounds of the different instruments to produce an often unrepeatable effect" (Turner 1986, 23).

Turner encourages ethnographers to study the interplay of performance codes, focussing on their syntactic relationships rather than their semantics:

> It is worth pointing out, too, that it is not, as some structuralists have argued, a matter of emitting the *same* message in different media and codes, the better to underline it by redundancy. The "same" message in different media is really a set of subtly variant messages, each medium contributing its own generic message to the message conveyed through it. The result is something like a hall of mirrors—magic mirrors, each interpreting as well as reflecting the images beamed to it, and flashed from one to the others. (Turner 1986, 23–24)

The polysemic nature of cultural performances "makes of these genres flexible and nuanced instruments capable of carrying and communicating many messages at once, even of subverting on one level what it appears to be 'saying' on another" (Turner 1986, 24). The performance paradigm is an alternative to the atemporal, decontextualized, flattening approach of text-positivism.

Rethinking the "world as text" to the "world as performance" opens up new questions that can be clustered around five intersecting planes of analyses:

1. *Performance and Cultural Process.* What are the conceptual consequences of thinking about culture as a *verb* instead of a *noun*, process instead of product? Culture as unfolding performative invention instead of reified system, structure, or variable? What happens to our thinking about performance when we move it outside of Aesthetics and situate it at the center of lived experience?
2. *Performance and Ethnographic Praxis.* What are the methodological implications of thinking about fieldwork as the collaborative performance of an enabling fiction between observer and observed, knower and known? How does thinking about fieldwork as performance differ from thinking about fieldwork as the collection of data? Reading of texts? How does the performance model shape the conduct of fieldwork? Relationship with the people? Choices made in the field? Positionality of the researcher?
3. *Performance and Hermeneutics.* What kinds of knowledge are privileged or displaced when performed experience becomes a way of knowing, a method of critical inquiry, a mode of understanding? What are the epistemological and ethical entailments of performing ethnographic texts and fieldnotes? What are the range and varieties of performance modes and styles that can enable interpretation and understanding?
4. *Performance and Scholarly Representation.* What are the rhetorical problematics of performance as a complementary or alternative form of "publishing" research? What are the differences between reading an analysis of fieldwork data, and hearing the voices from the field interpretively filtered through the voice of the researcher? For the listening audience of peers? For the performing ethnographer? For the people whose lived experience is the subject matter of the ethnography? What about enabling the people themselves to perform their own experience? What are the epistemological underpinnings and institutional practices that would legitimate performance as a complementary form of research publication?
5. *The Politics of Performance.* What is the relationship between

> performance and power? How does performance reproduce, enable, sustain, challenge, subvert, critique, and naturalize ideology? How do performances simultaneously reproduce and resist hegemony? How does performance accommodate and contest domination?

The most work has been done in Numbers One, Two, and Five, particularly One. Although we still need to think more deeply and radically about the performative nature of culture, Erving Goffman, Kenneth Burke, Dell Hymes, and a host of other social theorists have already set the stage. The expansive reach of conceptualizing performance as the agency for constituting and reconstituting culture, leads from performance as Agency to performance as ultimate Scene: "All the world's a stage." The popularity of Shakespeare's adage notwithstanding, we scarcely have begun to unpack and understand the radical potential of that idea.

Numbers Three and especially Four are the most deeply subversive and threatening to the text-bound structure of the academy. It is one thing to talk about performance as a model for cultural process, as a heuristic for understanding social life, as long as that performance-sensitive talk eventually gets "written up." The intensely performative and bodily experience of fieldwork is redeemed through writing. The hegemony of inscribed texts is never challenged by fieldwork because, after all is said and done, the final word is on paper. Print publication is the telos of fieldwork. It is interesting to note that even the most radical deconstructions still take place on the page. "Performance as a Form of Scholarly Representation" challenges the domination of textualism.

Turner advocated, practiced, and wrote about performance as a critical method for interpreting and intensifying fieldwork data (Turner 1986, 139–155). It is quite another thing, politically, to move performance from hermeneutics to a form of scholarly representation. That move strikes at the heart of academic politics and issues of scholarly authority. Talal Asad points in this direction:

> If Benjamin was right in proposing that translation may require not a mechanical reproduction of the original but a harmonization with **its *intentio,*** it follows that there is no reason why this should be done only in the same mode. indeed, it could be argued that "translating" an alien form of life, another culture, is not always done best through the representational discourse of ethnog-

> raphy, that under certain conditions a dramatic performance, the execution of a dance, or the playing of a piece of music might be more apt. (Asad 1986, 159)

If post-structuralist thought and the postmodern moment continue to open up received categories and established canons, more of this experimentation with scholarly form might happen. If the Performance Paradigm simply is pitted against the Textual Paradigm, then its radical force will be coopted by yet another either/or binary construction that ultimately reproduces modernist thinking. The Performance Paradigm will be most useful if it decenters, without discarding, texts. I do not imagine life in a university without books, nor do I have any wish to stop writing myself. But I do want to keep thinking about what gets lost and muted in texts. And I want to think about performance as a complement, alternative, supplement, and critique of inscribed texts. Following Turner and others, I want to keep opening up space for nondiscursive forms, and encouraging research and writing practices that are performance-sensitive.

Rhetorical Reflexivity

Far from displacing texts, contemporary ethnography is extremely interested in and self-conscious about its own text-making practices. There is widespread recognition of "the fact that ethnography is, from beginning to end, enmeshed in writing" (Clifford 1988, 25). These writings are not innocent descriptions through which the other is transparently revealed. "It is more than ever crucial for different peoples to form complex concrete images of one another," Clifford affirms, "as well as of the relationships of knowledge and power that connect them; but no sovereign scientific method or ethical stance can guarantee the truth of such images. They are constituted—the critique of colonial modes of representation has shown at least this much—in specific historical relations of dominance and dialogue" (Clifford 1988, 23). Geertz argues that even "the pretense of looking at the world directly, as though through a one-way screen, seeing others as they really are when only God is looking . . . is itself a rhetorical strategy, a mode of persuasion" (Geertz 1988, 141).

Ethnography is being rethought in fundamentally rhetorical terms. Many of the most influential books recently published in ethnography are meta-rhetorical critiques. It seems that everyone in ethnography nowadays is a rhetorical critic. Many ethnographers now believe that disciplinary authority is a matter of rhetorical strategy not scientific method. Geertz is perhaps most blunt about the essentially rhetorical nature of ethnography:

> The capacity to persuade readers . . . that what they are reading is an authentic account by someone personally acquainted with how life proceeds in some place, at some time, among some group, is the basis upon which anything else ethnography seeks to do . . . finally rests. The textual connection of the Being Here and the Being There sides of anthropology, the imaginative construction of a common ground between the Written At and the Written About . . . is the *fons et origo* of whatever power anthropology has to convince anyone of anything—not theory, not method, not even the aura of the professorial chair, consequential as these last may be. (Geertz 1988, 143–144)

Much of the current rethinking of ethnography has been sobered and empowered by vigorous rhetorical critique of anthropological discourse.

Geertz is foremost among ethnography's practicing rhetorical critics. His rhetorical criticism of E.E. Evans-Pritchard's (E-P) ethnographic texts is exemplary (Geertz 1988). He identifies E-P's stylistic token as "drastic clarity" (Geertz 1988, 68) that translates onto the page as "a string of clean, well-lighted judgments, unconditional statements so perspicuously presented that only the invincibly uninformed will think to resist them," a sort of "first-strike assertiveness" (Geertz 1988, 63). The rhetorical questions Geertz puts to E-P's texts are: "How (why? in what way? of what?) does all this resolute informing inform?" (Geertz 1988, 64) His "deep reading" of E-P yields these insights:

> *How he does it:* The outstanding characteristic of E-P's approach to ethnographic exposition and the main source of his persuasive power is his enormous capacity to construct visualizable representations of cultural phenomena—anthropological transparencies. *What he does:* The main effect, and the main intent, of this magic lantern ethnography is to demonstrate that the established frames of social perception, those upon which we ourselves instinctively rely, are fully adequate to whatever oddities the transparencies may turn out to picture. (Geertz 1988, 64)

According to Geertz E-P produces a "see-er's rhetoric" (Geertz 1988, 66). With E-P's texts, like all rhetorical practice, "the way of saying is the what of saying" (Geertz 1988, 68).

At a deep level, Geertz insightfully notes E-P's discussion of the Nuer and the Azande underwrite his own cultural ethos as much as they illuminate the other:

> . . . it validates the ethnographer's form of life at the same time as it justifies those of his subjects—and that it does the one by doing the other. The adequacy of the cultural categories of, in this case, university England, to provide a frame of intelligible reasonings, creditable values, and familiar motivations for such oddities as poison oracles, ghost marriages, blood feuds, and cucumber sacrifices recommends those categories as of somehow more than parochial importance. Whatever personal reasons E-P may have had for being so extraordinarily anxious to picture Africa as a logical and prudential place—orderly, straightforward and level-headed, firmly modeled and open to view—in doing so he constructed a forceful argument for the general authority of a certain conception of life. If it could undarken Africa, it could undarken anything. (Geertz 1988, 70)

By bringing "Africans into a world conceived in deeply English terms" he thereby confirmed "the dominion of those terms" (Geertz 1988, 70).

Geertz as rhetorical critic moves beyond formalist analysis and situates ethnographic texts within their distinctive institutional constraints and engendering professional practices:

> However far from the groves of academe anthropologists seek out their subjects—a shelved beach in Polynesia, a charred plateau in Amazonia; Akobo, Meknes, Panther Burn—they write their accounts with the world of lecterns, libraries, blackboards, and seminars all about them. This is the world that produces anthropologists, that licenses them to do the kind of work they do, and within which the kind of work they do must find a place if it is to count as worth attention. In itself, Being There is a postcard experience ("I've been to Katmandu—have you?"). It is Being Here, a scholar among scholars, that gets your anthropology read, published, reviewed, cited, taught. (Geertz 1988, 129–130)

Geertz weights the Being Here writing it down side of the axis. To be sure, ethnography on the page constrains and shapes performance in the field. But it is also true, I believe, that experiential performance sometimes resists, exceeds, and overwhelms the constraints and strictures of writing. It is the task of rhetorical critics to seek out these sites of tension, displacement, and contradiction between the Being There of performed experience and the Being Here of written texts.

This rhetorical self-reflexivity has helped politicize ethnography: "The gap between engaging others where they are and representing them where they aren't, always immense but not much noticed, has suddenly become extremely visible. What once seemed only technically difficult, getting 'their' lives into 'our' works, has turned morally, politically, even epistemologically, delicate" (Geertz 1988, 130). Ethnographic authority is the empowering alignment between rhetorical strategy and political ideology. Once shielded by the mask of science, ethnographers now have become acutely aware of the sources of their persuasive power:

> What it hasn't been, and, propelled by the moral and intellectual self-confidence of Western Civilization, hasn't so much had to be, is aware of the sources of its power. If it is now to prosper, with that confidence shaken, it must become aware. Attention to how it gets its effects and what those are, to anthropology on the page, is no longer a side issue, dwarfed by problems of method and issues of theory. It . . . is rather close to the heart of the matter. (Geertz 1988, 148–149)

Trinh enacts this struggle towards self-reflexive awareness of textual power in her book subtitled "Writing Postcoloniality and Feminism": " . . . what is exposed in this text is the inscription and de-scription of a non-unitary female subject of color through her engagement, therefore also disengagement, with master discourses" (Trinh 1989, 43).

It is ironic that the discipline of communication has been relatively unreflexive about the rhetorical construction of its own disciplinary authority. It would be illuminating to critique the rhetorical expectations and constraints on articles published in the *Quarterly Journal of Speech*, or *Communication Monographs*. What kinds of knowledge, and their attendant discursive styles, get privileged, legitimated, or displaced? How does knowledge about communication get constructed? What counts as an interesting question about human communication? What are the tacitly observed boundaries—the range of appropriateness—regarding the substance, methods, and discursive styles of communication scholarship? And, most importantly for critical theorists, what configuration of socio-political interests does communication scholarship serve? How does professionally authorized knowledge about communication articulate with relations of power? About the connection between a field of knowledge and relations of power, Michel Foucault offers this sobering insight: " . . . power produces knowledge . . . ; power and knowledge directly imply one another; . . . there is no power relation without the correlative constitution of a field of knowledge, nor any knowledge that does not presuppose and constitute at the same time power relations" (Foucault 1979, 27).

NOTES

I borrow the term "critical cultural politics" from James Clifford (1988, 147).

REFERENCES

Asad, Talal, ed. 1973. *Anthropology and the Colonial Encounter.* London: Ithaca Press.

Asad, Talal. 1986. "The Concept of Cultural Translation in British Social Anthropology." In *Writing culture: The Poetics and Politics of Ethnography,* edited by James Clifford and George E. Marcus, 141–164. Berkeley: University of California Press.

Ashcroft, Bill, Gareth Griffiths and Helen Tiffin. 1989. *The Empire Writes Back: Theory and Practice in Post-colonial Literatures.* New York: Routledge.

Bakhtin, Mikhail. 1986. *Speech Genres.* Edited by Caryl Emerson and Michael Holquist. Translated by Vern W. McGee. Austin: University of Texas Press.

Brummett, Barry. 1990. "A Eulogy for Epistemic Rhetoric." *Quarterly Journal of Speech* 76: 69–72.

Clifford, James. 1988. *Predicament of Culture: Twentieth Century Ethnography, Literature, and Art.* Cambridge: Harvard University Press.

Clifford, James and George Marcus, eds. 1986. *Writing Culture: The Poetics and Politics of Ethnography.* Berkeley: University of California Press.

Conquergood, Dwight, Paul Friesema, A. Hunter and J. Mansbridge. 1990. *Dispersed Ethnicity and Community Integration: Newcomers and Established Residents in the Albany Park Area of Chicago.* Evanston: Center for Urban Affairs and Policy Research, Northwestern University.

de Certeau, Michel. 1984. *The Practice of Everyday Life.* Translated by S. Randall. Berkeley: University of California Press.

Fabian, Johannes. 1983. *Time and the Other: How Anthropology Makes its Object.* New York: Columbia University Press.

Fernandez, James W. 1986. *Persuasions and Performances: The Play of Tropes in Culture.* Bloomington: Indiana University Press.

Fraser, Nancy. 1990. "Rethinking the Public Sphere: A Contribution to the Critique of Actually Existing Democracy." *Social Text* 25/26: 56–80.

Foucault, Michel. 1979. *Discipline and Punish: The Birth of the Prison.* Translated by Alan Sheridan. New York: Vintage Books.

Geertz, Clifford. 1973. *Interpretation of Cultures.* New York: Basic Books.

Geertz, Clifford. 1983. *Local Knowledge: Further Essays in Interpretive Anthropology.* New York: Basic Books.
Geertz, Clifford. 1988. *Works and Lives: The Anthropologist as Author.* Stanford: Stanford University Press.
Goffman, Erving. 1967. *Interaction Ritual: Essays on Face-to-Face Behavior.* New York: Anchor Books.
Goffman, Erving. 1989. "On fieldwork." *Journal of Contemporary Ethnography* 18: 123–132.
Jackson, Michael. 1989. *Paths Toward a Clearing: Radical Empiricism and Ethnographic Inquiry.* Bloomington: Indiana University Press.
Malinowski, Bronislaw. 1961. *Argonauts of the Western Pacific.* New York: E.P. Dutton.
Marcus, George E. and Michael M. J. Fischer. 1986. *Anthropology as Cultural Critique: An Experimental Moment in the Human Sciences.* Chicago: University of Chicago Press.
Miller, Christopher L. 1990. *Theories of Africans: Francophone Literature and Anthropology in Africa.* Chicago: University of Chicago Press.
Ricoeur, Paul. 1971. "The Model of the Text: Meaningful Action Considered as a Text." *Social Research* 38: 529–562.
Rosaldo, Renato. 1989. *Culture and Truth: The Remaking of Social Analysis.* Boston: Beacon.
Theunissen, Michael. 1984. *The Other: Studies in the Social Ontology of Husserl, Heidegger, Sartre, and Buber.* Cambridge: MIT Press.
Trinh, Minh-Ha T. 1989. *Woman, Native, Other: Writing Postcoloniality and Feminism.* Bloomington: Indiana University Press.
Turner, Victor. 1975. *Revelation and Divination in Ndembu Ritual.* Ithaca: Cornell University Press.
Turner, Victor. 1986. *The Anthropology of Performance.* New York: PAJ Publications.
Tyler, Stephen A. 1987. *The Unspeakable: Discourse, Dialogue, and Rhetoric in the Postmodern World.* Madison: University of Wisconsin Press.
Van Maanen, John. 1988. *Tales from the Field: On Writing Ethnography.* Chicago: University of Chicago Press.
Wagner, Roy. 1980. *The Invention of Culture* (Revised and Expanded Edition). Chicago: University of Chicago Press.

Rethinking Elocution

The Trope of the Talking Book and Other Figures of Speech

To read without uttering the words aloud or at least mumbling them is a "modern" experience, unknown for millennia. In earlier times, the reader interiorized the text; he made his voice the body of the other; he was its actor.

—MICHEL DE CERTEAU,
THE PRACTICE OF EVERYDAY LIFE

The performer sits under a spotlight surrounded by books on performance. She touches, smells, and tastes some of the books. She holds one of the books up to her ear. She notices you are there. She looks up to speak.

—D. SOYINI MADISON,
"PERFORMING THEORY/EMBODIED WRITING"

The intellectual currency of "performance" has stimulated a rediscovery of elocution by literary historians[1] and a resuturing of elocution and oral interpretation into the intertwining disciplinary genealogies of English, speech, theater, and performance studies (Jackson 1999; Lee 1999). Earlier historical studies of elocution and oral interpretation were written from a history of ideas perspective: the explication of theories and practices in order to trace a line of ideas, issues, debates, and pedagogies.[2] Perhaps the most influential example of this kind of scholarship is Wallace A. Bacon's 1960 article, "The Dangerous Shores: From Elocution to Interpretation," a metadisciplinary essay in which he named and thereby enacted a watershed moment for the field at midcentury. This signal publication—arguably the flagship essay for the new interpretation of literature movement—charted an historical course from elocution's "just and graceful management of the voice, countenance, and gesture" to a "modern view of interpretation as the study of literature through the medium of oral performance" (Bacon 1960, 149). Bacon theorized the performance of literature as a site for encountering and developing what he called a profound "sense of the other" (Bacon 1976). Drawing on two strands of Bacon's scholarship—his landmark historical research on elocution and his theoretical research on "a sense of the other"—I attempt to rethink and revive interest in elocution by investigating it from the perspectives of those "others" against whom it erected its protocols of taste, civility, and gentility.

Because the major theorists and exemplary practitioners written into the extant history of elocution are overwhelmingly white and privileged, I want to relocate elocution within a wider sociohistorical context of racial tension and class struggle. I approach the elocutionary movement from "below," from the angle of working-class and enslaved people who were excluded from this bourgeois tradition and disciplined by it but who nonetheless raided and redeployed it for their own subversive ends.[3] Drawing on slave narratives, working-class histories, and other historical documents, this essay excavates a hidden history and radical tradition of elocution and oral interpretation.

Voices That Matter

To reach the higher rungs of class respectability, voices had to be "legible," assessed in elocutionary terms of "clarity" and "purity of tone." Anna Russell's *The Young Ladies' Elocutionary Reader* described an uncultivated voice as smudged like a printer's error: "It resembles, in its effect to the ear, that presented to the eye, when the sheet has been accidentally disturbed in the press, and there comes forth, instead of the clear, dark, well-defined letter, executed distinctly on the fair white page, a blur of half-shade" (Russell 1853, 15). Elocution was tinctured with printer's ink. It would do for platform and social performance what printer's type did for scribal culture: systematize, standardize, and reproduce exemplary models in which the idiosyncrasy and excess of the oral could be repressed, regulated, and recirculated. Elocution developed and flourished in the 18th and 19th centuries during the crucial period of the rise of industrial capitalism and advance of science, reason, engineering, and commitment to progress and improvement. E. P. Thompson argued that the industrial "pressures towards discipline and order extended from the factory . . . into every aspect of life: leisure, personal relationships, speech, manners" (Thompson 1963, 401). As part of the same historical and cultural milieu, elocution drew from the same vocabulary: One of its early formations was called the "mechanical school" of elocution (Mattingly, 1972; Roach, 1985). Elocution expressed in another key the body discipline so characteristic of industrial capitalism, but this was a discipline imposed on the bourgeoisie, a way for them to mark "distinction" from the masses (Bourdieu 1984). Punning on the title of Walter Benjamin's (1969) well-known essay, we can think of elocution as the management of voice in the age of mechanical reproduction.

Elocution was designed to recuperate the vitality of the spoken word from rural and rough working-class contexts by regulating and refining its "performative excess" through principles, science, systematic study, and standards of taste and criticism (Butler 1997, 152). Textual enclosure was the technology of control; thus elocution, an art of the spoken word, was circumscribed by literacy. Ambivalently related to orality, elocution sought to tap the power of popular speech but curb its unruly embodiments and refine its coarse and uncouth features. It was the verbal counterpart, in the domain of speech, of the enclosure acts that confiscated the open commons so crucial to the hard-scrabble livelihood and recreation of the poor and privatized them for the privileged classes. Elocution seized the spoken word, the common currency to which the illiterate poor had open access, and made it uncommon, fencing it off with studied rules, regulations, and refinements. An art of linguistic enclosure, elocution's historical rise and development corresponded roughly with the legislative acts of enclosure and displacement, the "clearances," that produced "surplus populations" and cheap labor for urban factories (Marx 1930, 803–807). The pulpit and the lectern were the loci classici, exemplary sites of demonstration, but these capital sites extended to everyday speech and presentation of self. Elocution was practiced by professional public speakers and readers but was also embodied as a general social sign of gentility as the bourgeoisie conversed, read aloud, and entertained in their parlors. The hegemony of the pulpit and lectern extended into the habitus of the class-conscious home. Coextensive with sartorial codes, like dress it was a way of displaying social status and class background.

Elocution promoted a sizing up of bodies and auditing of voices, a critical scrutiny of "the grain of the voice" (Barthes 1985). There was a political economy of the voice: How one spoke was part of a circuit of comparison and exchange that produced social value, "the 'sonorous materiality' of words exchanged" (Certeau 1997, 102). Voices were "cultivated" and traded up. The thriving business of elocutionary lectures, training manuals, exercises, lessons, handbooks, workshops, and demonstrations pivoted on this trading up of voices and acquisition of "vocal superiority," vocal capital (Rush 1879, 578). According to James Rush, author of a key elocutionary text, *The Philosophy of the Human Voice,* "Intonation and other modes of the voice" betray class pretenders to "a cultivated ear" (Rush 1879, 480), to "the ear of a refined and educated taste" (Rush 1879, 518). Rush reveals that elocutionary proprieties were staked in overlapping class and racial tension with his choice of negative examples: "Hence with a Slavery agitator" and "an abolition preacher about the streets, there is equally an ignorant disregard to the proper, and certainly to the elegant uses of the voice" (Rush 1879, 480).

The opening scene of Harriet Beecher Stowe's best-selling novel *Uncle Tom's Cabin* (1852/1994) dramatizes the elocutionary surveillance and auditing of other bodies and voices. Stowe introduces one of her most contemptible characters, the slave trader Haley, by immediately subjecting him to a close critical examination of body, voice, and demeanor: "He was a short, thick-set man, with coarse, commonplace features, and that swaggering air of pretension which marks a low man who is trying to elbow his way upward in the world" (Stowe 1994, 1). *Air* was a key word grounded in the dramaturgy of social relations; it referred to a style of personal presentation, demeanor, that registered class tension, as in "putting on airs." Stowe encourages the cultivated reader to "catch" this slave catcher in the act of class pretension. She first tells us that his speech was "in free and easy defiance of Murray's Grammar" (Stowe 1994, 1) and then dramatizes his slips and class-marked dialect: "Yes, I consider religion a valeyable thing in a nigger, when it's the genuine article, and no mistake" (Stowe 1994, 2). Later, she describes him as someone who "slowly recited" texts: "He was not a remarkably fluent reader, and was in the habit of reading in a sort of recitative half-aloud" (Stowe 1994, 101). Haley's labored oral reading skills are in marked contrast to the elocutionary ability of light-skinned blacks, particularly Gassy: "She then read aloud, in a soft voice, and with a beauty of intonation" (Stowe 1994, 313).

Haley's "gentleman" interlocutor, Mr. Shelby, escapes critical inspection; the narrator keeps at a respectful remove and quickly merges him into the class habitus of his "well-furnished dining parlor": "Mr. Shelby . . . had the appearance of a gentleman, and the arrangements of the house, and the general air of the housekeeping indicated easy, and even opulent circumstances" (Stowe 1994, 1). Genteel bodies pass as unmarked norms of decorum, whereas "low-bred" and "vulgar" bodies are marked by their deviancy from bourgeois standards of taste.

Throughout the novel, Stowe articulates racial and class identity and moral character against norms of elocution in complex and troubling ways. The imbrication of colorism and elocution is particularly disturbing. The "full blacks" speak in thick dialect with "barbarous, guttural, half-brute intonation" (Stowe 1994, 300) whereas the light-skinned "mulatto" George Harris "talked so fluently, held himself so erect" (Stowe 1994, 10) and had a self-possessed "attitude, eye, voice, manner" of speaking (Stowe 1994, 172). Stowe's class animosity is expressed in grotesque descriptions of "low-bred" whites whose coarse features and elocutionary shortcomings correspond with moral flaws. These characters—Haley, Loker, and Legree—speak in dialect and are not quite white (Jacobson 1998). Stowe's detailed, head-to-toe inspections of working-class white bodies ironically mirrors the scene of invasive physical examination of black bodies for sale at auction (Stowe 1994, 289).[4]

Elocutionary protocols anticipated Judith Butler's (1993) theory of performativity as the reiteration, "citation," of a set of norms, but elocution would rework performativity as disembodied citationality into a re-embodied *recitationality* (Butler 1993, 14). The normative would become naturalized through habitual performance, and the hegemonic force is captured in Rush's (1879) description of elocutionary discipline as "frequent repetition" becoming "an eficacious [sic] habit" until "atention [sic] fading into habit" enables "the shore to be reached, and the life to be saved" (Rush 1879, 479). But the metaphor of swimming, "sucesfully [sic] employed in danger," reminds us that elocution was part of a punitive regime of body discipline and vocal discrimination (Rush 1879, 479).

The "natural school" of elocution demonstrates how hegemony works: that is, what is really cultured and acquired masquerades as "nature," thereby concealing its invention and artifice (Vandraegan 1949). The artistic bedrock of "natural" expression is revealed in Rush's observation that "the world of Taste goes to the Theater to hear the purest style of Elocution" (Rush 1879, 478). Although every inch a studied disciplining and remaking of body and voice to accrue class distinction, elocution was ideologically masked as "natural language" (Fliegelman 1993, 79–94). The uncultivated were then marked as aberrant and unnatural, corruptions of nature. Elocution wielded the double-edged sword of "nature" against the poor and untutored. Too little cultivation of taste and manners branded one as coarse and uncouth, a transgressor of "universal" laws of "truth, propriety, and taste" that were "drawn from nature" (Rush 1879, 477). On the other hand, too self-conscious a presentation of refinement led to charges of "afectation [sic]" (Rush 1879, 477). The upwardly mobile classes had to run an elocutionary gauntlet between "awkwardness" and "afectation," too little or too much art (Rush 1879, 477).

But it was the rerouting of literacy through oral communication, however refined and regulated, that rendered elocution vulnerable to penetration and pilfering from the very classes it was erected against. The spoken-word dimension of elocution provided for the "spillage" from the enclosed written word that the unlettered poor swept up and made their own (Linebaugh, 1992, 168). According to John Brewer (1997), the elocutionary practice of public readings mediated the divide between literate elite and illiterate laborers:

> Reading aloud, both in public and in private, was a universal practice that enabled non-readers to share in the pleasures of the literate. In homes, taverns, coffee houses, in fields and on the street, oral and literate cultures were married through the ministrations of the public reader. (Brewer 1997, 187)

Thompson's monumental history *The Making of the English Working Class* (1963) is replete with examples of "radical reading rooms" where "the custom of reading aloud the Radical periodicals, for the benefit of the illiterate" nurtured "the values of intellectual inquiry and of mutuality" (Thompson 1963, 743). Thompson includes the description of a remarkable, subversive oral reading at a meeting of an underground insurrectionary movement in a field near Sheffield in 1800: "[A]t 10 o'clock in the Evening—an orator in a Mask harangues the people—reads [aloud] letters from distant societies by the light of a candle and immediately burns them" (Thompson 1963, 474).

Henry Mayhew (1861/1968) amply documented "street elocution" and "street recitations" in his first volume of *London Labour and the London Poor*, thus making clear that the laboring classes and lumpenproletariat "pitched" and repackaged an elite performance form to their own subaltern needs and recycled it within the scrappy survival economy of the streets (Mayhew 1968, 232–238). They developed their own ethnoaesthetics and standards of evaluation; with a wink to his middle-class reader, Mayhew refers to the discriminating judgment of "a critical professor of street elocution" (Mayhew 1968, 232–238).[5]

The Trope of the Talking Book Reconsidered

In his pathfinding scholarship on the African American literary tradition, Henry Louis Gates identifies the "trope of the Talking Book" as "the central trope" (Gates 1988, 152), "the ur-trope," "the fundamental repeated trope" of the Anglo-African tradition that symbolized the tensions between the spoken word and the written word, the African's journey from orality to literacy (Gates 1988, 131, 198). He cites Olaudah Equiano's rendering of this trope in *The Interesting Narrative of Olaudah Equiano . . . The African: Written by Himself* (1789/1967) and a prototype for the genre of slave narrative:

> I had often seen my master and Dick employed in reading, and I had a great curiosity to talk to the books, as I thought they did, and so to learn how all things had a beginning: for that purpose I have often taken up a book alone, in hopes it would answer me, and I have been very much concerned when it remained silent. (Equiano 1967, 40)

Gates discusses this passage as an allegory for the struggle of blacks to insert their voice into white texts, to register a black presence in Western literature. The text does not speak to Equiano, according to Gates, because his black countenance and speech stand in Western texts as signs of absence. Gates either ignores or is unaware of the elocutionary milieu within which printed texts were generated, received, interpreted, and *performed*. Voice is not just a metaphor, as Gates would have it, and the vocal performance of texts is not just an allegory but a concrete material practice that suffused literacy in 18th- and 19th-century Anglo-American culture. Elocution illustrates Ngũgĩ wa Thiong'o's (1998) concept of "orature," that liminal space between speech and writing, performance and print, where these channels of communication constantly overlap, penetrate, and mutually produce one another. Although Gates has many insightful things to say about the trope of the talking book, he misses the obvious fact that Equiano was signifyin(g) on the widespread elocutionary practice of reading books aloud.

Black people in bondage had an ambivalent relationship with the elocutionary movement of white America. On the one hand, it provided them access to written and printed texts from which they were excluded by draconian legislation that outlawed literacy for enslaved people. One enslaved man had his eyes burned out for learning to read (Berlin et al. 1998, 280). Much valuable information was leaked through public readings and the practice of reading aloud in the domestic sphere. Although Sojourner Truth never learned to read, she was a great admirer of Walt Whitman's *Leaves of Grass* after first hearing it publicly read (Reynolds 1996, 148). And during the time of her enslavement, she engaged in insurgent eavesdropping, pressing her ear to the door of her mistress's room when confidential letters were read aloud (Truth 1850/1993, 41).

At the same time, white middle-class voice, gesture, and countenance were constructed against the black voice and body, the "savage" and "barbarous" (Rush 1879, 578, 579). Thomas Jefferson (1781/1993), well schooled in elocution, believed that racial "difference is fixed in nature" and contrasted the communicatively flexible and richly expressive blushing white countenance against the illegible opacity and blank unresponsiveness of the black face:

> Are not the fine mixtures of red and white, the expressions of every passion by greater or less suffusions of color in the one, preferable to that eternal monotony, which reigns in the countenances, that immoveable veil of black which covers the emotions of the other race? (Jefferson 1993, 238)

He equated blackness with impediment and incommunicability, the antithesis to elocutionary ideals of clarity, contrast, precision, emphasis, variety, fluency, distinction, and balance on vocal as well as visual registers. And, of course, Jefferson misread a complex, deliberate, embodied survival art of protective cover and veiling of feelings as an absence. Enslaved and other vulnerable people do not have the luxury of transparent, clear, direct, and open communication when interpersonal encounters are framed and reverberate with power (Scott 1990).

In an article in the *Chautauquan*, a journal connected with the 19th-century elocutionary lecture circuit, Sojourner Truth was described as a "grotesque figure" (Carter 1887, 479). In an *Atlantic Monthly* article titled "Sojourner Truth: The Libyan Sibyl," Stowe (1863) described Truth's vocal quality in terms of "the strong barbaric accent of the native African." For Stowe, Truth seemed "to impersonate the fervor of Ethiopia, wild, savage, the hunted of all nations." Mixing racial and class condescension with romanticism, she compared Truth's performance style to that of the French Jewish actress from an impoverished background, Rachel Felix, who "was wont to chant the 'Marseillaise' in a manner that made her seem the very spirit and impersonation of the gaunt, wild, hungry, avenging mob" (Stowe 1863, 477).[6] And Stowe actually performed Truth in dialect for the amusement of her Boston Brahmin social circle (Painter 1996, 154).

If we reconsider the trope of the talking book in early slave narratives as a sign of kidnapped Africans' initial encounter with the elocutionary practice of reading books aloud, then the racially charged tone of the first recorded example—*A Narrative of the Most Remarkable Particulars in the Life of James Albert Ukawsaw Gronniosaw, an African Prince, as Related by Himself* (1770/1996)—makes more sense. Gronniosaw's most painful and defining experience of racial difference was his exclusion from elocution, the refusal of the master's book to speak to him when he put his "ear down close upon it." Recently sold into slavery and new to the culture of "white folks," he was a keen observer of embodied signs who "watched every look" of his new master, a ship captain, so that he could adapt and survive within this new world. His master's custom of reading aloud to the ship's crew both startled and delighted him. "I saw the book talk to my master; for I thought it did, as I observed him to look upon it, and move his lips" (Gronniosaw 1996, 38). Admiration led to imitation, but when he tried to engage the book in dialogue, "open'd it . . . in great hope that it would say something to me," he was deeply disappointed that "it would not speak." He experienced this silence as a culminating moment of exile and excommunication and as a profound rejection of his humanity. Despondent, he concluded "that every body and every thing despis'd me *because I was black*" (Gronniosaw 1996, 38; italics added). His dawning racial consciousness and deep alienation emerged from the jarring encounter with elocution, the preeminent performance of whiteness.

Elocution existed in dialectical tension with minstrelsy, the most popular entertainment form of the 19th century (Lott, 1993, 4). Elocution had its framed events—public lectures, readings, recitations, orations, lyceum debates and declamations—but they were marketed as instruction more than entertainment. Unlike minstrelsy, the whole idea and motive for attending an elocutionary performance was to identify with, imitate, and extend the platform model of performance into social performance and the everyday performativity of whiteness. Whereas blackface minstrelsy was a theatrically framed mimicry and parody of blackness, elocution can be thought of as the performativity of whiteness naturalized. Exceeding the bounded performance event, elocution was an all-encompassing style of speaking and deportment that extended from the public sphere into the habitus of the home; hence the elocutionary training for "ladies," who otherwise were not encouraged to speak in public. (Ryan 1994) Because of its hegemonic reach and penetration—"the just and graceful management of the voice, countenance, and gesture"—elocution was more "popular," in the sense of pervasive, even than minstrelsy.

Antithetical in style, elocution and minstrelsy opposed and played off one another in striking and complex ways. Both performance traditions were enormously invested in voice, demeanor, and class difference. Elocution represented the high end, a respectable interest in vocal quality, dignified presence, and improvement for the rising classes. Minstrelsy expressed the low end, a disreputable fascination with vocal difference, burlesque bodies, and vulgar entertainment. Although their connection is seldom discussed, there was mutual acknowledgment, crossover, and some slippage between these contemporary performance formations. Popular elocutionary readers included "dialect pieces," such as Beecher's *Recitations and Readings: Humorous, Serious, Dramatic, Including Prose and Poetical Selections in Dutch, French, Yankee, Irish, Backwoods, Negro, and Other Dialects* (1874). The abolitionist lecture circuit, enfolded within elocutionary lecture circuit, titillated staid middle-class audiences by featuring speeches from fugitive and former slaves. Citing an antislavery newspaper account, John Blassingame documented that, during one of these speeches, the audience "cheered, clapped, stamped, laughed and wept, by turns" (Blassingame 1977, 123). After hearing the lecture of a fugitive slave, Lydia Maria Child observed that she had "seldom been more entertained" and that his "obvious want of education" and "the uncouth awkwardness of his language had a sort of charm" (quoted in Blassingame 1977, 151). John Collins, an agent of the American Anti-Slavery Society, noted in 1842 that "the public have itching ears to hear a colored man speak" (quoted in Blassingame 1977, 123).[7] Coincidentally, the Virginia Minstrels troupe, credited with developing the standard format for the full-fledged minstrel show, formed in the winter of 1842–43 (Lott 1993, 136).

At the opposite pole, minstrel shows included "lectures," along with songs and dances, in their repertory. These "lectures" were caricatures of elocutionary decorum. Black speech and bodies were made to look all the more ridiculous and degraded within the heightened frame of white bourgeois elocution. But these "lectures," along with the stock character of the well-spoken "interlocutor" who was "genteel in comportment" (Lott 1993, 140), were also send-ups of elocutionary propriety. W. T. Lhamon (1998) argues provocatively that in the early years of minstrelsy white lumpen youths identified with blackface as a way of defiantly signaling their disdain and distance from the bourgeois society that excluded and harassed them.[8]

A striking example that brings into sharp focus the dialectical relationship between elocution and minstrelsy is Stowe's strategic response to the minstrelization of *Uncle Tom's Cabin* in the hugely popular Tom shows (Bowman 2000). As a rebuttal to the sensationalized theatrical adaptations, she dramatized the novel as an elocutionary platform reading for the antislavery lecture circuit. Without recourse to copyright laws,

Stowe pitted her own adaptation for dignified solo lectern performance against the minstrelized stage adaptations that were proliferating to her dismay. To further exercise authorial control, she designed her adaptation expressly as a virtuoso vehicle for a designated elocutionary reader whom she had befriended. The title page of the 1855 adaptation reads, *The Christian Slave, a Drama, Founded on a Portion of Uncle Tom's Cabin. Dramatized by Harriet Beecher Stowe, Expressly for the Readings of Mrs. Mary E. Webb.* Trained by the Philadelphia professor of elocution, A. A. Apthorp, Webb drew large and enthusiastic audiences to her dramatic readings of Stowe's text. In Boston's Fremont Temple, she performed *The Christian Slave* to a packed house of 3,500 people, one of the largest audiences ever assembled in that place (Clark 1997, 342).

To complicate further the racialized class politics of *The Christian Slave* readings, Stowe's designated elocutionist, Mary E. Webb, was a woman of color, the daughter of an escaped slave and a "wealthy Spanish gentleman," and was dubbed the "Black Siddons" (Clark 1997, 342). One can only imagine how Webb was "read" as she publicly read from Stowe's lectern-mounted text, doing all the voices (27 characters), including white women and men, as well as black men and women, with some of the blacks and the low-class whites, such as Haley, speaking in thick dialect and the middle-class whites and some of the blacks, such as the light-skinned Cassy, speaking in elevated diction. Refracted through Webb's cultivated voice but racially marked body, Stowe's heteroglossic text must have taken on even more levels of mimicry and layers of "multiaccentuality" (Volosinov 1986, 23). The discreetly channeled thrill of cross-racial impersonation, imposture, and gender play that energized Webb's elocutionary readings needs to be read with and against the contemporary minstrel stage productions. In what ways were Webb's elocutionary readings of *The Christian Slave* a counterperformance to minstrelsy, and in what ways were they complicit with minstrelsy? How did the shadow of minstrelsy intensify the interplay of pleasure and subversion that simultaneously consolidated and unsettled the norms of elocution underpinning Webb's readings? Deliberately produced to trump minstrelsy, Webb's staged readings may have tapped its transgressive charge (Stowe interspersed scenes with songs, including "Way Down Upon the Swanee River"). But whatever else one can say about this politically complicated production, a black woman entered the public sphere as the literal embodiment of the trope of the talking book. The text did speak to and through a black voice and body, and Webb made enough money from her highly successful transatlantic reading tours to support her family, providing her husband with the economic security to leave his business and devote time to completing a novel (Clark 1997, 343).

If Webb's enactment of the trope of the talking book was constrained by white patronage and the protocols of elocution, then Sella Martin's signifyin(g) on this trope provides a remarkable example of black counterpublic reading that Gates does not consider. Martin recounts that, after being sold separately from his beloved mother at the age of 10, he worked as an errand boy in a hotel, where he learned all manner of things by eavesdropping on the guests: "I learned, too, from seeing them reading and writing, that they could make paper and the little black marks on it talk" (Blassingame 1977, 709). He made up his mind that he would learn this skill and set about cajoling and tricking the white boys to teach him the alphabet and how to read. He saw the liberatory potential of literacy, and after his first underground spelling lesson, "with the A B C ringing in my memory, I saw myself already writing a free-pass" (Blassingame 1977, 711). He practiced on found texts, "spelling signs and trying to read placard advertisements for runaway slaves" (Blassingame 1977, 710). Hearing him spelling out words all the time, the other slaves believed that he could read. One Sunday, three older slaves took him to the woods under the pretence of gathering wild grapes but, once there, pulled out a newspaper filched from the master and demanded that the young Sella read aloud a passage about abolitionists. Overwhelmed because he had only rudimentary spelling skills and had never attempted to read a newspaper before, but afraid of angering his companions by protesting lack of proficiency, he decided to fake it:

> This would be my excuse for looking over the paper with determination to read what I felt they would be pleased to hear, no matter though it should not be in the paper. I handled the paper with a trembling hand, and . . . to my great surprise, I made out this heading of a leading article: "Henry Clay an Abolitionist." I read on a little further. . . . Of course I did not make out fully all the long words . . . but I made a new discovery about my being able to read at all. . . . What I read, or pretended to read, gave the most intense satisfaction, and awakened the wildest hopes about freedom among my hearers. (Blassingame 1977, 711)

He becomes self-consciously literate in the transformative moment of reading aloud for a keenly listening audience. This scene is a rite of passage, a "breakthrough into performance": He accomplishes what he mimes and pretends (Hymes 1981, 79). Away from overseers, in the runaway space of the woods where his black compatriots are controlling the scene, the stolen text does talk to and through the young slave. This extraordinary example of the trope of the talking text gives new meaning to Certeau's subversive analogy of "reading as poaching" (de Certeau 1984, 165).

Word spread rapidly, and the same night the hotel kitchen where Martin worked was crowded with slaves from all around, petitioning him to read aloud "some book or newspaper which they had filched from their masters' libraries" (Blassingame 1977, 711–712). Thus was launched his underground career, his "regular task," of counterpublic "reading to the slaves": He became "an oracle among the slaves" who paid him to perform their poached texts.[9] These ongoing "clandestine" oral readings forged a fellowship of resistance, created "ties which bound" him "in a confederacy of . . . wrong-doing." And the solidarity forged in this insurgent performance space overrode even the master's authority. When his master discovered his illicit elocutionary activity and threatened him with flogging and the auction block—"Don't let me hear of your reading to the slaves again"—he disobeyed because of the reading-forged "ties that . . . it seemed safer to run the risk of being crushed by, than to attempt to break" (Blassingame 1977, 712).

While still enslaved, Frederick Douglass (1855/1969) also galvanized a secret slave counterpublic reading group that attracted as many as 40 members. "[H]olding it in the woods, behind the barn, and in the shade of trees," he read to them from *The Columbian Orator,* a popular elocutionary handbook of the day. Inside this subaltern performance space, "an attachment, deep and lasting" developed among the participants. In his autobiographical *My Bondage and My Freedom,* he says that when looking back on the experiences of his life, he recalled "*none* with more satisfaction" than this secret reading circle that constituted an empowering affective homosocial community: "the ardent friendship of my brother slaves. They were, every one of them, manly, generous and brave, yes; I say they were brave, and I will add, fine-looking" (Douglass 1969, 267–268).

By far the most inventive and radical example of signifyin(g) on literacy and refiguring the trope of the talking book comes from the obscure biographical sketch of Bartley Townsley (Gates does not include Townsley in his landmark study of the trope as key to how "the white written text" was made to "speak with a black voice" [Gates 1988, 131]). Worth quoting at length, Townsley's story is a dramatically compelling example of how enslaved people raided, short-circuited, and rerouted white texts, reciting them for their own subversive, liberatory ends:

> One night, when he had gone to bed and had fallen to sleep, he dreamed that he was in a white room, and its walls were the whitest he ever saw. He dreamed that some one came in and wrote the alphabet on the wall in large printed letters, and began to teach him every letter, and when he awoke he had learned every letter, and as early as he could get a book, he obtained one and went hard to work. One night very late, when he had come from his coal-kiln, he gathered his books as usual and began to try to spell, but it was not long before he came to a word that he could not pronounce. Now, thought he, what must I do? Then, remembering an old man who was on the farm, about fifty yards away, in a little old cabin, who could read a little, he thought he would go and ask him what the word spelt. The word was i-n-k. So he went quietly through the yard, for it was a very late hour of the night to be moving around, and reaching the cabin, he called him softly, Uncle Jesse! Uncle Jesse! Uncle Jesse! He said (the old man) who is that? Bartley. What do you want this time of the night? I want to know what i-n-k spells! The old man hallooed out, ink! He then returned to his cabin saying ink, ink, ink. After that night he never had any more trouble with ink. In 1852 he began to learn how to write well enough to write his own passes [to steal away]. (Carter 1969, 112–113)

It is difficult not to read this account as an allegory: the overwhelming whiteness of the enclosed room where he first encountered the alphabet, the symbolic significance of the word he found in the book but could not speak—i-n-k. In the dream where he first saw the writing on the wall, the pages of a book loomed as white walls of a room—the "whitest" he had ever seen—that engulfed him in whiteness. "Ink!" was the revelatory pronouncement that emptied literacy of whiteness and reinvested it with a distinctive black presence as it signified on the colloquialism, "black as ink." A strong black voice calling out "ink!" to him in the dark of night revealed the blackness that was inside texts all the time and that he had not been able to recognize in the blinding whiteness of the room. I-n-k performatively coalesced into "ink!" through transposition from the visual medium of the white page to the auditory register of Uncle Jesse's black voice. Through the synesthesia of recalling printed letters to vocality, first through his oral spelling, i-n-k, and then Uncle Jesse's robust calling, "hallooing out," he was able to hear/see the blackness that was inextricable from the material substance of printed letters. "Ink!" became the signifyin(g) password that liberated literacy from the "white room" and set it loose on the open road in the form of counterfeit freedom passes: "After that he never had any more trouble with ink."

Forgery, both literal and metaphorical, was the key operation and driving force behind slave literacy, and the source of slaveholders' anxiety about slaves learning to read and write. The counterfeit pass was the copy that was both a surrogation and theft of the master's textual power and a depletion of his capital investment. Elocution provided other opportunities for filching the master's texts in order to raid knowledge, reroute authority, and undermine power. We know from Sella Martin's narrative that slaves stole books and newspapers, but they also filched the spoken word. Thomas Johnson (1909) remembered: "While in slavery I would catch at every word that I heard the slave master use, and would repeat it over and over again until I had fixed it on my memory" (Johnson 1909, 40). They also closely studied demeanor and diction and filched elocutionary style. Johnson practiced speaking "with dignity of manner and with much dignity of diction" (Johnson 1909, 40). The acclaimed biographer William S. McFeely (1991) imaginatively reconstructs the young enslaved Frederick Douglass's elocutionary rehearsals:

> If he could say words—say them correctly, say them beautifully—Frederick could act; he could matter in the world. . . . Alone, behind the shipyard wall, Frederick Bailey [Douglass] read aloud. Laboriously, studiously, at first, then fluently, melodically, he recited great speeches. With *The Columbian Orator* in his hand, with the words of the great speakers of the past coming from his mouth, he was rehearsing. He was readying the sounds—and meanings—of words of his own that he would one day speak. (McFeely 1991, 34–35)

The secret always seeps, enclosures are poached, and hoarded knowledges escape the forms of those who would encrypt them.

Continuities

Recent work in black cultural studies calls for a "black performance studies" that puts performance at the center of black cultural politics and resistance (Diawara 1996, 304; Gilroy 1995). Black radical scholars are reclaiming oral interpretation of literature as an emancipatory pedagogy and performative cultural politics. bell hooks (1995) situates the performance of literature at the center of the "live arts" tradition that flourished within black working-class communities and historically links it to elocution: "The roots of black performance arts emerge from an early nineteenth century emphasis on oration and the recitation of poetry" (hooks 1995, 212). She grew up in that tradition and provides an insider view:

> As young black children raised in the post-slavery southern culture of apartheid, we were taught to appreciate and participate in "live arts." Organized stage shows were one of the primary places where we were encouraged to display talent. Dramatic readings of poetry, monologues, or plays were all central to these shows. Whether we performed in church or school, these displays of talent were seen as both expressions of artistic creativity and as political challenges to racist assumptions about the creative abilities of black folks. . . . In my household we staged performances in my living room, reciting poetry and acting in written or improvised drama. . . . I grew up in a working class family, where the particular skills of black art expressed in writing poetry were honored through the act of performance. We were encouraged to learn the works of black poets, to recite them to one another. In daily life, this was both a means of sharing our cultural legacy and of resisting indoctrination from Eurocentric biases within educational institutions that devalued black expressive culture. (hooks 1995, 211, 213)

Significantly, hooks turns to ethnography for the project of reclaiming and revaluing African American traditions of performed literature: "It is useful to think in terms of ethnographic performance when charting a cultural history of African-American participation in the performing arts" (hooks 1995, 213).

Autobiographies provide rich corroborative evidence for hooks's claims about the importance and pervasiveness of oral interpretation of literature in black working-class culture. One thinks immediately of Mrs. Bertha Flowers in Maya Angelou's (1970) *I Know Why the Caged Bird Sings,* who initiated the young Maya into the pleasures of literature. She loaned her books and instructed her to "read them aloud." Oral interpretation was mandatory, she insisted, because "words mean more than what is set down on paper. It takes the human voice to infuse them with the shades of deeper meaning" (Angelou 1970, 82). And when Mrs. Flowers performed literature, Angelou remembers the impact: "I heard poetry for the first time in my life" (Angelou 1970, 84).

In his autobiography *Voices and Silences,* James Earl Jones (1994) recounts his glorious experiences of reading Edgar Allen Poe aloud on an improvised stage in his high school gymnasium in Depression-era Michigan. Even more revealing is the passage in which he remembers his Uncle Bob Walker who loved to recite Shakespeare:

> He was a fine man, not endowed by society or economy with the chance to be highly educated. He worked in the foundry after his discharge from the army. He was unpretentious in his speech but he read Shakespeare with a full appreciation of the English language. I witnessed the joy he took in the words, and found it contagious. (Jones 1994, 66)

Jones dedicated his autobiography to his high school teacher of literature and oral interpretation.[10]

It is important to take an-*other* look at elocution and oral interpretation and to write revisionist histories that include the encounters and experiences of excluded others for at least three reasons: (1) it is long overdue; (2) it complicates in productive ways our understanding of disciplinary genealogies of performance studies; and (3) it provides compelling evidence and inspiring examples of how dispossessed people, in the word of Marta Savigliano (1995), "trick-back" on an apparatus of oppression, how they trip up and turn its overwhelming force and massive weight against itself and thereby leverage an alternative, provisional space of liberatory struggle (Savigliano 1995, 17).[11]

NOTES

1. See Fliegelman (1993), Looby (1996), and Portelli (1994). Gerald Graff's (1987) institutional history of English is also helpful, particularly chap. 3, "Oratorical Culture and the Teaching of English" (pp. 36–51). David Reynolds's (1996) cultural biography of Walt Whitman is also useful, especially chap. 6, "American Performances: Theatre, Oratory, Music" (pp. 154–93). Garry Wills's award-winning *Lincoln at Gettysburg* (1992) is a very accessible introduction to the elocutionary milieu of 19th-century America. See Cmiel (1990) for more detailed coverage of the same elocutionary ground.

2. See Bacon (1964), Bahn and Bahn (1970), Gray (1960), Howell (1959), Robb (1941), Thompson (1983), and Wallace (1954). For a notable exception from the intellectual history approach, see Mary Strine's (1983) important cultural study of Rush's *Philosophy of the Human Voice* (1879).

3. I am particularly indebted to Hobsbawm (1997), Thompson (1963), and Chauncey (1994). Methodologically, I have been influenced by recent work in historical ethnography, notably Comaroff and Comaroff (1991, 1992, 1997), Dening (1996), di Leonardo (1998), Poole (1997), and Savigliano (1995). See also the

splendid new performance historiography work of Fuoss (1999), Jackson (1999, 2000), Merrill (1999), Pollock (1998), and Roach (1985, 1996).

4. This essay is not the place, but Stowe's *Uncle Tom's Cabin* begs for a critical rereading from the perspective of the elocutionary milieu that engendered and permeated the novel. Stowe often uses voice, as well as hands—e.g., "delicately formed hand" (4), "a peculiar scowling expression of countenance, and a sullen, grumbling voice" (186)—as metonyms for character. She devotes extraordinary attention to vocal quality, countenance, and hands in both narrative summary and scenic description. And the novel is filled with scenes of characters reading aloud.

5. Cuban cigar makers hired lectors to read aloud literary and sociopolitical texts in the factory to stimulate their minds and provide relief from the mind-numbing labor of cigar rolling. The workers agreed on the reading materials in advance and paid the public reader out of their own pockets. This proletarian elocutionary tradition gained a reputation for being subversive, and in 1866 Cuba passed a law forbidding this practice in all factories. Cuban immigrants brought the tradition of the factory floor lector to America, where it continued until the 1920s. See Manguel (1996, 110–14).

6. Stowe (1863) refers to the actress only as "Rachel." I thank Lisa Merrill for identifying "Rachel" and pointing me to background materials.

7. This is the same John Collins who immediately recruited the fugitive Frederick Douglass to the abolitionist lecture circuit after hearing him speak spontaneously at the first antislavery convention he attended, barely three years after his escape from slavery. Douglass (1855/1969) recalled how Collins would introduce him on the circuit as a "graduate" from "the peculiar institution" of slavery, "*with my diploma written on my back!*" (359; emphasis in original).

8. In addition to the important scholarship on minstrelsy of Lott (1993) and Lhamon (1998), see that of Cockrell (1997), and Bean, Hatch, and McNamara (1996).

9. I am drawing on Nancy Fraser's important work on "counterpublics" in "Rethinking the Public Sphere" (1990). I connected Fraser's work on subaltern counterpublics with performance ethnography in "Rethinking Ethnography" (Conquergood, 1991, 189).

10. See also Rogers's (2000) biography of Barbara Jordan for detailed evidence of the persistence and importance of elocutionary activities in 20th-century black working-class communities. See especially chap. 4, "The Gift of the Voice" (35–59).

11. See also Lowe and Lloyd (1997) for a vigorous analysis of the "alternative" spaces that crack open or can be pried apart within the contradictions of late capitalism (1–32).

REFERENCES

Angelou, Maya. 1970. *I Know Why the Caged Bird Sings.* New York: Bantam.

Bacon, Wallace A. 1960. "The Dangerous Shores: From Elocution to Interpretation." *Quarterly Journal of Speech* 46: 148–52.

Bacon, Wallace A. 1964. "The Elocutionary Career of Thomas Sheridan (1719–1788)." *Speech Monographs* 31: 1–53.

Bacon, Wallace A. 1976. "Sense of Being: Interpretation and the Humanities." *Southern Speech Communication Journal* 41: 135–41.
Bahn, Eugene and Bahn, Margaret L. 1970. *A History of Oral Interpretation.* Minneapolis: Burgess.
Barthes, Roland. 1985. *The Grain of the Voice.* New York: Hill & Wang.
Bean, Annemarie, James V. Hatch and Brooks McNamara, eds. 1996. *Inside the Minstrel Mask: Readings in Nineteenth-Century Black Face Minstrelsy.* Hanover, NH: Wesleyan University Press.
Beecher, Alvah C., ed. 1874. *Beecher's Recitations and Readings: Humorous, Serious, Dramatic, Including Prose and Poetical Selections in Dutch, French, Yankee, Irish, Backwoods, Negro, and Other Dialects.* New York: Dick & Fitzgerald.
Benjamin, Walter. 1969. "The Work of Art in the Age of Mechanical Reproduction." In *Illuminations,* edited by Hannah Arendt, translated by Harry Zohn, 217–51. New York: Schocken.
Berlin, Ira, Marc Favreau and Steven F. Miller, eds. 1998. *Remembering Slavery: African Americans Talk About Their Personal Experiences of Slavery and Freedom.* New York: New Press.
Blassingame, John W., ed. 1977. *Slave Testimony: Two Centuries of Letters, Speeches, Interviews, and Autobiographies.* Baton Rouge: Louisiana State University Press.
Bourdieu, Pierre. 1984. *Distinction: A Social Critique of the Judgement of Taste.* Translated by Richard Nice. Cambridge, MA: Harvard University Press.
Bowman, Ruth Laurion. 2000. "Domestic(ating) Excess: Women's roles in *Uncle Tom's Cabin* and Its Adaptations." *Text and Performance Quarterly* 20: 113–29.
Brewer, John. 1997. *The Pleasures of the Imagination: English Culture in the Eighteenth Century.* New York: Farrar, Straus, Giroux.
Butler, Judith. 1993. *Bodies That Matter: On the Discursive Limits of Sex.* New York: Routledge.
Butler, Judith. 1997. *Excitable Speech: A Politics of the Performative.* New York: Routledge.
Carter, Edward R. 1888. *Our Pulpit Illustrated: Biographical Sketches.* Chicago: Afro-Am Press.
Carter, Harriet. 1887. "Sojourner Truth." *The Chautauquan* 7: 477–80.
Certeau, Michel de. 1984. *The Practice of Everyday Life.* Translated by Steven Rendall. Berkeley: University of California Press.
Certeau, Michel de. 1997. *The Capture of Speech and Other Political Writings.* Edited by Luced Giard, Translated by Tom Conley. Minneapolis: University of Minnesota Press.
Chauncey, George. 1994. *Gay New York: Gender, Urban Culture, and the Making of the Gay Male World, 1891–1940.* New York: Basic Books.
Clark, Susan F. 1997. "Solo Black Performance Before the Civil War: Mrs. Stowe, Mrs. Webb, and 'The Christian Slave.'" *New Theatre Quarterly* 13: 339–48.
Cmiel, Kenneth. 1990. *Democratic Eloquence: The Fight over Popular Speech in Nineteenth-Century America.* New York: William Morrow.
Cockrell, Dale. 1997. *Demons of Disorder: Early Blackface Minstrels and Their World.* Cambridge, UK: Cambridge University Press.
Comaroff, Jean and Comaroff, John L. 1992. *Ethnography and the Historical Imagination.* Boulder, CO: Westview.

Comaroff, Jean and Comaroff, John L. 1991. *Of Revelation and Revolution: Christianity, Colonialism, and Consciousness in South Africa* (Vol. 1). Chicago: University of Chicago Press.

Comaroff, Jean and Comaroff, John L. 1997. *Of Revelation and Revolution: The Dialectics of Modernity on a South African Frontier* (Vol. 2). Chicago: University of Chicago Press.

Conquergood, Dwight. 1991. "Rethinking Ethnography: Towards a Critical Cultural Politics." *Communication Monographs* 58 (1991).

Dening, Greg. 1996. *Performances.* Chicago: University of Chicago Press.

Diawara, Manthia. 1996. "Black Studies, Cultural Studies: Performative Acts." In *What is Cultural Studies?*, edited by John Storey, 300–306. London: Arnold.

di Leonardo, Micaela. 1998. *Exotics at Home: Anthropologies, Others, American Modernity.* Chicago: University of Chicago Press.

Douglass, Frederick. 1969. *My Bondage and My Freedom.* New York: Dover.

Equiano, Olaudah. 1967. *Equiano's Travels: The Interesting Narrative of the Life of Olaudah Equiano or Gustavus Vassa the African.* Edited by Paul Geoffrey Edwards. London: Heinemann.

Fliegelman, Jay. 1993. *Declaring Independence: Jefferson, Natural Language, and the Culture of Performance.* Stanford, CA: Stanford University Press.

Fraser, Nancy. 1990. "Rethinking the Public Sphere: A contribution to the critique of actually existing democracy." *Social Text* 25/26: 56–80.

Fuoss, Kirk W. 1999. "Lynching Performances, Theatres of Violence." *Text and Performance Quarterly* 19: 1–37.

Gates, Henry Louis, Jr. 1998. *The Signifying Monkey: A Theory of Afro-American Literary Criticism.* New York: Oxford University Press.

Gilroy, Paul. 1995. " . . . to be Real": The Dissident Forms of Black Expressive Culture." In *Let's Get It On: The Politics of Black Performance,* edited by Catherine Ugwu, 12–33. Seattle, WA: Bay.

Graff, Gerald. 1987. *Professing Literature: An Institutional History.* Chicago: University of Chicago Press.

Gray, Giles W. 1960. "What was Elocution?" *Quarterly Journal of Speech* 46: 1–7.

Gronniosaw, James Albert. 1996. "A Narrative of the Most Remarkable Particulars in the Life of James Albert Ukawsaw Gronniosaw, an African Prince, as Related by Himself." In *Unchained Voices: An Anthology of Black Authors in the English-speaking World of the Eighteenth Century,* edited by Vincent Carretta, 32–58. Lexington: University of Kentucky Press.

Hobsbawm, Eric. 1997. "On History from Below. In *On history,* 201–16. New York: New Press.

hooks, bell. 1995. "Performance Practice as a Site of Opposition." In *Let's Get It On: The Politics of Black Performance,* edited by Catherine Ugwu, 210–21. Seattle, WA: Bay.

Howell, Wilbur Samuel. 1959. "Sources of the Elocutionary Movement in England, 1700–1748." *Quarterly Journal of Speech* 45: 1–18.

Hymes, Dell. 1981. "Breakthrough into Performance." In *In Vain I Tried to Tell You: Essays in Native American Ethnopoetics,* 79–141. Philadelphia: University of Pennsylvania Press.

Jackson, Shannon. 1999. "Disciplinary Genealogies." Paper presented at the annual conference of Performance Studies international, University of Wales, Aberystwyth.

Jackson, Shannon. 2000. *Lines of Activity: Performance, Historiography, Hull-House Domesticity.* Ann Arbor: University of Michigan Press.

Jacobson, Matthew Frye. 1998. *Whiteness of a Different Color: European Immigrants and the Alchemy of Race.* Cambridge, MA: Harvard University Press.

Jefferson, Thomas. 1993. "Notes on Virginia." In *The Life and Selected Writings of Thomas Jefferson,* ed. Adrienne Koch and William Peden, 173–267. New York: Random House.

Johnson, Thomas L. 1909. *Twenty-Eight Years a Slave.* Bournemouth, UK: W. Math & Sons.

Jones, James Earl. 1994. *Voices and Silences.* New York: Simon & Schuster.

Lee, Josephine. 1999. "Disciplining Theater and Drama in the English Department: Some Reflections on 'Performance' and Institutional History." *Text and Performance Quarterly* 19: 145–58.

Lhamon, W. T., Jr. 1998. *Raising Cain: Blackface Performance from Jim Crow to Hip Hop.* Cambridge, MA: Harvard University Press.

Linebaugh, Peter. 1992. *The London Hanged: Crime and Civil Society in the Eighteenth Century.* Cambridge, UK: Cambridge University Press.

Looby, Christopher. 1996. *Voicing America: Language, Literary Form, and the Origins of the United States.* Chicago: University of Chicago Press.

Lott, Eric. 1993. *Love and Theft: Blackface Minstrelsy and the American Working Class.* New York: Oxford University Press.

Lowe, Lisa and David Lloyd, eds. 1997. *The Politics of Culture in the Shadow of Capital.* Durham, NC: Duke University Press.

Madison, D. Soyini. 1999. "Performing Theory/Embodied Writing." *Text and Performance Quarterly* 19: 107–24.

Manguel, Alberto. 1996. A *History of Reading.* New York: Viking.

Marx, Karl. 1930. *Capital* (vol. 1). Translated by E. Paul & C. Paul. New York: Dutton.

Mattingly, Alethea. 1972. "Art and Nature: The Mechanical School in England, 1761–1806." In *Studies in Interpretation,* edited by Esther M. Doyle & Virginia H. Floyd, 255–72. Amsterdam: Rodopi.

Mayhew, Henry. 1968. *London Labour and the London Poor* (Vol. 1). New York: Dover.

McFeely, William S. 1991. *Frederick Douglass.* New York: Norton.

Merrill, Lisa. 1999. *When Romeo Was a Woman: Charlotte Cushman and Her Circle of Female Spectators.* Ann Arbor: University of Michigan Press.

Painter, Nell Irvin. 1996. *Sojourner Truth: A Life, A Symbol.* New York: Norton.

Pollock, Della. 1998. *Exceptional Spaces: Essays in Performance and History.* Chapel Hill: University of North Carolina Press.

Poole, Deborah. 1997. *Vision, Race, and Modernity: A Visual Economy of the Andean Image World.* Princeton, NJ: Princeton University Press.

Portelli, Alessandro. 1994. *The Text and the Voice: Writing, Speaking, and Democracy in American Literature.* New York: Columbia University Press.

Reynolds, David. 1996. *Walt Whitman's America: A Cultural Biography.* New York: Vintage.

Roach, Joseph. 1985. "Nature Still, but Nature Mechanized." In *The player's passion: Studies in the science of acting,* 58–92. Newark, NJ: University of Delaware Press.

Roach, Joseph. 1996. *Cities of the Dead: Circum-Atlantic Performance.* New York: Columbia University Press.

Robb, Mary Margaret. 1969. *Oral Interpretation of Literature in American College and Universities: A Historical Study of Teaching Methods.* New York: Johnson Reprint.

Rogers, Mary Beth. 2000. *Barbara Jordan: American Hero.* New York: Doubleday Bantam.

Rush, James. 1879. *The Philosophy of the Human Voice: Embracing Its Physiological History; Together with a System of Principles, by Which Criticism in the Art of Elocution May Be Rendered Inteligible, and Instruction, Definite and Comprehensive* (7th ed.). Philadelphia: J. B. Lippincott.

Russell, Anna. 1853. *The Young Ladies' Elocutionary Reader.* Boston: James Munroe.

Ryan, Mary P. 1994. *Women in Public: Between Banners and Ballots, 1825–1880.* Baltimore: Johns Hopkins University Press.

Savigliano, Marta. 1995. *Tango and the Political Economy of Passion.* Boulder, CO: Westview.

Scott, James C. 1990. *Domination and the Arts of Resistance.* New Haven, CT: Yale University Press.

Stowe, Harriet Beecher. 1855. *The Christian Slave, a Drama, Founded on a Portion of "Uncle Tom's Cabin," Dramatized by Harriet Beecher Stowe, Expressly for the Readings of Mrs. Mary E. Webb.* Boston: Phillips, Sampson.

Stowe, Harriett Beecher. 1863. *Sojourner Truth, the Libyan Sibyl. Atlantic Monthly* 11: 473–81.

Stowe, Harriett Beecher. 1994. *Uncle Tom's Cabin (E. Ammons, Edition).* New York: Norton.

Strine, Mary. 1983. "Performance Theory as Science: The Formative Impact of Dr. James Rush's The Philosophy of the Human Voice." In *Performance of Literature in Historical Perspectives,* edited by David Thompson, 509–27. Lanham, MD: University Press of America.

Thiong'o, Ngũgĩ Wa. 1998. "Oral Power and Europhone Glory: Orature, Literature, and Stolen Legacies." In *Penpoints, Gunpoints, and Dreams: Towards a Critical Theory of the Arts and the State in Africa,* 103–28. Oxford: Clarendon.

Thompson, David. 1983. *Performance of Literature in Historical Perspectives.* Lanham, MD: University Press of America.

Thompson, E. P. 1963. *The Making of the English Working Class.* New York: Vintage.

Truth, Sojourner. 1993. *Narrative of Sojourner Truth.* Edited by Margaret Washington. New York: Vintage.

Vandraegan, Daniel E. 1949. *The Natural School of Oral Reading in England,1748–1828.* Unpublished doctoral dissertation, Northwestern University.

Volosinov, V. N. 1986. *Marxism and the Philosophy of Language.* Translated by Ladislav Matejka and I. R. Titunik. Cambridge, MA: Harvard University Press.

Wallace, Karl R., ed. 1954. *History of Speech Education in America.* New York: Appleton-Century-Crofts.

Wills, Garry. 1992. *Lincoln at Gettysburg: The Words That Remade America.* New York: Simon & Schuster.

III
Praxis

Health Theatre in a Hmong Refugee Camp
Performance, Communication, and Culture

A Hmong widow walks to a crossroad in Camp Ban Vinai, surveys the scene, and then settles herself on a bench outside the corner hut. Bracing her back against the split-bamboo wall, she begins to sing. At first softly, as if to herself, she sings a Hmong *khy txhiaj* (folksong). Aware of a gathering audience, she raises her voice to fill the space around her. She sings a lamentation, carving her personal anguish into a traditional expressive form. With exquisitely timed gestures, she strips and peels with one hand the branch of firewood she holds in the other. Tears stream down her face as she sings about the loss of her husband, her children, her house, her farm, her animals, and her country. She sings of war, and flight, and breaking, and of a time when she was a wife and mother in the Laotian village where silver neck-rings were worn. She punctuates each refrain by tossing away a sliver that her strong fingers have torn from the wood she holds across her lap as if it were a child.

The sad beauty of her singing attracts a crowd. She never makes eye contact but acknowledges the crowd's presence in her spontaneously composed verses, subtly at first, and then more confidently. She is both lamenting and entertaining. With nothing left to tear away, she makes the final toss of the last splinter, rises, and begins to sway with the rhythm of her song. People set out food for her. I give her the few baht I have in my pocket. Her face still wet, she breaks into a broad smile. Strange laughter interrupts her otherwise balanced verses.

She thanks us for listening to her sadness and tells us how happy it makes her to sing for us. Then she crosses the road to where I am standing and gives me a blue sticker the size of a nickel, with a crescent moon on it. It is one of the stickers the camp hospital puts on medicine bottles to indicate when the medicine should be taken, morning or night. With her thumb she presses it onto the page of my journal in which I am writing field notes on her performance. I notice that she has blue moons and golden suns stuck to her cheeks and forehead.

I came across this performance on my first day of fieldwork in Refugee Camp Ban Vinai in Thailand, where I had been assigned by the International Rescue Committee as a consultant for their environmental health education program. In many ways this opening image cathects the themes that would become salient in my fieldwork: performance, health, and intercultural exchange between refugees and expatriate health professionals.

I arrived in Thailand in February 1985 having just completed, with Taggart Siegel, a documentary on Hmong shamanism and the Sudden Unexpected Death Syndrome that has reached epidemic proportions among the Hmong resettled in the United States (Siegel and Conquergood 1985).[1] My intention was to do straightforward field research on cultural performance in refugee camps, particularly shamanism, but the refugee situation had become so politically sensitive in Thailand that all camps were closed to outsiders, particularly researchers. Therefore, I sought employment with the international aid voluntary agencies that administer health care and services to the camps. Fortunately I was hired by the International Rescue Committee (IRC) as a health worker in Ban Vinai, a hilltribe camp not far from the Mekong River that divides Thailand from Laos, and the oldest and largest refugee camp in Thailand (figure 1). During the time of my fieldwork the official population of the camp was 45,231 with an additional 2–3,000 undocumented "illegals" living in the camp without rice rations. I offered my services as an ethnographic consultant in exchange for the official papers that would legitimize my presence in the camp. My major assignment was to help design and direct an environmental health education program for this camp which was represented in many agency reports as the "filthiest," most "primitive," and "difficult" in Thailand.

Working with the refugees and a local Thai IRC employee, I helped design and direct a health education campaign based on native beliefs and values and communicated in culturally appropriate forms. Specifically, we started a refugee performance company that produced skits and scenarios drawing on Hmong folklore and traditional communicative forms, such as proverbs, storytelling, and folksinging, to develop critical awareness about the health problems in Ban Vinai.

The Ban Vinai Performance Company

Camp Ban Vinai may lack many things—water, housing, sewage disposal system—but not performance. The camp is an embarrassment of riches

Figure 1.

in terms of cultural performance. No matter where you go in the camp, at almost any hour of the day or night, you can simultaneously hear two or three performances, from simple storytelling and folksinging to the elaborate collective ritual performances for the dead that orchestrate multiple media, including drumming, stylized lamentation, ritual chanting, manipulation of funerary artifacts, incense, fire, dancing, and animal sacrifice (figures 2–6). Nearly every morning I was awakened before dawn by the drumming and ecstatic chanting of performing shamans (figures 7 & 8). During the day women everywhere would sew *pa ndau* (flower cloth), an intricate textile art that sometimes takes the form of embroidered story quilts with pictorial narratives drawn from history and folklore (figure 9). Performance permeates the fabric of everyday life in Ban Vinai.

A high level of cultural performance is characteristic of refugee camps in general. Since my work in Ban Vinai I have visited or lived for short

Figure 2: Funerary rites in Center #5 of the camp. (Photo by Dwight Conquergood: Courtesy of Northwestern University Archives)

periods of time in 11 refugee camps in Southeast Asia and the Middle East, not counting a shantytown for displaced people in Nigeria. In every one of them I was struck by the richness and frequency of performative expression. One explanation for this is that refugees have a lot of time on their hands to cultivate expressive traditions. But I think there are deeper psychological and cultural reasons for the high incidence of performance in the camps. Refugee camps are liminal zones where people displaced by trauma and crisis—usually war or famine—must try to regroup and salvage what is left of their lives. Their world has been shattered. They are in passage, no longer Laotian, certainly not Thai, and not quite sure where they will end up or what their lives will become. Betwixt and between worlds, suspended between past and future, they fall back on the performance of their traditions as an empowering way of securing continuity and some semblance of stability. Moreover, through performative flexibility they can play with new identities, new strategies for adaptation and survival. The playful creativity of performance enables them to experiment with and invent a new "camp culture" that is part affirmation of the past and part adaptive response to the exigencies of the present. Performance participates in the re-creation of self and society that emerges within refugee camps. Through its reflexive capacities, performance enables people to take stock of their situation and through

Figure 3: Spirit bridges used in soul-calling rituals. (Photo by Dwight Conquergood: Courtesy of Northwestern University Archives)

this self-knowledge to cope better. There are good reasons why in the crucible of refugee crisis, performative behaviors intensify.

And, of course, even before the Hmong became refugees, oral traditions and cultural performance were the primary ways of educating the young and promoting beliefs and values among adults, as is the case in most third world cultures (see Ong 1982). Any communication campaign that ignored the indigenous cultural strengths of performance would be doomed to failure.

There is always the danger, however, of appropriating performance and using it as an instrument of domination. I wanted no part of the puppet theatre approach used by some expatriates as simply another means to get refugees to do what bureaucrats think best for them. Instead, I hoped that performance could be used as a method for developing critical awareness as an essential part of the process of improving the health situation in the camp. My project was aligned with the popular theatre approach to development and political struggle that is being used with success throughout the third world, particularly Africa, Latin America, and Asia. This theatre movement frequently draws inspiration from Paulo Freire's fieldwork as documented in *Pedagogy of the Oppressed* (1986). Augusto Boal (1985) and Ross Kidd (1982, 1984) are perhaps the best-known names associated with the popular theatre,

Figure 4: Young tricksters with powder masks prepare to throw water on the author during the Thai New Year water-throwing festival. (Photo by Dwight Conquergood: Courtesy of Northwestern University Archives)

or people's theatre movement. Fortunately, a sizable body of literature is developing around this kind of third world theatre (Bustos 1984; Desai 1987; van Erven 1987; Eyoh 1986; Kaitaro 1979; Kidd and Byram 1978; Thiong'o 1981, 1983, 1986). In *Helping Health Workers Learn* (Werner and Bower 1982)—which is the companion volume to the widely distributed *Where There Is No Doctor: A Village Health Care Handbook* (Werner 1977)—there is an excellent chapter on politics, health, and performance entitled "Ways to Get People Thinking and Acting: Village Theater and Puppet Shows."[2] This work perhaps more than any other inspired my efforts in Ban Vinai.

The critical/political component of popular theatre enacts itself in the process of developing the performance as much as, if not more than, in the final presentation to an audience. The backstage processes of researching and developing culturally appropriate materials along with the participatory involvement of the people are experiential/processual dimensions as significant as any explicit "message" communicated in a skit or scenario. For popular theatre to work effectively as a tool of critical awareness and empowerment for oppressed peoples it must be rooted in and begin with their cultural strengths. Instead of aesthetic distance and

Figure 5: Unmarried Hmong women dance in a camp cultural revival center. (Photo by Dwight Conquergood: Courtesy of Northwestern University Archives)

other concepts of elite theatre, popular theatre is contingent upon what Kenneth Burke calls rhetorical processes of "identification" and "consubstantiality" (Burke 1969, 19–23).

The health worker who would use popular theatre must, perforce, become a participant fieldworker. Getting to know the people well is important not just as a technique for collecting appropriate materials and dramaturgical ideas to be worked into performance programs but as a way of earning their trust and respect. No matter how flashy and entertaining your health show, village people are wary of outsiders, experts who drop in for a day or two and then leave. Refugees, even more than villagers, have good reason to be skeptical of officials who hold themselves at a distance. The Hmong have a proverb: "To see a tiger is to die: to see an official is to become destitute" (Tapp 1986, 2). When a health worker gets involved, becomes part of the struggle, that speaks as forcefully as any line in a performance script. Ndumbe Eyoh said it clearly: "There seems to be no other better way than associating fully with them, meeting them in the villages, joining them in their daily chores and shar-

Figure 6: The leader of the Hmong cultural revival center performs a newly composed song about becoming refugees. (Photo by Dwight Conquergood: Courtesy of Northwestern University Archives)

ing with them their lifestyles" (Eyoh 1986, 23). That is why it was crucial for me to live in the camp with the Hmong, although that was considered a great oddity by the other expatriate agency workers who commuted from Chiang Kham village, an hour's drive away. Indeed, it was one of the camp rules that agency workers had to leave by 5:00 P.M. every day. Nevertheless, through delicate negotiations with the camp commander, a Thai colonel, I was able to stay overnight in the camp.

I hoped to break the pattern of importing the knowledge of "experts" and distributing it to the refugees, who were expected to be grateful consumers. I wanted to help demonstrate to both expatriates and refugees that *dialogical* exchange between the two cultures, the two worldviews and sensibilities, was possible (see Bakhtin 1981; Todorov 1984; Conquergood 1985).

One of the things that worked well for me as a health worker was to barter recommendations and health practices with traditional healers. This kept the program from being too one-sided. Because of the camp conditions, I personally had frequent trouble with intestinal disorders. For this discomfort, I went to the women herbalists who gave me a root to chew that was quite helpful. Early in my fieldwork I fell through a bridge and gashed my toe when a rotten board gave way. Herbalists treated my wound with soothing poultices from a glossy-leaved plant. Within a week the jagged wound had healed and I was able to go without a bandage. Because of the rugged terrain, however, I stubbed my toes repeatedly and reopened that wound more than once. I became quite dependent on the herbal healers—they knew that my trust and respect for their medicine was genuine. Their pleasure in my trust was overwhelming. Never have I received such devoted attention. However, when I came down with Dengue fever, a somewhat serious illness, I spent a week in a Singapore hospital taking advantage of the best that modern medicine had to offer in order to get back on my feet as soon as possible. My friends, of course, were curious about the hospital, and I shared the details of my treatment with them. What I tried to do in my fieldwork was enact an example of dialogical exchange, or barter, wherein each culture could benefit from the other, approaching health care issues within a both/and embrace instead of an either/or separation of categories; this approach was particularly important because the refugees were accustomed to having expatriates undermine, even outrightly assault, their traditions.

The first test was whether or not the Hmong would accept a popular theatre approach. Quite simply, could we gather an audience? That test came earlier than I had planned when five rabid dogs rampaged through the camp biting several children. The solution proposed by the camp commander was to go to the Thai market, buy five machetes, and kill all the dogs. To his great credit, the director of the International Rescue Committee in Ban Vinai persuaded the colonel against this course of action. He proposed instead that IRC use its funds to buy rabies vaccine and inoculate all the dogs in camp. The vaccine was purchased and IRC personnel were at their stations ready and poised with needles to vaccinate the dogs. No dogs arrived. The problem centered on communication. The Hmong were not boycotting the rabies program. They simply were baffled by this strange procedure, or unaware of it. There was no effective way of getting the word out as to where, when, and why dogs should be brought to the IRC stations for injections.

I had just arrived in camp and was beginning to establish rapport, recruit, and work with refugee performers/health workers. We had developed some characters based on stock figures in Hmong folklore and were designing and constructing costumes and masks. We had started improvisation and confidence-building exercises, but everything was still very tentative. The group was very young; all but one were under 20. We were just beginning to mesh as a group when the IRC director

Figures 7 and 8: An assistant balances a Ban Vinai shaman in ecstatic flight. (Photos by Dwight Conquergood: Courtesy of Northwestern University Archives)

approached me and asked for help with the rabies vaccination project. Time was running out. The camp dogs would have to be vaccinated soon or Ban Vinai might have a serious rabies epidemic.

I certainly did not feel confident about putting the fledgling actors to this kind of major test so soon. We met and discussed the seriousness of the situation and collectively decided what would be the best strategy for quickly communicating this important message to as much of the camp population as possible. We soon agreed on a grand, clamorous, eye-catching "Rabies Parade" that would snake its way through all the sections of the camp. The tiger costume—appliquéd cotton fabric with a long rope tail—was almost finished, so it was agreed that the tiger would be the lead figure in the parade (figure 10). The tiger is a trickster figure in Hmong folklore and mythology, a very dramatic and evocative character. We knew the tiger would draw attention, inspire awe. The tiger would be followed by a nature-spirit, a ragged costume with long colored strings for hair, that would sing and bang on a drum. That noise,

we hoped, would reach the people inside their huts and bring them out to see the commotion. We agreed that the chicken, a feathered costume with a striking cardboard mask that covered the entire head, would be the pivotal figure. After the dancing tiger and the clamorous nature-spirit got people's attention, the chicken would talk through a bullhorn and explain in terms the Hmong would understand the seriousness of rabies and why it was important for every family to round up the dogs and bring them for injections. The chicken couched all this in an appeal toward protecting the children and then gave specific instructions for each neighborhood in the camp as to where and when they should bring the dogs. It was culturally appropriate for the chicken to be the leading speaker because in Hmong lore chickens have divinatory powers. They are frequently offered up in spirit ceremonies as guides to lead the way to the sky kingdom. Three days after a baby is born, chickens are used in an augury ceremony to determine the child's future. Hmong naturally associate the chicken with divination because, as was explained to me, "Who is the one who knows first when the sun comes up every morning?"

We had some pep talks among ourselves to build confidence for going on the road the following morning. Not only would this be the performance company's first show, it would be the first time any member of our young group had performed in public. The ones who seemed to be the most extroverted were selected for the key roles of tiger, nature-spirit, and talking chicken. The rest would don masks and come along

Figure 9: A Hmong story quilt entitled "Viet Shoot Hmong." The Hmong use the story cloths to teach their children the tragic history of *neeg taw grog,* "war-broken people," or refugees. (Photo by Jerry Zbiral)

as backup and as moral support for their comrades. Without assigning them specific roles, I encouraged them to do whatever they felt comfortable with in the parade. This would be an opportunity for them to get exposure in front of an audience before assuming more demanding roles.

Our casting instincts for the critical roles of tiger, nature-spirit, and chicken turned out to be inspired. At first, everyone was extremely self-conscious and inhibited. I was prepared for the worst. But as we kept banging the drum and hanging together, some children began pointing their fingers and laughing at the listless tiger. This brought him to life. The young fellow turned out to be a natural acrobat. Drawing on the media influence of Chinese movies that Thai entrepreneurs show in the open air once a month, he created a highly physical "Kung-Fu Tiger" to

Figure 10: The tiger leads the 1985 Rabies Parade. (Photo by Dwight Conquergood: Courtesy of Northwestern University Archives)

the joy of the people who streamed out of their houses to see such a sight. The fellow playing the nature-spirit turned out to be quite a musician. In addition to the drum, he brought along a folk instrument, a reed pipe organ, that his grandfather had made. He spontaneously danced as he blew the pipes, a great hit with the crowd. The chicken enjoyed the importance of his role and took it quite seriously. Understanding the power of word-of-mouth networks, the young actor instructed his audiences to go and tell their neighbors and relatives what they had just heard.

In terms of ability to gather an audience, the Rabies Parade was a huge success. Also, the novice performers had acquitted themselves beyond my highest expectations. However, the real test of our communication effectiveness was whether or not the Hmong would bring their dogs to the vaccination stations.

The next morning, full of nervous anticipation, I staked out the first vaccination station. It was a heartwarming sight. Dogs came pouring in—on rope leashes, in two-wheel pushcarts, and carried in their owners' arms. We could not vaccinate them fast enough. I myself vaccinated scores of dogs. The vaccination stations became a sort of street theatre. As you can imagine, the dogs did not submit willingly to these injections. It is a rather intricate operation to hold a struggling dog up in the air—we had no veterinary tables—and get it injected properly. There was a lot of scuffling and abortive thrusts of the needle—the stuff of farce.

Also, with so many nervous dogs concentrated in one area, fights broke out. For a week this part of the rabies program performed before rapt audiences, drawing crowds equal to those for the parades. We vaccinated almost 500 dogs.

We took advantage of the performance company's initial outing to elicit direct audience feedback as part of the process of testing, developing, and refining our concepts. The drum that was used belonged to a shaman, and some of the older people objected to its use. When the young performer brought the gong from home, I recognized it as a shaman's and questioned the company about the appropriateness of using it. Everyone said there would be no problem, and that a shaman had donated it. In any event, we never again used a shaman's instrument in our performance.

Throughout the development of our health theatre programs we actively solicited feedback from Hmong elders. We received excellent, helpful criticism. After we had rehearsed our first set of acted scenarios we showed them to a Hmong leader. He critiqued the performers on three points: (1) the performers and stage managers not in costume should wear traditional Hmong clothes, and not Western-style T-shirts and trousers available in the camp through charity outlets; (2) the backup music for the dances should be authentic Hmong, not Thai or Western-influenced melodies; (3) the rhymed chants were a little off from the traditional Hmong prosody; he taught the young performers the correct speech patterns. These criticisms were very useful because many of the members of the performance company were quite young and had grown up in the camp, exposed to outside influences. Moreover, the critique demonstrated the concern of Hmong leaders for maintaining their cultural integrity against the forces of assimilation.

There was one other criticism regarding the masks and the tiger. The oldest member of the performance company declined to wear a mask of any kind. The masks were too real for him. He was unable to frame the wearing of a mask as make-believe and worried about problems with spirits as a consequence of wearing the mask. We, of course, gave him roles that did not require wearing a mask and he remained a dedicated and important member of the performance company. But, soon after the Rabies Parade, a few of the people said that the masks and the tiger were scary and worried that some of the children's spirits might be scared away and they would fall sick. This response struck terror in me. As many anthropologists have noted, the political influence and power of shamans lies in their role as interpreters of the source and cause of illness. Shamanic ceremonies for a patient are in two phases: first, the divination/diagnosis, then the cure (see Conquergood 1989). A shaman can influence the politics of a village by interpreting certain actions as the cause of illness or calamity. There is no lack of children falling sick every day in Ban Vinai. Fever and diarrhea are prevalent. Hundreds of children had enjoyed our parades. If one shaman attributed the sickness of one child to spirit-flight precipitated by the parade, the Ban Vinai health and performance company would be destroyed. One accusation could ruin us.

It was a tense week for me, but no accusations came. However, we decided to modify our staging techniques based on this feedback. Powerful characters like the tiger would no longer play directly to the audience in open form. Using theatre-in-the-round staging, we would direct the energies of the tiger and other masked characters inside the circle, using onstage focus. We would have these dramatic characters interact in an animated way with one another, but not directly confront the audience.

However, we did not want to lose the power of open-form communication, so we needed a narrator character who could safely and directly address audiences. Proverbs are an important communication form in all oral cultures and particularly popular with the Hmong (see Conquergood 1986). We wanted to use a character who could recite health proverbs and tell stories and who would have a special rapport with small children. Almost a quarter of the camp's population is under the age of five, the most vulnerable group with a high rate of disease and death. Appealing to them would also be a way of involving their parents; Hmong families are tightly knit and children are greatly loved. This led to the creation of our most successful character who became the symbol for the entire health communication program: the beloved Niam Tsev Huv (Mother Clean), our cleanliness clown (figure 11). She was the collective creation of the entire performance company. Inspired by Peter Schumann's Bread and Puppet Theatre, I introduced the idea of a huge muppet figure constructed on a bamboo frame (figure 12). The performance company took it from there. Someone designed her face, a pleasant smile painted on a cloth-stuffed dummy's head tacked atop the bamboo frame; someone else did her costume, a colorfully striped dress that made her look larger than life; another member made her hair out of dyed yarn. The performance company worked collectively on all phases of the performance process, from research for scenarios to composing songs and proverbs to costume construction. Except for the tiger's mask which I purchased in Loei, the provincial capital, all of the costumes and props were handmade from local materials.

The performer who eventually assumed the role of Mother Clean

Figure 11: Dwight Conquergood performs with Mother Clean in 1985. (Photo by Lw Vang)

was a late starter—not one of the precocious three who emerged during the Rabies Parade. Several members of the company tried out the role, but he was the one who brought Mother Clean to life. Mother Clean, as he created her, was as gentle and loving as she was physically huge and imposing. She was a narrator-character who set the stage for the performance and, during the performance, could negotiate back and forth between direct address to the audience and dialog with onstage characters. Mother Clean particularly loved little children and always had special words for them. They adored her; sometimes during a performance they would run on stage to peek underneath her muppet skirts. Mother Clean always handled these moments with tender dignity, improvising skillfully. She also was very, very funny. Adults would double over with laughter at her antics. The incongruity between her size and her feigned daintiness was very farcical. Mother Clean grew in popularity so that the sight of her coming down the camp road would immediately draw a huge crowd for a performance. As she would walk through the camp, small children would shout her name. Hundreds of T-shirts were printed with her image in the Ban Vinai Print Shop run by a Japanese Refugee Relief Agency (figure 13). The camp literacy project used her image on

Figure 12: The frames for the muppets are constructed out of split bamboo wicker. (Photo by Dwight Conquergood: Courtesy of Northwestern University Archives)

posters. She was perhaps the most visible figure with the highest name recognition in the camp and she became the linchpin of our communication campaign. People believed that Mother Clean was on their side and the side of their children and they listened to what she told them about health and sanitation.

Performance, Garbage, and the Environmental Setting

Once we had demonstrated that performance was an appropriate and successful way of communicating with the Hmong, we set out to work on the environmental health problems of the camp. Ban Vinai has serious hygiene and sanitation problems. The cause, however, lies in the environmental circumstances, not any innate character flaw of the Hmong. Simplistic health messages imported from Western middle-class notions of cleanliness simply would not work for Ban Vinai. What was needed was a health education and consciousness-raising program that was sensitive to the history and specific environmental problems and constraints of the camp.

Figure 13: A Mother Clean T-shirt printed in the Ban Vinai print shop. (Photo by Dawn Murrey)

Ban Vinai is located in an isolated, hilly region of northeast Thailand, the poorest sector of the country. The camp has a population larger than any city in this remote area of Thailand, surpassing even Loei, the provincial capital. It is the most populous refugee camp in Asia. All these people are crowded onto about 400 acres of undeveloped land. The camp space is intensively used because refugees are forbidden to go outside the camp without the express permission of Colonel Vichitmala, the Thai camp commander. Armed guards enforce this policy. During the time of my fieldwork more than one refugee was shot for venturing outside the camp.

The overcrowding in the camp, not to mention the sanitation level, is compounded by large numbers of animals. The Hmong were sturdy peasant farmers before they became refugees. Resourceful by nature, they supplement their diet by raising a variety of animals within the confines of the camp. Purchased as inexpensive chicks, and a valuable ceremonial animal, chickens scratch about everywhere. Every family seems to have at least half a dozen. Ducks and geese are also raised. Pigs are a common sight, and dogs and goats roam freely throughout the camp. Because space is at such a premium, there is little room for separate livestock pens. During the day they roam outside and at night they are often brought inside the house. In one of the thatched huts where I regularly slept overnight, I shared a corner with seven chickens—they were kept underneath wicker baskets at night—and the neighbor's pig. Inside many of the homes of very poor families you could find guinea pigs scurrying about, an inexpensive source of protein. Ban Vinai boasts a herd of more than 20 dairy cows, a gift from a well-meaning but uninformed charitable organization with the intention of raising the nutritional level of the camp. The Hmong do not drink milk; like many Asians, some are lactose intolerant. Because the cows were donated for the common good, no individual is authorized to butcher them. Therefore, completely useless, the cows wander freely throughout the camp, contributing to the hygiene and sanitation problems of the camp.

Housing is extremely crowded and inadequate. The United Nations High Commissioner for Refugees built 395 tin-roofed buildings, each one with ten small rooms. The camp was established in 1975 for 12,000 refugees; the population has nearly quadrupled since then. The 1984 birthrate was 5.5 percent, one of the highest in the world. Twenty-five percent of the Ban Vinai population was born in the camp. The refugees have responded to the housing shortage by building more than 2,250 thatch/bamboo huts. But it costs more than $50 for the materials to build a house. That kind of money is hard to come by in a refugee camp, so extended families crowd together in congested living quarters. During the rainy season, some of these dirt-floor huts are in danger of getting washed away so families use partially buried discarded glass bottles to bank up the earth around their huts.

Camp Ban Vinai is the largest gathering of Hmong in the world. The tragic events of war and global politics have led to this artificial urbanization of the Hmong with dizzying speed. Traditionally, the Hmong lived in small mountaintop villages in the forbidding terrain of northern Laos where they tended their animals and grew dry rice and corn in fields cleared from the forest. F.M. Savina reported that the Hmong in Laos "do not seem to like big settlements. They prefer to live in little groups making up hamlets rather than real villages" (1930:182). A peaceful mountain people who kept to themselves, they had little contact with even the lowland-dwelling Lao, much less the rest of the world, until they were pulled into the war in Southeast Asia. In the 1960s they were recruited by the CIA and trained by the Green Berets as anticommunist guerilla fighters.[3] In proportion to their population, they suffered casualties 10 times higher than those of Americans who fought in Vietnam (Cerquone 1986). When U.S. forces withdrew in 1975, Laos collapsed and came under the rule of a government hostile to the Hmong who were viewed as collaborators with the hated enemy. Thousands fled their beloved mountain homes to seek asylum in Camp Ban Vinai, just across the Mekong in Thailand. Almost overnight they were thrown into a densely populated camp with no time to develop the adaptive cultural traditions and folkways, not to mention garbage disposal systems, that societies in the West have had centuries to evolve. It is any wonder, then, that there would be severe environmental health problems in Ban Vinai?

Moreover, there is no running water or adequate sewage disposal in the camp. The camp commander lists the water shortage as one of the major problems. Water has to be carried long distances in buckets balanced on shoulder yokes or in 10-gallon cans strapped to the back, a job usually done by teenagers. Sewage disposal is also a chronic problem. There are not enough pit toilets for the camp population. The latrines are distributed unevenly throughout the camp and are clustered together in long rows—convenient if you happen to live close to a cluster but the trade-off is the overwhelming stench. Because there is a shortage of toilets, they are kept locked and families have to obtain keys from the camp administration. Keys get lost, and there are never enough keys to go around, particularly for all the children. Further, you need to bring along a bucket of water to flush the shallow pit, water that is scarce and has to be carried on the back of some family member. Obviously, there are many disincentives for using the pit toilets; the stench alone is often a deterrent. Because gaining access to and using the pit toilets is a rather complex operation, most small children (one-fourth the population) simply cannot manage.

I go into detail about the camp toilets in order to give an infrastructural explanation for what has become a topos in reports about Ban Vinai from Western journalists and visiting relief workers. Ban Vinai is notorious for the image of refugees relieving themselves in the open space. This act, so shocking to "sophisticated" sensibilities, functions discursively as a sign of "the primitive." Before I left Bangkok en route to Ban Vinai, I heard stories about this behavior from other aid workers and came across this motif in written reports as well as oral anecdotes. This recurrent image is psychologically and rhetorically interesting for what it reveals about our discursive projections of the Other. My observations are that the Hmong are a very modest people. The act does not occur with the frequency the stories imply. However, you have only to spend three days and nights in the camp in order to understand the environmental circumstances that produce such behavior even occasionally. Living in the camp with the refugees and experiencing these environmental constraints and indignities was instructive for me.

The following excerpt from an unpublished report written by an agency health worker is representative:

> The first week I arrived in Ban Vinai, a refugee city, a city without discipline, I strolled around the camp and realized the important need for basic health education. No one looks after the children playing cheerfully in the streams. The streams in which they defecate, take a bath, and throw garbage including drainage from houses and toilets. The refugees use sticks for cleaning after defecation and throw them behind the toilets. When it rains, the sewage goes into the streams. Also, a lot of children wear nothing when it rains.

Instead of blaming the Hmong for the poor health conditions, our performance company situated the problem in the environmental setting. Instead of didactic health messages instructing the Hmong to change their behavior, we developed performances that would stimulate critical awareness about the camp environment, particularly how it differed from the natural mountain villages of the Hmong in Laos. Once their radically changed living conditions could be brought to consciousness through performance, the Hmong might understand the need for changing some of their habits to adapt to this altered situation. Such a line of thinking was not alien to them. One man offered me an environmental explanation for the high suicide rate in Ban Vinai. He argued that, in their homeland, family tensions and pressures could be relieved by the troubled person leaving home temporarily to stay with relatives or friends in the next village until the situation cooled down. Without this outlet in Ban Vinai, pressures sometimes mount until suicide seems the only escape. Also, there is a traditional Hmong proverb that encourages adjustment to change of venue: "When you cross a river, take off your shoes/When you move to another place, you must change your headman" (Conquergood 1986).

We mounted a series of performances focused on the problem of garbage in the camp (figures 14, 15, 16). The first thing we had to do was problematize "garbage." In a traditional Hmong village, garbage would not be the problem it was in Ban Vinai. If all disposable waste is organic, and you live in a small hamlet on a windswept mountain slope, then pitching waste out the door is not a problem. It becomes instant feed for

Figure 14: The Garbage Troll (standing, left) performs during Garbage Theme Month 1985. (Photo by Dwight Conquergood: Courtesy of Northwestern University Archives)

the household pigs or is biodegradably reabsorbed into the natural ecology of the environment. Within the context of a crowded refugee camp, however, traditional ways of waste disposal entail radically different consequences. We wanted to get this message across without demeaning the people, suggesting that they were dirty.

Our "Garbage Theme" month featured Mother Clean in one of our most successful scenarios. Drawing on the *poj ntxoog* evil ogre character from Hmong folklore, we created an ugly Garbage Troll in soiled ragged clothes and a mask plastered with bits of garbage and dirt (figure 14). The Garbage Troll would lumber into the center of the playing space and begin dramatizing the behavior we wanted to discourage—peeling eggs and other food and throwing the waste on the ground, picking up dirty food from the ground and putting it into his mouth, and so forth. After a few minutes of this improvisation, the tiger would charge on stage and rebuke the troll for such unseemly behavior. The tiger would growl and snarl and pounce at the impassive troll, all the while making verbally explicit how bad this behavior was. The tiger would give up and leave but then the pig would run out on stage and fuss at the troll for his disgusting conduct. The young performer who played our pig was a gifted clown and there would be much farcical business between the pig and the Garbage Troll until the troll drove the pig away. Then the chicken would follow suit and sagely admonish the troll about the environmental consequences of his behavior and how he would make children sick by throwing garbage all about. The troll would respond by throwing more garbage on the ground and at the chicken, driving the latter away.

From a considerable distance, Mother Clean would slowly sweep toward the dirty Garbage Troll. The children forming a circle around the playing space would have to open up their ranks to permit Mother Clean's passage. They would call out, warning her to beware of the nasty Garbage Troll. But Mother Clean would be unaware of the danger; absorbed in sweet thoughts she would sing to herself and dance as daintily as her bulk would permit. The children in the audience would increase the volume of their warning cries until Mother Clean heard and caught sight of the Garbage Troll. Unafraid, slowly, triumphantly she would sweep toward the nasty troll huddling in the dirt making menacing noises. She'd reach down, pull him up by his hands, then, in a moment of redemptive grace, remove his dirt-face mask and wash his face and hands. Transformed, the troll and Mother Clean danced as music was played from our battery-operated cassette player. Tiger, pig, and chicken rushed back on stage to dance and sing with Mother Clean and the redeemed troll.

Our health workers, wearing sandwich-board posters with the health theme boldly lettered, would join the circle, and Mother Clean would slowly spell out and read the poster proverbs for those in the audience who were nonliterate (figures 15 & 16). She would talk and invite comment and discussion about the theme.

The theme we developed in proverb form and painted on the sandwich-board posters was this:

Thaum peb nyob pem roob cua thiab nag
    Tshoob yam khoom qias neeg pov tseg.
Tam sim no muaj neeg coob coob nyob hauv zos vib nai,
    Peb txhua leej txhua tus yuav xyuam xim
Cheb yam khoom qias neeg kom huv si

[When you lived in the mountains
    The wind and the rain cleaned the garbage.

Figures 15 and 16: Health workers wearing sandwich-board posters join the performance circle. Mother Clean slowly spells out and reads the garbage theme proverbs for those in the audience who are nonliterate. (Photos by Dwight Conquergood: Courtesy of Northwestern University Archives)

Now with so many people in Ban Vinai
    We all must be careful to clean up the garbage]

Mother Clean would lovingly amplify the message of the proverb, explaining how a small village on a mountain slope with plenty of space for everyone could absorb organic refuse naturally through the elements of wind and rain. She pointed out that Ban Vinai is very different from the mountaintop villages in which the Hmong used to live. Consequently, customs and habits, particularly regarding garbage, needed to change accordingly. She exhorted a change in behavior without degrading the people whom she was trying to persuade, locating responsibility in the environmental circumstances. Everyone could agree that indeed Ban Vinai was very different from their former home. After establishing that premise, Mother Clean then could make the point about the need for adaptive response to this new situation.

This scenario was staged three or four times a week, each time in a different section of the camp. In this way we could reach most of the

camp population in a month's time. Each day we would find a wide place in the road, or a clearing between houses, and use that empty space for the performance. One of the company members would walk around the area with a bullhorn announcing the performance. The performances were so popular that we sometimes had crowd control problems, with people pressing in so close that there was no room for the performers to move. One of the company members, usually the one who made the initial announcements over the bullhorn, would serve as "house manager." He would draw a large circle on the ground with a pointed stick and declare that area the players' space, off-limits to curious children. This strategy worked, except for the occasional dog that wandered on stage.

It was hard work performing in the open air under the tropical sun. I admired the dedication of the refugee performers. I was particularly touched by the young man who played Mother Clean. Lee Neng (his name means "human being" in Hmong) was malarial and every month or so would run a fever, have a stomachache, and pass blood in his urine.

I insisted that he not perform during these bouts and proposed that we use an understudy when he was sick. Besides, the roles of the pig, chicken, and tiger were passed around among the company members. But Lee Neng knew that he had a special rapport with the children and that his character Niam Tsev Huv was doing good in the camp, helping the little children so that they would not get sick so often. He said it made him feel very good when he was Niam Tsev Huv and he refused to surrender the role, even when he was ill. Sometimes he was so weak he could barely be heard. I would give him aspirin and lighten the performance schedule when I knew he was feverish.

We included a participatory dimension to the performances by teaching health and sanitation songs to the children. Initially, young children performers were trained as role models who traveled around the camp with our troupe, singing and dancing the sanitation songs (figure 17). However, we incurred "labor problems" with the young actors when their parents complained about the taxing performance schedule. We discontinued the Chorus of Children and used members of the performance company, particularly the young women, as sanitation song leaders.

The children of the camp loved to learn and sing these sanitation songs. They particularly enjoyed a call and response style of singing in which the audience would alternate the singing of verses with a leader, Mother Clean or one of the refugee health workers. We put some of the songs on cassette tapes, and distributed them throughout the camp in that way as well. Most of the Hmong have access to battery-operated cassette players because many of them correspond with relatives resettled in the West by sending cassettes through the mail. I also gave cassettes of these songs to the "Hilltribe Broadcast Program," Radio Thailand. Later, when I toured their studios and facilities in Chiang Mai and interviewed the Hmong broadcasters, they reported that the Ban Vinai Health Songs were very popular with their listening audience.

Here is a sample health song composed for our campaign:

Yog koj mus yos hav zoov tsam ysov tom
  Yog koj tsis ntxuav muag ntxuav tes, taw ibce
Koj yuav tau kab mob
  Yog koj mus torn tej hav tsaub liab koj yuav tau mob

[If you play in the jungle
  The Tiger will bite you
If you don't wash your hands, face, and body
  You will fall ill]

Figure 17: The Chorus of Children singing and dancing sanitation songs. (Photo by Dwight Conquergood: Courtesy of Northwestern University Archives)

Another sanitation song, "Using the Latrine," turned out to be one of the most durable songs in the repertoire. Mother Clean led a parade of 40 singing children throughout the camp, with the message visually reinforced on posters that graphically depicted the appropriate behavior (figure 18). There was follow-up to the parade with activities such as coloring pictures and a game called "Take Your Small Brother or Sister to the Latrine." Once again, reaching and involving the children was an important way of communicating with adults.

Mother Clean was the anchor for the performance company. A variety of performance materials and activities could be organized around her character. She seemed to embody something very appealing to the

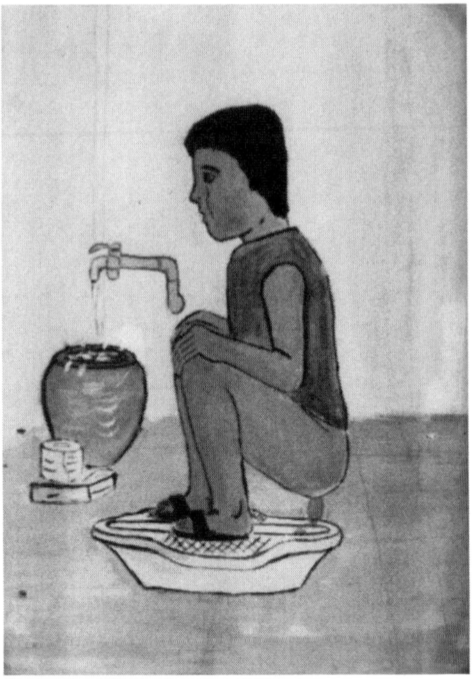

Figure 18: One of the vividly illustrated posters carried by Mother Clean and the performance company in the 1987 Using the Latrine Parade. (Photo by Dwight Conquergood: Courtesy of Northwestern University Archives)

Hmong. Adults as well as small children were delighted by her messages. I will never forget the image of a very thin, elderly man doubled over his walking stick with uncontrollable laughter during Mother Clean's performance. His neighbors told me they had not seen him laugh in a long time.

Expatriate Health Professionals and the Hmong: Perceptions of Difference, Disorder, Dirt, and Danger

The more I learned about the history and cultural dynamics of the camp, the more I came to believe that the expatriate health professionals needed consciousness-raising messages as much as the Hmong. The Hmong are perceived by Western officials and visiting journalists as the causal, producing agents of the unsanitary and unhealthy conditions in the camp. Instead of seeing the Hmong as struggling within a constraining context of historical, political, and economic forces that have reduced them from proud, independent, mountain people to landless refugees, the Hmong are blamed for their miserable condition. In her brilliant and incisive analysis of refugee assistance programs, Barbara Harrell-Bond notes this sad pattern: "[I]t is alarming to observe that assistance programmes are dominated by an ethos in which the victims of mass exodus are treated as the villains" (1986:305). It is easier to scapegoat than to historicize a complex problem.

I began to collect the phrases used regularly to describe the Hmong by agency officials who worked in Ban Vinai. The word I heard most often was "filthy," followed closely by "dirty," and often part of a cluster of terms that included "scabies," "abscesses," "feces," and "piles of garbage." A phrase regularly employed to cover a multitude of perceived sanitation sins was the following, "They're one step out of the Stone Age, you know." A meaning-packed word heard about the Hmong almost every day was "difficult," and its ramified derivatives: "difficult to work with," "the most difficult group," "set in their ways," "rigid," "stubborn," "you cannot get through to them," "backward." One dedicated humanitarian agency employee who had worked with the Hmong for several years told me that "the hand of God is on this place," but as for the Hmong living here, "they're a fearful lot . . . you cannot work with them." These perceptions surface in official discourse as well. Senator Alan Simpson, ranking minority member of the Senate Subcommittee on Immigration and Refugee Affairs, visited Ban Vinai for a day during the time of my fieldwork. He introduced a new metaphor into this complex of discursive denigrations of the Hmong. He called the Hmong "the most indigestible group in society" (1987:4). Ambassador Jonathan Moore, the new U.S. Coordinator for Refugee Affairs, was more diplomatic when, in a 1987 interview, he singled out the Hmong as "the people with special problems" (1987:5).

The dialectic between the perception of "difference" and "dirt" is interesting. I suggest that so much focus on the "dirtiness" and "difficulty" of the Hmong is actually an expression of Western expatriates' uneasiness when confronted with Difference, the Other. A Western aid official's encounter with the Hmong is a confrontation with radical difference—in cosmology, worldview, ethos, texture of everyday life. The difference is exacerbated if the relief workers are devout Christians. The three relief agencies that have been in charge of the camp hospital have all been Christian organizations which have perceived the animism of the Hmong as "devil worship."

For medical health officials with a professional commitment to the tenets of Western science, the equally strong Hmong belief in spirits and shamans challenges fundamental Western assumptions about the nature of the world. What is frustrating for agency workers is that the acceptance and cooperation of the Hmong are essential for the successful delivery of health care programs and services. The Hmong are the clear majority in Camp Ban Vinai, of course, and they continue to control their symbolic universe. Much to the distress of agency workers, they have not acquiesced to the new scientific epistemology presented to them as a "superior" form of knowledge. Visible affirmations of their traditional way of understanding the world are displayed everywhere. Here are excerpts from a report by Dr. Ronald Munger, an epidemiologist who did research in Ban Vinai:

> The striking issue in regard to traditional Hmong health practices is how visible these practices are in Ban Vinai Refugee camp in Thailand. [. . .] Shamanism was widely practiced. [. . .] There were other more common everyday rituals which reflected pervading belief in the spirits in every aspect of life. Ritual figures or heads of sacrificed animals set on poles were common. Wooden boards on the floor at the doorway of a home were intended to confuse unwanted spirits and prevent them from entering the house. [. . .] Pleasing the spirits was a primary goal. For example, bracelets, necklaces, and other devices were often placed on babies and small children to contain the spirit of that person and avoid its loss. [. . .] Many Hmong homes [. . .] contained small altars with the items needed to interact with spirits. There were buffalo horns [. . .] rings and rattles used during rituals. (1984)

All this display of "difference" and "strangeness" is quite dramatic to Western eyes and makes a vivid impression. Unfortunately, as Tzvetan Todorov reminds us, "The first, spontaneous reaction with regard to the stranger is to imagine him as inferior, since he is different from us" (Todorov 1984, 76). All too easily, "difference is corrupted into inequality" (Todorov 1984, 146).

Mary Douglas' ideas about the social relativity and symbolic functions of dirt help explain how "Difference" and "Dirt" are conjoined in perceptions of the Hmong. Inspired by William James' insight that dirt is "matter out of place" (Douglas 1966, 164), she argues:

> [D]irt is essentially disorder. There is no such thing as absolute dirt: it exists in the eye of the beholder. [. . .] Dirt offends against order. Eliminating it is not a negative movement, but a positive effort to organise the environment. (Douglas 1966, 2)

Perceptions of what is clean and unclean are contextually variable and culturally specific. Habits of cleanliness and rites of purification are the manifest expressions and protections of deep structures and fundamental classificatory schemes that maintain order and help hold a society together. People and actions that disturb order, violate categories, mess up the system are branded unclean: "The unclear is the unclean" (Turner 1967, 97). Labeling someone or something "dirty" is a way of controlling perceived anomalies, incongruities, contradictions, ambiguities—all that does not fit into our categories, and therefore threatens cherished principles. "Dirt," then, functions as the mediating term between "Difference" and "Danger." It is the term that loads the perception of "Difference" with a moral imperative, and enables the move from description to action, from "is" to "ought." Defining something as unhealthy, harmful, dangerous establishes the premise for "moving in," for control, making it "licit to intervene [. . .] in order to exercise the rights of guardianship [. . .] to impose 'the good' on others" (Todorov 1984, 150). Perception, language, and politics cathect in the encounter with the Other: "the perception of the other and that of symbolic (or semiotic) behavior intersect" (Todorov 1984, 157; see also Foucault 1973; Said 1979).

The communication between expatriate camp officials and the refugees in Ban Vinai is so clouded by the perceptual transformations which I call the Difference-Disorder-Dirt-Danger Sliding Continuum, that other explanations for the poor health conditions of the camp get filtered out. I quote a revealing passage from one of the monthly reports submitted to the Bangkok office by a Ban Vinai health officer:

> Three refugees in Center Five had just died before my arrival. [. . .] We walked around that area. It was muddy; piled with garbage, sticks thrown behind toilets and sludge appeared from place to place. [Agency] garbage pits and sewage treatment lagoons were situated above and close to the buildings. "It's a horrible smell when the wind blows especially from that garbage pit down to our houses, sometimes we can't eat anymore," [a refugee said]. [. . .] [He] asked me to convey this problem to [the agency], hoping we could move the pits to another place. However, [the agency] can't move it at all because of the limitations of land and budget.

This is a remarkable passage. After the obligatory fecal imagery of the toilets, mud, sludge, and ooze, there is almost a recognition scene. The health official notes the "garbage pits" and "sewage treatment lagoons" his agency has situated dangerously close to the living quarters. The refugee accompanying him on this site tour follows up on the perception and complains. We are presented with a marvelous glimpse of a refugee talking back to a camp official, resisting the unhealthy and degrading circumstances in which he and his people are caught. The responsibility for the problem almost gets shifted from the refugees to the environment, with the expatriate agencies even held accountable for contributing to the creation of a harmful scene.

This rupture in the discursive text about refugees gets sealed off quickly, however. Scarcely a page later, the perceptual blinders are back in place: "Even though some have had public health training, it is evident that the training has had little effect—their homes are untidy and stuffy and their children are dirty. They have no picture of community." We are comfortably refocused on the dirtiness of the refugees. This ideology of blaming the victims, and thereby legitimizing domination and control over them, is displayed transparently in the final section of the report, ominously subtitled "Submission for Discipline":

> We all realize that even though lots of refugees have been trained about hygiene and sanitation by volags [voluntary agencies], they still behave as they used to. [. . .] No refugees really take care of the environment. [. . .] They live freely wandering around without any responsibility.
>
> In my own opinion it'll take a long time to change their habits which detract from their health. One thing that might help is a 'system of discipline'. [. . .] For example, the refugees can be told what will happen if they throw garbage everywhere, defecate into the streams, etc.
>
> It's an idea that we might think about carefully and which might work in the future.

This text is paradigmatic of the documents produced by the bureaucracy and institutional apparatus of refugee relief agencies. It is an avatar of the twin themes of discursive power and institutional control that Michel Foucault discussed in *The Birth of the Clinic: An Archaeology of Medical Perception* (1973) and *Discipline and Punish: The Birth of the Prison* (1977). Because the "limitation of land and budget" forecloses the consideration of infrastructural change in the camp environment, attention is diverted to the "change [of] their habits which detract from their good health." Refugee subjects are discursively represented in a way that reduces them to the unhealthy and/or passive Other who is to be managed, administered, and if need be, changed. Their resistance, interpreted as recalcitrance, only legitimizes and further sustains the institutional power and authority that are enacted upon them. Harrell-Bond deconstructs the strange, self-reinforcing logic that underpins refugee programs in Africa where she did fieldwork: "Often interpretations of compassion seem to define those in need as helpless, and then work in ways which makes sure that they are useless" (Harrell-Bond 1986, 82).

One of the motives that would prompt doctors and nurses to volunteer for stressful work in an alien, harsh environment is concern for the refugees' souls as well as their physical bodies. I heard horror story after horror story from the refugees about people who went to the hospital for treatment, but before being admitted had their spirit-strings cut from their wrists by a nurse because "the strings were unsanitary and carried germs." Doctors confidently cut off neck-rings that held the life-souls of babies intact. Instead of working in cooperation with the shamans, they did everything to disconfirm them and undermine their authority. Shamans were regarded as "witch doctors." Here are the views of a Finnish nurse who worked in Ban Vinai: "They have their bark and root medicines and rites to appease the spirits. Most of it is worthless, and some of it is positively harmful" (Evans 1983, 110). Is it any wonder that the Hmong community regarded the camp hospital as the last choice of available health care options? In the local hierarchy of values, consulting a shaman or herbalist, or purchasing medicine available in the Thai market just outside the entrance to the camp, was much preferred and more prestigious than going to the camp hospital. The refugees told me that only the very poorest people who had no relatives or resources whatsoever would subject themselves to the camp hospital treatment. To say that the camp hospital was underutilized would be an understatement.

As I critique my work in the camp I realize that I should have developed more consciousness-raising performances specifically for the expatriate health professionals. They needed to develop a critical awareness about health problems in the camp at least as much as did the Hmong. Directing most of the performances to the Hmong resulted in a one-sided communication campaign and subtly reinforced the prevailing notion that the Hmong were primarily responsible for the bad conditions.

I did develop one performance event that was designed especially for the agency health workers, the *IRC Health and Sanitation Celebration* (figures 19–21). All the voluntary agency personnel were invited to a showcase of skits from the refugee performance company culminating in a shared meal. The ostensible purpose of this event was to let the other agency workers know what we were doing so that they would not be surprised if they came across one of our health shows in the camp. The implicit agenda was to promote better understanding of Hmong culture and traditions. To this end, we capped the series of performance sketches by bringing a Hmong shaman on stage who enacted a traditional soul-calling ceremony of blessing and tied string around the wrists of expatriate personnel who voluntarily came up to the stage (figure 21). Given the history of hostility between shamans and the hospital, this was a radical move. Those who participated in this intercultural performance found it deeply moving. However, they were a small, self-selected group who were already the most open-minded. Most of the expatriate guests politely remained in their seats but observed attentively. The most dogmatic agency workers—for example, the Christian nurse who refused to allow any Thai calendars in her ward because they had pictures of the Buddha—did not even attend this event.

I should have been more assiduous in attempts to reach the expatriate personnel who were most ethnocentric in their dealings with the Hmong. My sympathies were with the refugees. My interests and energies were devoted to understanding and working with the Hmong. It was easier to identify with the Hmong; the dogmatic Christians became the Other for me.

It is important to speak out against the repressive practices of some refugee relief agencies, however, in the interest of searching for a solution to this sad situation, I do not want to substitute one scapegoat for another. I agree with Harrell-Bond that "it is unproductive to blame" the agency fieldworkers for the enormous communication breakdowns that occur in refugee camps. By nature a refugee camp is a highly volatile, stressful, politically intense, multicultural arena, usually located in a harsh environment. In matters of communication and intercultural sensitivity, relief workers "are not trained. Within the agency bureaucracy they are not rewarded for involving themselves with individuals. In fact, fieldworkers are often warned against 'getting involved'" (1986:305). The agency workers I met in Ban Vinai were all dedicated, caring people. Even though they commuted to the camp from a Thai village an hour away, their living conditions there were quite basic. Many of the workers were volunteers, working in the camp at considerable personal sacrifice. The problem cannot be so easily contained at the level of the agency personnel. The root of the problem goes much deeper into institutional bureaucratic practices and the ideologies that empower and sustain them.

The ideal is for the two cultures, refugees' and relief workers', to enter into a productive and mutually invigorating dialog, with neither side dominating or winning out, but both replenishing one another (see Bakhtin 1981). Intercultural performance can enable this kind of dia-

IRC Health and Sanitation Celebration

THEME

When you lived in the Mountains
The Wind and the Rain cleaned the Garbage.
Now with so many people in Ban Vinai
We all must be careful to clean up the Garbage

Thaum peb nyob pem roob cua thiab nag
Tshoob yam khoom qias neeg pov tseg.
Tam sim no muaj neeg coob coob myob hauv zos vib nai,
Peb txhua leej txhua tus yuav xyuam xim
Cheb yam khoom qias neeg kom huv si

PROGRAM

1. SCENARIO—"Mother Clean and the Garbage Troll"—*Niam Tsev Huv*
2. SANDWICH BOARD DISPLAY OF POSTERS (thanks to JSRC)
3. DANCING FOOD—Singing Vegetables, Meat, and Fruit—*Yam Qav Noj Muaj Zog*
4. CHORUS OF CHILDREN—Tiny tots sing and dance a medley of sanitation songs
5. PANTOMIME—Enactment of Theme Message
6. STORY-BOARD THEATRE—*Nyiam Huv Ntxim Siab*—"Housecleaning is Wonderful!" (a story adapted from the Yao the Orphan cycle of Hmong tales)
7. DEMONSTRATION OF GAME—*Yam Khoom Qhia Neeg*—"Flee the Garbage Dragon!"
8. SAMPLE BROADCAST AUDIOTAPE
9. *Hu Plig Khi Tes*—Traditional Hmong Ceremony of Blessing and String-Tying for participants, workers, and guests of IRC. The ceremony will be performed by Thoj Txooj Neeb, Hmong shaman
10. EVERYONE EAT AND ENJOY!

Figure 19: Program for the 1985 Health and Sanitation Celebration sponsored by the International Rescue Committee.

Figures 20 and 21: Singing and dancing zucchini and squash encourage children to eat their vegetables in the "Nutrition Show" for the 1985 Health and Sanitation Celebration. (Photos by Dwight Conquergood: Courtesy of Northwestern University Archives)

logical exchange between Self and Other. Eugenio Barba talks about performance as "barter":

> Otherness is our point of departure. Imagine two very different tribes, each on their own side of the river. Each tribe can live for itself, talk about the other, praise or slander it. But every time one of them rows over to the other shore it is to exchange something. One does not row over to teach, to enlighten, to entertain, but rather to give and take: a handful of salt for a scrap of cloth. [. . .] Otherness is our meeting point. (Barba 1986, 161)

As a medium of exchange, performance draws us to the margins, the borders between Self and Other. Bakhtin affirms: "The most intense and productive life of culture takes place on the boundaries" (Bakhtin 1986, 2). Conceived of as barter, a site of exchange, performance is a key to understanding "how the deeply different can be deeply known without becoming any less different" (Geertz 1983:48). The value of the exchange is in the encounter, the relations that are produced, not the objects: "It is

the act of exchanging that gives value to that which is exchanged, and not the opposite" (Barba 1986, 268).

Postscript

I returned to Camp Ban Vinai for a brief follow-up visit in September 1987, anxious to see what had become of Mother Clean and the Ban Vinai Performance Company during the two years since my departure. IRC had hired a Thai university graduate who worked with me on the health education program and she was to take over the project after I left. Although she left IRC to work for another agency in the camp, Mother Clean and the performance approach to working with refugees survived this transfer to another agency. I was delighted to see that Mother Clean had been fully integrated into the culture of Camp Ban Vinai. Literacy textbooks produced in the camp print shop were illustrated with images of Mother Clean (figure 23). Mother Clean hand puppets were made in the camp and used for entertainment and instruction (figure 24). Mother

Figure 22: A Hmong shaman stands on stage and prepares to tie spirit-strings around the wrists of Western agency relief workers attending the Health and Sanitation Celebration. (Photo by Lw Vang)

Clean puzzles delighted children (figure 25). The ultimate test was that Mother Clean had been invited by the Hmong leaders to perform at the New Year Festivities, the most important and elaborate celebration of Hmong culture.

The character had been through three reincarnations and several performers in the two years I had been gone. Two bamboo frames and costumes had been worn out by heavy use. Her yarn hair was more purple than I had remembered it, but other than that she looked very much the same as when I left in 1985. I was pleased to see her again, as well as the young man who currently performed her. Nuanjan Charnwiwatana, the Thai worker in charge of the program after I left, told me that during her change of employment from IRC to another agency, there was a period of time when Mother Clean did not perform. She said that children would come to the IRC office in camp and ask worriedly, "Where is Mama Clean? Is Mama Clean sick?" And they had begun to ask about Mother Clean's children. Construction was underway during my visit for a child-sized Mother Clean, and the performance company talked of eventually having a Mother Clean family. Mother Clean's success as a

Figure 23: By 1987 Mother Clean is used to illustration a literacy textbook designed for the refugees in Camp Ban Vinai. (Photo by Dwight Conquergood: Courtesy of Northwestern University Archives)

communicator had reached personnel in other refugee camps, and I was told that she had been cloned for some of these.

A new participatory theatre strategy was highly successful: Mother Clean now made home visits. The performers were quite confident with the character and could improvise lines that directly addressed the problems of a particular household or neighborhood in the camp. These home visits also involved a great deal of interaction between Mother Clean and her hosts. The home visits were still highly entertaining because Mother Clean would have to maneuver her considerable bulk through the crowded living quarters and underneath low-hanging thatched eaves. This required a good deal of awkward bending and turning on Mother Clean's part and sometimes she would get stuck in a narrow passageway, to the glee of the onlookers.

It was heartening to see Mother Clean still being performed by Hmong actors, supporting Hmong identity, and blending with Hmong cultural traditions which still flourished in the camp. My return visit was celebrated by a shamanic performance. Hmong friends positioned me on a shaman's bench in front of his altar, tied me with a cord to a live pig, while the shaman circled me chanting and beating a gong. The pig's

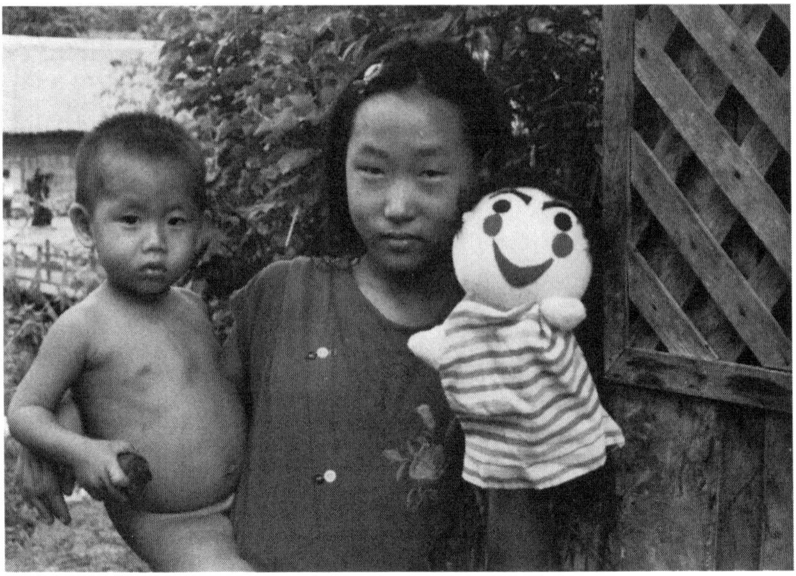

Figure 24: A big sister uses a Mother Clean hand puppet to entertain and teach her brother about healthy living in the camp (1987). (Photo by Dwight Conquergood: Courtesy of Northwestern University Archives)

souls were released on my behalf through a deft cut at the throat, while the shaman covered his face with a dark veil and entered ecstatic trance, leaping back and forth between the bench and the ground.

Conditions had not improved in the camp since 1985. If anything, the camp was even more tense. There was a new camp commander who imposed more rules and restrictions. The presence of soldiers was greater. Throughout my stay during 1985 I was never stopped by the military. My second day in camp during the return visit I was challenged by a patrol. The camp was even more crowded, particularly with "illegals," estimated to be as many as 10,000. Still, it was gratifying to see the Mother Clean character bringing some joy to the camp inmates, particularly the children, while attempting to address in a positive way the difficult situation.

NOTES

1. More than 100 Hmong refugees, almost all men, have died suddenly. Autopsy reports show no cause of death (see Holtan 1984; Munger 1986).

2. *Helping Health Workers Learn* should be read as a model of praxis. It is

Figure 25: A Mother Clean puzzle made by refugee craftspeople in Camp Ban Vinai (1987). (Photo by Dwight Conquergood: Courtesy of Northwestern University Archives)

designed for village health workers, but it has much to say about action and reflection, the development of a critical consciousness. Although the authors draw extensively on the methods of Freire, they provide an incisive critique of his work. I recommend this book particularly for academics whose social and critical theories get abstracted from the lived struggles of poor people.

3. Through the Freedom of Information Act a CIA film depicting the recruitment, training, and guerilla warfare of the Hmong in Laos is now available. This media text documents how the Hmong were recruited and used by the CIA during the war in Southeast Asia. It sets forth vividly the political-historical circumstances that led ultimately to the Hmong becoming refugees.

REFERENCES

Bakhtin, Mikhail. 1981. *The Dialogic Imagination.* Edited by Michael Holquist. Translated by Caryl Emerson and Michael Holquist. Austin: University of Texas Press.

Bakhtin, Mikhail. 1986. *Speech Genres.* Edited by Caryl Emerson and Michael Holquist. Translated by Vern W. McGee. Austin: University of Texas Press.

Barba, Eugenio. 1986. *Beyond the Floating Islands.* New York: Performing Arts Journal Publications.

Boal, Augusto. 1985. *Theatre of the Oppressed.* Translated by Charles A. and Maria-Odila Leal McBride. New York: Theatre Communications Group.

Burke, Kenneth. 1969. *A Rhetoric of Motives.* Berkeley: University of California Press.

Bustos, Nidia. 1984. "Mecate, the Nicaraguan Farm Workers' Theatre Movement." *Adult Education and Development* 23: 129–40.

Cerquone, Joseph. 1986. *Refugees From Laos: In Harm's Way.* Washington, DC: U.S. Committee for Refugees, American Council for Nationalities Service.

Conquergood, Dwight. 1985. "Performing as a Moral Act: Ethical Dimensions of the Ethnography of Performance." *Literature in Performance* 5: 1–13.

Conquergood, Dwight and Paja Thao. 1989. *I Am a Shaman: A Hmong Life Story, with Ethnographic Commentary.* Minneapolis, MN: Center for Urban and Regional Affairs, Southeast Asia Refugee Studies.

Conquergood, Dwight. 1986. "Hmong Proverbs: Texts and Ethnographic Commentary." In *The Hmong World.* New Haven, CT: Yale University, Council on Southeast Asia Studies.

Desai, Gaurav. 1987. "Popular Theatre, Participatory Research and Adult Education in Africa: A Preliminary Bibliography." Unpublished manuscript, Northwestern University.

Douglas, Mary. 1966. *Purity and Danger: An Analysis of the Concepts of Pollution and Taboo.* London: Routledge & Kegan Paul.

Erven, Eugene van. 1987. "Philippine Political Theatre and the Fall of Ferdinand Marcos." *The Drama Review* 31. 2: 58–78.

Evans, Grant. 1983. *The Yellow Rainmakers.* London: Verso.

Eyoh, H. Ndumbe. 1986. *Hammocks to Bridges: Report of the Workshop on Theatre for Integrated Rural Development.* Yaounde, Cameroon: BET & Co.

Foucault, Michel. 1973. *The Birth of the Clinic: An Archaeology of Medical Perception.* Translated by A. M. Sheridan Smith. New York: Pantheon.

Foucault, Michel. 1977. *Discipline and Punish: The Birth of the Prison.* Translated by Alan Sheridan. New York: Pantheon.

Freire, Paulo. 1986. *Pedagogy of the Oppressed.* New York: Continuum.

Geertz, Clifford. 1983. *Local Knowledge: Further Essays in Interpretive Anthropology.* New York: Basic Books.

Harrell-Bond, Barbara. 1986. *Imposing Aid: Emergency Assistance to Refugees.* New York: Oxford University Press.

Holtan, Neal, ed. 1984. *Final Report of the SUNDS Planning Project.* St. Paul, MN: St. Paul–Ramsey Medical Center.

Kaitaro, Tsuno, ed. 1979. "Theater as Struggle: Asian People's Drama." *Ampo* ii, nos. 2–3 (special issue).

Kidd, Ross. 1984. *From People's Theatre for Revolution to Popular Theatre for Reconstruction: Diary of a Zimbabwean Workshop.* Hague: Centre for the Study of Education in Developing Countries.

Kidd, Ross. 1982. *The Popular Performing Arts, Non-formal Education and Social Change in the Third World: A Bibliography and Review Essay.* Hague: Centre for the Study of Education in Developing Countries.

Kidd, Ross, and Martin Byram. 1978. *Popular Theatre and Participation in De-*

velopment: Three Botswana Case Studies. Gaborone: Bosele Tshwaraganang Publications.

Moore, Jonathan. 1987. "Interview with Jonathan Moore: U.S. Coordinator for Refugees." *Refugee Reports* 8: 1–5.

Munger, Ron. 1986. "Sleep Disturbance and Sudden Death of Hmong Refugees: A Report on Fieldwork Conducted in the Ban Vinai Refugee Camp." In *The Hmong in Transition.* New York: Center for Migration Studies.

Munger, Ron. 1984. "Synopsis of Comments to the Wilder Foundation Refugee Projects." *Final Report of the SUNDS Planning Project,* edited by Neal Holtan, 37–39. St. Paul, MN: St. Paul-Ramsey Medical Center.

Ong, Walter. 1982. *Orality and Literacy: The Technologizing of the Word.* London: Methuen.

Said, Edward. 1979. *Orientalism.* New York: Vintage.

Savina, F.M. 1930. *Histoire des Miao.* Hong Kong: Societe des Missions Etrangeres de Paris.

Siegel, Taggart, and Dwight Conquergood, producers. 1985. *Between Two Worlds: The Hmong Shaman in America.* Video-documentary. 28 mins. Siegel Productions.

Simpson, Alan. 1987. Quoted in "Senate Holds Midyear Hearings on FY 87 Refugee Admissions." *Refugee Reports* 8: 4.

Tapp, Nicholas. 1986. *The Hmong of Thailand: Opium People of the Golden Triangle. Indigenous Peoples and Development Series Report No. 4.* London: Anti-Slavery Society.

Thiong'o, Ngũgĩ wa. 1983. *Barrel of a Pen: Resistance to Repression in Neo-Colonial Kenya.* Trenton: Africa World Press.

Thiong'o, Ngũgĩ wa. 1986. *Decolonising the Mind: The Politics of Language in African Literature.* London: J. Currey.

Thiong'o, Ngũgĩ wa. 1981. *Detained: A Writer's Prison Diary.* London: Heinemann.

Todorov, Tzvetan. 1984. *The Conquest of America: The Question of the Other.* New York: Harper & Row.

Turner, Victor. 1967. *The Forest of Symbols.* Ithaca, NY: Cornell University Press.

Werner, David. 1977. *Where There Is No Doctor: A Village Health Care Handbook.* Palo Alto, CA: Hesperian Foundation.

Werner, David, and Bill Bower. 1982. *Helping Health Workers Learn.* Palo Alto, CA: Hesperian Foundation.

Life in Big Red

Struggles and Accommodations in a Chicago Polyethnic Tenement

I have lived long enough amidst you to know something about your circumstances; I have devoted to their knowledge my most serious attention. I have studied the various official and non-official documents as far as I was able to get hold of them—I have not been satisfied with this, I wanted more than a mere abstract knowledge of my subject. I wanted to see you in your own homes, to observe you in your every-day life, to chat with you on your condition and grievances, to witness your struggles against the social and political power of your oppressors.

—FRIEDRICH ENGELS, *THE CONDITION OF THE WORKING CLASS IN ENGLAND* (1845)

At 10:00 A.M. on August 16, 1988, Bao Xiang, a Hmong woman from Laos, stepped out the back door of her top-floor Big Red apartment and the rotting porch collapsed beneath her feet. All summer long I had swept away slivers of wood that had fallen from the Xiongs' decrepit porch onto mine, one floor below. Six households were intimately affected by Bao Xiong's calamity, because we shared the same front entrance and stairwell, and our respective back porches were structurally interlocked within a shaky wooden framework of open landings and sagging staircases that clung precariously to the red-brick exterior of the Chicago tenement. The six households included two Hmong, one Mexican, one Puerto Rican, one Mexican–Puerto Rican, and myself, a white male ethnographer from Northwestern University. Ethnically our wing represented much of the rest of Big Red, where other first-generation Hmong, Mexican, and Puerto Rican families were joined by refugees and migrants from Cambodia, Iraq, Lebanon, and Poland, as well as an elderly Jew and Appalachians and African Americans who had been displaced from gentrifying neighborhoods of the city, such as Uptown. Big

Red mirrored the global forces of displacement and migration that had grouped such ethnically diverse working-class residents in one dilapidated building.

Although separated by language, ethnicity, and cultural background, the polyglot residents shared the commonplaces of daily struggle embodied in Big Red. By sharing the same crowded living space, they were forced to interact across ethnic lines and cultural traditions. The distinct smells of several ethnic cuisines wafting from kitchens pungently accented the sounds of many voices and languages in the corridors and public spaces, collectively creating a richly sensuous experience of overlapping difference for anyone climbing up and down the back staircases. After reaching your landing, more often than not, you parted your way through damp clothing hanging from the clotheslines that crisscrossed back porches and extended the laundry of one household onto the threshold of another, your progress punctuated by the robust greetings, cries, and laughter of children.

Within minutes of arriving home on the day that the Xiongs' porch collapsed, I heard versions of the story from most of the neighbors whose back landings were structurally connected with Bao Xiong's. A Puerto Rican grandmother was relieved that her neighbor had come to no serious harm but worried about the future safety of the children, particularly her grandchildren. A young Mexican mother anxiously pointed out the loose and missing railing on her porch, and how her wash had been ruined by all the dust and falling debris. Then Bao Xiong joined us, uninjured but still shaken. She kept repeating to the small circle of neighbors: "Oh-h-h, very, very scared. Only me. Happen only to me. Why me? Oh-h-h, very scared." For her, the physical mishap was fraught with metaphysical meaning. She was not interested so much in why or how the porch collapsed. It is in the nature of things that they decay and fall. She sought explanation for the meaning-laden conjunction between the fall of the porch, and her stepping outside the back door. In her worldview, the precise timing of these two events was no mere coincidence, and she consulted the divination powers of a Hmong shaman who lived in another wing of Big Red.

Providing substandard housing to a mix of people from all over the world, Big Red became a highly contested site of convergence and friction between the forces of global resettlement and local redevelopment. More than an inhabited physical space, Big Red itself inhabited discursive space, became a site of cultural production and political struggle.

"Inhabited space—and above all the house," argues Pierre Bourdieu, "is the principal locus" for those socially constituted motivating princi-

Figure 1: Front entrance to Big Red. (Photo by Dwight Conquergood: Courtesy of Northwestern University Archives)

ples that generate and coordinate cultural practices (Bourdieu 1977, 89). Bourdieu investigates the "premises"—both physical and figurative—on which people dwell and practice everyday life. His study of Kabylian housing demonstrates how the house is a threshold of exchange for both the incorporation and the objectification of a cultural ethos, those dispositions that enable and constrain practice (Bourdieu 1990, 271–283). He uses the terms "*habitus*" and "class *habitus*" to name these "durably inculcated" dispositions and tastes that are a consequence of one's position within socioeconomic space (see also Bourdieu 1984, 169–225; 1990, 271–83).

The house is a privileged site for Bourdieu because it is an enclosure with thresholds and openings, and thus epitomizes the "dialectic of the internalization of externality and the externalization of internality" (Bourdieu 1977, 72). Recently there has been a resurgence of interest among anthropologists in this insideoutside dialectic, in the interpenetrations between global forces and local particularities. George Marcus and Michael Fischer pose the challenge of "how to represent the embedding of richly described local cultural worlds in larger impersonal systems of political economy" and argue that these broader outside forces "are as much inside as outside the local context" (Marcus and Fischer 1986, 77–78). Leith Mullings has called similarly for an anthropology of the city that complexly registers demographic, political, and economic pressures on urban lifeways (Mullings 1987, 9; see also Sanjek 1990).

Urban housing is just such an intersection between macro-forces and micro-realities. Housing encompasses intimate and collective as well as public space, and is situated between the deeply personal and the highly political.[1] Housing is both a physical structure and an ideological construction. It structures propinquity, shapes interactions, and provides a compelling issue around which people mobilize.

Big Red, a dilapidated tenement where I lived for twenty months in northwest Chicago's Albany Park neighborhood, intersects a distinctively local life-world with larger political-economic forces. In Albany Park, with its deteriorating housing stock—87 percent built before 1939—and a high density of four hundred large multiunit buildings, the issue of housing looms large (Royer 1984, 37). This analysis begins by situating Big Red within the larger context of Chicago's Albany Park neighborhood, a port-of-entry for many new immigrants and refugees. It then explores the struggles of accommodation and tactics of resistance within Big Red, and concludes with the documentation of domination and displacement accomplished by agents of civil society through the rhetoric of transgression and redevelopment.

Big Red and the Transformation of Albany Park

> Since the 1960s till now we've had everything moving in or moving out and I can't tell you "who," because there was no "who." The big buildings were deserted. There's a big building down there called Big Red. It's horrible. It was turned into a slum.
>
> —RUTH, LONGTIME RESIDENT OF ALBANY PARK

Most urban sociologists note that Chicago is "America's most segregated city" (Squires et al. 1987, 94; Fremon 1988, 124) and journalists echo this theme (McClory 1991, 16). The South Side and the West Side of Chicago are primarily African American. Albany Park is located on the Northwest Side of Chicago, an area that historically has been predominantly white (see figure 1). During the 1970s and particularly the 1980s the ethnic composition of Albany Park shifted, not from white to black but from white to an emergent third category in the racial and ethnic geography of Chicago, "immigrant" or "diverse." The extraordinary ethnic diversity of Albany Park parallels that of many Chicago North Side neighborhoods that have received substantial numbers of new immigrants and refugees from hemispheres of the South and the East. In the aftermath of the 1990 census, Albany Park is now a site of redistricting struggles to create a new ethnic ward for Asians or Latinos as a result of population growth through immigration (see Hinz 1991b; Quinlan 1991).

Housing has played a key role in the ethnic recomposition of neighborhoods like Albany Park. On March 25, 1964, Anthony Downs delivered a speech before the Chicago Real Estate Board titled "What Will Chicago's Residential Areas Be Like in 1975?" He forecast "many changes" in Chicago's residential neighborhoods, using three structural factors as causal predictors: the impact of rising real incomes, combined with the aging of the housing stock, and the impact of ethnic changes. "In older areas of the city," Downs explained, "older and less-well-maintained housing will become increasingly difficult to market to rising-income families. As a result, the housing in many of these so-called 'gray areas' will gradually shift to the market for either complete redevelopment or occupancy by lower-income groups, particularly nonwhites" (Downs 1964, 4). His general predictions about neighborhoods with aging housing stock have come to pass, even though he did not foresee how the category "nonwhites" would expand significantly as a result of the 1965 Immigration Law and the 1980 Refugee Act.

Historical Processes and Demographic Changes

Back in 1907, the completion of the Ravenswood Elevated public transportation line that terminated at the Lawrence and Kimball intersection at the center of Albany Park stimulated a building boom, and the population grew at a stunning rate (see table 1). Population growth and housing construction continued apace into the "roaring twenties." The building boom was over by 1930 and the Great Depression of that decade: "by 1924 Albany Park reached residential maturity. Since 1930 there has been little residential development, and, in fact, after a slight increase in population during the 1930s, the community has lost population" (Albany Park Community Area 1982, 17).

Throughout much of the twentieth century, Albany Park could be characterized, in the words of one resident, as "a step-up-and-then-out" community. After 1912 Russian Jewish immigrants augmented the original population of Swedes, Germans, and Irish. By 1930 Russian Jews were the majority among foreign-born whites. In 1934, when the population of 55,822 had almost reached its zenith (see table 1), it was almost 100 percent white. There were 43 listed under "Negro" and 43 listed under "Other." It was a community predominantly of first- and second-generation immigrants: 27.4 percent foreign-born white, and 43.8 percent native white of mixed or foreign-born parents, according to "Population and Family Numbers."[2]

An uncatalogued archival paper in the Albany Park Branch of the Chicago Public Library dating from the 1960s, "Changes in Population in Albany Park Area," interpretively summarizes the history of Albany Park's transitional population:

> Presently Alb Pk. [sic] is in the midst of the second population change since the war and its third in the last 40 years. Original settlement was Scandinavian, German and English. In the 1920's and 1930's a middle class Jewish population came in and was succeeded by a lower income Jewish population. Now a non-Jewish population is moving in and the Jewish population is moving away. Population is now mostly either middle aged or older. Few young families come into the area . . . Between the years 1950 and 1960 Albany Park lost 30% of its child-bearing population. Community now has a larger number in proportion of older women. Young people are of high school and college age and will be marrying and moving away during the next few years. This makes an unstable community.

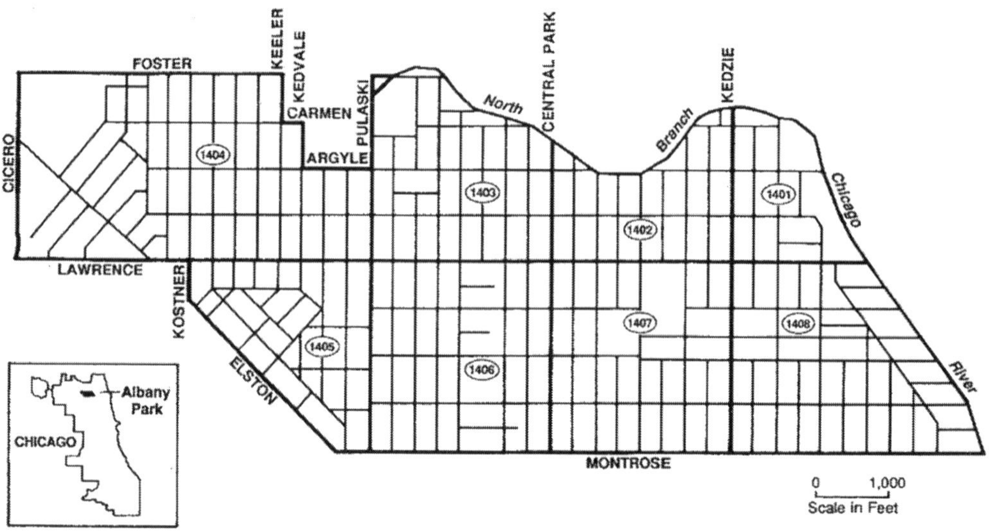

Figure 2: Community Area 14, Albany Park.

From 1940 to 1980 the population of Albany Park declined 18.7 percent, but during the 1980s it grew 7.4 percent (see table 1).

Moreover, the ethnic diversity of the neighborhood increased dramatically during the decade of the 1980s. From an immigrant but overwhelmingly white neighborhood, Albany Park has changed to a neighborhood with a majority of nonwhites during the 1980s. At the same time that the total population of the neighborhood boomed 7.4 percent, the number of whites declined 40 percent, blacks increased 500 percent, Latinos increased 73.4 percent, and Asians increased 83.6 percent (tables 2, 3). According to the 1990 census figures, African Americans now make up 3.4 percent, Latinos 31.8 percent, and Asians 24.1 percent of the population of Albany Park (see Hinz 1991a). With twice as many Asians as in Chinatown on the near South Side, Albany Park is now the city's biggest Asian neighborhood (Quinlan 1991).[3]

The total population of Chicago declined 7.4 percent. The number of whites declined 20.1 percent, blacks declined 8.4 percent, Latinos increased 29.3 percent, and Asians increased 41.2 percent. Although in 1980 Chicago already had a majority of minorities, by 1990 whites had slipped from being the predominant group for the first time since the city was founded (see table 4).

Demographic data from the neighborhood schools vividly reflect the out-migration of the Jewish population in the 1960s and early 1970s

Table 1. Albany Park Population, 1910–90

Year	Total Population	Year	Total Population
1910	7,000*	1960	49,450
1920	26,076	1970	47,092
1930	55,577	1980	46,075
1940	56,692	1990	49,501
1950	52,995		

Sources: U.S. Bureau of the Census; *Local Community Fact Book: Chicago Metropolitan Area, 1980.*

*Estimated

Table 2. Albany Park Population by Race and Ethnicity, 1970–90

Year	Total	White	Black	Latino	Amer. Indian	Asian	Other
1970	47,092	45,969	30	2,852	86	875	132
1980	46,075	34,070	279	9,074	257	6,502	4,967
1990	49,501	20,458	1,681	15,738	212	11,939	132

Source: U.S. Bureau of the Census.

Table 3. Ethnic Composition of Albany Park by Census Tract, 1970–90.

Census Tract	Year	Total	White	Black	Latino	Asian
1401	1970	3,762	82%	0.2%	14%	3.8%
	1980	4,096	28.4%	1.7%	27.6%	42.3%
	1990	3,987	23%	6.7%	34.9%	35.4%
1402	1970	5,270	88.9%	0%	8.6%	2.5%
	1980	5,499	44.5%	0.8%	20.5%	34.2%
	1990	5,873	31.3%	5.1%	27.8%	35.8%
1403	1970	6,217	93.1%	0.1%	4%	2.8%
	1980	6,352	66%	0.5%	16.2%	27.3%
	1990	6,944	37.8%	1.9%	25.9%	34.4%
1404	1970	6,123	98.4%	0%	1%	0.6%
	1980	5,467	91.2%	0%	3.5%	5.3%
	1990	5,479	78.2%	0.1%	9%	12.7
1405	1970	3,398	98.2%	0%	1.2%	0.6%
	1980	2,946	84.9%	0%	7%	8.1%
	1990	3,044	71.5%	0.6%	17.6%	10.3
1406	1970	7,326	92.1%	0%	5.7%	2.2%
	1980	6,904	59.1%	0.7%	17.9%	22.3%
	1990	8,011	39.3%	3.2%	34.5%	23%
1407	1970	7,724	91.2%	0.1%	6.4%	2.3%
	1980	7,640	40.1%	0.8%	28.2%	30.9%
	1990	8,782	29.8%	3.4%	47.1%	19,7%
1408	1970	7,272	88%	0.1%	8.5%	3.4%
	1980	7,171	44.5%	0.3%	27.9%	27.3%
	1990	7,381	39.1%	2.8%	40.4%	19.7%

Sources: U.S. Bureau of the Census; *Local Community Fact Book: Chicago Metropolitan Area, 1980.*

Table 4. Chicago's Population by Race and Ethnicity, 1950–90

Year	White	Black	Latino	Asian	All Races
1950	3,078,110	492,265	33,415	17,172	3,620,962
1960	2,602,748	812,637	110,000	25,019	3,550,404
1970	1,977,280	1,102,620	247,343	42,116	3,369,359
1980	1,321,359	1,187,905	422,063	73,745	3,005,072
1990	1,056,048	1,087,711	545,852	104,118	2,783 ,726

Source: U.S. Bureau of the Census.
Note: The total for all races is not necessarily the total for the other four categories since some individuals may be counted in two columns.

and the arrival of new immigrants and refugees. In 1959 Roosevelt High School had been 70 percent Jewish; in 1965 it was still 60 percent Jewish ("Schools," n.d., uncatalogued archive, Albany Park Branch Library). By 1988, however, Roosevelt High School was 39.17 percent Latino, 24.01 percent white, 22.29 percent Asian, and 14.2 percent black.[4] This pattern intensifies at the level of a feeder elementary school. In 1959 Hibbard Elementary School had been 95 percent Jewish, and in 1965 it was 80 percent Jewish ("Schools," n.d., uncatalogued archive, Albany Park Branch Library). Although I do not have precise 1988 data for Hibbard, its students are overwhelmingly new immigrants, with more than fifty languages and dialects spoken.

The middle-class Jewish population has been replaced not only by immigrants and refugees from all over the world but also by a large number of Appalachian and working-class whites (Royer 1984, 37). Public Aid statistics show that whites living in census tracts dominated by nonwhites receive public assistance in disproportionate numbers to their percentage of the population. Three tracts illustrate this pattern: in Census Tract 1401, whites represent 20 percent of the population and 31 percent of Public Aid recipients; in 1403, whites represent 38 percent of the population and 57 percent of Public Aid recipients; in 1407 whites represent 27 percent of the population and 42 percent of Public Aid recipients.[5] Whites in Albany Park have a fertility rate of 70, compared to the citywide fertility rate of 52 for whites. Albany Park ranks ninth among Chicago's seventy-seven neighborhoods in the fertility rate of white women, and demographers connect high fertility rate among white women with low level of education (Bousfield 1989, 16–18).

The northeast corner of Albany Park, Census Tract 1401 (known on the streets as "Little Beirut") has been the vanguard of Albany Park's demographic change (see map and tables 3, 5, 6). Little Beirut has the greatest population diversity, density, and residential deterioration in Albany Park. With its high concentration of large, multiunit apartment buildings owned by absentee landlords, it is the gateway for new immigrants into Albany Park. In 1970, Little Beirut was 36.1 percent foreign-born, compared to 22.2 percent for Albany Park as a whole. In 1980, 54 percent of the Little Beirut population was foreign-born, compared to 36.3 percent for Albany Park (Royer 1984, 36). The Latino population of Albany Park—now quickly closing the gap with whites (table 5)—settled first in Little Beirut. Even though Census Tract 1407, the most populous in Albany Park, now has the highest percentage of Latinos, 47.1 percent, in 1970 it had only 6.4 percent, compared to 14 percent Latino in Little Beirut. In 1970, when Albany Park was only 8.5 percent nonwhite, Little Beirut was 18 percent nonwhite. Viewed in light of Albany Park changes over time, Little Beirut has been a bellwether more than an anomaly. Perhaps that is why it commands such interest from established residents; more than just a dramatic contrast, it functions as an augury of things to come.

Viewed within the "ethnographic present," however, Little Beirut appears to be the extreme case, even within a demographically interesting neighborhood like Albany Park. Whereas census figures for Albany Park reflect a fall in white population, from 91.5 percent in 1970 to 40.7 percent in 1990, whites in 1990 are still the largest group overall. In Little Beirut, however, whites, at 23 percent, are ranked third—behind Asians, who are the largest group with 35.4 percent, followed closely by Latinos with 34.9 percent of the 1990 population. Little Beirut has the largest

Table 5. Ethnic Composition of Chicago, Albany Park, and Census Tract 1401,* 1970-90

	White (%)	Black (%)	Latino (%)	Asian (%)
Chicago				
1970	59	33	7	1
1980	44	39	14	3
1990	38	39	19	4
Albany Park				
1970	91.5	0.1	6.1	2.3
1980	65	0.6	20	14
1990	40.7	3.4	31.8	24.1
Census Tract 1401*				
1970	82	0.2	14	3.8
1980	28.4	1.7	27.6	42.3
1990	23	6.7	34.9	35.4

Sources: U.S. Bureau of the Census; Local Community Fact Book: Chicago Metropolitan Area 1980.

*The "Little Beirut" area where Big Red is located.

Table 6. Census Tract 1401* Births by Ethnicity, 1979–87

Year	Total	White	Black	Latino	Asian	Amer. Indian	Unknown
1979	104	34	2	32	35		1
%		32.69	1.92	30.77	33.65		.96
1980	114	44	2	38	29	1	
%		38.6	1.75	33.33	25.44	0.88	
1981	117	40	2	41	31	3	
%		34.19	1.71	35.04	26.5	2.56	
1982	108	31	5	32	39	1	
%		28.7	4.63	29.63	36.1	0.93	
1983	128	41	8	42	36	1	
%		32.03	6.25	32.81	28.13	0.78	
1984	129	33	11	34	49	2	
%		25.58	8.53	26.36	37.99	1.55	
1985	122	30	12	21	59		
%		24.59	9.84	17.21	48.36		
1986	115	30	10	19	55	1	
%		26.09	8.7	16.52	47.83	0.87	
1987	104	22	13	28	38	2	1
%		21.15	12.5	26.92	36.54	1.92	0.96

Source: City of Chicago, Department of Planning. I am grateful to Marie V. Bousfield, City Demographer, for releasing these unpublished data.

*The "Little Beirut" area where Big Red is located.

concentration of African Americans, 6.7 percent of the population, compared to 3.4 percent for Albany Park as a whole (see table 5). Little Beirut had a higher percentage of Asians than any other census tract in the city, except two in Chinatown (Flores, Bousfield, and Chin 1990, 19). According to 1990 census figures, however, Census Tract 1402, immediately east of Little Beirut, now has a higher percentage of Asians (see table 3).

Little Beirut has the highest percentage of Public Aid recipients among Albany Park's eight census tracts: 13.19 percent, compared to 7.89 percent for Albany Park (see table 7). In 1980, only 15.9 percent of its housing units were owner-occupied, compared to 31.8 percent for Albany Park. The rate of overcrowding (more than one person per room)—perhaps the statistic most revealing of poverty—is 20.1 percent in Little Beirut, compared to 9 percent for Albany Park as a whole.

Middle-class white residents define Little Beirut as the alien, threatening "Other" of Albany Park. Here is the interpretive assessment of a young Jewish real estate agent, the grandson of longtime residents of Albany Park, who now works there:

> That's a war zone. That's the nastiest area in Albany Park. You don't even want to be there at night. Shit—that's the worst. All those big

Table 7. Percent of Albany Park Population on Public Assistance* by Census Tract, 1988.

Census Tract	%	Census Tract	%
1401	13.19	1405	4.21
1402	12.85	1406	7.83
1403	7.21	1407	8.16
1404	2.12	1408	6.85
Albany Park	7.89		

Sources: I am grateful to Marie V. Bousfieid, City Demographer for Chicago, for releasing the unpublished data on Public Aid Cases by census tract for 1988. The population estimates for 1988 were taken from *Areas at Risk: Chicago's Potential Undercount in the 1990 Census,* City of Chicago, Department of Planning, March 1990.

*Total Public Aid Cases.

> rental units—no one has a commitment to the property. I almost sold a two-unit on Ainslie. We were ready to close, a Vietnamese woman. But she had a brother who lived in the area. She said she just wanted to check with him before she closed on the deal. Oh man! He told her, "Don't even consider it. Don't even think about it. You don't want to even think about being here at night."

A municipal report describes Little Beirut thus: "Housing conditions . . . are poor, and this area has physically declined. Deferred maintenance, disinvestment and the deterioration of Kedzie Avenue have created the perception that this is not a good place to live. Gang related incidents and graffiti reinforce this image" (Albany Park Community Area 1982, 40). A white policeman confided: "Let me put it to you this way: I'm carrying a gun, and I wouldn't come into this armpit of the district."

Established residents cast their positive images of Albany Park against the negative Other of Little Beirut and, by extension, Big Red. Through synecdochic extensions, Little Beirut absorbs and intensifies most of the tensions reverberating around the historic transformations of Albany Park. Little Beirut is on the edge of Albany Park, literally and figuratively, and the edges, margins, and borders of a culture are always intensely contested zones charged with power and danger (Douglas 1966; Bakhtin 1986). People need concrete symbols through which they can grasp elusive meanings and discharge deep and contradictory feelings. Big Red is a particularly powerful symbol for the middle class, because it cathects property and people. The disturbing signifying powers of Big Red contradict other signs of neighborhood revitalization.

Commercial and Economic Development

Established residents formed the North River Commission (NRC)[6] in 1962 out of three powerful community institutions—Swedish Covenant Hospital, North Park College and Seminary (the Swedish Covenant Church), and Albany Park Bank—to forestall neighborhood decline and decay that was already evident. In the late 1970s, Albany Park hit bottom. In 1977 there was a 29 percent vacancy rate on the commercial strip, which included seven adult bookstores, three massage parlors, an X-rated movie theater, and a predominance of used-furniture and secondhand thrift stores. The number of home sales plunged from 1,122 in 1979 to 580 in 1980. In 1977, however, the Lawrence Avenue Development Corporation (LADCOR), an arm of NRC, invented the Streetscape Program and persuaded the city of Chicago to fund it. In 1978 Lawrence Avenue became the first commercial area in Chicago under this program to receive new trees, street and pedestrian lights, and benches without advertisements at a cost of more than $7 million to the city (Corral 1990, 15).

In 1981 LADCOR spurred the city to launch the Facade Rebate Program. The plan provides a 30 percent cash rebate for property owners or tenants who renovate storefronts in accordance with guidelines set by LADCOR and the city. In Albany Park, 192 of 750 storefronts have been renovated through this program, representing $2.5 million in storefront improvements. No other neighborhood in the city even comes close to matching Albany Park's participation in the Facade Rebate Program. Other commercial strips such as Howard Street and Devon Avenue to the north have renovated ten to twenty storefronts through this program ("Looking Good Getting Tougher" 1989, 1).

Strategically planned large-scale commercial developments followed the success of the Streetscape and Facade Rebate programs. The Albany Park Shopping Center at the run-down intersection of Lawrence and Kedzie avenues opened in February 1987, creating more than eighty jobs. In September 1988, two blocks west at the corner of Lawrence and Kimball avenues, Kimball Plaza opened with another eighty jobs. In February 1989 Dominick's Finer Foods opened at the corner of Lawrence Avenue and Pulaski Road (an area previously described as an eyesore), creating more than 350 jobs. In May 1990, Albany Plaza Shopping Center opened on the 4900 block of Kedzie, the block immediately north of Albany Park Shopping Center, bringing another eighty jobs (Corral 1990, 16).

The revitalization of the Lawrence Avenue commercial strip has been a remarkable success. By 1988 the Albany Park community area was generating $8.3 million annually in federal income taxes, more than $900,000 in state income and sales taxes, and more than $180,000 in local taxes (Corral 1990, 16). In 1987 there were 541 bank loans totaling $41 million. This level of bank lending compares favorably with those of three other ethnically diverse North Side neighborhoods: Rogers Park, 456 loans totaling $46.3 million; Uptown, 458 loans totaling $45.5 million; Lincoln Square, 455 loans totaling $36.3 million. There is a big difference, however, when one compares Albany Park to an affluent neighborhood like Lincoln Park: 1,655 loans totaling $229.8 million (Kerson 1990, 88).

The annual number of residential sales has climbed 125 percent, from a 1980 low of 580 to a 1989 high of 1,307 (Corral 1990, 27). The average value of an Albany Park house in 1990 is $94,976, a 62.54 percent increase over the 1980 average of $59,395. Within Albany Park considerable variation in housing stock has developed, particularly if one looks at Ravenswood Manor, an insulated "yuppie" corridor in the southeast corner of Albany Park between Sacramento Street and the river; there the average value of a house jumps to $188,931, nearly double the rest of Albany Park (Meyers and DeBat 1990, 41).

The dramatic turnaround of Albany Park's shopping district during the 1980s coincided with a startling climb in the number of jobs in the larger Chicago area. As reported in the *Chicago Tribune* on April 22, 1990, "Between 1986 and 1989, the Chicago area racked up a stunning increase of 12.8 percent in jobs, the region's longest and largest sustained upturn in employment in more than two decades" (Goozner 1990, 1). The number of jobs in the six-county Chicago area reached just under 3 million in March 1989, an increase of 340,000 jobs since March 1986. The biggest gains were in the suburban counties, but Chicago added more than 56,000 jobs to bring city employment to 1.18 million, the highest level since 1981. This increase reflects a growth rate of 5 percent (Goozner 1990, 1). Nearly half of all new jobs are concentrated in what is called the Super Loop, the downtown area and the areas immediately north along the river and Michigan Avenue (Goozner 1990, 8).

Community leaders link the health of a neighborhood's commercial strip to the condition of its housing stock. The executive director of the powerful NRC explains the theory behind the redevelopment of Albany Park:

> Twelve years ago, the officers and volunteers of the North River Commission advanced a premise, then unknown and immedi-

> ately ridiculed. That premise was that older, lower income, predominantly multi-family areas that suffer from slum and blighted conditions, do so beginning with the commercial strip or main street of the area. Up until then, the accepted wisdom was that decay began with deferred maintenance and ultimately abandonment of large multi-family buildings. . . . Our conclusion was that if you successfully change the look of the main street from decay to prosperity, and if you provide hundreds and even thousands of employment opportunities, then the housing market can be stimulated into rehabilitation. (Cicero 1988, 8)

The NRC "premise" takes what a poststructuralist would call a social semiotic approach, which stimulates housing within a web of interactive signifying practices arising from and feeding back into a matrix of political-economic power. Altering the signifiers in one venue has consequences for another domain. Changing "the look of the main street from decay to prosperity" stimulates the "rehabilitation" of "slum and blighted conditions" along the residential side streets. "Every text, being itself the intertext of another text," Barthes affirms, "belongs to the inter-textual" (Barthes 1979, 77; see also Hodge and Kress 1988).

Just one-half block north of the renovated facades of the commercially revitalized Lawrence Avenue, and only two streets west of affluent Ravenswood Manor, stands Big Red. Located on Albany Street, and officially named "Albany Apartments," the sprawling red-brick building opposes the official image of Albany Park. It belies the shopkeeper prosperity of Lawrence Avenue and threatens the "suburb within the city" tranquillity of Ravenswood Manor. Weighted down with history, Big Red is a drag on the development programs that attempt to disconnect or erase the past and to propel Albany Park towards a bullish future. Behind the incompletely and ambivalently achieved "streetscape" program, Big Red stubbornly presents other signs, other meanings about Albany Park. Big Red disrupts the discourse of success and revitalization. It challenges the ideology of progress and development. Its deteriorated structure overflows with a mix of poor Third World refugees and migrants alongside working-class African Americans and Appalachians. It stands as a document of the geopolitical and political-economic structures—of violence and oppression—that caused such a heteroglot group of people to ricochet from their multiple respective homelands and re-collect themselves in a dilapidated tenement side by side with this country's socioeconomically displaced and marginalized people. "Within an ever more integrated world," Eric Wolf observes, "we witness the growth of ever more diverse proletarian diasporas" (Wolf 1982, 383).

Dwelling within Big Red

Everyday life invents itself by poaching in countless ways on the property of others.

—MICHEL DE CERTEAU,
THE PRACTICE OF EVERYDAY LIFE (1984)

I moved into Big Red in December 1987 in order to begin research for the Changing Relations Ford Foundation project.[7] At the time I moved in to the A2r apartment, previously occupied by an Assyrian family, I was the second white resident. An elderly Jewish man lived in C2L. The ethnic breakdown for the other 35 units was 11 Hmong, 10 Mexican, 10 Assyrian, 2 Sino-Cambodian, 1 Puerto Rican, and 1 Puerto Rican–Mexican mixed (see figure 2). During the twenty months I lived in Big Red, the ethnic mix was enriched by African Americans, Appalachian whites, more Puerto Ricans, and new immigrant Poles (see figure 3). I lived in Big Red until the end of August 1989, when along with all my A stairwell neighbors I was displaced and that wing of Big Red was boarded up. I rented an apartment just one block north of Big Red and continue to live in Little Beirut and interact with my Big Red networks at the time of this writing.[8]

Initial inquiries about renting an apartment pulled me immediately into interactions with other tenants. Beyond the "Apartment for Rent" sign, there was no formal assistance for prospective tenants: no rental office, telephone number, or agency address. Yet every vestibule and stairwell was unlocked, open, and filled with friendly people. All the business of renting the apartment was conducted informally, through face-to-face interactions with other residents. In twenty months, I never signed or saw a lease. It was a few months before I actually saw the absentee owner. The word-of-mouth way of getting information brought me into contact with a number of neighbors who graciously shared with me what they knew and ventured outside in the bitter chill of Chicago December nights to track down the janitor. Sometimes we would find the janitor, sometimes we would not: he held down another full-time job in order to make ends meet. Sometimes when we found him he would not have the keys.

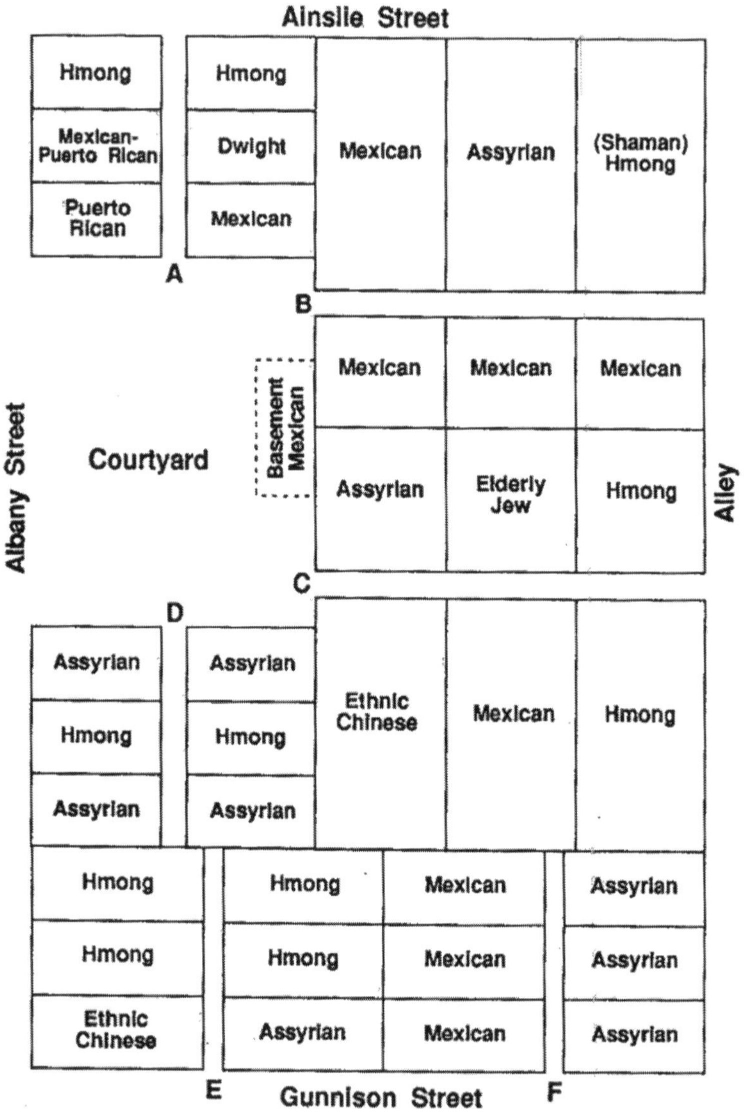

Figure 3: Big Red ethnic makeup, December 1988.

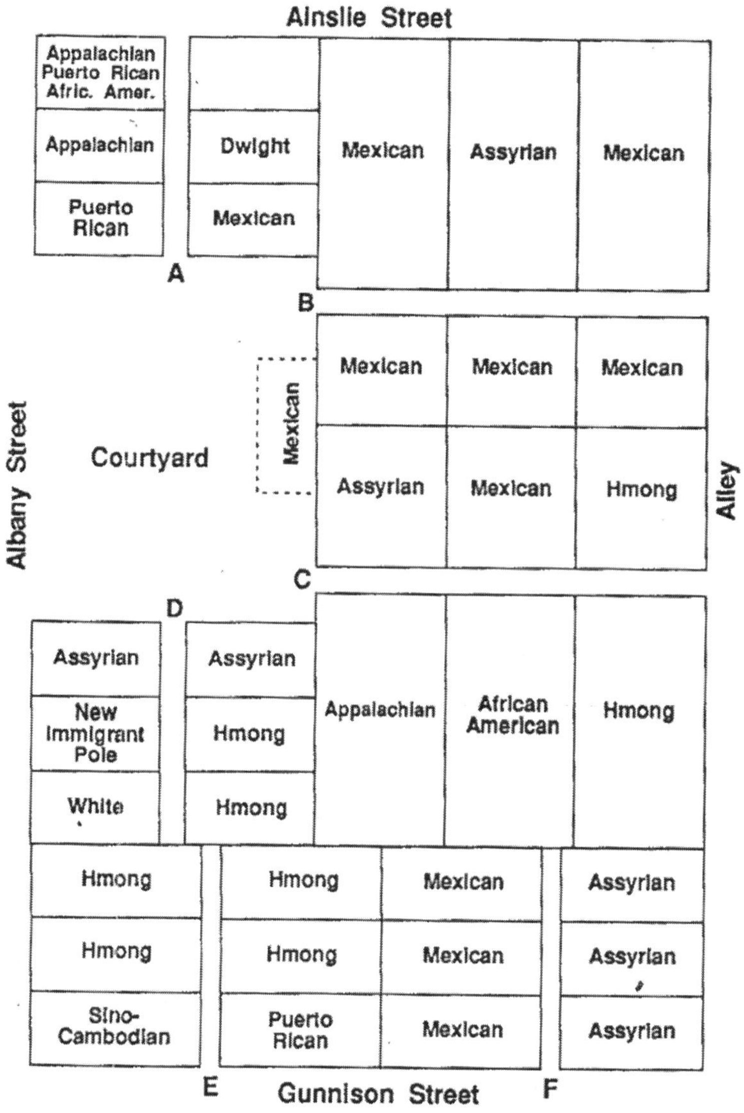

Figure 4: Big Red ethnic makeup, summer 1989.

From one perspective, the rental management of Big Red was highly inefficient and required unnecessary trips, long waits, and delays. On the other hand, the absence of a managing authority made all the residents interdependent. By the time I was ready to move in, I was on friendly terms with several neighbors and had received offers of help with the move, including the loan of a car.

The physical dilapidation of Big Red is even more apparent from the inside than the outside, but it is mitigated by the warmth and friendliness of the people. Indeed, the chronic state of disrepair, breakdowns, and emergencies requires for survival a neighborly interdependence unheard-of in efficiently managed middle-class properties. Crises create community, but this is particularly true when the crisis relates to physical space that people share over time. When the plumbing on the third floor leaks through the second floor ceiling with every toilet flush, the residents of those two floors get to know one another in intimate ways.

It is the human quality of life in Big Red that eludes outsiders. The following NRC memo (1989) captures coldly the physical state of disrepair in Big Red. Even though it notes that "the building is currently fully occupied by low-income families," it discursively evacuates the human element, forgetting that people transform a tenement into a home:

> Due to neglect by the previous owners over the past 15 years, the property has declined into a critical state of deterioration. The building has suffered severely from a lack of any capital improvements. The mechanical systems are only partially operative or not performing at all. Prior attempts at building security have been feeble so that the apartments and common areas are open to abuse by anyone willing to gain access. The major apartment components are functionally obsolete and that, coupled with cosmetic neglect, greatly limits the marketability of the apartments and presents potential health and safety hazards. A few recent examples include a total lack of hot water, the collapsing of a back porch, rats and roach infestation, and small arson fires in the vestibules.

From the inside, one gets a more detailed experience of the building's deterioration, but that is complemented with a complex understanding of how people maintain human dignity within difficult structures. A casual inspection would reveal scores of housing-ordinance violations but might not capture their meaning in the day-to-day lives of the urban working class and under- and unemployed. The children complain of mice in their beds. Housewives trade stories of "roaches in my refrigerator." They make stoic jokes about this indignity, dubbing them "Eskimo roaches." They say that the roaches move more slowly but can survive in the cold, "just like Eskimos." One day I opened my refrigerator and discovered a mouse scurrying around inside. The refrigerator was decrepit, and the door did not always stay shut. There were jokes about "super-rats" so big that the traps would have to be "anchored." These and other vermin stories about aggressive mice and flying cockroaches resemble "fish stories." Through exaggeration and shared laughter they made the situation more bearable.

Minor disasters related to the dilapidation of Big Red brought residents together across ethnic lines. In early July 1988, Shajiba, an Assyrian mother of four from across the courtyard, stepped into her bathtub and the bathroom ceiling fell on her head. Not just some falling plaster, the entire ceiling rotted out and collapsed around her. Her husband, Daniel, ran to summon me. By the time I arrived, several neighbors had gathered in the bathroom to witness this most recent outrage. They asked me to take pictures of the bathroom with its debris-filled bathtub.

Almost every household had its own disaster tale. The neighbors did not search for small talk about the weather when they met in the stairwells, courtyards, and open back porches. They exchanged intimate, urgent concerns about shared hardships in Big Red. They inquired whether the Younans' (Assyrian) toilet still overflowed every time it was flushed, whether Bravo Xiong's (Hmong) ceiling had leaked during last night's rain, whether Mrs. Montalvo (Mexican) and her five children had a refrigerator yet. And there was the problem of the sweatshop operating out of the basement. When filling rush orders for surgical scrub suits, the Cambodian women worked all night, keeping some of the neighbors awake. Scraps from the sweatshop filled one of the two building dumpsters, aggravating the garbage-collection problem. The physical hardships and indignities of life in Big Red created a common experience and shared understanding that united the diverse ethnic groups. Coping strategies were the topics for talk among the residents of Big Red.

To limit the story of Big Red to appalling physical conditions would be misleading. Michel de Certeau in *The Practice of Everyday Life* investigates the creative and manifold "tactics" ordinary people use to resist the "strategies" of the strong—the hegemonic forces of governments, armies, institutions, and landlords. He illuminates the myriad ways vulnerable people "operate" within dominant structures and constraints, what he calls "the art of making do." To illustrate his intellectual project, he uses the metaphor of "dwelling":

> Thus a North African living in Paris or Roubaix [France] insinuates *into* the system imposed on him by the construction of a low-income housing development or of the French language the ways of "dwelling" (in a house or a language) peculiar to his native Kabylia. He superimposes them, and, by that combination, creates for himself a space in which he can find *ways of using* the constraining order of the place or of the language. Without leaving the place where he has no choice but to live and which lays down its law for him, he establishes within it a degree of *plurality* and creativity. By an art of being in between, he draws unexpected results from his situation. (de Certeau 1984, 30)

Even highly vulnerable people are not simply contained by the structures, both physical and socioeconomic, within which they find themselves. Through imagination and human energy they contest and create "dwelling spaces" inside even forbidding structures.

The tenants of Big Red exploited the marginality, illegalities, and transgressive nature of Big Red in manifold ways. They turned the owner's negligence, which bordered on the criminal, to their advantage. While they suffered, to be sure, from the owner's neglect and lack of building maintenance, they also used his irresponsibility to circumvent typical middle-class restrictions, rules, and "tastes" pertaining to residential life, such as in the use of stairwells, courtyards, and alleys. Hmong women roped off a section of the front courtyard and planted a vegetable garden during the summer of 1988. The rest of the courtyard was an intensively used social space: the center was a playground for a group I will call the Courtyard Kids, while the fence between sidewalk and courtyard served as a volleyball net for teenage girls. The back area bordering on the alley was converted into an unofficial parking lot and open-air garage for working on old cars that were always in need of repair. Some back stairwells were used to sell drugs during the summer of 1989, when dealers set up operations in two Big Red apartments.

The back area also was used for weekend *bracero* alley parties. Whereas the courtyard and front sidewalk of Big Red were informally designated spaces for the evening sociability of women and children, the back alley, at night and on weekends, was a masculine space, so marked by one section of the back wall used as a urinal. This was the time when *braceros* shared the price of a case of beer, with a sensitively enforced code that those who were unemployed or newly arrived would be graciously exempted from any pressure to contribute. For those holding jobs, it was a source of esteem to assume a greater responsibility for financing these parties. This was a time for dramatizing the hardy manliness of their jobs by complaining about sore backs, tight muscles, blisters, and cut hands. Friendship networks of exchange and sharing developed at these alley parties. It was a sign of my acceptance when I first was invited to join these parties and then allowed, after initial protest, to contribute to the cost of a case of beer. Soon afterward, the three neighbors who worked at the Easy Spuds potato-chip factory began offering me free sacks of potatoes that they brought from work. Both the tools and the labor that helped me mount the steel security gate across my back door came from contacts made at the *bracero* parties. The front stairwells and lobbies were prime sites for display of gang graffiti, and during the winter the stairwells were used as spillover rooms for social drinking, talk, and smoking. In some respects, the residents had more autonomy and scope for use of Big Red than would have been possible within a better maintained, middle-class building.

The Courtyard Kids

De Certeau's discussion of spatial practices is eloquently apt for the Courtyard Kids: "To practice space is thus to repeat the joyful and silent experience of childhood; it is in a place *to be other and to move toward the other*" (de Certeau 1984, 110; emphasis in original). Big Red lacks many material amenities but is rich in children. Its families typically are large. For example, I shared my stairwell with two families with six children each, two families with four children each, and another family with three children. Mrs. Gutierrez, who lived in my stairwell, had reared nine children in Big Red; all of them visited frequently with a retinue of grandchildren in tow. Across the courtyard, an Assyrian family had ten children.

Children naturally are threshold-crossers and boundary-blurrers. Curious, inquisitive, spared the self-consciousness that descends at adolescence, children are most open to others. Although there was a great deal of interaction among all the groups within Big Red, the free-for-all mingling of ethnicities was most intense among the Courtyard Kids, even when they played up the block at River Park.

The courtyard, extending into surrounding sidewalks and the street, was their space. There were no Nintendos in Big Red. As apartments were crowded and without air conditioning, the courtyard was far more inviting and exciting than any private apartment. In the shared public space of the courtyard, twenty to thirty kids, sometimes more, could organize games of dodgeball or improvise mud fights. Even in the cold Chicago winters, the courtyard was the place where the children of Big Red passed the time, throwing snowballs and building snowmen (see Suttles 1968, 75–77).

What few toys or items of sports equipment the children possessed, they shared with the group. The one football in all of Big Red belonged to a little Hmong boy in my stairwell. This football was enjoyed by all the children in hotly contested courtyard games between "Assyria" and "Chinatown." Actually, the team on which one played had more to do with the time one joined the game than ethnicity. Mexicans, Puerto Ricans, whites, Cambodians, Assyrians, African Americans—all played interchangeably for "Assyria" or "Chinatown." Mothers served as courtyard monitors, using English to resolve disputes in the larger group and using their native language when checking their own children. The mothers clustered at the sidelines and chatted among themselves while observing the play of the Courtyard Kids. Sometimes a mother would join a game as a player, particularly if there were no other women in the courtyard with whom to visit. Often I saw Mexican, Hmong, Assyrian, and (later during my tenure) Appalachian mothers visiting among themselves while sharing child-supervision responsibilities. Mothers also cooperated in feeding the hungry children after a period of vigorous play. As a result, the Hmong children were introduced to pita bread from the Assyrian households, and this became one of their favorite foods. One white mother of three who moved into Big Red in 1989 was quickly absorbed into the nurturing network constituted around the Courtyard Kids. She proudly remarked how all the kids called her Mom.

When an African-American family moved into Big Red during 1989, no one commented except white families. At first, an Appalachian family made some racist remarks, and the white mother whom all the Courtyard Kids called Mom joked that her mother had said, "Those Black kids better not start calling me grandma!" But her son soon started playing with the African-American child, and that opened up relations between the two households. The white family helped their African-American neighbors find a new job. The white and African-American fathers began working together on back-alley mechanical repairs for their weather-beaten cars. One day the white mother saw the eight-year-old African-American son doing some mischief, and she took him by the hand and returned him to his mother's apartment, where both women scolded him. On another occasion, passing through the alley, I saw the teenage son from the white family carrying sacks of groceries up the back stairwell and inside the apartment for the African-American family.

During the summer of 1988, there was only one bicycle in Big Red, and it was broken. The Courtyard Kids often talked wistfully about owning a bicycle. One kid told me that his father said that maybe when he graduated from eighth grade the family could afford a bicycle. In the meantime, the Courtyard Kids made do with taking turns riding Tony's borrowed bicycle. Tony (Assyrian), who lived across the street, was called "rich" because he owned both a bicycle and a skateboard.

The sixteen-year-old son of the white family that moved into Big Red during the winter of 1989 had "street connections" that opened up a source for used bicycles priced at ten dollars or less. By May 1989, every Courtyard Kid owned a bicycle. That summer the courtyard became the site of much bicycle trading and dealing. The wheeling and dealing in used bicycles drew in East Indian and Pakistani kids from across the street and Cambodian kids from around the corner, as well as a large circle of Latino, white, African-American, Assyrian, and Hmong children. The Courtyard Kids developed and honed entrepreneurial and mechanical skills as they swapped bikes and borrowed tools from neighbors to tear down bikes, trade parts, and customize their purchases. It was an exciting time. The courtyard was abuzz with the talk of bike culture: "wheelies," "ollies," "bunny-hops," "cherry-pickers," and "mags." Not only did all the Courtyard Kids own bicycles, but it seemed that each one owned a different bike each week. By the end of the summer of 1989, ten-year-old Stevie (Assyrian) had owned seven different bicycles.

It is not easy to raise a large family in the conditions of Little Beirut. Parents seek, share, and welcome help from others, particularly with the counsel, care-giving, and even disciplining of the children. Mrs. Gutierrez, referring to African-American kids from across the street, represents the community pattern of shared parenting: "I feel sorry for them. They don't have any money. I talk to them like a mother. When they ask me for money, I say, 'You be good, I'll give you a quarter! But if I see you do something bad, no more quarters!"

My rapport with many of the households was established through the nurturing network constituted around children. Men are important participants in this network as well as women. The *bracero* alley parties, for example, were off-limits to women, but children frequently inserted themselves briefly into the circle for a hug or a whisper before scurrying off with change to purchase a treat from the musical ice-cream trucks that ply the streets in the evening. As I passed through the courtyard daily and became a more familiar figure, the Courtyard Kids began calling out to me for acknowledgment, attention, and advice. They announced the news of the day and shared their successes and concerns:

"Hey Mr. Dwight, it's my birthday today," "These are my cousins—they're living with us now because my uncle died," or "Mr. Dwight, Frankie failed second grade." Parents told me time and again to help them watch their children: "You see my kid do something wrong, catch him—talk to him." Courtyard Kids asked me to accompany them to school on the day parents were required to pick up report cards, so that their parents would not have to take off half a day from work. Several times I accompanied a mother to the school principal's office when a child was in trouble. I also went to the police station with (and sometimes without) the parents to sign out teenagers who had been picked up for misdemeanors. This nurturing network expresses one of the strongest ethics of Little Beirut culture: children are cherished. Gang leaders in the area affirmed the community norm: "We look out for the little kids; we be watching that nobody messes with the little kids."

Not counting middle-class residents, only one person ever complained about the Courtyard Kids and challenged their access to the courtyard. This example underscores the power of this norm, while demonstrating the scrappy resourcefulness of the Courtyard Kids. In the spring of 1989 the absentee landlord hired an Appalachian man as the new on-site janitor for Big Red. He had been a day laborer before he moved into Big Red and lobbied successfully for the job of janitor. He seized this opportunity to make something out of the position. One of his first acts was to buy (with his own money) a flashing neon sign that said "Building Manager" and mount it in his window. As a way of undercutting his pretensions, the residents nicknamed him Mr. Jethro, after the television character from "Beverly Hillbillies."

Although in his income level, dress, speech, and apartment decor Mr. Jethro was as far away from the middle class as any other Big Red resident, he had aspirations for finer things. He soon announced to everyone that he was "taking the building back." By that he meant that he would introduce more middle-class standards of taste and notions of public space. Entirely on his own initiative, and out of his meager wages, he bought "Keep off the Grass" signs and strung them with ropes around the courtyard. Next he mounted "No Parking" signs for the back alley. He roped off the intensively used social spaces by the back stairwells and the sites of evening *bracero* parties for his announced plans of cultivating grass and shrubs.

Soon Mr. Jethro entered into battle with the Courtyard Kids in his attempts to "take back" the courtyard and transform it into a lawn. The kids did not surrender their playground without a fight. They threw eggs at his window, set his door on fire twice, broke all the windows of his car, then dropped marbles into the oil spout and ruined the engine. He was not seen for two weeks; his wife explained that he was in bed "with the nerves." Then he emerged from his apartment one day, rallied, and one more time attempted to chase the kids off the grass. All of a sudden, Pit Bull's brother (Pit Bull is a well-known Puerto Rican gang member), with his namesake dog, bounded into the courtyard and menaced Mr. Jethro. Pit Bull's brother and other gang members warned Mr. Jethro about what would happen to his "skinny ass" if he ever mistreated the Courtyard Kids again. Mr. Jethro was admonished to fight like a man, if he wanted to fight, and that no man worth anything would yell at little kids. The gang members shoved Mr. Jethro around a little bit to clinch their point, then left.

At that moment, Mr. Jethro dropped his beautification campaign and became quite conciliatory toward the Courtyard Kids. On one of the hot Sundays later in the summer he hooked up a water sprinkler in the middle of the courtyard for the kids to run and splash through. He brought a lawn chair out to the sidewalk, where he spent a pleasant afternoon watching the kids cavort around the sprinkler. For the July Fourth weekend he mounted a huge American flag outside his front window and clamped a spotlight on the sill so that the flag was illuminated at night. Next to the flag he positioned a menu-board sign that he had purchased at a flea market with this lettered message: "Have a Happy and Safe Fourth of July Weekend."

The Art of Making Do: On Kinship, Kindness, and Caring

Tenants stretched scant resources by "doubling up," a common practice enabled by the irregular management of Big Red. In order to save money on rent, two or three families shared a single apartment. The one-bedroom apartment directly above me was home to a Hmong family with three small children, and another newlywed couple with an infant, plus the grandmother. Nine people (five adults and four children) shared this one-bedroom apartment. The one-bedroom basement apartment sheltered two Mexican sisters. One sister slept with her four children (ranging in age from seven to sixteen years old) in the single bedroom, while the other slept with her three small children in the living room. The Assyrian family of twelve lived in a three-bedroom apartment. A

Mexican family with six children shared a one-bedroom apartment. These "doubling up" arrangements probably would not be permitted in middle-class-managed buildings.

Perhaps the most vivid example of this practice is the large heteroglot household that lived above me during the summer of 1989. Grace, an Appalachian mother of six children with a Puerto Rican husband, lived with Angel, her Puerto Rican "business" partner, who brought along his girlfriend, his younger brother just released from prison, the brother's girlfriend, and his African-American friend (who before the summer was over went to prison), as well as a single pregnant mother and her best girlfriend—fifteen people in one three-bedroom apartment. The household was anchored by Grace's Public Aid check and Angel's street hustling activities. Two years earlier, Grace had been homeless, living on the streets with her six children; the girls had panhandled and the boys had stolen food and cigarettes from stores. She had a network with street people, and Angel was plugged into the prison culture, so three to five extra people would "crash" at the apartment at any given time. This household was the most multicultural one in Big Red, embracing whites and African Americans who cohabited with several Latinos and one Filipino. The illicit life-style of street hustling and drugs brought together these several ethnic groups in strikingly intimate ways. Their unruly household had many problems, but racism and prejudice never surfaced.

The gathering together of extended families and the creation of "fictive kin" (Rapp 1987, 232) are primary tactics for "making do" within Big Red. A twelve-year-old Assyrian Courtyard Kid articulated this conventional wisdom: "It's good to have friends and relatives nearby so you can borrow money when you need it." Indeed, the culture of Big Red was characterized by an intimacy of interactions across apartments, expressing in part the kinship networks that laced together these households. When I surveyed the apartments at the end of my first year of residence, I discovered that every household but two (one of those being mine) was tied by kinship to at least one other apartment in Big Red. The young Mexican family with three small children directly below me in A1r, for example, had strong ties to the B stairwell. The husband's widowed mother lived in B1L, along with his sister, thirty-year-old single brother, and three cousins. His older brother lived across the hall from the mother in B1r, with his five children. Their cousins lived in B3r. Further, the three brothers and half-brothers all worked at the same place: the Easy Spuds potato-chip factory in Evanston. The families all ran back and forth from one another's back porches. Raul in A1r had three children, Salvatore in B1L had five, and two or three children always stayed with the single adults and grandmother in B1L, so there were many cousins to play with, circulate outgrown clothing among, share transportation, and collectively receive parenting from multiple care-givers. The grandmother in B1r had high blood pressure (one of the first things I was told when introduced) and was always surrounded by caring relatives. Maria, the daughter-in-law from A1r, spent so much time with her frail mother-in-law in B1L that it took me some time before I figured out in which apartment Maria actually lived.

The functional importance of this propinquity with immediate relatives became clear when Maria told me about her husband Raul's being laid off from work for seven months. One can get through such a crunch with immediate family close by. This supportive net of family is extended by several friendships with other Latino families in Big Red, as well as more friends and family in or near Albany Park. A more financially successful older brother who is a delivery-truck driver regularly visited from near Hoffman Estates. He had purchased a shiny new Ford truck with a camper cover that was shared with the Big Red kin for shopping trips.

Aurelio (Mexican), who lived across the hall from me in A2l, had a sister with a large family who lived in B2r. Over the summer, two of his younger brothers arrived from Mexico without papers, and they lived with his sister. Aurelio had eight sisters and seven brothers; all but the youngest lived in or near Albany Park. Three brothers and their families lived on Whipple Street around the corner; they and their children visited back and forth all the time. They pooled resources for major family celebrations. For example, Alfredo, Aurelio's baby boy, was baptized with four other cousins; a huge party and feast in the church basement followed for all the extended family and friends. All the working brothers and sisters cofinanced the *quinceañera* debutante celebration for Aurelio's niece; Aurelio bought the flowers. Thanksgiving 1989 was celebrated jointly with six turkeys. My first week in Big Red I could not find anyone with the key to get my mailbox unlocked. Gabriel, one of Aurelio's brothers from Whipple, passed by, pulled out a knife from his pocket, and forced it open for me. That incident represented the quality of life in Big Red, the back-and-forth visiting between households and the spontaneous offering of assistance.

Aurelio's family was also tied strongly to the financially strapped family (two sisters rearing their seven children together without husbands) in the basement of B. I think they were cousins, or maybe just good friends, but everyone in A2l looked out for the extended family in the basement because there was no father. The older sister did not speak English.

Alberto, the kid from C2r, practically lived with Aurelio. At first he told me that they were cousins, then later that they really were not blood cousins, but like adopted family because they had lived close together for so long. They had been at Whipple together and then had both moved to Big Red. The same is true for Raul and Hilda, directly below me, and their relatives in B stairwell: they had come from Whipple along with Aurelio. The president of the Whipple block club, a white woman, remembered Aurelio and his relatives; she had had an altercation with them that led to a court hearing and the breaking of all the windows on two sides of her house. She described the entire group negatively as "clannish."

Another example of a kin network in Big Red was the Assyrian family with ten children in D1r. They were on Public Aid with monthly rent of $450. Unable to afford a telephone or transportation, they were among the most needy, even by Big Red standards. In this case it was the wife who articulated the kinship lines. Her sister and husband lived two floors above them in D3r. The sister drove them to church, which was the hub of their social and economic sustenance (they obtained free meals there and clothes for the kids). The mother lived with the sister on the third floor, but every time I visited the family in D1r, the mother was there helping with caring and cooking for the ten kids, the oldest of whom was sixteen. The wife's brother lived just around the corner on the Gunnison side, in E1r. The brother's apartment was one of the more nicely furnished in Big Red. The D1r family depended on the brother for telephone use. The Assyrian family directly across the hall from them were cousins. The first time I was invited to this family's home for Sunday dinner, the children had picked leaves from trees in River Park; the mother stuffed the leaves with rice and served them with yogurt made from the powdered milk that is distributed once a month at the Albany Park Community Center.

The two ethnic Chinese families from Cambodia were intimately connected. The wife in E1L was the eldest daughter of the family in C1r, and both families helped manage the sewing shop in the basement.

The Hmong are noted for their kinship solidarity. Because they lived on the top floors, by and large, they could leave their doors open. Related families faced one another and shared back and forth, one apartment becoming an extension of the other. The kids ran from one apartment to the other, ate together, and blurred the household boundaries.

The Hmong in the United States have not assimilated to the model of the nuclear family. My observations of the Latino and Assyrian families suggest the same, but the extended-family pattern was strongest among the Hmong. The Hmong neighbors directly above me had an apartment the same size as mine, one bedroom. It housed five adults—two brothers, their wives, and a grandmother—as well as the four small children of the older brother (the oldest child is eight) and the baby of the younger brother. They got along handsomely in this one-bedroom apartment. The kids skipped down to my apartment frequently for cookies. They were extremely happy children, polite and very well behaved.

This same Hmong family in A3r, the Yangs, demonstrated remarkably the importance of having kinfolk nearby. In December, when their Hmong neighbors across the hall moved to an apartment just across the street because they had suffered for a month with a waterless toilet (it was this same family whose back porch had collapsed in August), the Yangs could not bear to be alone on the top floor of our stairwell. Within two weeks they moved just across the courtyard to the D3l apartment in order to be close to their cousins living one floor below them in D2l. The mother explained that they had moved because she needed kin nearby to help with child care. This was the family's third move within Big Red in order to achieve close communal ties with relatives. Their understanding of "closeness" differed from that of white established residents. First, the Yangs' departing friends from A3l had only moved across the street, still in the 4800 block of Albany, within sight and shouting distance. Further, their cousins in D2l were in the same building, just across the courtyard. The Yangs, however, wanted a degree of intimacy that required side-by-side proximity to relatives or friends.

Even families from different ethnic groups expressed their friendship in "the idiom of kinship" (Stack 1974). The Mexican family in C2r told me that their new downstairs neighbors (Appalachian) in C1r were their "cousins." They claimed knowledge of a family tree that traced the Appalachians' family roots back to Spain, where the connection was made with the Mexicans' forebears. When I pressed the Mexican teenager who told me this, he did not know the specifics. But that did not seem to matter; he was delighted to have "relatives" living directly below him. He informed me that his neighbors—he calls them "hillbillies"—had told his family that they were also related to me, tracing their Irish side to my Scots background.

This interconnectedness with intimate others is highly functional for the people of Big Red. Carol Stack notes: "The poor adopt a variety of tactics in order to survive. They immerse themselves in a domestic circle of kinfolk who will help them. . . . Friends may be incorporated into one's domestic circle" (Stack 1974, 29). Notwithstanding the unpleasant physical conditions, Big Red was an extraordinarily pleasant and human place to live because of the densely interlaced kin and friendship networks. My neighbors were not self-sufficient; therefore, they did not privilege self-reliance in the same way that the white middle class does. Sometimes they had difficulty making it from one paycheck to the next. They worked at connecting themselves to one another with reciprocal ties of gift-giving and the exchange of goods and services, as well as the less tangible but extremely important mutual offerings of respect and esteem. What Jane Addams observed almost a century ago still applies to Big Red: "I became permanently impressed with the kindness of the poor to each other; the woman who lives upstairs will willingly share her breakfast with the family below because she knows they 'are hard up'; the man who boarded with them last winter will give a month's rent because he knows the father of the family is out of work" (Addams 1910, 123–24).

This ethic of care and concern for one another cuts across ethnic groups. The older sister of the Cambodian-Chinese family in C1r cut the hair of Latino neighbors, and the Latino youths in turn "looked out for" her family. I was amazed when the sixteen-year-old Mexican from the basement apartment walked through the courtyard on her way to the high school prom. She was beautifully dressed, with all the accessories. I knew that this household of nine sharing a one-bedroom apartment did not have the resources to finance such an outfit. I learned later that the dress had been borrowed from an aunt, the shoes from a neighbor, the purse from a cousin, and the hair-bow from another neighbor, and that her hair had been styled by the Cambodian neighbor.

This ethos of solidarity was expressed in the common greeting—used by Latino, Hmong, Assyrian—"Where are you going?" "Where have you been?" "I haven't seen you for a while." They expected answers and explanations. They were interested in one another's business. It was from the Mexicans that I learned the Hmong paid $20 a month for their garden plots in the vacant lot down the street. An Assyrian man I had not yet met knocked on my door one day and asked me whether I could help him patent an invention. He explained, "I look through your window and see all the books and thought you must have a book on this."

Taking my cue from neighbors, I started a back-porch "garden" in June 1988. Within the first week of setting out the pots, I had gifts of seeds and cuttings from four of my immediate neighbors.

One of the poignant examples of interethnic sharing deserves a full transcription. Ching, a small eight-year-old Hmong boy from E3r, approached me one day in the courtyard:

CHING: Mr. Dwight, do you know Julio [twenty-year-old Mexican resident of Big Red]?

DC: Yes.
CHING: [obviously troubled] Is he gang?
[In order not to violate street ethics, I deflected Ching's question.]
DC: Why are you worried about that, Ching?
CHING: [staring at ground, voice sad] Because he's my friend.
DC: He's my friend too. How is he your friend, Ching?
CHING: Because he's nice to me. He always gives me lots of toys, the toys he used to play with when he was a kid.
DC: Why do you think he's in a gang?
CHING: Because people say he's gang.

As the example of Ching makes clear, people value the intangibles of friendship and caring as much as the tangibles of money, food, or toys that change hands. That is not to depreciate the real need for material support. Julio's hand-me-down toys are the only ones Ching has. Ching's family moved into Big Red because they had lost their savings on a house they bought. The house had been burglarized twice, and they had lost everything. The father told me that they had moved into Big Red to recoup, to start over again.

The other Courtyard Kids were as poor as Ching. One day as I was passing through the courtyard Azziz (Assyrian) came running up to me, calling out, "Hey Mr. Dwight. Today's my birthday. I'm thirteen. I'm a teenager. Tony [cousin who lives across the hall] and I have the same birthday. He's twelve. So my dad said that we can't afford to do two birthdays. So this year we will do his. And next year they will do mine." I spontaneously decided to take Azziz and his eleven-year-old brother for the treat of his choice. He chose McDonald's. Before placing his order, he conferred with me about the total price, worried that I might not be able to afford his Big Mac, fries, and small Coke. The boys told me that this was the third time in their life they had been out to eat.

All the Courtyard Kids were very conscious of the price of things. When I returned from shopping, they rushed to carry my grocery bags and ask the prices of items. Often one or two of them walked to the grocery store with me. They had a clear sense of price differentials at the local stores. Pao, an eight-year-old Hmong boy informed me: "Dominick's is cheaper than Jewel's, but Aldi's is the cheapest. Vanilla wafers are 79 cents and at Dominick's they're $1.09. But bags [at Aldi's] are 4 cents so we just carry the stuff in our hands." Observing me as I bought a newspaper, a Courtyard Kid remarked, "Newspapers is wasting your money, isn't it, Mr. Dwight? 'Cause you can get the news free from TV."

My neighbors have borrowed a variety of things from me: money for milk, newspapers, pliers, dustpan, toilet paper, flashlight, books, suitcases, hair dryer, Band-Aids, aspirin, toothache medicine, videocassettes, earache medicine, and clothes. Not everyone who borrows from me lives in Big Red. Propinquity affects the frequency and intensity of borrowings. The Mexican–Puerto Rican family directly across the hall from me borrowed the most costly items. The two teenage girls borrowed my camera. But that came after months of interaction. When Aurelio returned to Mexico for a short visit and Carmen's telephone stopped functioning, she borrowed my unit and plugged it into the outlet in her apartment. She did not directly ask to borrow it. She met me in the stairwell and asked me first whether I could fix her defunct telephone. Then she confided how frightened she was at night, being alone with six children. When I offered her the use of my telephone, she was appreciative but worried that sometimes I had to go out in the evening and she would be stranded. Finally, I recognized her indirect request and offered her my entire telephone. She protested but soon gratefully accepted the offer. This family also requested my services as a photographer at the joint baptism of their baby son Alfredo and four of his cousins, as well as the *quinceañera* celebration of Aurelio's goddaughter. Carmen asked me whether on washdays she could extend her clothesline across my back porch.

In return, the family did many favors for me. They kept an eye on my place when I was away. They gave my rent to the landlord, thus freeing me from having to stay home on rent-collection days. They offered me rides in their car when they saw me walking on the street. They cooked meals for me and shared their intimate family problems and life celebrations with me: baptisms, birthdays, cotillions. Aurelio invited me to the alley parties of the *braceros*. During the water shutoff in June, they began looking for another affordable apartment; finding a building that had two vacancies, they suggested that I could move with them. When they actually moved in November because of a fight with the landlord, I bought the floor-to-ceiling steel security gate Aurelio had installed on his back door. He and a nephew mounted it for me.

I was the recipient of manifold kindnesses from other neighbors throughout Big Red. The Hmong who lived directly above me gave me a hand-embroidered textile wall hanging and a beaded window hanging they had made. Mrs. Gutierrez (Puerto Rican), the "dean" of Big Red, was concerned about mail getting stolen from my mailbox with its defective lock. Consistent with her senior woman-in-the-building status, she took charge of the situation. Without consulting me, she instructed the Puerto Rican mailman, whom she had known for years, to put all my mail in her box—she has one of the few locked mailboxes. Then she would espy me from her window as I walked through the courtyard and would station herself at the top of the stairwell, smiling grandly with my mail in hand. Until another neighbor showed me how to fix my lock, I was dependent on Mrs. Gutierrez for my mail.

The Big Red ethos of familiarity and reciprocity continues, for even though many of us have been displaced from the building, we still live in the area. In early July 1990, two teenagers (Assyrian and Mexican) hailed me as I carried a bag of groceries down one of the streets of Little Beirut. Consistent with local custom, they examined what was in my bag and said, "Thanks, Dwight," as they reached for two yogurts. There was no need to ask for the food. The nature and history of our relationship enabled them to assume this familiarity. Two days later, as they were riding around the neighborhood, they spotted me again and pulled the car over; the Assyrian fellow leaned out the window and offered me some of his food: "Hey Dwight, you want some of this shake?" These two incidents capture the quality of life in the Big Red area. At a micro-level, every day is filled with a host of significant kindnesses and richly nuanced reciprocities. To use a term from the streets, people are "tight" in Little Beirut (meaning tightly connected, not "tight" with their money). These micro-level courtesies provide a buffer against the macro-structures of exclusion and oppression. They enable people to experience dignity and joy in structures like Big Red, refashioning them into "dwellingplaces."

The fine-grained texture of the daily acknowledgments and courtesies that characterize life in Big Red provides a counterpoint to the blunter treatment the residents sometimes receive when they enter the system controlled by established residents and bureaucracies. Teenagers expelled from school have asked me to accompany their mothers to the principal's office for reinstatement because when the mother went alone, as one student put it, "they did not see her." In a communication system that required a different style of assertiveness, she was invisible. When I accompanied Mexican and Guatemalan mothers to school offices or police stations, all the attention and eye contact would be directed toward me, the white male. One time, after the high school principal had been persuaded to give one of my young neighbors a second chance, the mother gratefully extended her hand to thank him. But the principal reached right past her to shake my hand. Quite literally, he did not see her. A short, dark-complexioned Mexican woman, she had three factors that contributed to her invisibility: race, gender, and class.

Sometimes the erasure is not so subtle. While standing in line at the

Perry Drugstore checkout line, one of my Assyrian neighbors gave me an updated report on her finger, which had been bitten by a rat as she slept in Big Red. Although the bandage had been removed, the finger still looked as if it had been slammed in a car door. The cashier, a white woman in her late fifties, treated my neighbors very curtly at the checkout. Before the Assyrian woman was out of earshot, and as the cashier was ringing up my purchases, she began talking to the neighboring cashier, also an older white woman. Here is what the two of them said, in full hearing of the Assyrian woman, her husband, her granddaughter, and me:

CASHIER 1: Can you believe it? If my father were alive to see what's happened to the neighborhood!
CASHIER 2: I know. Don't get upset.—
CASHIER 1: I hate getting upset first thing in the morning.
CASHIER 2: They're not worth it.
CASHIER 1: I know I shouldn't let them upset me.
CASHIER 2: They're not worth it. They're trash.

Tactics of Resistance

The residents of Big Red coped with their oppressive circumstances typically through circumventions, survival tactics, and seizing opportunities. They did not have the power and clout to confront the system head-on. They survived via connections, evasions, street-smart maneuvers, making end-runs around authority. De Certeau describes the "tactical" thinking of people everywhere who must find space for themselves within oppressive structures:

> The space of a tactic is the space of the other. Thus it must play on and with a terrain imposed on it and organized by the law of a foreign power. . . . It does not, therefore, have the options of planning general strategy and viewing the adversary as a whole within a distinct, visible, and objectifiable space. . . . It must vigilantly make use of the cracks that particular conjunctions open in the surveillance of the proprietary powers. It poaches in them. It creates surprises in them. It can be where it is least expected. It is a guileful ruse. (1984, 37)

The Big Red tenants turned the "absenteeism" of the landlord to their advantage to enact spatial practices and temporal rhythms that would not have been tolerated in well-managed buildings. They had their tactics for dealing with the landlord. Mrs. Gutierrez from time to time would unleash a blistering tongue-lashing on him. She always announced to neighbors, days in advance, that she was going to "really shout at him this time." She would gather more complaints from the neighbors, gradually building up steam for one of her anticipated confrontations, and then, at the opportune moment, she would "really let him have it." Though none could match the explosive force of Mrs. Gutierrez, I overheard many women as they stood on back porches and denounced him.

Perhaps the best example of tactical resistance unfolded when the city shut off the water supply to Big Red because the landlord was $26,000 in arrears for payment. This action was taken at the end of June 1988, during a summer in which Chicago broke its previous record for days in which the temperature rose above 100 degrees Fahrenheit. During the three days of the water shutoff, temperatures soared to 105 degrees.

Attempts to work within the system were ineffectual. I contacted NRC, the powerful community organization, but it could do nothing to remedy the immediate crisis. I personally called several agencies and officials in the city, including the Water Department. It is legal, within the City of Chicago, to shut off water supply for a large building as a method of collecting debt payments. The only result my flurry of telephone calls produced was that a city inspector did visit Big Red during the time we were without water, wrote a report, sympathized with us, then drove away. We never heard from him again. If we had depended on his official intervention, Big Red would still be without water. What all the city bureaucrats told us was that they did not have the authority to turn the water back on until the debt was cleared, or at least a partial payment was deposited. The owner, of course, was unaffected by the city's action. Never easy to reach, insulated in his lakefront condominium, he did not even know that the water had been shut off.

By the third day without water, the situation was intolerable. The gross inconvenience, the outrage of having no water for drink, bathing, or flushing the toilet, intensified by the 105-degree heat, incited radical action. It is hard to say whose idea the final solution was, because I think we came to it collectively. I remember that we were all standing in the courtyard, quite bedraggled and exhausted. Mrs. Yang, the Hmong mother from C3l, kept insisting, "We have to do something!" Spontaneously, we decided to take action into our own hands, dig down to the water main, and turn the water back on ourselves. This action was not only unauthorized, it was illegal.

This plan required several steps of coordinated action across lines of ethnicity, gender, and age. The hue and cry raised during the first day of the water shutoff drew in the white Democratic precinct captain, who lived one block north of Big Red. He became involved in the day-to-day drama of the water crisis as it unfolded. He donated his tools and garage workshop for the Hmong smiths to fashion a custom wrench to turn on the water valve. Mexican, Hmong, and Assyrian residents of Big Red all took turns with the digging. This activity attracted several "sidewalk supervisors," many of whom were homeowners from across the street, others just passersby, including African Americans and whites. The diggers reached the water main only to find the valve sheathed in an eighteen-inch sleeve filled with dirt. A Puerto Rican woman volunteered her vacuum-cleaner hose, and extension cords were plugged into the nearest apartment outlet, which happened to be Assyrian. The Hmong ran back and forth with the white precinct captain to fashion the wrench that would turn the valve. This took several attempts. Once they got it to fit, the next problem to be solved was determining what manipulation turned the water on. A full turn? Half turn? To the right or left? The water company does not make it easy for unauthorized people to take control of their water supply. An elderly Assyrian woman was stationed in the window to check her sink and report the results of each trial turn: "Nothing yet—yes, a trickle, do that again—no, nothing O.K., that's it."

It was close to midnight by the time the water flowed. Everyone was exhilarated. Several of the men went to the Mexican *bracero* bar down the street on Lawrence to celebrate. No one bought his own beer. Everyone crossed over and spent his money buying someone else's beer, although in the end there was an equal distribution of monies. There was much camaraderie, backslapping, handshaking, and clicking of bottles.

The audience of this drama was enlarged by a front-page story in the *Chicago Tribune*, "In Crisis, Immigrants Learn Who Their True Friends Are." Several follow-up stories and editorials appeared in the Lerner neighborhood newspapers, all supporting the pluck of the Big Red residents and condemning the conditions that allowed a building full of vulnerable people to go for a prolonged time without water during the worst of Chicago's summer heat wave. Spokespersons for the Water Department went on record to say that no legal action would be taken against the Big Red residents who circumvented the law to regain control of their water supply.

This crisis tightened the community. In a crisis, boundaries are suspended or become porous. The sixth month into the project, I had made headway in meeting my Big Red neighbors, but most of the meaningful interaction had been with neighbors sharing my stairwell. By the time the water was turned back on, I had been inside thirty-five of the thirty-seven apartments. The shared hardship of going without water during one of Chicago's most notorious heat waves threw Big Red into a "communitas of crisis," a heightened sense of "we-feeling" (Turner 1977, 154). It was easy to approach anybody sharing that experience. Residents who had not previously met were greeting one another with warm familiarity by the end of the second day. This crisis transformed my position in the building from semi-outsider to an informal advocate of sorts. It accelerated trust and rapport with neighbors by a great leap.

The homeowners across the street and across the alley rallied in very kind and generous ways. These same people had been known to complain about the condition of Big Red and how this huge building overrun with children did nothing to enhance property values on the block. Nevertheless, one homeowner across the alley bought a connection for his garden hose so that it would reach into the first-floor windows and people would not have to lug buckets. Across the street, another family built a temporary brick walk across their yard to provide a more direct route for women and kids carrying heavy buckets of water from their outdoor faucet. One homeowner tried to charge people for the water, and he immediately became the scapegoat against whom everyone united in contempt.

The Big Red water crisis demonstrated clearly that even though marginalized people are highly vulnerable, they are not passive (Clifford 1988, 16). This incident is only one dramatic example of myriad tactics and highly creative forms of resistance employed by the weak (Scott 1990).

The Rhetoric of Transgression and Redevelopment

> We look at the material solidity of a building . . . and behind it we see always the insecurity that lurks within a circulation process of capital, which always asks: how much more time in this relative space?
>
> —DAVID HARVEY, *CONSCIOUSNESS AND THE URBAN EXPERIENCE* (1985)

On August 1, 1989, the president of Oakwood Development Company, who was also president of the Albany Park Landlords' Association, took control of Big Red. The absentee owner had failed to make his mortgage payments, and the building was being cited in criminal housing court because of building-code violations and physical deterioration due to his negligence. Notices had gone up warning of another water shutoff because of the owner's failure to pay the water bill. The court appointed Superior Bank as receiver. With NRC urging, the bank appointed Oakwood Development Company as manager of Big Red. Empowered by the state and allied with community organizations, an Oakwood Development crew used sledgehammers to break into the basement of Big Red to take charge of the utility meters and other facilities.

Almost immediately after the takeover, Oakwood and staff interviewed various residents and quickly pinpointed two drug-dealing apartments, the busiest one being the apartment above me that Bao Xiang and her family had formerly occupied. Oakwood used the crisis of drug trafficking as an excuse to evacuate the entire stairwell. With hindsight, I believe the drug dealers, who were real, became the lever Oakwood deployed to start emptying Big Red as quickly as possible.

When Oakwood took control in August, Big Red was fully occupied and still had a vital building culture and ethos of solidarity. Within four months, half of the Big Red households were displaced. One year later, thirty-one of the thirty-seven apartments were vacant (figure 4). Empty and boarded up, Big Red looms like a ghost building. The wrenching violence of this intervention was muted in the euphemisms that Oakwood and NRC used to describe their actions: "turning the building around," "turning the neighborhood around."

Oakwood, a multimillion-dollar company that specializes in managing low-income rental properties, works closely with NRC. The NRC director of housing development lives in an Oakwood building. Oakwood and NRC estimate that it will require a $1.5-million loan to purchase and rehabilitate Big Red. NRC Housing Development is working on getting a low-interest loan package through Chicago Equity Fund[9] and Community Investment Incorporation. The NRC Housing Development director explained the plans for Big Red: "We want to make it a community project—bring together Oakwood experience and profit-making know-how with NRC philosophy and provide quality rehab for poor people. Make it a good solid community, *but integrated with the rest of the community*" (emphasis mine). The partnership of Oakwood's "profit-making know-how with NRC philosophy," united against the market individualism of "slumlords" as much as the transgressive tenants, is a classic example of the complex way investment property mirrors "the internal tensions within the capitalist order" and anchors a coalition between private investment and the public sector in advanced capitalist societies (Harvey 1985, 61). The absentee landlord of Big Red was displaced along with the residents: his locks were smashed with Oakwood sledgeham-

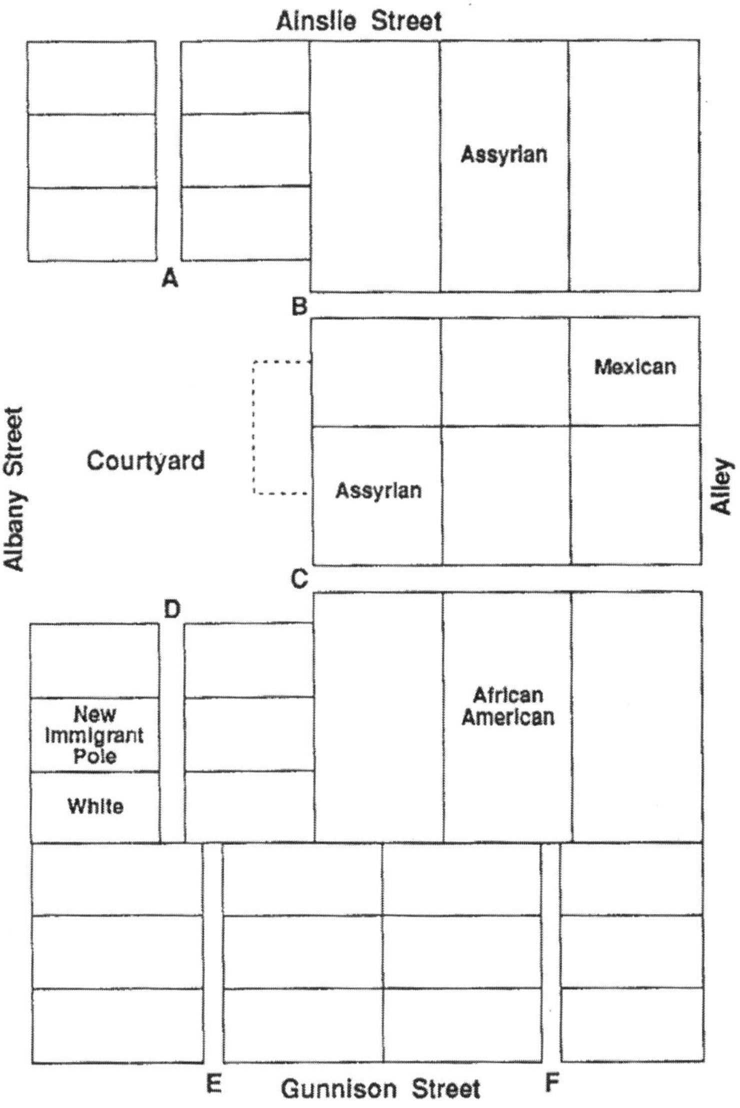

Figure 5: Big Red occupancy, summer 1990.

mers on the day of takeover. The competitive tensions and profit-making dictates of capitalism are softened, elided, and simultaneously enabled by the moral rhetoric (NRC's "philosophy") of community organizations concerned with the public good. Community organizations like NRC produce strategic definitions of "the public good," "quality of life," and "good solid community" that are advantageous to capital development. "Community," David Harvey argues, "plays a fundamental role in terms of the reproduction of labor power, the circulation of revenues, and the geography of capital accumulation" (Harvey 1985, 252; see also 255–57).

NRC brought Big Red to the attention of a subcommittee of the U.S. Congress. Frank Annunzio, U.S. Representative for the district encompassing Albany Park, chairs the Subcommittee on Financial Institutions, which oversees the Federal Deposit Insurance Corporation (FDIC). In order to guarantee that Superior Bank would not sell Big Red to the highest bidder without a rehabilitation entailment—"slumbanger types who would rent to multiple families that would overrun the place," according to NRC staff—NRC pressured Annunzio, who was waging a tough reelection fight because of the savings and loan scandal. He needed the support of Patrick O'Connor, Fortieth Ward alderman; NRC worked through O'Connor, who then pressured Annunzio. Annunzio was reelected, but at the time of this writing Big Red still awaits repairs.

The NRC phrase "but integrated with the rest of the community" codes the middle-class anxiety about Big Red. Big Red transgressed the system by remaining outside it. With an unresponsive absentee landlord and an array of mostly new-immigrant working-class tenants, Big Red eluded middle-class strategies of containment and control. The plurality, fluidity, and openness that made Big Red accessible and accommodating to new-immigrant and working-class tenants were among the very qualities that the middle class finds forbidding. Situated in the center of Little Beirut, Big Red focused and displayed middle-class fears and ambivalences about difference, density, deterioration, and demographic change.

The domination and displacement of the residents of Big Red were underwritten by a rhetoric of redevelopment. Before the Big Red residents were physically vacated, they were discursively displaced. Drastic measures in the service of capitalism were discursively mediated as desirable and natural inevitabilities. Defined as dirty, disorderly, deteriorating, and dangerous, Big Red became ripe for redevelopment, making it "licit to intervene . . . in order to exercise the rights of guardianship . . . to impose 'the good' on others" (Todorov 1984, 157). To legitimate the wholesale disruption and displacement of families, the community organizations, in league with real estate interests, defined Big Red as the alien, transgressive Other that threatened civil order and neighborhood stability (see Stallybrass and White 1986; Skogan 1990).

The rhetoric of transgression turns on a symbolic equation of dirt with danger. Mary Douglas helps us understand the symbolizing powers of dirt. Inspired by William James's insight that dirt is "matter out of place" (Douglas 1966:164), she argues: "Dirt is essentially disorder. There is no such thing as absolute dirt. . . . Dirt offends against order. Eliminating it is not a negative movement, but a positive effort to organize the environment" (Douglas 1966, 2). That which is out of place, marginal, different, and therefore dirty gets charged with danger and becomes subject to the moral imperative for correction, rehabilitation, development, all in the name of restoring order.

The rhetorical valences among these loaded terms can be schematized as a triangle with disorder at the apex and dirt and danger forming the base (figure 5). Density and deterioration are intensifying links in the extended causal chain that sets up development as a moral necessity. Underneath all these terms is difference, that which cannot be spoken without disrupting the discourse of liberal pluralism upon which the rhetoric of redevelopment draws. The president of Oakwood Development, for example, takes pride in being "a socially conscious real-estate developer" ("His Niche Is Low-Income Housing" 1990, 1). Sanitized celebrations of "diversity" elide deep fears of difference. Local commercial boosterism promotes Albany Park's diversity as a "salad bowl," "mosaic," "orchestra," "symphony," and "bouquet" of cultures, but these metaphors invoke emblematic icons of the middle-class containment and taming of difference. Fredric Jameson critiques this form of "liberal tolerance":

> Much of what passes for a spirited defense of difference is, of course, simply liberal tolerance, a position whose offensive complacencies are well known but which has at least the merit of raising the embarrassing historical question of whether the tolerance of difference, as a social fact, is not the result of social homogenization and standardization and the obliteration of genuine social difference in the first place. (Jameson 1991, 341)

Anxiety about dirt and disorder sets the stage for the elimination of difference and mobilizes efforts to patrol boundaries and purge the environment.

The discourse of transgression legitimates official systems of surveillance, reform, enforcement, and demolition. A proposal from the Report

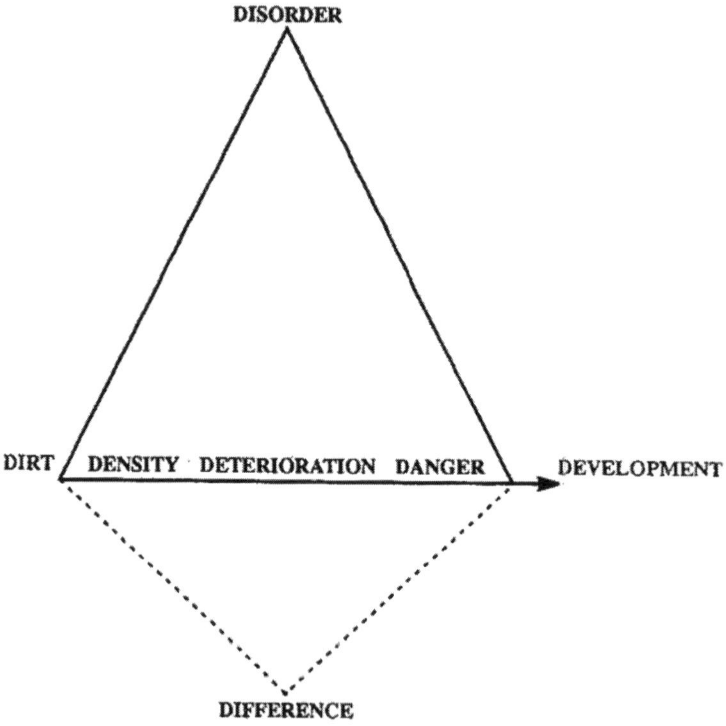

Figure 6: Configuration of key terms in the rhetoric of transgression.

of the Albany Park Planning Committee, an NRC group, vividly clarifies the connection between discourse and power (Foucault 1979): "We propose that the City use its powers of condemnation to inspect, acquire, demolish and prepare for redevelopment." (Uncataloged archive, 1980, 3)[10] The rhetoric of transgression features three definitional strategies for classifying buildings and areas as dirty, dangerous, and therefore in need of redevelopment: (1) metaphors of disease and decay, (2) images of flux and instability, and (3) temporal retardation. These three strategies interact in complex and mutually reinforcing ways.

Community activists deploy organic metaphors of disease and decay to identify targeted buildings and urban areas with dangerous powers of pollution and contagion (Sontag 1979). The NRC Housing Development director called Big Red a "blight" on the neighborhood. Likewise, "cancer," "epidemic," and "plague" are frequently invoked terms of contamination. This trope is rhetorically potent because it imparts a sense of life-threatening urgency through images of rapidly spreading infection, debilitation, and death. The executive director of NRC unequivo-

Figure 7: Back view of Big Red with decrepit porches facing alley. The graffiti on back walls and garage mark the contested turf of rival gangs in and around "Little Beirut." "Pee Wee RIP" is a "Rest in Peace" death mural that commemorates a fifteen-year-old Latin King who was killed the summer of 1990. Ten "RIP" death murals were inscribed on the walls of Big Red during the time I lived there. Gangs communicate in a complex code of symbols, icons, and acronyms. They invert and reverse the letters that stand for hostile gangs as a way of debunking rivals. The *R* and the *P* are inverted because they stand for the Royals and the Popes, two gangs currently at war with the Latin Kings (*LK*), the dominant gang in "Little Beirut." Whipple and Ainslie are the names of two streets whose intersection, one-half block from Big Red, is a popular "hang-out" for Latin Kings. (Photo by Dwight Conquergood: Courtesy of Northwestern University Archives)

cally defined Big Red as casting a deathly presence over the neighborhood: "Big Red is the dead heart of the neighborhood. It's where it's situated. It's the dead heart of the neighborhood. It casts a pall over the entire neighborhood."

Gangs and drugs are particularly potent signs of urban disease that create revulsion and dread among citizens. A civic report notes that "youth gangs and drug trafficking are the scourges of certain portions of Albany Park" and laments "the growing cancer of crime and drug activity" along the Kedzie corridor (Albany Park Community Area 1982, 37, 39). Oakwood Development initially used the fear of drugs and gangs to "clean out" Big Red. The A stairwell where I lived was the first to be evacuated, because it included a drug apartment and was covered with gang graffiti. I attended a meeting with the police and Oakwood staff. The police lieutenant described how drugs spread through a neighborhood like a metastasizing disease: "It infects the whole building, then the block goes, then the neighborhood."

The trope of contagious disease gathers resonance and intensity within a wider circulation of contemporary cultural meanings that connect the health of the body politic to the strength of the immune system. Donna Haraway has written brilliantly about the "semantics of defense and invasion" in "immune system discourse":

> My thesis is that the immune system is an elaborate icon for principal systems of symbolic and material "difference" in late capitalism . . . . the immune system is a plan for meaningful action to construct and maintain the boundaries for what may count as self and other in the crucial realms of the normal and the pathological. (Haraway 1989, 4)

The boundary anxiety of "immune system discourse" renders confrontations with difference more acute. The symbolism of the vigilant immune system appeals to "the rules of purity, propriety and continuous production which govern bourgeois reason" (Stallybrass and White 1986, 107).

This pathologizing of buildings and blocks as diseased bodies with dead hearts is an indirect way of stigmatizing the tenants, the socioeconomically least advantaged classes, caught in this "spatial entrapment" (Harvey 1985, 40). In *The Politics and Poetics of Transgression,* Peter Stallybrass and Allon White insightfully discuss this "metonymic chain of contagion which led back to the culture of the working classes" (Stallybrass and White 1986, 138). The associative link between perceptions of decay and class difference is patent in the following phrase: "older, lower income, predominantly multi-family areas that suffer from slum and blighted conditions" (Cicero 1988, 8). Density, crowding, households' "doubling up" in Big Red and other "multi-family areas," and "bands of teenagers congregating on street corners" (Skogan 1990, 2) are economically constrained spatial practices of the poor that affront middle-class norms of privacy, polite society, and property management. "Spatial practices," David Harvey argues, "become imbued with class meanings. . . . They take on their meanings under specific social relations of class, gender, community, ethnicity, or race" (Harvey 1989, 223).

The rhetoric of transgression and redevelopment combines the bacterial metaphor of spreading contagion with kinetic images of flux and instability to depict dangerous disorder. An official report warned that the deteriorated conditions of housing in Little Beirut "will create a spill-over effect that will spread to the areas of good housing in Albany Park" (Albany Park Community Area 1982, 42). A neighborhood "in transition" associated with "demographic change," dizzying "turn-over," and the "downward spiral" of property values is constructed as the dangerous, unbalanced Other that threatens the "stability" of "good solid" communities: "The single-family homes in Ravenswood Manor have served as *anchors* in keeping property values *stable* in Albany Park" (Pennelle 1989, 1; emphasis mine). One of the stated goals of NRC is "to manage the demographic transition so that whole streets aren't turning over at the same time" (Albany Park Community Area 1982, 44).

Topsy-turvy visions of upset and turnover are complemented by destabilizing imagery of ooze, spillover, and flood, particularly when applied to people, with the most commonly used descriptor of demographic change: "influx." In addition to property, the NRC is vigilant about people: "The attempt to stabilize the Kedzie corridor is also being fought on a different front—monitoring the influx of poor people into the area who are being displaced from other neighborhoods" (Albany Park Community Area 1982, 44). Sometimes these migratory Others are discursively imagined as a "wave" that threatens to overwhelm an established neighborhood. An NRC spokesperson reassured the community: "The current wave of low-income residents will only be temporary; the long-term prospective is positive" (Pennelle 1989, 2). Multifamily low-income courtyard buildings are described as "overflowing" with people, especially children.

Class difference gets constructed symbolically along the axes of stable/unstable, solid/fluid, balanced/teetering, dry/wet, long-term/temporary, established/mobile. As I learned from living more than three years in Little Beirut (the first twenty months in Big Red), economically disadvantaged people, for a variety of reasons, have to move frequently. One of the most powerful ways of demeaning people is to call them "transient." Henry Mayhew opens his monumental nineteenth-century four-volume study, *London Labour and the London Poor,* with one grand binary opposition that proposes "wandering"—that is, instability, transience—as the universally defining characteristic of the poor:

> Of the thousand millions of human beings that are said to constitute the population of the entire globe, there are—socially, morally, and perhaps even physically considered—but two distinct

> and broadly marked races, viz., the wanderers and the settlers—the vagabond and the citizen—the nomadic and the civilized tribes. . . . Moreover it would appear, that not only are all races divisible into wanderers and settlers, but that each civilized or settled tribe has generally some wandering horde intermingled with and in a measure preying upon it. (Mayhew 1968, 1)

Wanderers, transients, nomads, migrants, and refugees are unattached to a "proper place" (de Certeau 1984) and thereby threaten order because they "transgress all settled boundaries of 'home'" (Stallybrass and White 1986:129). Nomination, the rhetoric of naming, is a strategy of containment for these drifters: "It is the task of nomination to fix a *locus proprius* for them, and to set limits for their drifting" (De Certeau 1986, 72).

The NRC uses the stigma of transience to differentiate the "deserving poor" from the "undeserving poor." An expansive quote from a commission staffer is revealing:

> Our vice-president has an expression: "There are poor people and there are slobs." Well, we're not interested in the slobs. We're not interested in people who don't want to live between four walls: . . . We're interested in poor folks who need to live here because they're poor. We are concerned that they, in fact, will be a part of the community and observe property rights. But there are concerns about people who move in and out of the community, people who are floaters, who will take and will not give. We'd like to see them move in and out of the community. That's their problem; we're beyond the point where we're gonna sit and commiserate with them. (Albany Park Community Area 1982, 44)

"Floaters" and "transients"—also named "slobs" and "trash"—embody the instability of the "transitional" neighborhoods they pass through and upset. No one wants to recognize that their nomadic practices are economically constrained.

It should be pointed out that the same kinetic imagery of circulation, movement, and mobility, when aligned with entrepreneurial interests, takes on a positive valence. The circulation of capital is construed as dynamic, and mobility is celebrated insofar as it is upward. Instead of "transient," nomadic capitalists are considered to be "on the fast track." Those in control of the production of images are able to play it both ways with the imagery of Motion: dynamic and directional for the ruling classes, disintegrative and anarchic for the subordinate classes. The rhetorical deployment of kinetic imagery underpins a "politics of representation" (Shapiro 1988) that is used both to displace certain groups of people and to keep them in a subordinate place.

Like motion, time is strategically manipulated in the discourse of redevelopment. As a term, "development" has the same temporal ring as "growth," "progress," "modernization"—a sense of advancing confidently through time toward improvement, fulfillment, and enlightenment. In *Keywords,* Raymond Williams charts the political career of "development" and notes that its late-nineteenth-century use in connection with industry and commerce was preceded by its eighteenth-century association with the new biology, when it became the virtual equivalent of "evolution," in the "specialized sense of *development* from 'lower' to 'higher' organisms" (Williams 1983:121; see also 102–4). Development becomes the temporal transposition of a moral hierarchy that is spatialized along a high/low vertical axis and a forward/backward horizontal plane.

Aligned with the forces of nature and fueled by trade and industry, the rhetorical power of development as an idea about time takes on quasireligious tones with the emergence, in the twentieth century, of "progress" as a "god term," a "rhetorical absolute." Richard Weaver argues: "By a transposition of terms, 'progress' becomes the salvation man is placed on earth to work out; and just as there can be no achievement more important than salvation, so there can be no activity more justified in enlisting our sympathy and support than 'progress'" (Weaver 1953, 212–13). Anything that impedes progress, any building or urban area that is labeled as in need of redevelopment, suffers the stigma of regression, temporal retardation. It is perceived as delaying and retarding the natural order and progression of time and therefore as a legitimate target for intervention.

The rhetoric of urban redevelopment, therefore, is a "temporal setup" (Clifford 1988, 16) with strategies and consequences similar to those of the development programs imposed on the Third World: "an often generous idea of '*aid* to the *developing* countries' is confused with wholly ungenerous practices of cancellation of the identities of others, by their definition as *underdeveloped* or *less developed,* and of imposed processes of *development* for a world market controlled by others" (Williams 1983, 104). In *Time and the Other,* Johannes Fabian analyzes how global policies of imperialism and colonialism "required Time to accommodate the schemes of a one-way history: progress, development, modernity (and their negative mirror images: stagnation, underdevelopment, tradition). In short, *geopolitics* has its ideological foundations in *chronopolitics*" (Fabian 1983, 144). Urban redevelopment attempts the temporal reversal of areas that drag neighborhoods backward in time, in the direction of decay, decomposition, and death, away from millenarian renewal. Redevelopment erases and rewrites history on the urban landscape.

In its strategic manipulation of time, the rhetoric of transgression and redevelopment resonates with the puritan jeremiad, a classic American form of public discourse much studied by rhetoricians (Bercovitch 1978; Johannesen 1985; Murphy 1990). The secular discourse of urban "renewal," "revitalization," "redevelopment," and "restoration," like the puritan jeremiad, castigates the current state of decline and promises a shining future through correction and reform. As Richard Johannesen reminds us, the prophet Jeremiah used discourse "to root out, to pull down, and to destroy, and to throw down, to build, and to plant" (Johannesen 1985, 159). The contemporary rhetoric of urban redevelopment participates in a discursive formation with a long history of instrumental force. The discourse of economic revitalization profits from the jeremiadic undertones of moral redemption and rebirth.

The "chronopolitics" of redevelopment plays out in other ways. Big Red has stood empty since summer 1990 while Oakwood Development and NRC wait for the best interest rate and loan package for rehabilitation. In the meantime, the former tenants have been forced to relocate to substandard housing nearby. "Those who can afford to wait," Harvey notes, "always have an advantage over those who cannot" (Harvey 1985, 23). The president of Oakwood Development stated this time-based philosophy in a press interview: "And that's our philosophy; it's long-term. We own about 12 properties and we've sold two since 1975. We're hanging on for long-term gain" ("His Niche Is Low-income Housing," 1990, 1). One of Oakwood's most effective methods of emptying Big Red was the five-day notice that warned tenants of eviction when their rent was late. Oakwood trapped and displaced the Big Red tenants with these "temporal nets" (Harvey 1985, 29) while the company profits from "appreciation over time" ("His Niche," 1).

The people of Big Red have been displaced, but not erased. Victims of the bourgeois "will to refinement" (Stallybrass and White 1986, 94) that purged the building, strained household resources, and dispersed the Courtyard Kids, most have redistributed themselves within Little Beirut with their friendship networks still intact. The culture of Big Red survives in remnants and fragments.

It is now starkly clear that all the initial talk from Oakwood and NRC about "making Big Red a safer and more pleasant place to live" did not include the people of Big Red in that vision. Indeed, my Big Red neighbors were perceived as part of the problem that had to be removed. The public statements of both Oakwood Development and NRC champion "the rights of poor people to decent housing." The people of Big Red, however, did not fit into the class of the deserving poor, a category that includes only those who embrace middle-class values.

Walter Benjamin's insight, "There is no document of civilization which is not at the same time a document of barbarism" (Benjamin 1969, 256; see also Brenkman 1987, 3), can be transposed in the case of Big Red to "There is no act of redevelopment which is not at the same time an act of violence and oppression." In the words of Harvey, "The perpetual reshaping of the geographical landscape of capitalism is a process of violence and pain" (Harvey 1985, 29). The sturdy tenants who had coped successfully with the gross negligence and greed of a slumlord, and made homes, reared children, and created an interdependent culture of warmth and neighborliness, were no match for the outside agents of middle-class order and stability who branded Big Red as a symbol of incivility, thus legitimating drastic measures of control and correction.

NOTES

1. For an engagingly written study of the politics of housing and development in Chicago see Gerald D. Stades, *The Man-Made City: The Land-Use Confidence Game in Chicago* (Chicago: University of Chicago Press, 1990). See also Gregory D. Squires, Larry Bennett, Kathleen McCourt, and Philip Nyden, *Chicago: Race, Class, and the Response to Urban Decline* (Philadelphia: Temple University Press, 1987). For an excellent study of the black migration to Chicago and its impact on the city, see Nicholas Lemann, *The Promised Land: The Great Black Migration and How It Changed America* (New York: Knopf, 1991).

2. Uncatalogued archival material, Chicago Public Library, Albany Park Branch. Scattered throughout the Albany Park Branch Library in file cabinets and desk drawers are minutes of committee meetings, North River Commission memoranda, old newspaper clippings and photographs, flyers and leaflets, and unpublished reports from key neighborhood institutions and groups. I am grateful to the librarians who helped me locate these materials.

3. The "Asian" category includes Middle Easterners.

4. "Racial and Ethnic Composition, Roosevelt High School," Chicago Public School System, unpublished report.

5. I am grateful to Marie V. Bousfield, city demographer for Chicago, Department of Planning, for access to these unpublished data.

6. For a history of NRC, see Stades 1990:115–18.

7. The Northwestern colleagues with whom I worked on the Ford Foundation Changing Relations Project were Paul Friesema, Jane Mansbridge, and Al Hunter, assisted by graduate students Mary Erdmans, Jeremy Hein, Yvonne Newsome, and Yung-Sun Park. I wish to acknowledge support from the Ford Foundation, which funded the Changing Relations project through the Research Foundation

of the State University of New York, Grant 240–1117-A. The Center for Urban Affairs and Policy Research (CUAPR) at Northwestern University facilitated the work of the Chicago team of the Changing Relations project, I thank the staff of CUAPR for their expertise and cheerful support. I am particularly grateful to my colleague Jane Mansbridge, who carefully read earlier drafts of this chapter and offered many helpful criticisms and suggestions.

8. The conditions and people of Big Red can be seen in segments of two documentaries: *America Becoming,* produced by Dai-Sil Kim-Gibson for the Ford Foundation, and *The Heart Broken in Half,* produced and directed by Taggart Siegel and Dwight Conquergood.

9. Chicago Equity Fund is a not-for-profit loan company for low-income housing funded by a group of Chicago millionaires, who get a special tax break in exchange for the entailment that money go toward housing that will be designated low-income for fifteen years.

10. For important studies of the relationship between discourse and power, see Edward Said, *Orientalism* (New York: Vintage, 1979); V. Y. Mudimbe, *The Invention of Africa: Gnosis, Philosophy, and the Order of Knowledge* (Bloomington: Indiana University Press, 1988); Christopher Miller, *Blank Darkness: Africanist Discourse in French* (Chicago: University of Chicago Press, 1985); Nancy Fraser, *Unruly Practices: Power, Discourse, and Gender in Contemporary Social Theory* (Minneapolis: University of Minnesota Press, 1989); John Dorst, *The Written Suburb: An American Site, an Ethnographic Dilemma* (Philadelphia: University of Pennsylvania Press, 1989); and Robert Scholes, *Textual Power* (New Haven, Conn.: Yale University Press, 1985).

REFERENCES

Addams, Jane. 1960. *Twenty Years at Hull-House.* New York: Penguin.

Albany Park Community Area. 1982. *Chicago Comprehensive Needs Assessment,* Vol. 2. Chicago: Melaniphy and Associates.

Bakhtin, Mikhail M. 1986. *Speech Genres.* Edited by Caryl Emerson and Michael Holquist. Translated by Vern McGee. Austin: University of Texas Press.

Barthes, Roland. 1979. "From Work to Text." In *Textual Strategies: Perspectives in Post-structuralist Criticism,* edited by Josue V. Harari. Ithaca, N.Y.: Cornell University Press.

Benjamin, Walter. 1969. *Illuminations.* Edited by Hannah Arendt. Translated by Harry Zohn. New York: Schocken.

Bercovitch, Sacvan. 1978. *The American Jeremiad.* Madison: University of Wisconsin Press.

Bourdieu, Pierre. 1977. *Outline of a Theory of Practice.* Translated by Richard Nice. Cambridge, U.K.: Cambridge University Press.

Bourdieu, Pierre. 1984. *Distinction: A Social Critique of the Judgement of Taste.* Translated by Richard Nice. Cambridge, Mass.: Harvard University Press.

Bourdieu, Pierre. 1990. *The Logic of Practice.* Translated by Richard Nice. Stanford, Calif.: Stanford University Press.

Bousfield, Marie. 1989. *Births by Race in Chicago's Community Areas, 1979–87.* Chicago: Department of Planning, City of Chicago.

Brenkman, John. 1987. *Culture and Domination.* Ithaca, N.Y.: Cornell University Press.

Cicero, Joe. 1988. "Commercial Revitalization Stimulates Rehab Interest." *North River News,* 8.

Clifford, James. 1988. *The Predicament of Culture: Twentieth-Century Ethnography, Literature, and Art.* Cambridge, Mass.: Harvard University Press.

Corral, Luis M. 1990. "Neighborhoods: Albany Park Cleans Up Its Act." *Chicago Enterprise,* May, 15–16, 27.

De Certeau, Michel. 1984. *The Practice of Everyday Life.* Translated by Steven Rendall. Berkeley: University of California Press.

De Certeau, Michel. 1986. *Heterologies: Discourse on the Other.* Translated by Brian Massurni. Minneapolis: University of Minnesota Press.

Dorst, John. 1989. *The Written Suburb: An American Site, an Ethnographic Dilemma.* Philadelphia: University of Pennsylvania Press.

Douglas, Mary. 1966. *Purity and Danger: An Analysis of Pollution and Taboo.* London: Routledge and Kegan Paul.

Downs, Anthony. 1964. *What Will Chicago's Residential Areas Be Like in 1975?* Chicago: Chicago Commission on Human Relations.

Engels, Friedrich. 1987. *The Condition of the Working Class in England.* New York: Penguin.

Fabian, Johannes. 1983. *Time and the Other: How Anthropology Makes Its Object.* New York: Columbia University Press.

Flores, Raymundo, Marie Bousfield, and Eugene Chin. 1990. *Areas at Risk: Chicago's Potential Undercount in the 1990 Census.* Chicago: Department of Planning, City of Chicago.

Foucault, Michel. 1979. *Discipline and Punish: The Birth of the Prison.* Translated by Alan Sheridan. New York: Vintage.

Fraser, Nancy. 1989. *Unruly Practices: Power, Discourse, and Gender in Contemporary Social Theory.* Minneapolis: University of Minnesota Press.

Fremon, David K. 1988. *Chicago Politics Ward by Ward.* Bloomington: Indiana University Press.

Goozner, Merrill. 1990. "A Startling Climb in Area's Jobs." *Chicago Tribune,* 22 April, 1, 8.

Haraway, Donna. 1989. "The Biopolitics of Postmodern Bodies: Determinations of Self in Immune System Discourse." *Differences* 1: 3–43.

Harvey, David. 1985. *Consciousness and the Urban Experience: Studies in the History and Theory of Capitalist Urbanization.* Baltimore: Johns Hopkins University Press.

Harvey, David. 1989. *The Condition of Postmodernity.* Oxford: Basil Blackwell.

Hinz, Greg. 1991. "Census Reveals Huge Changes." *News Star* (Chicago Lerner Newspaper), 26 February, 1, 4.

Hinz, Greg. 1991. "An Extra Ward for North Side?" *News Star* (Chicago Lerner Newspaper), 5 March, 1, 5.

Hodge, Robert, and Gunther Kress. 1988. *Social Semiotics.* Cambridge, U.K.: Polity.

Jameson, Fredric. 1991. *Postmodernism: Or, The Cultural Logic of Late Capitalism.* Durham: Duke University Press.

Johannesen, Richard L. 1985. "The Jeremiad and Jenkin Lloyd Jones." *Communication Monographs* 52:156–72.

Kerson, Roger, ed. 1990. *The Chicago Affordable Housing Fact Book.* Chicago: Chicago Rehab Network.
Lemann, Nicholas. 1991. *The Promised Land: The Great Black Migration and How It Changed America.* New York: Knopf.
Marcus, George E., and Michael M. J. Fischer. 1986. *Anthropology as Cultural Critique. An Experimental Moment in the Human Sciences.* Chicago: University of Chicago Press.
Mayhew, Henry. 1968. *London Labour and the London Poor* (Vol. 1). New York: Dover.
McClory, Robert. 1991. "Segregation City." *Chicago Reader,* 30 August, 1, 16, 18–20, 22–23, 26, 28.
Meyers, Gary S., and Don DeBat. 1990. *The Chicago House Hunt Book.* Chicago: Chicago Sun-Times.
Miller, Christopher. 1985. *Blank Darkness: Africanist Discourse in French.* Chicago: University of Chicago Press.
Mudimbe, V. Y. 1983. *The Invention of Africa: Gnosis, Philosophy, and the Order of Knowledge.* Bloomington: Indiana University Press.
Mullings, Leith, ed. 1987. *Cities of the United States: Studies in Urban Anthropology.* New York: Columbia University Press.
Murphy, John M. 1990. "'A Time of Shame and Sorrow': Robert F. Kennedy and the American Jeremiad." *Quarterly Journal of Speech* 76: 401–14.
Pennelle, Sandra. 1989. "Prices Force Families to Live Together." *News Star* (Chicago Lerner Newspaper), 8 November, sec. 2, pp. 1–2.
Quinlan, Donal G. 1991. "'Polite' Minority Finding Its Voice." *News Star* (Chicago Lerner Newspaper), 2 April, 1, 7.
Rapp, Rayna. 1987. "Urban Kinship in Contemporary America: Families, Classes, and Ideology." In *Cities of the United States. Studies in Urban Anthropology,* edited by Leith Mullings. New York: Columbia University Press.
Royer, Ariela. 1984. "Albany Park." In *Local Community Fact Book: Chicago Metropolitan Area, 1980,* edited by Chicago Fact Book Consortium. Chicago: Chicago Review Press.
Said, Edward. 1979. *Orientalism.* New York: Vintage.
Sanjek, Roger. 1990. "Urban Anthropology in the 1980's: A World View." *Annual Review of Anthropology* 19:151–86.
Scholes, Robert. 1985. *Textual Power.* New Haven, Conn.: Yale University Press.
Scott, James C. 1990. *Domination and the Arts of Resistance.* New Haven, Conn.: Yale University Press.
Shapiro, Michael J. 1988. *The Politics of Representation.* Madison: University of Wisconsin Press.
Skogan, Wesley G. 1990. *Disorder and Decline: Crime and the Spiral of Decay in American Neighborhoods.* New York: Free Press.
Sontag, Susan. 1979. *Illness as Metaphor.* New York: Vintage.
Squires, Gregory D., Larry Bennett, Kathleen McCourt, and Philip Nyden. 1987. *Chicago: Race, Class, and the Response to Urban Decline.* Philadelphia: University of Pennsylvania Press.
Stack, Carol B. 1974. *All Our Kin: Strategies for Survival in a Black Community.* New York: Harper and Row.
Stallybrass, Peter, and Allon White. 1986. *The Politics and Poetics of Transgression.* Ithaca, N.Y.: Cornell University Press.

Suttles, Gerald D. 1968. *The Social Order of the Slum.* Chicago: University of Chicago Press.
Suttles, Gerald D. 1990. *The Man-made City: The Land-Use Confidence Game in Chicago.* Chicago: University of Chicago Press.
Todorov, Tzvetan. 1984. *The Conquest of America.* New York: Harper and Row.
Turner, Victor. 1977. *The Ritual Process: Structure and Anti-Structure.* Ithaca, N.Y.: Cornell University Press.
Weaver, Richard. 1953. *The Ethics of Rhetoric.* South Bend, Ind.: Regnery Gateway.
Williams, Raymond. 1983. *Keywords: A Vocabulary of Culture and Society,* rev. ed. New York: Oxford University Press.
Wolf, Eric. 1982. *Europe and the People without History.* Berkeley: University of California Press.

Homeboys and Hoods
Gang Communication and Cultural Space

> Kings is not only like a gang, it's a family. Everybody cares about one another. You can never leave one behind. Everywhere we go we watch each other's back. We never leave nobody running behind. . . . 'Cause, see, the same way we watch their back, they're watching our back. When he (gestures toward Shadow, his friend) walks in the street and I'm walking on the other side of the street, I'm watching his back and he's watching mine. That's how we watch our own. That's the way you gotta do it. You gotta watch each other's back. We're all family, we're all Latin Kings. And see right there on the wall (points toward graffito on nearby wall) you can read over there by that crown over there with the LK—it says "Amor." And "amor" right there means love. Amor stands for a lot of things. It stands for, uh, the A stands for Almighty, the M stands for Masters, the O stands for Of, the R, Revolution—'cause that stands for Almighty Masters Of Revolution. See, amor.
>
> —LATINO BOY TALKING TO DWIGHT CONQUERGOOD ON A CHICAGO ROOFTOP (JUNE 1989)[1]

Gangs give new meaning to group communication. For gangs, *esprit de corps* is an overarching goal and much celebrated achievement of *all* communication praxis. More than a discursive context, the gang as group is a way of being in the world, both modus vivendi and moral vision. Although gangs span a remarkable range of organizational structures that vary in terms of complexity—from a neighborhood adolescent street corner society to a city-wide supergang that controls the urban drug market[2]—in-group solidarity remains a defining characteristic. For gangs, conventional typologies of communication, such as interpersonal and small group, are inadequate. I coin the term *intracommunal communication* to capture the group-centered cosmology and communitarian ethic of street gangs.

My focus on intracommunal communication practices extends Lannamann's (1991) important critique of the ideological commitment of mainstream communication research. Lannamann noted that academic research on interpersonal communication presupposes the individual as the locus of personhood, leading to a focus on cognitive operations that renders invisible the wider social and historical fields of power within which all human communication is embedded. I would add that this privileging of the individual in communication research both reflects and reifies the "ontological individualism" that Bellah et al. (1985) and Gans (1988) identified as a defining characteristic of middle-class America.[3] Indeed, the intensely communal ethos of gangs threatens bourgeois individualism and accounts for the anxiety-ridden demonizing of them in media images of the "pack," the "mob," and "wilding" group—middle-class nightmares of communalism run amok (see Conquergood, 1992a).[4]

Cultural Communication of Gangs

Anthropologist Mary Douglas (1982a) argued for a dynamic, communication-centered understanding of social formations that are constituted and sustained by appeals to the greater value of the group, as opposed to those that are premised on the sanctity of individualism:

> Every time a member appeals successfully to the paramount need to ensure the survival of the group, its being in existence can be used as a more powerful justification for controlling individuals. . . . Each basic principle, the value of the group, the value of the individual, is the point of reference that justifies action of a potentially generative kind. (Douglas 1982a, 198)

Douglas critiqued "passive voice theories" that construe culture as a static entity floating above the everyday communicative interactions, arguments, and rhetorical struggles of living people "who actively make their own environment" (Douglas 1982a, 1, 189). She reconceptualized culture "in the active voice": Culture is both the fecund residue of past communicative interactions and the dynamic resource for ongoing communicative activities; in other words, meanings are both "deeply embedded [in history] and context-bound," and they are dynamically "generated, caught, and transformed" (Douglas 1982a, 189).

Communication practices of "real live human beings" become the crucible of culture—the generative site where culture gets made and remade. As Douglas explained:

> For the cognitive activity of the real live individual is largely devoted to building the culture, patching it here and trimming it there, according to the exigencies of the day. In his [or her] very negotiating activity, each is forcing culture down the throats of his [or her] fellow-[wo]men. When individuals transact, their medium of exchange is in units of culture. (Douglas 1982a, 189)

The virtue of Douglas' theory of culture is that it restores agency to individual actors as they negotiate their everyday world, while providing a communication-centered framework for understanding how individuals become predisposed to act in culturally patterned ways—what she calls "cultural bias." She is interested in comparative discursive configurations of cultural bias produced by:

> moral judgments, excuses, complaints and shifts of interest reckoned as the spoken justifications by individuals of the action they feel required to take. As their subjective perception of the scene and its moral implications emanates from each of them individually, it constitutes a collective moral consciousness about [wo] man and his [or her] place in the universe. The interaction of individual subjects produces a public cosmology capable of being internalized in the consciousness of individuals, if they decide to accept and stay with it. (Douglas 1982a, 199–200)

Douglas (1982a, 1982b) set forth a grand typology of four cultural contexts, and compared and contrasted their distinguishing moral visions and cosmological biases: rugged individualists, isolated insulates, hierarchical organization members, and bonded communitarians (commitment to the group is strongest with bonded communitarians).

Clearly, gangs are exemplars of the bonded communitarians. Their communication pulls against the dominant cultural bias of competitive individualism in the larger society. Celebrations of interconnectedness and rituals of "phatic communion" (Burke 1984) create these strong attachments. The street aphorism, "Hook up or pull up" ("pull up" in street argot means "to leave," "depart," "make an exit") stands in contradistinction to the middle-class enjoinder "Pull yourself up by your bootstraps." The street saying projects a view of the social world as a web of interconnections, whereas the latter references a vertical hierarchy of upward mobility. During the time of my fieldwork, one of my working-class neighbors from South America noted disapprovingly that "American [middle-class] culture is a do-it-yourself tool-kit." Contrast middle-class self-reliance with Latino Boy's affirmations about the communal, familial caring and nurturance of gang culture as echoed and elaborated by another young Chicago gang member quoted by sociologist Padilla (1992):

> We call ourselves a family, but, you know, when you really think about it we're also a team. And if you want to lose, play alone. . . . Myself, I have gotten busted by the police several times because I was alone. I couldn't see them coming. When you're with your boys you have more eyes to check out what's going on—you can see the cops; you can see the opposition. But when you are by yourself sometimes you feel scared. . . . In the Diamonds we teach the young guys; *we practice how to be together all the time* [italics added]. We think that that's our strength. Other people have money. We have each other. (Padilla 1992, 108)

Scarcely could one have a clearer enunciation of the communitarian ethos rooted in a social environment where self-sufficiency, individuation, and independence are dysfunctional and even dangerous.

Douglas (1982a) noted that strong-group social formations maintain their solidarity primarily by producing rhetorical visions of a hostile outside world that threatens to violate the integrity of the group. Bonded communitarians are boundary vigilant; border maintenance between in-group and out-group areas and alignments is a constant activity and source of anxiety. "The social experience of the individual," Douglas explained, "is first and foremost constrained by the external boundary maintained by the group against outsiders" (Douglas 1982a, 205).

The need to mobilize and heighten group consciousness by creating a strong boundary against the outside world accounts for the densely coded and deliberately opaque nature of gang communication. Gangs rely heavily on nonverbal channels of communication: hand signs, color of clothing, tilt of a baseball cap, brand of tennis shoes and style of lacing, whistles, visual icons (both in graffiti murals and body tattoos), mode of crossing arms, and earrings. These nonverbal channels of communication are incomprehensible to outsiders who lack the necessary "local knowledge" to decipher their meanings (Geertz 1983). Gang graffiti is inscrutable to outsiders because it draws on an elaborate system of underground symbols, icons, and logos, the nuanced meanings of which can be keyed according to certain semiotic manipulations: inversions, reversals, and fractures. Middle-class citizens driving through the so-called "inner city" look at a graffiti-covered wall as meaningless gibberish and a sign of social disorder, whereas the local homeboys look at the same graffiti mural and appreciate the complex meanings and messages it artfully conveys. Instead of a mindless mess, gang graffiti, at least in the Chicago neighborhoods where I have conducted research, display an efflorescence of semiosis (see Conquergood 1992a).[5]

The verbal communication of gangs is likewise coded in a variety of ways so that meanings are camouflaged. Gangs draw richly on street slang, a class-marked discourse that already sets them apart from mainstream "respectability." In addition, they develop a special argot and set of shibboleths peculiar to gangs, with certain terms and phrases that circulate only within specific gangs. Examples include *violation,* shortened typically to V, as in take your V, a term referring to intragang discipline, the administering of corporal punishment for infractions of the gang's cultural norms, and during rites of initiation into gang membership. In Chicago, the Vice Lords, one of the oldest and largest supergangs, use *All is well* as their password, whereas their archrivals, the Disciples, use *All is one.* The "What you be about?" challenge is the verbal equivalent of throwing down the gauntlet, whereby a gang member when encountering a suspected rival on unfamiliar territory demands that he or she declare gang allegiance. Much more than a simple question, "What you be about?" uttered in a hostile, intimidating tone is often the prelude to a fight, and functions communicatively as what Austin (1962) called a "performative utterance."

A common rite of greeting and leave-taking among Chicago's Latin Kings gang is to proclaim "Amor!" This, of course, is the Spanish word for *love,* but as Latino Boy explained in the epigraph to this chapter it is also an acronym for Almighty Masters Of Revolution. The complete title for the gang, Almighty Latin Kings Nation, is a complicated acronym that stands for the following:

> *A* *L*ove *M*easured *I*n *G*reat *H*armony *T*owards *Y*ahve
> *L*atin *A*merican *T*ribe *I*lluminating *N*atural
> *K*nowledge, *I*ndestructible *N*obility and *G*lowing *S*trength
> *N*atural *A*llies *T*ogether *I*n *O*ne *N*ucleus

The Black Gangster Disciples identify themselves as BOS, standing for Brothers Of the Struggle. Secret acronyms as well as special argot are thus developed and designed precisely to circumscribe group boundaries, heighten in-group consciousness, and exclude outsiders.

The most verbally explicit written genre of gang communication—the underground manifestos and charters that spell out the rules, rituals, and symbolism for each gang—are guarded carefully and hidden from the gaze of the uninitiated. It was only after 3 years of intense participant-observation fieldwork that I earned the rapport to be shown one of these secret documents. The first of these typescript manuscripts I saw had a handwritten proscription encircled at the top of the title page: "For real _______ [name of gang] only." One of the "laws" set forth in the manifesto underscores the role of communication in sustaining a tight external boundary: "Nation affairs are to be kept within the Nation and are not [to] be discussed in the presence of anyone outside the Nation." Another "law" also proscribes communication and attests to the fact that members know that "gangs" have become a highly saleable media commodity: "No member shall conduct an interview with any person from the news media concerning Nation affairs without the approval of the ________ [respected leaders]." In the constitution of another large Chicago gang, the first law likewise concerns communication boundaries and sets forth what de Certeau (1986) called the "politics of silence": "All members must respect and participate in maintaining a code of silence within our family" (de Certeau 1986, 225).[6]

The need for silence, secrecy, and circumspection is intensified because the line between insiders and outsiders is slippery and shifting. Once one looks closely at gangs, it becomes evident that borders are constructed on multiple and mobile fronts. Actually, borders absolutely criss-cross the entire domain of gang culture because gangs set themselves apart from mainstream society, as well as from one another. Intergang conflict and border disputes over turf heighten and intensify the boundary anxiety and vigilance between and among gangs, and all this takes place within the larger context of outside surveillance and hostility from police and other agents of civil society. Bakhtin's (1990) radical rethinking and resituating of culture along boundaries and borders instead of organic centers is a remarkably apt spatial image for understanding the dynamics of gang cultural processes:[7]

> A cultural domain has no inner territory. It is located entirely along boundaries, boundaries intersect it everywhere, passing through each of its constituent features. The systematic unity of culture passes into the atoms of cultural life—like the sun, it is re-

> flected in every drop of this life. Every cultural act lives essentially on the boundaries, and it derives its seriousness and significance from this fact. Separated by abstraction from these boundaries, it loses the ground of its being and becomes vacuous, arrogant; it degenerates and dies. (Bakhtin 1990, 274)

In the following section, I map some of the principal boundaries and intersections that constitute gang cultures.

Organizational Linkages and Gang Systems

One of the benefits of studying natural groups at ground level is an ability to capture structural complexities, transformations, and processual dynamics that would not be manifest in zero-history, "ad hoc groups manufactured from classroom students" for academic research (Fisher 1978, 230). Gangs have been studied both as organizations (e.g., Jankowski 1991; Padilla 1992) and groups (e.g., Miller 1980; Morash 1983; Short & Strodtbeck 1974; Vigil 1988a). Indeed, struggles over definitions of what constitutes a gang are still engaged in the scholarly literature (Horowitz 1990). Instead of *either* an organization or a group process, I argue that gangs are *both.* Gangs are complex border cultures that at any given moment in time slide between the categories of *organization* and *small group.* It is that slide along this continuum that distinguishes gang experience. I believe the definitional arguments say more about a given researcher's theoretical and methodological focus than the realities of gang life. For example, Jankowski (1991) studied 37 gangs in three cities, so it makes sense that he focused on macrostructures of gangs as hierarchical organizations with entrepreneurial goals. On the other hand, Vigil (1988a, 1988b) drew on his own personal experience of growing up in a Los Angeles barrio to deepen his participant-observation research of barrio gangs, which explains why he picked up on the microdynamics and group processes of gang experience. Interestingly, both Jankowski and Vigil researched gangs in Los Angeles during approximately the same time period. I attribute their contrasting definitions of gangs to their different perspectives, which predisposes them to pick up qualities of gang life at different points between the organization-group continuum.

Although here I emphasize the small group dimension of gangs, I hope to make clear that the face-to-face familiarities of the street-corner homeboys are embedded within, enabled, and energized by the organizational resources of the supergang confederations—the "gang nations" to which they are linked or "hooked up." In Chicago, there are two major confederations of gangs: People and Folks. These supragang alliances developed in the Illinois prison system during the early 1980s in an attempt to minimize factionalism and intergang warfare. Instead of scores of street gangs all fighting one another for turf and honor, two major coalitions were consolidated to absorb all the internecine hostilities and rearticulate them along one fundamental Us/Them divide: the symbolically constructed border between People and Folks. The Folks Nation is composed of (a) the Black Gangster Disciple Nation, the largest Chicago street gang; (b) the Simon City Royals, one of the oldest White gangs; (c) the Maniac Latin Disciples; and (d) several other street gangs. The People Nation is composed of (a) Vice Lords, the oldest and one of the largest gangs in Chicago; (b) the Latin Kings, the oldest and largest Latino gang; (c) the Gaylords, a White gang; and (d) several others (see Table 1).

This organization of all Chicago street gangs into two grand gang nations in the early 1980s was anticipated a decade earlier: Jeff Fort, leader of the Blackstone Rangers street gang, organized several African-American gangs on Chicago's South Side into the Black Peace Stone Nation, referred to commonly as the Black P Stone Nation. Here again, the goal was to reduce conflict by forging solidarity among several gang factions. In response to the greatly expanded and consolidated power of the Black P Stone Nation, the Black Disciples likewise forged a coalition with several other gangs to create the Black Gangster Disciple Nation under

Table 1. Chicago Street Gangs Aligned with Nation

People Nation	*Folks Nation*
Latin Kings	Black Gangster Disciples
Vice Kings	Simon City Royals
Bishops	Ambrose
Gaylords	Ashland Vikings
Insane Unknowns	Braziers
Latin Counts	Imperial Gangsters
Latin Saints	Insane Popes
Cobrastones	La Raza
Pachucos	Latin Eagles
Future Puerto Rican Stones	Latin Lovers
Spanish Lords	Maniac Latin Disciples
	Orchestra Albany
	Party People
	Spanish Cobras
	Two Sixers

Note: This list is selective, not comprehensive. The four largest street gangs in Chicago are Black Gangster Disciples, Vice Lords, Latin Kings, and Simon City Royals.

the leadership of David Barksdale. The emergence of these two major coalitions during the late 1960s and early 1970s signaled a shift in self-identification from street gang to "nation," and reflected the revolutionary rhetoric of the times.

I want to emphasize that the boundary between People and Folks Nations is constructed symbolically. It is not based on race, ethnicity, or major geographic area (i.e., Chicago was not divided into South Side for Folks Nation and North Side for People Nation). Although branches of gangs certainly are territorially based, my point is that both People Nation and Folks Nation gang branches are distributed throughout the city, thus making Chicago a patchwork quilt of continuously alternating Nation turf. Most remarkably, the organization of all street gangs into one of two Nations cuts across and subsumes race and ethnicity. Both Nations are multiracial and multiethnic ensembles. A look at the histories of some of these gangs underscores the extraordinary integrative achievement of the Nation confederations. As noted earlier, one of the oldest and largest White gangs, the Simon City Royals, forged solidarity with the Black Gangster Disciple Nation in the formation of the Folks Nation. However, another long-standing White gang, the Gaylords, did not join the Simon City Royals in lining up under the Folks Nation. Instead, the Gaylords aligned with the People Nation, and thus became major allies of the Latin Kings. This alignment is all the more remarkable given the racist history of the Gaylords: Their gang name is an acronym standing for Great American Youth Love Our Race Destroy Spics. Now the Gaylords join their People Nation confederates the Latin Kings and the Future Puerto Rican Stones to fight the Folks-aligned Popes, another historically White gang whose name, like the Gaylords, is a racist acronym: Protect Our People Eliminate Spics. In these internation fights, the Popes are backed up by their Folks compatriots: the Spanish Cobras and the Latin Eagles.

The next level of organization, after the Nation confederations and special multigang alliances, is that of the gangs themselves.[8] Individual gangs can range in size from 6 to more than 1,000 members. Many gangs now affix Nation to their title. In some cases this acknowledges the size and scale of organizational complexity of a gang (e.g., the Almighty Latin King Nation), whereas in other cases it is simply self-aggrandizing (e.g., Pee Wee Future Puerto Rican Stones Nation). Whereas the People versus Folks alignment determines coalition partners and fighting allies, the particular gang is the primary source of social symbolism, identification, and meaningfulness for gang members. The larger gangs have the organizational savvy to know that people are mobilized best in units small enough to encompass co-residence, which provides frequent face-to-face interactions. Therefore, the large gangs subdivide into multiple branches, also called *sections* or *chapters*. The primary unit in Chicago's gang organization is the turf-based branch, named after the street corner where the local homeboys hang out. As soon as a branch grows too large to accommodate the face-to-face intimacies that are the highly prized and defining quality of gang life, it subdivides into more manageable units, typically no more than 50 "heads" (members).[9] For example, the Almighty Latin King Nation embraces more than a dozen branches, each one named after the intersection that serves as the focal point for that turf: Lawrence/Kedzie Kings, Beach/Spaulding Kings, Columbia/Ashland Kings, Montrose/Paulina Kings, Rockwell/Leland Kings, Whipple/Wabansia Kings, Berwyn/Winthrop Kings, Clark/Bryn Mawr Kings, Broadway/Winona Kings, Lawrence/Washtenau Kings, Leavitt/Schiller Kings, and so forth. Each branch uses the colors and iconography of the gang. The Latin Kings branches use black and gold colors and a five-point crown, which follows the overall Nation symbology and numerology. All People use a cross with two dots; inverted pitchforks; the left side of the body in nonverbal communication; and number five in graffiti (either explicitly, e.g., "5," or in icons of five-point stars and five-point crowns), throwing up one hand with five fingers spread, lacing up five eyelets of tennis shoes, and so forth.

Each branch has its own set of officers, and it exercises a great deal of autonomy in the day-to-day activities of the homeboys. The gang manifestos and constitutions referred to previously are designed to share traditions and assure continuity across multiple sections. Some of them contain charts of the organizational structure of the gang, delineating hierarchies of power and various roles. These include, in the case of Latin Kings, the offices of Incas, Coronas, Caciques, and Crown Councils. Other gangs name their officers Chairman, Governor, Lieutenant Governor, Ambassador, and so forth. The most common leadership title at the branch level is Prez, short for President. Typically, there is more flexibility in the leadership structure at the level of the branch than at the gang level. Academics might be surprised to know that these underground documents contain sound advice about organizational communication. Here are some examples: "No one person should be required to manage more than six (6) to ten (10) members." Most manifestos encourage adaptive flexibility at the level of branch/section: "There is no ideal organizational structure that fits the needs of every single [branch]. . . .

Whatever structure you finally choose, let it be flexible enough to accommodate the growth of your section. . . . Don't be afraid to change your structure when it is necessary."

All these documents also emphasize the centrality of communication. One gang charter actually has a subsection titled "Communication and Meetings"[10]:

> If you don't communicate effectively, you won't lead effectively. Leadership involves getting things done through people. How well you do this, this will be determined by your ability to communicate. You have to look upon communication as your most valuable asset, other than your own personal communication methods there is one primary way that a section can communicate with its members. The primary way is through: Meetings!

These written documents inscribe what I hear on the streets. Mex, one of my neighbors in the Big Red tenement where I lived for the first 20 months of my fieldwork, explained: "It's all organization and communication. You gotta have communication" (see Conqucrgood 1992b).

The branch or section is the generative center of gang life, and the texture of everyday experience for the homeboys of a local branch is constituted by interactive group processes. A Latin King shows respect to all Latin Kings from every branch, but the real blood-brother bonding is cemented within the shared space of the "hood." Recall the quote of the young gang member cited earlier: "In the Diamonds, we teach the young guys: *we practice how to be together all the time* [italics added]" (Padilla 1992, 108). This quote points to the importance of generational boundaries within branches. Several age cohorts with separate and overlapping responsibilities are nested within a gang branch. They are identified by names such as Seniors (over 20), Juniors (late teens), Pee Wees (14–16), Shorties (12–13), and Wannabes (10–11). Younger cohorts of gangs also are called Futures, and Baby, as in Baby Kings, Baby Cobras, and so forth. An age cohort is often initiated, "V'd in," as a group, given its own set of leaders (e.g., the Prez [president] of the Lawrence and Kedzie Pee Wee Latin Kings), thus appropriating and strengthening the bond that age-mates already share. Differences in age are sometimes the source of tensions within the hood, just as they are in the larger society. A member of an older cohort once complained to me about the immaturity of the Pee Wees: "These young bloods be messin' up the neighborhood. They're crazy, too wild, starting trouble all the time. Then we have to take care of it. They be nothing but trouble." However, the age sets within a branch enable intense cross-cohort bonding. Older gang members form powerful mentoring relationships with the Shorties and young bloods. The Latin Kings name this relationship as "making a King," and I heard one Senior announce with pride, "Shadow's my boy—I made him a King." These cross-cohort bonds provide status and respect for the older partner, and attention, guidance, and nurturance for the Shorties.

The microunit of gang structure is the clique—the tight bond between two or three members of a cohort that is inseparable. One can be a member of more than one clique, and these cliques, like all close friendships, can change and reconfigure over time. Although these dyads and triads are not formal units of gang structure, their existence nonetheless is marked by informal talk and joking. People on the streets acknowledge this special relationship: "You looking for Richie? Find Little Man, he'll be with Little Man." Sometimes the clique partners are teased good-naturedly and referred to jokingly as "girlfriends." Partners make metarelational references, such as "Ghetto Boy—he's my homey, my homz, he's my main man—I'm down for that brother."

Gangs need to be understood as large systems of multiple embedded and mutually implicated units, each one impinging and shaping the contours of experience for all the others (see Fig. 1). With permeable boundaries and interdependence with immediate context, gangs are exemplars of what Putnam and Stohl (1990) called "bona fide groups." The fundamental external boundary is the hostility-charged border between People and Folks Nations. However, my point in mapping the larger gang system is to reveal all the intricate intersections and boundaries of difference *inside* Nations that constitute and crisscross identities. Latin Kings and Vice Lords are both lead gangs in the People N: They "ride" together, but at the same time they are different. It is important both to signal solidarity with one another while simultaneously negotiating their own ramified boundaries. It is not unusual for tensions to erupt sometimes between gangs of the same nation. During 1988–1989, fighting broke out between the La Raza and Ambrose gangs, both members of the Folks Nation. The dispute escalated into a war that drew in the Two Sixers and the Party People gangs on the side of La Raza, and the Satan Disciples on the side of Ambrose. I want to emphasize that all five Chicago gangs embroiled in the conflict were members of the Folks Nation.

There are also internal tensions and occasional rivalries among the various branches within the same gang. Some street gangs originated as breakaway sections from established gangs. For example, the Spanish Cobras broke from the Maniac Latin Disciples, and the Future Puerto Rican Stones away from the Latin Kings. Each branch contests for pride

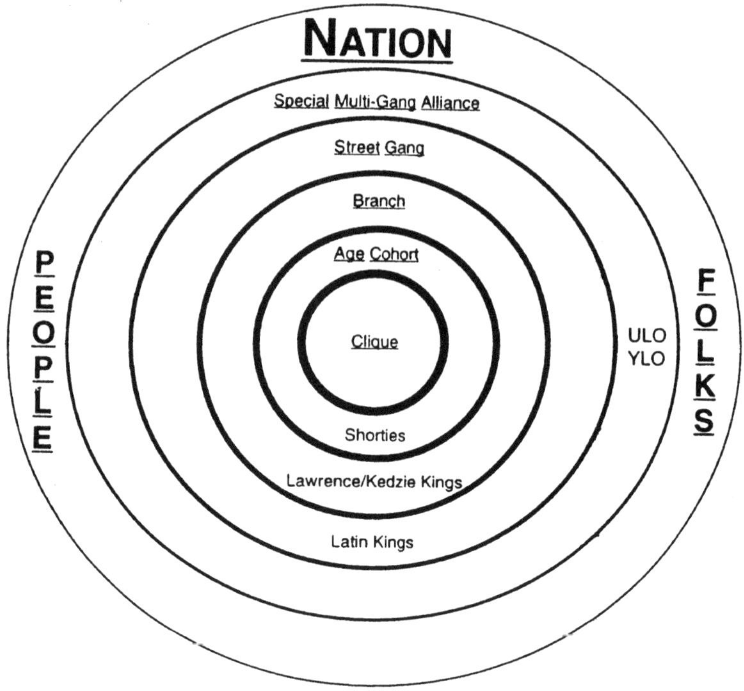

Figure 1: The gang system

of place within overall reputation of the gang. Because the branch is the heart of gang life and the site of primary loyalty and affection, gang members often code graffiti displays to designate their specific branch affiliation, in addition to their gang identification. In the hood of the Lawrence and Kedzie branch of the Latin Kings where I lived during most of my fieldwork, I frequently saw graffiti from other Latin King branches. That is not the same kind of insult as when a rival Folks gang entered the hood and "splashed" the walls, but it is a bit of a boundary transgression.

It is not uncommon for gang members to switch allegiance from one branch to another within the same gang. This border-crossing practice is called "turning sections." From time to time gang members also change gangs. This is relatively unproblematic as long as the new gang is, of course, a member of the same Nation. These transfers between gangs come about typically as a result of a gang member's family moving to another neighborhood. I also know individual gang members who have changed from Folks to People Nation gangs, and vice versa. This practice, unlike turning sections, is an unspeakable transgression of the fundamental binary opposition on which gang identity pivots, and therefore cannot be countenanced. Such major threshold crossings are deep, closely guarded, dangerous secrets. I am sure that my confidantes felt safe to unburden themselves with me only because of my liminal relationship to gang culture. Because I know a great deal about gangs, I can serve as an appreciative audience able to absorb the full impact of these dramatic self-disclosures. At the same time, I am not a part of the culture: As participant-observer ethnographer I am both insider and outsider. An even more radical border crossing takes place when entire gangs switch affiliation between Nations. At one time the Latin Saints were a Folks gang (originally a breakaway gang from the Spanish Cobras) that changed to People. During the summer of 1991, the Insane Deuces switched from People to Folks as a result of their intranation fighting with the Latin Kings. Unlike individual crossovers, when an entire gang switches Nation allegiance it is a public act that is discussed widely, with repercussions for the entire gang system.

To convey the dynamism and volatility within the overall gang system, I summarize the life cycle of one particular group with which I have been involved throughout the course of my fieldwork. I moved into the Big Red tenement in December 1987. The exterior walls and the interior stairwells were inscribed with graffiti proclaiming that Big Red was in the heart of Latin King turf, specifically the Lawrence/Kedzie branch of the Almighty Latin King Nation. There were other affiliate People gangs, such as the Assyrian Eagles and the Future Puerto Rican Stones, whose turf overlapped with that of the Lawrence and Kedzie Kings. After a few months, new graffiti, LNN, which stood for the Latin Knights Nation, a new gang (they substituted N for the K of Knights to differentiate their logo from the Latin Kings), started appearing on neighborhood walls. The Latin Knights were an emergent gang, a loose collection of more than a dozen local 14-year-old Mexican, Puerto Rican, Assyrian, African American, and White youths all constellated around a charismatic 17-year-old leader. The Latin Knights were associated closely with the Latin Kings. They adopted the Latin King handshake and crown symbolism, but sustained their own LNN graffiti. By the summer of 1988, they had ordered their own custom-made Latin Knights baseball caps.

In October 1988, the Latin Kings were hanging out in the park with several Latin Knights when they were attacked allegedly by the Simon City Royals, whose hood is just to the north. Two Kings were wounded, and a third youth, who was not a King and just socializing with them, was killed during the attack. This killing sent shock waves through the community that resulted in the incorporation of the Latin Knights into the Lawrence and Kedzie Kings. On December 9, 1988, 13 of the Latin Knights were "V'd in" as Pee Wee Kings. Their charismatic leader became the prez of the Pee Wee cohort. In effect, the Latin Knights were a "wannabe" gang, an imitation of formal street gangs without the ensuing responsibilities of a full-fledged gang. It had provided a liminal space for neighborhood youths to experiment and play with gang symbolism and traditions without a full commitment to the larger system. The Latin Kings in the area were not very pleased about the prospect of sharing the neighborhood with another gang, even a friendly one that emulated them. However, the killing in the park created a crisis that clarified and consolidated boundaries. The Latin Knights saw the advantage of relinquishing their autonomy and joining a larger established group, while the Lawrence/Kedzie Kings seized this opportunity to deal with the mildly annoying presence of the Knights by incorporating them in toto as a Pee Wee cohort.

This Pee Wee cohort became very active and assertive within the branch, and soon began to chafe under what they perceived as the stodginess of older gang members. By the summer of 1990, there was increasing generational tension within the Lawrence/Kedzie branch. As early as the summer of 1989, I began noticing graffiti announcing a new Whipple/Ainslie branch of the Latin Kings (see Fig. 2). Whipple and Ainslie is a street corner in back of the Big Red tenement where I lived. Thus, it looked like the Lawrence/Kedzie branch was splitting in half, with Big Red situated on the fault line. However, this fission was prevented by skillful mediation within the branch across cohorts. The cohorts united in common struggle against the Insane Popes, the enemy Folks gang on their eastern boundary. They invaded and conquered a portion of the Popes' territory, thereby extending the Latin Kings' turf two blocks east. Most importantly, the border war against the Popes gang absorbed internal tensions and consolidated the Lawrence/Kedzie branch of the Latin Kings.

In May 1991, a minor war broke out between the Lawrence/Kedzie Kings and the Future Puerto Rican Stones with whom they had cohabited for years. Latin Kings and Future Puerto Rican Stones' graffiti would often be displayed side by side on the same walls. A single family might include one brother who belonged to the Kings and another brother who belonged to the Stones. However, in early May 1991, a King disrespected the girlfriend of a Stone, inciting the Stone to shoot out the windows of the apartment building where the King lived. This incident escalated quickly into a war. Recall that the Future Puerto Rican Stones had originated as a breakaway branch from the Latin Kings more than

Figure 2: In addition to the tattoos and graffiti, this Latin King is reppin' to the left—the privileged side of the body for all People Nation gangs—by crossing his right hand over his left wrist. This specific mode of reppin' is called "crossing up," and can be performed in another way by crossing the right hand over the torso so that it grasps the left upper arm. Folks Nation gangs rep to the right. (Photo by Dwight Conquergood: Courtesy of Northwestern University Archives)

a decade ago, and no doubt old tensions and imperfectly resolved issues from the past resurfaced during this breach. There was intense fighting within the branch during most of May, with several exchanges of gunfire, but fortunately no one was killed, and only one person received a minor wound in the leg. What is interesting about this crisis once again is the way it clarified and realigned boundaries. Several members of the original Latin Knights who had become Pee Wees impatient with the older Latin Kings had drifted over to the Stones. Before the war, this slippage was not very remarkable because the Stones and the Kings of the Lawrence/Kedzie branch are "tight"—they "ride together." However, the war forced people to take sides, and everyone remarked particularly about the Kings-turned-Stones who were now shooting at Kings. The charismatic leader of the original Latin Knights was one of these frustrated Kings who, as prez of the Pee Wee cohort, had led the movement to create his own Whipple/Ainslie branch. After that failed, he turned Stone. By the end of May, a truce was negotiated. Because no one on either side had been killed, it was relatively easy for both sides to resolve the dispute in a face-saving way.

I provide this historical detail about the processual dynamics within one branch of the larger gang system to make the point that borders and boundaries are continuously negotiated, clarified, reconstructed, and contested. Examined at the microlevel of everyday interaction, the gang system is more like a dynamic zone of contest and struggle than a fixed, static, hierarchical structure.

Gangs and Cultural Space

The heart of gang life, the branch, is what Turner (1982) called a "star group"—the group "with which a person identifies most deeply and in which he [or she] finds fulfillment of his [or her] major social and personal strivings and desires" (69). Embedded within a larger system, the branch provides an encircling web of support, attachment, and solidarity against a hostile world. The group is galvanized communicatively through the figurative and physical deployment of space (see Lefebvre, 1991). Every branch is rooted in a clearly bounded territory called the hood. For example, the Lawrence/Kedzie branch of the Latin Kings inhabits the neighborhood of Chicago bounded by Foster Street to the north, Montrose Street to the south, the north branch of the Chicago River to the east, and Kimball Street to the west. Within this territory, particularly near the boundaries, graffiti announce self-consciously, "LK Camp," "This is King's World" (see Fig. 2). The communicative task of the gang group is to transform marginal, somewhat forbidding urban space into a hood to make a world of meaning, familiarity, adventure, and affective intensity through ritual, symbol, and dramaturgy.

Carey's (1989) view of communication as ritual is particularly helpful for understanding the intracommunal cultural practices of gangs. For Carey "communication is a symbolic process whereby reality is produced, maintained, repaired, and transformed" (23). Through communication we "produce the world by symbolic work and then *take up residence* [italics added] in the world so produced" (85). I am struck by Carey's analogy between ritual communication and homemaking, inhabiting, "tak[ing] up residence." Carey is not alone in using the metaphors of *home* and *habitation* when theorizing about cultural communication. de Certeau (1984) wrote evocatively about the everyday practices of marginal people struggling to cope within forbidding social structures as "dwelling," making a "dwelling place" within dominant space. Bourdieu (1977) developed his complex cultural theory around the idea of "habitus." hooks (1990) wrote about the task of "making homeplace" as the construction and maintenance of "spaces of care and nurturance" (42). Bachelard (1969) argued that the image of "the house is one of the greatest powers of integration for the thoughts, memories and dreams of [wo]mankind . . . It is body and soul. It is the human being's first world. Before he [or she] is 'cast into the world,' . . . [wo]man is laid in the cradle of the house" (6–7).

Gang youth articulate and experience their hood through imagery of home and family. They name themselves *homeboys, homeys, homz, bloods,* and the preferred term of intracommunal address is *bro,* short for brother. Bro is a term of endearment, communitas, an expression of "we feeling," asserting that you are an extension of myself (see Turner, 1977). Powerfully significant, this term marks a move to trust and intimacy, and it is not used idly. I moved into Big Red mid-December 1987, but it was June 14, 1988, before anyone addressed me as "bro." It took 6 months of intensely participative fieldwork to earn the trust signified by this relational marker. However, once one has earned this epithet, it is used liberally to lend emotional warmth as well as stylistic rhythm to verbal exchanges: "Hey bro, anybody steal your bicycle, bro, you tell us, bro, we'll get it back for you, bro. Hey bro, we'll even get you a better one."

Most outsiders, whose image of gangs is shaped by media demonology, would be surprised to hear the preponderance of gang terms rooted in nurturance and domestic tenderness. The entire hood is symbolized as a homeplace filled with bros and bloods, with specific apartments and domiciles referred to as "cribs" and "cradles." The nicknames that gang members give themselves and one another alternate between menacing and affectionate epithets. For every Hit Man and Pit Bull nickname there is a long line of Spanky, Teddy Bear, Baby Face, Hush Puppie, Kool Aid, Little Man, Pee Wee, Polio, and other diminutives. The hood is imagined as a space of warmth and well-being.

The key term in gang communication is reppin', short for representing. It refers to a repertoire of communication practices whereby gang members enact, and thereby constitute, their gang identity. Reppin' encompasses everything from wearing the signifying gang colors, throwing up hand signs, and calling out code words to inscribing elaborate graffiti murals (see Figs. 2–10). However, there is a deeper meaning undergirding all of these representations. As one neighbor explained to me, "It is throwing up your love—it is all about love." I quote from one of the underground manifestos: "Our struggle is to show love to each other. . . .

Figure 3: Street gangs inscribe the urban landscape with elaborate, complex, and deeply meaningful symbolism. The bodies of gang members, in addition to urban walls, are important sites for these signifying practices. Here, Ghetto Boy reps his identity by hand signing (throwing down the Folks Nation with a digital icon of an upside-down pitchfork) and by wearing his baseball cap with the bill raked to the left. The cap can be worn with the tilted bill in front or back, but the back position intensifies the rep. Also, the strength of a rep is calibrated by the degree of the angle (e.g., a slight tilt to the left is interpreted as not as strong [audacious] as a wide angle rake to the left). (Photo by Dwight Conquergood: Courtesy of Northwestern University Archives)

We all understand the love and meaning behind representing. We all know who we are, and what we stand for. If in any place or situation you cannot represent, well, we know one doesn't have to hit his chest to be 100% loyal to this almighty family."

The Latin Kings frequently write on walls and call out "amor," and "King Love." They say that the five points of their crown stand for Love, Honor, Obedience, Sacrifice, and Righteousness. Their manifesto enjoins members to honor and respect "the Sacred Colors" of black and gold "for they represent the people we love and live for." Reppin' truly is an example par excellence of what Burke (1984) called "secular prayer . . . *the coaching* of an attitude by the use of mimetic and verbal language" (322). The attitude that is danced continuously throughout the representational practices within the hood is that of loving commitment, bonding.

The elaborate and stylized rites of handshaking—much more developed than the perfunctory middle-class two and one-half pumps—enact performatively this blood-brother bonding. Most gangs in Chicago have their own specific and elaborately choreographed rites of handshaking. For example, the Latin Kings "shake on the crown"; the crown, of course, is the centerpiece of their iconography (see Fig. 4). "Shaking on the crown" entails a graceful series of coper-formed hand gestures that represent digitally the Latin King crown. These choreographed handshakes, performed both as rites of greeting and leave-taking, often include a kiss of the coparticipants' fingertips joined to form the crown (see Fig. 6). These rites culminate in both partners throwing their right fist on their "heart" (chest), kissing their fingertips, and then tapping their heart with tips of fingers extended in the shape of a crown. Called the "national salute," this performance can be repeated a dozen times in the course of traversing a single block if many brothers happen to be out on the streets. The manifesto has a section entitled "National Salute": "A fist upon our heart, it means, "I DIE FOR YOU" for you are flesh of my flesh, blood of my blood, son of my mother who is the Universal Nature and follower of Yahve who is the Almighty King of Kings; it also means Love—Strength—Sacrifice."

As a participant-observer, I have firsthand experience with how these rituals of phatic communion texture street life into a tightly knit fabric of familiarity. It sometimes has taken me an hour just to walk a few blocks to the bus stop, particularly on weekend evenings when all the brothers, sisters, and local characters are out on the streets, seeing and being seen, acknowledging one another's presence, and self-consciously commenting on and thereby cementing relationships. Even if you have seen someone the day before, or earlier in the same day, you perform these rites of affiliation all over again. Not to do so is to commit one of the cardinal sins of life in the hood: disrespect. In a mainstream world where residents of the inner city have been marginalized socioeconomically and stripped of human dignity, the reciprocal courtesies of street politesse help restore respect, repair the loss of face, and redress the daily humiliations of poverty and prejudice.

The social indignities and status deprivations that the homeboys and other low-income people endure when they venture into mainstream society *as* bus boys, dishwashers, janitors, and common laborers are more fearsome than physical suffering or death. The *Latin King Manifesto*

Figure 4: Two versions of the "throwing the crown" rep. The youth on the upper ledge combines a digital three-point crown with a "crossing up" to the left side of his body. The youth on the lower level performs a two-hand variant of "throwing up the crown." Note also his baseball cap tilted to the left, his left foot "turned out" to the left, and his Converse high-top tennis shoes. The Converse brand is popular with People Nation gangs because of the five-point star logo on the heel. (Photo by Dwight Conquergood: Courtesy of Northwestern University Archives)

includes a section entitled "Fearlessness," which speaks to the need of "freedom from such fears as hunger, *humiliation* [italics added], wrath and criticism of others." The fear of hunger points to the real material needs of this community, but I find it most interesting that hunger is followed immediately by humiliation, which points to social indignities and denigrating communication processes. "Physical death" is actually last on this list of fears. My reading of the manifesto corroborates my field observations, where fear of losing face or the social death of erasure equals and sometimes overrides the real physical dangers of the streets. Within this context of stigmatizing poverty and prejudice, *disrespect,* a term loaded with intensely charged meanings, is a breach of the cherished norms of restorative warmth and reciprocal affirmations of self-

Figure 5: An elaborate death mural displayed to commemorate the killing of a 16-year-old Guatemalan youth who was beaten to death in an alley not far from this site. (Photo by Dwight Conquergood: Courtesy of Northwestern University Archives)

worth. The manifesto of another Chicago gang spells out this principle: "Disrespect is a very serious violation of the principals [sic] of law of our amalgamated Order,—and will be judged according[ly]. Therefore, it will not be tolerated." I once observed one of my Latin King neighbors approach another homeboy, put his arm around his neck, and apologize: "Was I disrespecting you last night, bro? I'm sorry, man. I was wasted [drunk]. I'm sorry, bro."

A particular form of disrespect is to "leave me hanging." To leave someone hanging refers specifically to the failure to return a handshake (because one has not seen the extended hand) and coperform these manual choreographies, and, more evocatively, to fail to weave someone into the intracommunal webs of talk and sociability that keep people "hooked up." Just as homeboys "watch each other's back" and "never leave nobody running behind" when physically running on the streets, they likewise "look out" for one another communicatively, always taking care that everyone is included in the loop. When I thanked my friend Roadrunner

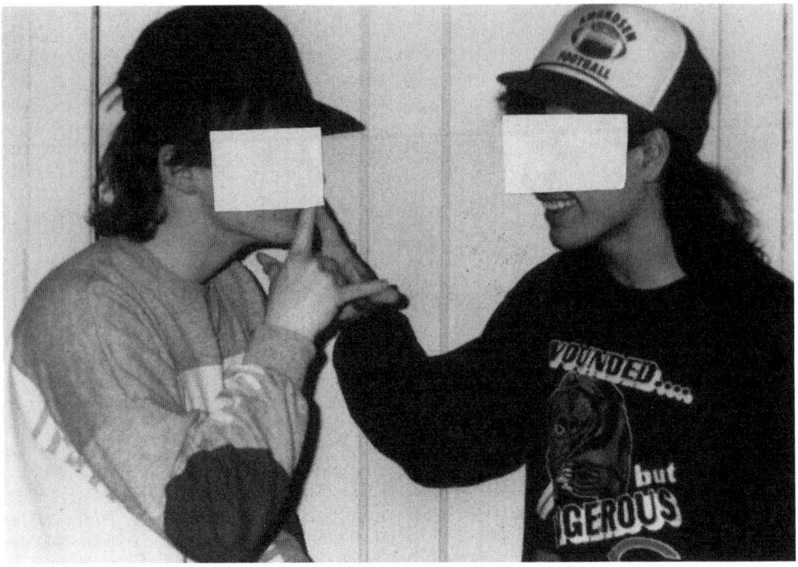

Figure 6: No biological brothers could be closer than these two Latin Kings who are "shaking on the crown." This particular clique demonstrates the cross-ethnic bonding. The youth on the left is White, his *bro* on the right is Mexican. (Photo by Dwight Conquergood: Courtesy of Northwestern University Archives)

for follow-up information, he responded metaphatically: "Sure, Dwight, I wouldn't leave you hanging." One keeps hooked up through communication that provides "not [just] information but confirmation" of ongoing interaction and togetherness, "the sacred ceremony that draws persons together in fellowship and commonality" (Carey, 1989, 19, 43).

Gang communication is all about "keeping in touch" through the tactile talk of handshakes and the metaphatic rites of "hanging out" on the corner, "hanging together," and "being together," "being tight" (as in tightly connected, not tight with your money). As an ethnographer, particularly during the first 3 years of fieldwork, it was important for me to be out on the streets in order to get enmeshed in the daily dramas of the neighborhood. Periodically I had to withdraw from the streets to write papers and attend conferences. The homeboys took note of my absence and chided me thus: "Where have you been? Be around, Dwight, be around the hood, so we can see you, so we can be with you." They wanted me to be out and about, not necessarily because they had something to tell me, but, quite simply, so that they could "see me, be with me," so that

Figure 7: The cross with three points astride an inverted *LK* (Latin Kings) and crown announce that this street corner is Folks turf. (Photo by Dwight Conquergood: Courtesy of Northwestern University Archives)

we could co-experience the hood—our shared and overlapping cultural space. Intracommunal communication is rooted in co-presence.

In contrast to intracommunal communication, interpersonal communication conjures a map where discrete persons are linked together via terminals that enable and control communication flow that does not infringe on personal space. On the other hand, gang communication is all about blending and merging identities into the group: "The Brotherhood of man, blending like the waves of one ocean, shining as the sun, one soul in many bodies . . . all our powers and all our desires thrown into the mission of human service and united into one Single Gold Sun" (*Latin King Manifesto*). The homeboys are keenly aware of class difference in communication style, and are critical of what they take to be the tepid, distant, interpersonal mode of the middle class. Using "White people" as an index for "middle class," a Guatemalan youth facing deportation proceedings because he was an "undocumented, illegal alien" complained to me during trial recess about the yuppie lawyers, middle-class social workers, and courtroom personnel involved with his case: "I don't understand white people, Dwight. How they look, how they talk, how they dress, how they carry themselves. If they gonna put me away,

Figure 8: This graffito fuses and simultaneously inverts the iconography of both the Latin Kings and Future Puerto Rican Stones gangs. Framed by two *K*s, the left one reversed (standing for King Killers), this wall stakes out Folks turf. (Photo by Dwight Conquergood: Courtesy of Northwestern University Archives)

lock me up, I'd rather be locked in a cage with wild animals, than with white people, Dwight. I can't breathe around white people, Dwight."[11] Against a dominant world that displaces, stifles, and erases identity, the homeboys create, through their communication practices, a hood: a subterranean space of life-sustaining warmth, intimacy, and protection.

In addition to the pleasures of communal fellowship, there is a survival function in this communitarian ethos of tightly laced connections with trusted and intimate others. Precisely because the streets are dangerous and densely coded, survival chances improve when one is immersed in a group, among multiple companions all helping and watching one another's back. The rugged individualism and self-reliance much admired in the suburbs would be suicidal for someone who needed to negotiate the street life of the inner city. I quote at length from one of the underground gang manifestos that enunciates clearly how the communitarian ethic is anchored in a need for collective vigilance and shared perceptions and responses to situations that arise:

> Communication among our brothers is our greatest virtue, for what one brother misses in his sight, another brother can carry

Figure 9: The cross with three dots and *I-P-N* on the roof proclaim that this park clubhouse is the turf of the Insane Popes Nation. In addition to the dramaturgical breaking of the upside-down crown every time the door is opened, the Latin Kings are debunked further by the inverted 5 underneath the window. The inverted *LC* underneath the left window is a put-down of the Latin Counts, another People Nation gang aligned with the Latin Kings. (Photo by Dwight Conquergood: Courtesy of Northwestern University Archives)

> the blind to see the light of a situation; as in understanding, teach our brothers understanding until they are capable of being the prophet. . . . Our guard is to be up at all times and we are to strike first if need be, because for our people to be struck at first is a sure sign of being lax.
>
> It is always best to be in the presence of another brother at all times, if not, for best results let another brother know of your whereabouts, in case of any occurrence that may come about. . . . Any revengious act of a brother is not tolerated, especially an act alone—consult other brothers in the surroundings to make the wisest decision as a whole, never leaving any brother in the dark.

My findings are corroborated by Padilla (1992), who also conducted field research with Chicago gang members: "To them individual behavior leads to obliteration" (108).

Figure 10: A miniature death mural for Negro, a slain brother who was loved greatly within the Lawrence and Kedzie hood. (Photo by Dwight Conquergood: Courtesy of Northwestern University Archives)

The privileging of group communication has made gang members very responsive to certain communication technologies, especially the pager-beeper. In the section of the gang with which I have worked most closely, influential members all carry these paging devices.[12] Indeed, this technology has facilitated new methods of extending my fieldwork research. Particularly now that I am spending more time teaching and writing than earlier in the fieldwork, I am able to keep in close touch with key consultants even on days when I am teaching in Evanston and they are running on the streets of Chicago. I can page them from my Northwestern University office, and they return my calls from public telephones on the street.[13]

Through interlaced networks of intracommunal communication, street youth build a hood, producing a "space that may be grasped, that may be defended against adverse forces, the space we love" (Bachelard, 1969, xxxi). They "throw up their love" for and within this communal space by writing on its walls. One Latin King described gang graffiti in this way: "We write our love on the wall." As I discussed earlier, dense coding and secrecy are hallmarks of gang representational practices because the external boundary between in-group and out-group is of paramount importance. I want to emphasize that secrecy, in addition to closing out others, has an enclosing function. Experienced from within, secrecy shelters and intensifies bonding. According to Feldman (1991): "In a colonized culture, secrecy is an assertion of identity and of symbolic capital. Pushed to the margins, subaltern groups construct their own margins as fragile insulations from the 'center.' Secrecy is the creation of centers in peripheries deprived of stable anchorages" (Feldman 1991, 11).

Street youth take pleasure in the symbolic capital, collusions, and interpretive intimacies that radiate from the ornamental and esoteric graffiti inscriptions with which they embellish their hood. Figures 2–4 visually make the important point that the hood is an *embodied* space, a living space of sensuous communication. The tattooed and signifying bodies of gang members become mirrors and mobile extensions of the graffiti-inscribed walls. Figure 3 displays the remarkable dialectic between illumination and shadow, comprehensibility and camouflage, that characterizes gang representations. "Here the Sun Shines" refers to the radiant symbol of the Latin Kings, the "Single Gold Sun." The graffito proclaims that this is the hood of the Latin Kings: that this cultural space will be enlightened by the ideals and values of the King brothers and sisters. For insiders, it is a center of light, glowing with meaningfulness. All the intricate graffiti decorating this rooftop wall are simultaneously the source and result of the shining strength of King Love that suffuses this hood.

Much of the interpretive glow of this wall depends on the meanings that are hooded—hooded in the sense of masked, and also in the sense of limited to members of the hood, hood-specific. Staying with the "Here the Sun Shines" proclamation, an outsider would not know that the *R* in Here is inverted to "throw down" the Royals, a rival Folks gang. Likewise, the *T* in The is figured as an inverted pitchfork to debunk the Disciples, whose major icon is the pitchfork. If you look closely, you can see seven other inverted pitchforks in this photograph. A large one with spiked tines is directly underneath *HERE*, another one is the *T* in Chiquito, with a free-floating one underneath the *T* in Chiquito. A large thin one with spiked tines is just to the right of Ghetto Boy, standing on the ledge, with a fifth one with dots underneath the three tines to the right of that one. A sixth one is underneath *J.J.* in the upper right, and the seventh one is the hand sign Ghetto Boy is throwing down. On the left side of the wall, there is a five-point star for the People Nation astride a reversed *D*. The backward *D* stands for the Disciples, the lead gang of the Folks Nation, and the hyphenated *K* stands for Killers. Through a strategy of affirmation by negation, the Latin Kings clear representational space for their own Nation identity by eliminating alien others, thus reminding one of the *terror* that is part of the consolidation of all territory,[14] to say nothing of the violence inherent in representation (see Armstrong and Tennenhouse 1989; Conquergood 1991b). In addition to reversals and inversions of acronyms and icons, gangs symbolically pollute the other by breaking a symbol. Just to the right of the five-point star in Figure 3 there is a heart with wings, another icon of the Disciples, broken grotesquely in half. On the right half of the fractured line, where the other half of the heart should be, there is instead the broken half of a six-point star, the symbol of the Folks Nation. This reppin' of the self by negating the other inspired the emotionally resonant title for the documentary based on my fieldwork, *The Heart Broken in Half* (Conquergood and Siegel 1990).

Figure 4 is dominated by the resplendent five-point crown of the Latin Kings, which is mirrored in two versions of hand-signing the crown—one with two hands, and the other with the extended thumb, index, and fifth fingers of the right hand thrown over the left side of body. Digital reps configure a three-point crown, also used by the Latin Kings, as can be seen in Figure 3. An icon of any crown is insufficient to represent the Latin Kings because a Folks Nation gang, the Imperial Gangsters, also rep with a crown, but a six-point crown. One can see an upside-down six-point crown broken in half just to the left of the youth standing on the ledge in Figure 4. In the upper-right corner of the graffiti wall in Figure 5, one can see the same polluted Folks Nation crown conjoined across a fracture line, with the broken half of a six-point star directly above the inverted and reversed letters *M-L-D*, thus defiling the Maniac Latin Disciples. The reversed *C* hyphenated with *K* stands for Cobra-Killers. The Spanish Cobras are the alleged slayers of my neighbor Negro, who is eulogized in this graffiti memorial by writing his name above *R-I-P*, Rest in Peace. The full name of the street gang allegedly responsible for slaying Negro, COBRA, is spelled out underneath the large *LK* acronym of the Latin Kings. The *C* is reversed, of course, to defame the Cobras, the *B* is reversed to put down the Braziers, the *R* inverted to defile the Royals, and the upside-down *A* inside the *O* is actually a complex inversion of the logo of the Orchestra Albany gang. Orchestra Albany, Royals, and Braziers are all gangs aligned with the Folks Nation.

Figures 7, 8, and 9 demonstrate how the same symbolic scapegoating takes place—on the other side of the People/Folks oppositional boundary. I photographed Figs. 7 and 8 just six blocks west of Big Red, across Kimball street, a major border street between People and Folks gangs. In Fig. 7, the hood is marked as Folks turf by displaying a cross with three dots atop an inverted and reversed *LK* over an upside-down crown. The semiotic pollution in Fig. 8 is also intricate. Here, a three-point crown, a Latin King icon, has been fused with a pyramid topped with an encircling moon, the symbol of the Future Puerto Rican Stones, a close affiliate of the Latin Kings. This double-fused icon has been inverted with a reversed and upside-down *S* in the middle. Double *K*s, standing for King Killers, frame this image, with the *K* standing for King reversed.

Figure 9 represents a highly imaginative and theatrical innovation on this basic principle of affirmation by negation. Here, a park clubhouse claimed by the Insane Popes, arch enemies of the Latin Kings, features a door that has been incorporated visually into an image of an upside-down Latin King crown. Thus, when people open and walk through the door, they, perforce, break and violate, ostentatiously, the symbol of the Latin Kings.

Figure 10 speaks poignantly to the coarticulation of secrecy, sacrifice, and solidarity. It depicts one of the many death murals that appeared throughout the Lawrence/Kedzie Kings hood commemorating young Negro, my neighbor, a 16-year-old Guatemalan youth who was murdered during my second year of fieldwork. His violent death is transmuted rhetorically into heroic sacrifice for the group. Death murals like the one in Fig. 10 become mnemonic sites for storytelling and legend making that function as didactic dramas that sacralize commitment to the hood and all that it embraces. Latino Boy eulogizes Negro while standing in front of a "Negro RIP" mural:

> He died being a King. He fought with a lot of Folks and they finally got him. But, see, Negro Rest In Peace means he used to fight for all of this and he believed in the crown and all of this is his [gesturing toward graffiti displays]. This is all his, it belongs to him. All these walls. We will always know that Negro will always live in our hearts. We wrote his name all over this neighborhood and everywhere we go we see something that reminds us of him. And before he died Negro told us that he would like to die in this neighborhood. He died still throwing up the crown, you know, he threw it up until the last minute of his breath.

The death of Negro activates the cultural memory of the group, brings into sharpest focus its most radiant symbols, and becomes a generative source for strengthening cohesion and commitment.

In a profound way, this tiny death mural painted on one of the narrow edges of a bridge can be thought of as an emblematic image for the world-making capacities of the hood. It is a miniature, designed to enclose, concentrate, clarify, control, and intensify meaning. All reppin' practices can be thought of as metonymies and condensation symbols for the hood. They represent it in a heightened, stylized, and focused way. The hood that Negro embodies and, paradoxically, enlivens in death is a miniature world excavated and constructed out of subjugated knowledges and marginal materials. At every level of refraction, the hood represents an enclosed space, a microworld, for the nurturance of agency, intimacy, and meaning. The very forces that threaten to rip it asunder—sudden violence and death—are appropriated and absorbed as value-clarifying and community-building moral dramas of heroic sacrifice and solidarity.

Conclusion: Gangs, Communication, and Public Policy

Gangs are preeminently a communication phenomenon. I have devoted much of this chapter to a description of how street youth build a sheltering world of mutual support and well-being, a hood, through complex and creative communication practices. However, the intracommunal cultural space of the hood needs to be understood as an adaptive response and bulwark against dominant spaces and structures of exclusion and oppression. No ethnography of gang "group communication in context" would be complete without interrogation of the macrocontexts of communication that have created the "gang problem."

My communication-centered approach to gangs builds on sociologist Becker's (1963) powerful insight that deviance is first and foremost a *rhetorical construction*—a label deployed by agents of civil society to control and contain the "dangerous classes." Becker argued that "the central fact about deviance" is that "it is created by society" (Becker 1963, 8). He explained:

> I do not mean this in the way it is ordinarily understood, in which the causes of deviance are located in the social situation of the deviant or in "social factors" which prompt his action. I mean, rather, that *social groups create deviance by making rules whose infraction constitutes deviance,* and by applying those rules to particular people and labeling them as outsiders. From this point of view, deviance is not a quality of the act the person commits, but rather a consequence of the application by others of rules and sanctions to an "offender." The deviant is one to whom that label

> has successfully been applied; deviant behavior is behavior that people so label. (Becker 1963, 8–9; see also Reiman 1984; Stallybrass and White 1986)

Becker's social construction theory of deviance anticipates the best of post-structuralist theory, which conjoins discourse analysis with political economy (see di Leonardo 1993). The gang members among whom I lived were labeled, *textualized,* but these were not postmodern texts of infinite open-endedness and free play. Instead, these were hard-edged texts in the bulging files of police and prosecutors that underscored the authority and power of surveillance, control, and incarceration. My friends and field consultants were incisive deconstructivists of the connections between language and power. One of my neighbors, a 20-year-old Guatemalan, had already been arrested 26 times, mostly for "Disorderly Conduct" and "Mob Action." Facing deportation proceedings as an "*undocumented,* illegal alien," he showed me the "Criminal History" section of his court file, and explained: "*Disorderly Conduct*—that means walking down the street if you're a person who looks like me. I just be walking down the street. *Mob Action*—that means standing on a street corner with your friends. If you're a gangbanger, they can pick you up just for standing on the corner with your friends."

The grandmother of a slain youth quoted in a *Chicago Tribune* article likewise articulated a subtle understanding of labeling theory, and how it applied, with devastating consequences, to her grandson: "School officials labelled him a gang member. It was hard for him to break that label, she said. So he lived up to it, friends say" (Thomas 1991, 5).

Before they tattoo their bodies with gang insignia, urban youth are always already inscribed and branded by stigmatizing images of poverty, prejudice, and pathology, which are produced by the official discourse of the media, legal system, and public policy institutions—those authorities and experts who have the power to know, name, and label. Gangs are constructed in public discourse as the cause, effect, and aberrant response to social disorder and urban decay. The demonized figure of the violent gangbanger is the sensational centerpiece in a self-righteous morality play called "the urban underclass" playing currently mainstream media and social-policy institutions (see Reed 1992; Williams 1992). Little more than a lurid sideshow, this script locates the problems of the inner city in the so-called pathological behavior of its rogues gallery of residents: gangbangers, muggers, drug dealers, welfare mothers, pregnant teenagers, and other social defectives. This blame-the-victim focus on individual behavior resonates ideologically with bourgeois individualism. Moreover, it diverts attention away from the political and economic macropatterns of exclusion and displacement, which shape the microtextures of everyday struggle for poor and socially marginalized people (see Hagedorn, 1988; Massey and Denton, 1993; Sullivan, 1989; Williams, 1988). The figure of the gangbanger as personification of urban pathology rhetorically deflects scrutiny away from the root causes of poverty and crime: (a) deindustrialization; (b) disinvestment; (c) economic polarization; (d) residential segregation; (e) real estate speculation and gentrification; and (f) the abandonment, neglect, and collapse of civic institutions (i.e., public schools, social services, youth programs), all in the name of retrograde "fiscal responsibility." The urban rites of "hanging out" on street corners and "holding down the hood" cannot be understood apart from the enforced leisure that is a consequence of the staggering unemployment rate for minority youth. The children of entire neighborhoods are viewed as disposable by legislators and policymakers. The so-called "disorder" of the inner city is linked directly to the stability of the affluent suburbs: "mainstream spaces such as suburbs, *are also active agents* in the destabilization of ghetto communities" (Venkatesh 1993, 8).

"Imagery and symbols—rhetorics," di Leonardo (1990) reminded us, "are themselves material facts" (4). Zatz (1987) provided a stunning case study of the material consequences of the rhetorical imagery surrounding Chicano youth gangs in Phoenix, Arizona. Based on a multimethodological study that included media analysis, interviews, and examination of police and court records, she concluded:

> [I]t was the social imagery of Chicano youth gangs, rather than their actual behavior, that lay at the root of the gang problem in Phoenix. The imagery of gangs as violent converged with that of Mexicans as "different." With the convergence of these images, the potential threat of disorder and of contempt for law escalated to the point at which a "moral panic" ensued. This is not to say that there were no Chicano youth gangs and no gang-related crimes. There were and are. But there was also the usual gamut of regular street crime, corporate crime, and so forth, without any specialized "squads" in place to combat them. (Zatz 1987, 153–154)

These media-fomented "moral panics" help redirect material resources (to say nothing of compassion and good will) away from educational and employment programs that could help these youngsters and toward the much more costly buildup of a state apparatus of surveillance, control, and punishment: gang squads, jails, and prisons (see Hall, Critcher, Jefferson, Clarke and Roberts, 1978).

If communication is part of the creation of the "gang problem," then communication must be part of the solution. My research calls for a radical reorientation of the many gang-intervention programs that deploy fear appeals and shame tactics aimed at scaring street youth out of gangs. One antigang program in Chicago uses a large poster that features a herd of sheep mindlessly congregated in front of a graffiti-inscribed wall (note, again, the animal imagery and the anticommunal bias). Perhaps the most unsavory antigang message is the public service announcement that is part of the city of Evanston, Illinois, antigang campaign, in which members of African-American street gangs are compared to the Ku Klux Klan. The fundamental flaw of these communication strategies (to say nothing of their dubious content) is that by directing messages exclusively to gang members they reinforce the ideology that individual poor and minority youth are the locus of responsibility for the "gang problem." Instead of targeting and further stigmatizing individual gang members, the work of communication needs to be redirected toward rallying and awakening communities and public policymakers to a sense of social justice and responsibility to these youngsters and their families. An initial, concrete step would be to think about jobs, instead of jails, as a preemptive (instead of punitive) response to gangs. Hagedorn (1988) asked the founder of a major Milwaukee gang what would be the most effective way of dealing with gangs; he responded, unhesitatingly, "Give 'em jobs" (Hagedorn 1988, 166). I agree with Reed (1992): "I do not want to hear another word about drugs or crime [or gangs] without hearing about decent jobs, adequate housing, and egalitarian education in the same breath" (Reed 1992, 38).

NOTES

1. The field research for this chapter is part of a larger ethnographic study of Chicago's Albany Park neighborhood, a working-class community that has become a port of entry for refugees and new immigrants. The Chicago field study is part of a Ford Foundation national project, "Changing Relations: Newcomers and Established Residents in Six U.S. Communities," that was funded through the Research Foundation of the State University of New York, Grant 240–1117-A (see Lamphere 1992). I am grateful to the Ford Foundation, Northwestern University's Center for Urban Affairs and Policy Research, and the Illinois Humanities Council for financial support of my work. In December 1987, I moved into the large Big

Red tenement in a notorious quarter of this neighborhood called "Little Beirut," and lived in that area until June 1992. (In August 1989, Big Red was evacuated and boarded up due to its severe state of deterioration and disrepair, so I moved into another flat one block north.) I am committed to ethnographic research methods that are intensely participative and critically engaged (see Conquergood 1991a).

2. Padilla's (1992) recent research and Thrasher's (1927) classic work are representative studies situated at opposite ends of this continuum of gang structures.

3. For an incisive critique of Bellah et al. (1985), see di Leonardo (1991).

4. Bourdieu (1977), like Lannamann (1991), critiqued the individualist bias of much social research. He argued that "'interpersonal' relations are never, except in appearance, *individual-to-individual* relationships and that the truth of the interaction is never entirely contained in the interaction" (81). His critique of social psychology for ahistorical and superficial understanding of context is pertinent for much of the research on small group communication:

This is what social psychology and interactionism and ethnomethodology forget when, reducing the objective structure of the relationship between the assembled individuals to the conjunctural structure of their interaction in a particular situation and group, they seek to explain everything that occurs in an experimental or observed interaction in terms of the experimentally controlled characteristics of the situation (81).

5. Police refer to gang graffiti in deeply insulting animal imagery, such as "dog and fire hydrant" marking of turf. I quote from the Chicago Police Department (1991) information booklet entitled *Street Gangs:* "Gang graffiti is not a youthful prank. It puts forth a strong message from the gang that they control the area, much like a wild animal marking his boundaries" (1).

6. Conducting and publishing research on an underground, somewhat secret social group is riddled with ethical dilemmas, conundrums, and predicaments. I must negotiate continuously the delicate boundary between respect and sensitivity to my field consultants, and the need to write the fullest, most complex ethnographic account of their communication practices that my data support. My struggle about how to handle the secret manifestos foregrounds the ethicopolitical problematics of fieldwork. They are amazing exegetical documents in which gangs spell out their credo, moral vision, and symbolism, thus providing emic explanations, indigenous interpretations, and metacultural analyses from the people themselves. Any ethnographer aspiring to Geertz's (1973) ideal of rendering "thick descriptions" of another way of life would be foolish to ignore these documents. Further, because I want to contest and counter the mainstream media demonology about gangs (i.e., that they are all drug-crazed, sociopathic, subhuman, vicious killers) with a more complicated picture of gang life, these manifestos are key texts for highlighting the thoughtful, creative, and humane aspects of gang culture—the very characteristics that are erased in the prevailing media representations of gangs so that only the violent *and* sensationalist (and I would add, highly marketable) images dominate. However, my ethnographic predicament is that these documents are secret. I wish I could say to beginning ethnographers that there is always an easy, clear-cut answer that resolves every fieldwork dilemma. I can share only my ethical struggles and uneasy decision to quote from these underground documents. I do so in support of telling a more complex and ethnographically valid story that will deepen understanding of gang culture and,

I hope, contribute in some small way to the advancement of more enlightened public policies and humane intervention programs for street youth. When faced with the ethicopolitical problematics of field research, I find it helpful to read how other ethnographers struggle with similar contradictions and ambivalences that arise inevitably in many fieldwork projects. I particularly recommend the monographs of Feldman (1991) and Lavie (1990), two ethnographers who have conducted difficult fieldwork in politically charged research sites.

7. Boundaries and borderlands, and conjunctions and commotions are now the staples of postpositivist and poststructuralist ethnography (see Anzaldua 1987; Clifford 1988; Rosaldo 1989).

8. An example of a special multigang alliance is the Young Latino Organization (YLO), or United Latino Organization (ULO), a coalition of several Folks Nation street gangs that includes the Spanish Cobras, Latin Disciples, Latin Eagles, and Imperial Gangsters. The YLO/ULO alliance is pitted against the Latin Kings, one of the largest People Nation street gangs.

9. One of the most significant findings of my fieldwork is that turf (territory) overrides race and ethnicity as the primary determinant of gang identification. Both researchers and laypersons have taken unproblematically the title of a street gang as a reliable indicator of racial and ethnic composition, and have generalized that gangs are organized along racial lines. This is true only when a local neighborhood is racially segregated, such as when the Latin Kings emerged in the 1960s in a section of Chicago that was predominantly Latino, hence the title Latin Kings. However, in the multicultural new immigrant and refugee neighborhood where I lived and conducted fieldwork, the Lawrence and Kedzie branch of the Latin Kings embraced a rainbow coalition of Mexican, Puerto Rican, Guatemalan, Salvadoran, Panamanian, as well as African American, White, Assyrian, Filipino, Lebanese, Palestinian, Korean, Vietnamese, Lao, and others. The vice prez of this branch of the Latin Kings is an Assyrian refugee born in Iraq, and another high-ranking member is a displaced Appalachian youth born in West Virginia, whose street tag is Blanco, which, of course, is Spanish for White. Newly formed branches of the Latin Kings in some of southwest Chicago's predominantly White working-class neighborhoods have a membership that is predominantly White. The local street gang will be ethnically homogeneous only if the neighborhood is residentially segregated. The names of street gangs often point more to a stark history of residential segregation in Chicago than they do the current realities of gang membership (see Massey and Denton 1993). If the neighborhood is ethnically mixed, then the local gang will mirror this same diversity, regardless of whether it is named Latin Kings or Future Puerto Rican Stones. I could give many examples of how gang identity subsumes and rearticulates racial and ethnic boundaries, but the following example must suffice: in April 1991, a Future Puerto Rican Stone, who actually was a Romanian refugee youth, was killed in my neighborhood allegedly by a Spanish Cobra, who actually was a Vietnamese youth.

10. For an anthropological study of meetings as key sites of organizational communication, see Schwartzman (1989).

11. See Dyer (1988) and hooks (1992).

12. I certainly am aware that drug dealers also make heavy use of these pager/beepers to coordinate their business, or, "beez neez" as they say on the streets. Although some street gangs are involved heavily in drug trafficking, some are

not. Further, within a single branch, some members might deal drugs, some will not, and there will be others who go back and forth. That is to say, during an economic crisis they will fall back on the underground economy of drugs to "make their money," and then will take factory jobs and other legitimate employment when opportunity arises. Because the dominant media demonology conflates gangbangers and drug dealers into one master devil figure (e.g., the NBC Special, "Gangs, Cops, and Drugs"), I must emphasize that I know many committed gang members who neither deal nor consume drugs. The two Latin Kings who communicate with me via pager/beepers are not drug dealers; they invest in this technology to keep "hooked up" with King brothers and friends. The general public might be surprised to know that several manifestos contain "gang laws" that expressly forbid the use of hard drugs. I quote from one: "The use of what is commonly known as angel dust, glue, LSD (acid), heroin, downers and free-basing is unlawful, and cannot be sold in our communities." In the neighborhood where I conducted research, "bow" (marijuana) was used freely and sold by gang members, but hard drugs were frowned upon.

13. In Latin King numerology 5 is sacred, therefore most identification numbers are some combination that contains the numeral 5. The identification number they gave me, for example, is 005.

14. I want to thank my colleague Rick Maxwell for pointing me to this etymological connection.

REFERENCES

Anzaldua, Gloria. 1999. *Borderlands/La Frontera: The New Mestiza.* San Francisco: Ante Lute Books, 1999.

Armstrong, Nancy and Leonard Tennenhouse. 1989. *The Violence of Representation: Literature and the History of Violence.* London and New York: Routledge.

Austin, J.L. 1962. *How To Do Things With Words.* London: Oxford University Press.

Bachelard, Gaston. 1969. *The Poetics of Space.* Translated by Maria Jolas. Boston: Beacon Press.

Bakhtin, Mikhail. 1990. *Art and Answerability.* Translated by Vadim Liapunov. Edited by Michael Holquist and Vadim Liapunov. Austin, TX: University of Texas Press.

Becker, Howard. 1963. *Outsiders: Studies in the Sociology of Deviance.* New York: Free Press.

Bellah, Robert N., Richard Madsen, William M. Sullivan, Ann Swidler, and Steven M. Tipton. 1985. *Habits of the Heart: Individualism and Commitment in American Life.* New York: Harper & Row.

Bourdieu, Pierre. 1977. *Outline of a Theory of Practice.* Translated by Richard Nice. Cambridge, U.K.: Cambridge University Press.

Burke, Kenneth. 1984. *Attitudes Toward History* (3rd edition). Berkeley, CA: University of California Press.

Carey, James. 1989. *Communication as Culture: Essays on Media and Society.* Boston: Unwin Hyman.

Chicago Police Department. 1991. *Street Gangs.* Chicago: Author.
Clifford, James. 1988. *The Predicament of Culture: Twentieth-century Ethnography, Literature, and Art.* Cambridge, MA: Harvard University Press.
Conquergood, Dwight. 1991a. "Rethinking Ethnography: Towards a Critical Cultural Politics." *Communication Monographs* 58: 179–94.
Conquergood, Dwight. 1991b. "'For the Nation!' How Street Gangs Problematize Patriotism." In *Peacemaking through Communication,* edited by Rod Troester, 8–21. Annandale, VA: Speech Communication Association.
Conquergood, Dwight. 1992a. *On Reppin' and Rhetoric: Gang representations* (CUAPR working papers no. 92–19). Evanston, IL: Northwestern University, Center for Urban Affairs and Policy Research.
Conquergood, Dwight. 1992b. "Life in Big Red: Struggles and Accomodations in a Chicago Polyethnic Tenement." In *Structuring Diversity: Ethnographic Perspectives on the New Immigration,* Edited by Louise Lamphere, 95–144. Chicago: University of Chicago Press.
Conquergood, Dwight [Producer] and Taggart Siegel [Producer and Director]. 1990. *The Heart Broken in Half* [Videotape]. Chicago: Siegel Productions; New York: Filmmakers Library.
de Certeau, Michel. 1984. *The Practice of Everyday Life.* Translated by S. Randall. Berkeley: University of California Press.
de Certeau, Michel. 1986. *Heterologies: Discourse on the Other.* Translated by Brian Massurni. Minneapolis: University of Minnesota Press.
di Leonardo, Micaela. 1993. "Who's Really Getting Paid?" *The Nation.* 14 May, 672–76.
di Leonardo, Micaela. 1990. "Habits of the Cumbered Heart: Ethnic community and women's culture as invented traditions." In *Golden Ages, Dark Ages: Imagining the Past in Anthropology and History,* edited by Jay O'Brien and William Roseberry, 234–56. Berkeley: University of California Press.
Douglas, Mary. 1982. *In the Active Voice.* London: Routledge & Kegan Paul.
Douglas, Mary. 1982. *Essays in the Sociology of Perception.* London: Routledge & Kegan Paul.
Feldman, Allen. 1991. *Formations of Violence: The Narrative of the Body and Political Terror in Northern Ireland.* Chicago: University of Chicago Press.
Fisher, B. Aubrey. 1978. *Perspectives on Human Communication.* New York: Macmillan.
Gans, Herbert. 1988. *Middle American Individualism: The Future of Liberal Democracy.* New York: Free Press.
Geertz, Clifford. 1983. *Local Knowledge: Further Essays in Interpretive Anthropology.* New York: Basic.
Geertz, Clifford. 1973. *The Interpretation of Cultures.* New York: Basic Books.
Hagedorn, John M. 1988. *People and Folks: Gangs, Crime and the Underclass in a Rustbelt City.* Chicago: Lakeview Press.
Hall, Stuart, Chas Critcher, Tony Jefferson, John N. Clarke and Brian Roberts. 1978. *Policing the Crises: Mugging, the State, and Law and Order.* New York: Macmillan.
hooks, bell. 1990. "Homeplace: A Site of Resistance." *Yearning: Race, Gender and Cultural Politics.* Boston: South End Press.
Horowitz, Ruth. 1990. "Sociological Perspectives on Gangs: Conflicting Defini-

tions and Concepts." In *Gangs in America,* edited by C. Ronald Huff, 37–54. Newbury Park, CA.

Jankowski, Martin Sanchez. 1991. *Islands in the Street: Gangs and American Urban Society.* Berkeley: University of California Press.

Lamphere, Louise (ed.). 1992. *Structuring Diversity: Ethnographic Perspectives on the New Immigration.* Chicago: University of Chicago Press.

Lannamann, John W. 1991. "Interpersonal Communication Research as Ideological Practice." *Communication Theory* 1: 179–203.

Lavie, Smadar. 1990. *The Poetics of Military Occupation.* Berkeley: University of California Press.

Lefebvre, Henri. 1991. *The Production of Space.* Oxford: Blackwell Publishers. Print.

Massey, Douglas and Nancy Denton. 1993. *American Apartheid: Segregation and the Making of the Underclass.* Cambridge, MA: Harvard University Press.

Miller, Walter. 1980. "Gangs, Groups and Serious Youth Crime." In *Critical Issues in Juvenile Delinquency,* edited by David Shichor and Delos H. Kelly, 115–38. Lexington, KY: Lexington Books.

Morash, Merry. 1983. "Gangs, Groups, and Delinquency." *British Journal of Criminology* 23: 309–35.

Padilla, Felix. 1992. *The Gang as an American Enterprise.* New Brunswick, NJ: Rutgers University Press.

Putnam, Linda and Cynthia Stohl. 1990. "Bona Fide Groups: A Reconceptualization of Groups in Context." *Communication Studies* 41: 248–65.

Reed, Adolph. 1992. "The Underclass as Myth and Symbol: The Poverty of Discourse about Poverty." *Radical America* 24: 21–40.

Reiman, Jeffrey. 1984. *The Rich Get Richer and the Poor Get Prison: Ideology, Class, and Criminal Justice* (2nd edition). New York: Wiley.

Rosaldo, Renato. 1989. *Culture and Truth: The Remaking of Social Analysis.* Boston: Beacon.

Schwartzman, Helen. 1989. *The Meeting: Gatherings in Organizations and Communities.* New York: Plenum.

Short, James F. and Fred L. Strodtbeck. 1974. *Group Process and Gang Delinquency.* Chicago: University of Chicago Press.

Stallybrass, Peter, and Allon White. 1986. *The Politics and Poetics of Transgression.* Ithaca, N.Y.: Cornell University Press.

Sullivan, Mercer. 1989. *"Getting Paid": Youth Crime and Work in the Inner City.* Ithaca, NY: Cornell University Press.

Thomas, J. 1991. "Evanston Copes with Surge in Gangs." *Chicago Tribune.* 12 August section 2, 1, 5.

Thrasher. Frederic. 1927. *The Gang: A Study of 1313 Gangs in Chicago.* Chicago: University of Chicago Press.

Turner, Victor. 1977. *The Ritual Process: The Human Seriousness of Play.* New York: PAJ Publications.

Venkatesh, Sudhir. 1993. *Black Gangs and the Reconstitution of "Community" in an Urban Ghetto.* Unpublished manuscript, University of Chicago.

Vigil, J. D. 1988a. "Group Process and Street Identity: Adolescent Chicago Gang Members." *Ethos* 16: 421–45.

Vigil, J.D. 1988b. *Barrio Gangs: Street Life and Identity in Southern California.* Austin, TX: University of Texas Press.

Williams, Brett. 1992. "Poverty Among African Americans in the Urban United States." *Human Organization* 51: 166–74.

Williams, Brett. 1988. *Upscaling Downtown: Stalled Gentrification in Washington, D.C.* Ithaca, NY: Cornell University Press.

Zatz, Marjorie S. 1987. "Chicano Youth Gangs and Crime: The Creation of a Moral Panic." *Contemporary Crises* 11: 129–58.

Lethal Theatre

Performance, Punishment, and the Death Penalty

I'm not going to struggle physically against any restraints. I'm not going to shout, use profanity or make idle threats. Understand though that I'm not only upset, but I'm saddened by what is happening here tonight . . . . If someone tried to dispose of everyone here for participating in this killing, I'd scream a resounding, "No." I'd tell them to give them all the gift that they would not give me, and that's to give them all a second chance. . . . There are a lot of men like me on death row—good men—who fell to the same misguided emotions, but may not have recovered as I have. Give those men a chance to do what's right. Give them a chance to undo their wrongs. A lot of them want to fix the mess they started, but don't know how. . . . No one wins tonight. No one gets closure.

—NAPOLEON BEAZLEY[1]

There will be no lasting peace either in the heart of individuals or in social customs until death is outlawed.

—ALBERT CAMUS (1995, 234)

Like it or not, you are putting on a show.

—JOHN WHITLEY[2]

Show, spectacle, theatre, these representational media are central to the rituals of state killing.

—AUSTIN SARAT (2001, 242)

In 1975 Michel Foucault published *Discipline and Punish: The Birth of the Prison,* a landmark book that opened with two astonishing chapters, "The Body of the Condemned" and "The Spectacle of the Scaffold," harrowing accounts in gruesome detail of the performance of capital punishment in the premodern era (Foucault 1979). These chapters served as points of departure for charting the historical shift from the dramatic infliction of corporal and capital punishment to modernity's more subtle and insidious infiltrations of power through mechanisms of discipline linked with knowledge. Punishment transformed, Foucault argued, from a theatre of violence and repression to a medical model of rehabilitation metonymically connected to other normalizing mechanisms and internalized techniques of coercion, compliance, and surveillance. According to Foucault, the performance of power in modern society has changed radically from spectacular capital punishments—that point at which the violence of the state is most nakedly displayed—to undercover capillary penetrations, insinuations, secretions, and circulations of power that is difficult to flesh out. He closed the book with the confident claim that "we are now far away from the country of tortures," the spectacle of the scaffold, because contemporary legal punishment "appears to be free of all excess and all violence" (Foucault 1979, 307).

I reread *Discipline and Punish* in the summer of 2001, during the same time that I traveled twice in eight days to Terre Haute, Indiana, to march and stand in vigil outside the prison death chamber to protest the serial executions of Timothy McVeigh and Juan Raul Garza, the first federal prisoners put to death since 1963. I found Foucault's opening chapters on executions more resonant and familiar than later chapters titled "The Gentle Way of Punishment." Emotionally drained from attending the June 11 and June 19 executions, I kept writing "not in June, 2001" in the margins of passages about how modern judicial punishment had advanced well beyond the deployment of raw, physical force. I drew an incredulous exclamation point across from this passage in the conclusion: "There is nothing in it now that recalls the former excess of sovereign power when it revenged its authority" on the body of the condemned (Foucault 1979, 302).

To be fair, Foucault wrote *Discipline and Punish* in 1975, at a time when the medical model of rehabilitation was in the ascendancy in penological thought and practice. The death penalty was rarely deployed, and France, along with the rest of Europe, was on the verge of abolishing capital punishment for good. Although it is amazing to think of it now, the United States was in step with and even ahead of the international community on the issue of the death penalty. In 1975, there were no executions in the US, not even in Texas. In 1972 the Supreme Court in Furman vs. Georgia had declared capital punishment—"as then practiced," which proved to be a fatal loophole phrase—"cruel and unusual punishment" and therefore unconstitutional. Many assumed that the death penalty had been abolished for good, instead of temporarily suspended. After World War II and the shock of Holocaust atrocities, executions had declined steadily. In 1965, the same year that Britain abolished the death penalty, there were seven executions, compared to the peak decade of the depression-ravaged 1930s when there were 167 executions a year on average. Then in the next year, 1966, there were two, and the following year, 1967, only one. No executions were performed in the five years leading up to the Supreme Court's formal ruling against the death penalty in 1972, and in particular the Federal government had not executed anyone since 1963. From the vantage point of May 2002 (the time of the final draft of this article), when we have already put 31 people to death in the first five months of this year, it is astounding to think that from 1968 through 1976 there was not a single execution in America.[3]

How have we come so far from the social sensibility that Foucault indexed in *Discipline and Punish*? Since 1975 there has been a major shift of societal attitudes toward punishment. Current support for the death penalty hovers between 70 and 75 percent, having peaked at 80 percent in 1994, the year of the conservative Republican takeover of Congress. As of April 1, 2002, there are 3,701 men and women—including 83 juvenile offenders—awaiting execution on Death Row compared to 334 in 1972 when the Supreme Court struck down the death penalty.[4] So deep is the revanchist enthusiasm for spectacles of the scaffold that when Senator Dianne Feinstein, the former mayor of San Francisco, ran for governor of California in 1990 she displayed images of the San Quentin gas chamber in her television campaign commercials. She came from behind to win the Democratic primary by nineteen percent after campaigning on the slogan, "the only Democrat who supports the death penalty" (Bessler 1997, 146).

Especially with the resurgent popularity of capital punishment, it is important to remember that the history of the death penalty in the United States has been one of challenge and contention.[5] Almost from the beginning, capital punishment has been a fraught and contested performance practice. The performance genealogy of executions periodically requires fresh blood to keep this macabre tradition alive. Contemporary defenders of capital punishment shore up its shaky premises, not by logic or rational argument, but by invoking scapegoats, poster boys for the death penalty: Timothy McVeigh, John Wayne Gacy, Jeffrey Dahmer, Richard Speck—and now Osama bin Laden and his henchmen. With each exemplary monster executed, capital punishment is legitimated and revitalized. Thus it is no surprise that George W. Bush, who has presided over 156 executions during his relatively short time in public life, issued executive orders very soon after September 11, 2001, to create military tribunals designed to expedite executions with an efficiency and speed that would exceed that of Texas (The White House 2001). Theatre and performance studies have an ethical as well as intellectual obligation to examine this resurgent theatre of death that anchors conservative politics in the United States. The very word "execute" means to accomplish, to carry out, and to perform, to do. "Execution" also means "a mode or style of performance" (*The American Heritage Dictionary of English* 2000). The death penalty cannot be understood simply as a matter of public policy debate or an aspect of criminology, apart from what it is pre-eminently: performance.

Performance Rituals of State Killing

Executions are awesome rituals of human sacrifice through which the state dramatizes its absolute power and monopoly on violence. We know from the anthropological record that a key to the efficacy of rituals is their capacity to embrace paradox, to gloss contradictions, to mediate profound oppositions, tensions, ambivalences, anxieties. The ritual frame is elastic enough to encompass conflict and chaos, yet sufficiently sturdy to channel volatile forces and disruptive tensions into an aesthetic shape, a repeatable pattern. Rituals draw their drama, dynamism, and intensity from the crises they redress. A host of important anthropologists, notably Victor Turner, Mary Douglas, Clifford Geertz, Roy Rappaport, and others, have noted that ritual performance proliferates along social faultlines, pressure points, cracks in the system, the jagged edge of belief.[6] Rituals carry their weight and earn their cultural keep by restoring, replenishing, repairing, and re-making belief, transforming vague ideas, mixed feelings, and shaky commitments into dramatic clarity and alignment. As embodied performances, rituals incarnate and make visible abstract principles and inchoate concepts—such as "Justice." What is Justice? Justice is an abstraction, a spirit that commands tremendous faith, power, and huge investments both economic and emotional. Like religion and other powerful abstractions, Justice—to paraphrase Victor Turner—lives only in performance, "only in so far as its rituals are 'going concerns'"; Justice can be seen only when it is acted out (Turner 1986, 48). All the interlocking rituals of criminal punishment—arrest, detention, interrogation, trial, conviction, incarceration, execution—are performed so that citizens can see "justice done": "All of justice is a stage; it is the appearance—the ritual—that is the meaningful thing" (Johnson 1998, 20).

Moreover, rituals are neither static nor discrete. They draw their meaning, structure, style, and affective resonance from the traditions they reenact. But they never simply repeat a given form, but, like all "restored behavior," they reverberate within the traditions they simultaneously reinvent and re-deploy for historically situated needs and purposes.[7] The ritual replaying of traditional form always plays with, and plays off and against, the performance genealogy that it recites.[8] Rituals of execution in the United States are part of a dynamic performance genealogy that has undergone profound shifts in feeling, form, and dramaturgy. The seismic shift has been from the public, open-air, communal, hortatory rituals of redemption in colonial and revolutionary era America to the privatized, elite, class-stratified rituals of retribution and exclusion that were created in the early nineteenth century to accommodate an emergent middle-class ethos of restraint, propriety, gentility and new standards of bourgeois taste and refinement. Beginning in the 1830s, execution rituals moved from the public square where they drew diverse audiences numbering in the thousands to inside prison walls where, withdrawn from public view, they became private performances for a small, homosocial, invitation-only audience of elites. Historian Louis Masur summarizes the wider social significance of this change in the mise-en-scène of execution rituals:

> The creation of private executions [during the 1830s] . . . was an act charged with multiple meanings: it marked the triumph of a certain code of conduct and set of social attitudes among the middle and upper classes; it symbolized a broader trend toward privatization and class segmentation; it turned the execution of criminals into an elite event centered around class and gender exclusion. (Masur 1989, 6)[9]

The withdrawal and relocation of executions from the public green to censored enclosures signaled a major shift in structures of feeling about criminals and capital punishment.

To understand better this profoundly meaningful change in dramaturgy, let us examine the execution rituals characteristic of early America. Public hangings in seventeenth- and eighteenth-century New England were mass spectacles that drew the largest audiences ever assembled for any occasion. Especially in Puritan New England, with no maypoles, carnivals, staged theatre, or even Christmas celebrations, a public hanging was an avidly attended "Tragical Spectacle" (Mather 1704). For the 1686 execution of John Morgan, crowds began gathering in Boston a week before the hanging. According to John Dunston, a bookseller from London visiting Boston at the time, some "have come 50 miles to see it" (Dunston 1966, 295). On the morning of March 11, more than 5,000 people jammed into Boston's Second Old North Church to see the condemned prisoner prominently seated in front of the pulpit to hear Cotton Mather preach his execution sermon, a key part of the dramaturgy of hanging day rituals. When the floor and walls of the church gallery began to crack and buckle under the tremendous weight and pressure of the crowd, Mather interrupted his sermon to move the audience to Samuel Willard's Third Old South Church, which had a larger gallery (Dunston 1966, 296). And the outdoor staging of the gallows accommodated multitudes who could not squeeze into the church or were inclined to skip the sermon. One scholar estimated that executions in colonial New England attracted as many as 12,000 spectators (Minnick 1968). In terms of sheer audience size, executions were the most popular performance genre in seventeenth- and eighteenth-century America: "Well into the nineteenth century, execution crowds still outnumbered crowds gathered for any other purpose" (Banner 2002, 25).[10]

Puritan executions were elaborately staged and exquisitely paced ritual dramas seething with suspense, tension, ambivalence, crisis, reversals, revelations, and breathtaking spectacle. The hanging day ritual included the public procession from the jail to the church, where the prisoner was displayed as a "sorrowful spectacle" and embodied "example," a focal point and prop for the minister's fiery execution sermon (Mather 1715). The celebrated ministers appointed to preside at these high profile events rose to their greatest oratorical heights, knowing that they were addressing the largest audiences of their careers, and given the magnitude of an execution, the sermons were often published and sold, thus circulating in print to an ever widening audience.[11]

After the sermon, there was the doleful parade to the gallows, which often took one or more hours. The prisoner typically was carried slowly through the crowd elevated on a cart, sometimes with a rope around his or her neck, and with the coffin conspicuously alongside. At the gallows, there were more speeches and audible prayers, and often hymns were sung communally to pitch the emotions of the audience. Then the sheriff read the death warrant aloud. All of the dramaturgy at the foot of the gallows was designed to anticipate, draw out, and heighten the spellbinding moment when the prisoner climbed the ladder and, precariously perched, delivered a speech to the rapt audience thronged below. This long-awaited speech from the prisoner—who, more often than not, was a young servant or slave, a person of little or no education and low social standing—could eclipse the rhetorical grandeur of the elite, Harvard-trained minister-orators. The "last Dying Words" (Rogers 1701, 147) of the condemned gathered compelling presencing powers precisely because they were uttered from a space of death and disappearance that impressed on the audience the urgency of their vanishing: "I am upon the brink of Eternity" (Phelan 1993). Then the hood was lowered and the noose tightened around the neck. To clinch the climactic force of the condemned's dying speech, the hangman kicked the ladder out from under the prisoner's feet, and, as one historian put it, "then came a riot of motion" (Banner 2002, 44).

The suspense that excited and transfixed execution audiences was not about the temporal plot or unfolding physical action—the hanging day scenario was well known and predictably choreographed. All the suspense hovered over the fate of the prisoner's immortal soul. What riveted audience attention was whether or not the condemned had truly repented, and, even if so, would her or his faith hold fast under the tremendous distress and horror of "the present circumstances for Terrification" (Rogers 1701, 144)? Executions, like every other temporal aspect of life in Puritan New England, were inserted within a cosmic spiritual drama of sin and salvation. The real suspense was not about anything so mundane as whether the condemned would get a last-minute reprieve, but would the condemned confess convincingly, manifest true repentance, and be able to deliver an affecting dying speech that would serve as warning to sinners and inspiration to the sanctified? If that happened—no easy feat, by any measure—then the worst malefactor could hope for eternal life. Puritan audiences scrutinized the body and speech of the condemned for "Signals of Divine Grace," and when they recognized true penitence then they could interpretively reframe the hideous torture of a hanging into a catalyst for salvation: "This Serves only to draw the Curtain, that thou mayst behold a Tragick Scene, strangely changed into a Theater of Mercy" (Rogers 1701, 2, 118).[12]

To appreciate better the complex theatricality of executions in early America, let us look more closely at one particular case. On July 31, 1701, Esther Rodgers, a twenty-one-year-old indentured servant convicted of infanticide, was hanged outside the town of Ipswich before a crowd estimated between four and five thousand (Rogers 1701, 153). She had confessed to fornication, "Carnal Pollution with the Negro" with whom she worked in the same household, and to killing the "bastard" newborn "begotten in Whoredom" (Rogers 1701, 124). After arraignment and imprisonment for this heinous crime, she confessed to another, earlier murder: when she was seventeen she had fallen into "that foul Sin of Uncleanness, suffering my self to be defiled by a Negro Lad" and she had killed that mixed-race baby as well. In between the two pregnancies, she had lived in a tavern, "giving my self up to other wicked Company and ways of Evil" (Rogers 1701, 123). A vast multitude of spectators assembled at the gallows, the largest audience "as was scarcely ever heard of or seen upon any occasion in any part of New England" (Rogers 1701, 2). They had come "to behold the Tragical End" of this young but "very great Criminal" (Rogers 1701, 2, 142). In addition to the notoriety and sexual-racial sensationalism of her crimes, part of the draw could have been the circulating reports of her "marvelous change" from the pastors and pious townspeople who had visited and ministered to her during her eight months in prison awaiting execution (Rogers 1701, 3). As one of the ministers attested: "a poor Wretch, entering into Prison a Bloody Malefactor, her Conscience laden with Sins of a Scarlet Die . . . she came forth, Sprinkled, Cleansed, Comforted, a Candidate of Heaven" (Rogers 1701, 118).

For all its "antitheatrical prejudice," Puritan life was saturated with a performance consciousness that delighted in transformations, metamorphoses, reversals, astonishing wonders, and the language of theatrical representation: "tragical spectacle," "tragick scene," "tragick end," "theater of mercy" (Barish 1981). Everyday people and events could become spectacles, displays, signs, examples, monuments. Esther was depicted as "a Pillar of Salt Transformed into a Monument of Free Grace" (Rogers 1701, 118). But Puritan ways of seeing increased the dramatic tension because any "monument of grace" was unstable and fallible, always in danger of falling, of debasing itself, of shape-shifting into "a Monument of Shame and Ignominy" (Danforth 1674). The drama of the fall and the relentless conflict with evil suffused the workaday world where everyday action, gesture, and speech suddenly could shimmer with spiritual significance to the discerning eye. The execution sermon provided a figural proscenium arch, the theological frame, through which a Puritan audience viewed a public hanging. Puritan ministers endeavored, at great discursive length, to turn the earthly scene of capital punishment into a shining morality play, a vivid acting out of the allegory of divine wrath and judgment, and, if the ritual succeeded, "an Instance of Converting Grace and Mercy" (Rogers 1701, 3). They uplifted the physical action of the state "Business of Death" onto a sacred plane of performative metaphors, images, and symbols (Rogers 1701, 119).[13] Thus when describing the vast multitude of thousands gathered to watch Esther Rodgers hang, one minister commented, "Which could not but put all serious and thoughtful Spirits in mind of the Great and General Assembly that will appear at the Great Day to receive their final Sentence" (Rogers 1701, 2).

Puritan theology underpinned robust "interpretive communities" of active spectators for whom, in a very deep sense, all the world was a stage, a place for seeing.[14] They inculcated "watchfulness"—of themselves and their neighbors—as part of the habitus of daily life (Williams 1699, 7). According to their Calvinist outlook, everyone was innately depraved, and conversion, never final, was an arduous and incessant struggle. For several weeks prior to her execution, Esther Rodgers consistently enacted the role of an exemplary sinner, showing all the signs of repentance and conversion. Nonetheless, she emerged from prison on the morning of her execution as a "*Candidate* of Heaven," her salvation by no means yet assured (Rogers 1701, 118; emphasis added). She still had to face the greatest and most severe test and trial of her newfound faith. The sabbath before her hanging she had dictated a written message to be read aloud in church enlisting the support and prayers of the congregation, "that the Lord would Strengthen and Uphold her, and carry her through that hard and difficult Work when called thereunto, that she may not be dismayed at the Sight and Fear of Death" (Rogers 1701, 133). These same congregants formed part of the vigilant and expectant circle of spectators around the gallows who scrutinized every move she made. Everyone wondered: what was the state of her mind, heart, and soul as she looked death in the face? Had she accomplished the laborious work of conversion sufficiently?

And if these questions were not already in many spectators' minds, they certainly would have been stirred up by the attending clergy who continuously questioned her conversion as they cross-examined her throughout the grim proceedings. Toward the end of his execution morning sermon, the Reverend Rogers challenged her:

> But what preparation hast thy Soul made to appear at Gods Tribunal before this Day be ended? . . . Hast thou desired and laboured for Holiness to Sanctify thee, as well as Righteousness to justify thee? What means hast thou used to get thy Soul purged as well as sin pardoned . . . ? Hast thou waited and prayed with David, Psal[m] 51. *Wash me throughly from my sins, purge me with Hyssop* . . . or hast thou thought a few Tears sufficient for this? (Rogers 1701, 115–16)

And as she walked the long "dolorous way" to the gallows, the accompanying ministers pressed her with frightening questions, "mixing with words of Consolation, something of Terrour":

> O Esther, How can your heart abide! Don't you here behold terrible displayes of Justice: you are surrounded with Armed men. . . . The terrible place and Engines of Destruction, are but a little before us, where you must in a few Minutes Expire; and there lyes your Coffin that must receive your perishing Body: How can you bear the sight of all these things? (Rogers 1701, 119, 144)

And even after she had climbed the scaffold ladder, and delivered a deeply moving speech to the audience of thousands, and an even more emotionally pitched and passionate prayer, and after the sheriff had tied the blindfold over her face, just moments before he placed the noose over her head, another attending minister, Reverend Wise, stepped forward and took that moment to cross-examine her again: "Now is the great Crisis of Time. Does your Faith hold in God and Christ still? She answers, *God be thanked it does, God be thanked.*" Then, with the rope around her neck, and after her final, almost frantic, outcry—"O Lord Jesus, Now Lord Jesus, I am a coming . . . ." (Rogers 1701, 152)—even at that most vulnerable, plaintive moment, as she waited for the drop, "Lifting up her Hands to Heaven," the unflappable Reverend Wise stepped forward again, and extended her only the conditional comfort of the subjunctive mood: "If your Hopes can lay hold upon the irresistible Grace and Mercy of God in Christ, and [if] you can cast your self into His Armes, you are Happy for Ever. And so we must bid you Fare-Well" (Rogers 1701, 152).

The Ipswich pastors seized the occasion of Esther Rodgers's execution to dramatize and drive home the point that conversion was a moment-by-moment contingency: at any instant mortals could be "assaulted with Temptations to Unbelief or Fear" (Rogers 1701, 132). Esther died a saint, but throughout the protracted drama of her execution-cum-salvation her state of grace was both affirmed and deferred, contrapuntally played out and kept in agonizing suspense right up until the end. The processual, equivocal, anxious, contested dynamics of conversion heightened the tension and turned a familiar execution scenario into a cliffhanger. The moral drama was heightened and made compelling by this deep interplay between knowing, and not knowing, for sure.

Further, Puritan sermons were filled with warnings against dissemblers, hypocrites, and charlatans who masqueraded piety: "Lyars: Such as are deceitful, and dissembling, who speak otherwise then they think; and do otherwise then they speak; such as accustom themselves to speak falsly" and those who are "partial and feigned in their repentance" (Williams 1699, 12, 37). Esther Rodgers was a person who knew how to keep secrets, how to feign and hide: she had concealed not one, but two pregnancies, carried the babies to term, secretly delivered, and no one knew, not even the fathers. And she had successfully covered up the first murder. At least one supporter felt the need to preempt questions about the sincerity of her jailhouse conversion: "Neither shall any need to question the truth of the repentance of the person Condemned, and after Executed, from the shortness of the time of her Experiences: The Thief that Commenced Converted on the Cross . . . is a proof of the possibility hereof" (Rogers 1701, 3).

The ambivalence of her spiritual condition, the gap between closure and uncertainty that the ministers pried open, also provided a space for multiple ways of seeing and other spectatorial positions unbounded by Puritan orthodoxy. Executions encouraged spectators to gaze intently at the body on display and granted extraordinary ritual license for the condemned, especially if they were women, to make spectacles out of their bodies.[15] Just as the sentence of death had to be "executed on her body," so also the signs of grace had to be manifested bodily (Rogers 1701, 133). Execution audiences closely monitored the prisoner's gesture, carriage, countenance, demeanor, deportment, vocal intonation, inflection, timber. An "admiring observer" noted Esther's "Composure of spirit, Cheerfulness of Countenance, pleasantness of Speech, and a sort of Complaisantness in Carriage towards the Ministers who were assistant to her" (Rogers 1701, 153). But was there slippage in the frames through which she was viewed? And did even a pious allegorical reading pivot on a doubling of vision, an interplay of perspectives that saw her as both a wanton woman and an aspiring Christian? She had been, until very recently, a harlot. Everyone knew the sexual nature of her crime and her "scarlet" past. She had confessed that she was a creature wholly given over to "lust" (Rogers 1701, 122). Reverend Rogers reminded her, and everyone else, in his morning execution sermon: "Thy ways have been all filthy, thy whole Walk, a walk after the Flesh; thy course a course of filthy Communication and Conversation" (Rogers 1701, 114).

With that phrase still ringing in their ears, how did spectators view her "Walk" to the gallows? Her choice to forego the customary cart and to "walk on foot" (Rogers 1701, 143)? How did they observe the moving body of this young, sexually active woman, surrounded by men, as it paraded by them? Was she a walking palimpsest, the imprint of her harlot past shadowing and alternating with her Christian image? Which image came into sharper and more sustained focus for whom, at what points in the procession? How did bystanders interpret her vivacious physicality, especially the remarkable moment when she responded to a minister's question by "turn[ing] about, and looking him in the face with a very smiling countenance" (Rogers 1701, 144)? What did various spectators make of the moment when she stumbled upon first seeing the gallows, and then, after this "Reluctancy of the Flesh," her recovery when "she lift up her Feet, and Marched on with an Erected, and Radiant Countenance" (Rogers 1701, 119)? How did different audience members construe "the very affecting Gestures" with which she took her leave of the ministers at the foot of the gallows (Rogers 1701, 146)? How did they watch her as she paused, composed herself, "and so without stop or trembling went up the Ladder"? And what went through their minds during the physically delicate moment of "turning herself about" on the narrow ladder so that she could face the crowd? And how did they take in her spectacularly displayed body, especially when she arched it, "being bid [by the sheriff] to lean her Head back upon the Ladder, to receive the Halter" (Rogers 1701, 152)?

We can be sure that profane ways of looking commingled with pious perspectives within this huge gathering. The sheer size of the crowd, numbering in the thousands, must have created a social effervescence. Executions in England during the same time period were rowdy, rambunctious, "carnivalesque" affairs.[16] And the large number of young people in the audience—"great Numbers whereof were expected" and their large presence was "accordingly" noted—must have charged the event with libidinal energy (Rogers 1701, 113). Puritan sermons reverberated with warnings about "youthful lusts" (Danforth 1674, i). The massive ideological pressure of the execution sermons attests indirectly to the excitement and desire that the preachers struggled so forcefully to rein in and control. If we read these official documents against the grain of their orthodoxy, we can understand that all the appeals to "serious and thoughtful spirits" were pulling against other, more unruly and irreverent dispositions (Rogers 1701, 2). Moreover, sensuality was not banished from Puritan piety. Recent historical research disputes the stereotype of the dour, sexually repressed Puritans and argues that they exuberantly "conjoined earthly and spiritual passion" and that a striking aspect of their religious life was "the eroticisation of the spiritual" (Godbeer 2002, 55).

Execution audiences were encouraged to identify deeply with the condemned as fellow sinners. They did not shrink in moral revulsion from even the most despised and heinous criminals. The typical response was "there but for the grace of God, go I." At the 1674 execution of Benjamin Goad for sodomy, Samuel Danforth vehemently denounced his horrid and unnatural "lasciviousness" but then reminded the audience: "there are sins with the Spectators, as well as with the Sufferers. . . . If we ransack our own hearts . . . we shall finde such sins with us . . . . The holiest man hath as vile and filthy a Nature, as the Sodomites . . ." (Danforth 1674, 10). This way of seeing encouraged a deeply sympathetic, theatrical identification in which the spectators could imaginatively exchange places with the condemned, instead of holding themselves aloof in distanced judgment. The ideal spectator at executions became a deeply engaged, co-performative witness.

The Puritan structure of feeling that embraced wrongdoers as members of the same moral community in need of repentance was superseded in the nineteenth century by a gothic view of criminals as "moral aliens" and "moral monsters."[17] The dramaturgy of executions changed from large-scale public rituals of redemption and reincorporation to exclusive, privatized rituals of retribution and expulsion. This new, bourgeois structure of feeling about criminals is registered powerfully in an 1848 *American Whig Review* article, "On the Use of Chloroform in Hanging" (Peck 1848).[18] Criminals are now seen as "miserable wretches whom we simply wish to cast contemptuously out of existence" (Peck 1848, 295). Class lines are now sharply drawn and patrolled by social performances of civility and respectability, all based on bodily deportment: "the rude have one species, the refined another" (Peck 1848, 286). A "gentlemanly nation" should be "severe towards crime"; therefore the respectable classes "must overcome sympathy" (Peck 1848, 291) to criminals who are "aliens to the race":

> The reason should condemn them, the fancy recoil from them, and the pride scorn them. All that can spring from the deepest determination to wipe out such stains from humanity, or express the universal strong disgust which they inspire, should be brought to bear against them. Mankind are bound to affect towards them the manners of loathing and horror. (Peck 1848, 292)

Peck proposed chloroforming prisoners before hanging them, not out of any compassion for the condemned, but because some of the loathsome creatures had the bad manners to struggle and convulse while being executed, "thus tending to disturb the nervous peace, which is the support of refinement." A botched execution was "against good manners, and unbecoming in a civilized Christian people" (Peck 1848, 296).

Coming midway between the 1701 execution of Esther Rodgers and the 2001 executions of Timothy McVeigh and Juan Raul Garza, Peck's pivotal document registers the profound shift in structure of feeling about the death penalty and prefigures the modern interest in new methods and technologies for sanitizing death. Although Peck's idea to anesthetize criminals before executing them was not adopted in his day, it resurfaced in 1977 when Oklahoma invented lethal injection as the preferred mode of capital punishment for the modern age. The lethal injection protocol includes a first dose of sodium pentothal, which puts the prisoner to sleep, followed by a muscle relaxant that paralyzes the lungs, and then potassium chloride that stops the heart (see Johnson 1998). Putting the prisoner to sleep before killing him or her is more about cosmetics than compassion; it keeps up the appearance of decency, protects the witnesses from messy scenes, and masks the violence of state killing with a humane medical procedure.

The Magical Realism of Modern Capital Punishment

The multibillion dollar business of incarceration with its ramified rituals of punishment provides the bodies—and they are disproportionately racialized and working-class bodies—that serve as the concrete referents for society's ideas about "justice," "law and order," and "public safety" (Taussig 1997, 187).[19] Executions anchor belief in the criminal justice system, dramatizing in an especially vivid way that "something is being done," that the system is in control, order has been restored. Foucault argued: "without the right to kill, would the judicial system be anything more than a public utility a bit less efficient than the post office? The right to kill is the last emblem of its supremacy" (Foucault 1994, 435–436). Never has Foucault's insight been demonstrated more clearly than in the FBI bungling of the McVeigh evidence in the most high-profile capital trial in recent history; the FBI lost 4,400 documents, evidence that should have been turned over to the defense team. This was such a breach of due process that Attorney General John Ashcroft had to issue a one-month stay of execution (Johnston 2001). If the judicial system can break down and bungle a case of this magnitude, under an international media spotlight, imagine what happens with everyday prosecutions. This crisis of confidence was redressed by speedy review, and within a few weeks the McVeigh execution bandwagon was back on track and a new death warrant signed for June 11. These events dramatically drive home Foucault's larger point that executions justify Justice, that they provide a satisfying sense of closure and cover for a shaky system that pretends to be infallible. Northwestern University's Center for Wrongful Convictions has documented more than one hundred cases of men and women who were sentenced to death and then exonerated. In Illinois, 13 men in recent years have been freed from death row; that is one more than the state has executed since the United States reinstated capital punishment in 1976. One of these released men, Anthony Porter, came within 48 hours of being put to death; he had already ordered his last meal and been measured for his coffin.[20]

Contemporary execution rituals work their magic and derive their efficacy from the effusive power of the effigy. Here I draw together Joseph Roach's performance theory of the effigy in *Cities of the Dead* with Michael Taussig's rereading of the anthropological literature on effigies and magic in *Mimesis and Alterity*.[21] Effigies are crudely fashioned surrogates that bear little resemblance to the person for whom they stand in. They produce magical power from parts, pieces, effluvia, operating on principles of contiguity and synecdoche—the piece, the part that stands for the whole—more than likeness or resemblance. Effigies are rough fabrications made from distorted parts of a person, often excrements such as saliva, blood, hair, fingernail parings, semen, fingerprints, footprints, which are then performatively deployed to put the real person in harm's way. An effigy is the fusion of image and body, symbol and source, the figurative and the physical. Because a jury will never vote to kill a human being, the fundamental task of the prosecutor is to turn the accused into an effigy composed of his or her worst parts and bad deeds. Before they are strip-searched and strapped down to the execution gurney, the condemned must first be stripped of all human complexity and reduced to human waste, the worst of the worst. These waste parts are then crafted onto prefabricated figures: stereotypes of the violent criminal, cold-blooded killer, animal, beast, brute, predator, fiend, monster. Thus a young, attractive, completely rehabilitated, devoutly spiritual Karla Faye Tucker was transformed into an effigy, a scarecrow, and methodically put to death as "the Pick-Axe Killer." These effigies take on manifest powers and become not just surrogates for the accused, but stand-ins for crime and all anti-social forces of evil that threaten law and order. When the Federal government strapped Juan Garza onto a gurney on June 19, 2001, and stuck a needle into the calf of his right leg, it was not killing a loving father of young children who was much, much more than the single worst thing that he had ever done. They were sticking pins into an effigy: "Drug Kingpin," the headlines blared on execution day. And they did this in the name of Justice and for the sake of Order to ward off omnipresent social dangers and the specter of crime.

Race figures prominently in the construction of these effigies. Glaring racial disparities at every level of the death penalty system are shocking and egregious. Of the 760 people put to death since capital punishment was reinstated in 1977, 44 percent have been minorities, when minorities are only 29 percent of the population. And this disproportion is even more skewed if we focus on blacks: 35 percent of the people executed were black, when blacks are only 12 percent of the population (Table 1). And 43 percent of the prisoners currently on death row are black (Table 2). The racial profile of people put to death becomes even more stark when we look at juvenile offenders. First, I need to point out that the United States is one of a small number of countries in the world that still has a juvenile death penalty. Not only is the US out of step with other western democracies that long since have stopped putting their citizens to death—abolition of the death penalty is a condition of membership in the European Union—but also only five countries that still retain capital punishment execute minors: Iran, Nigeria, Pakistan, Saudi Arabia, and the United States. And no nation in the world has reported executions of minors since 1997, except the United States: we have executed seven juvenile offenders since 1998, three in 2000, one in May, 2002 (Napoleon Beazley, the young African American man, whose last words I quoted in the epigraph for this essay). Not even China, the world leader in number of executions per year, still executes juvenile offenders. Of the 38 states with death penalty statutes, 23 authorize the execution of children; 18 states allow the execution of children as young as 16 (Table 3). Texas has executed 11 of the 19 juvenile offenders who have been put to death since 1985, and 64 percent of that group were minorities (Table 4). And 26 of the 83 juvenile offenders currently awaiting execution are on Texas's death row: 85 percent of them are minorities (Table 5).[22]

Furthermore, if we look at other jurisdictions in addition to the 38 states with death penalty statutes, the racial disparities are even more glaring. The United States military has its own death penalty statute, and 86 percent of the military prisoners on death row are minorities (Table 6). This statistic does not augur well for the military tribunals that President Bush has authorized by executive order to adjudicate capital cases in the wake of September 11. The federal government also has its own death penalty statute that authorizes the execution of prisoners in the name of every citizen in the nation. 87 percent of the prisoners on federal death row are minorities (Table 7). Because of these statistics, the federal

Table 1. Race of 760 Defendants Executed, 1977–2002

			(US pop.)
White	430	56%	(71%)
Minority	330	44%	(29%)
Black	265	35%	(12%)
Latino	50	7%	(12%)
Other	15	2%	(5%)

U.S. Census 2000
Execution count up to February 19, 2002

Table 2. Race of Death Row Inmates

Minority	54%
Black	43%
Latino	9%
Other	2%
White	46%

January 1, 2002

Table 3. Juvenile Death Penalty

23 of the 38 Death Penalty States Permit the Execution of Minors

Minimum Age

16	(18 states)
17	(5 states)
18	(15 states)

Table 4. 19 Juvenile Offenders Executed Since 1985

Texas Executed 11

7 Minority	64%
6 Black	
1 Latino	
4 White	36%

May, 2002

Table 5. 83 Juvenile Offenders on Death Row

26 on Texas Death Row	
22 Minority	85%
11 Black	42%
10 Latino	39%
1 Asian	4%
4 White	15%

February, 2002

government went to great lengths to assure that McVeigh would precede Mexican-born Garza to the federal death chamber. The federal government had not put anyone to death in thirty-eight years, so whoever inaugurated the newly built state-of-the-art federal execution chamber in Terre Haute, Indiana—strategically chosen as the geographic "crossroads of America"—would attract extraordinary media attention. Garza originally had been scheduled to go to the gurney first, August 5, 2000, but two stays of execution pushed back his date to June 19, 2001, behind Timothy McVeigh who was scheduled for May 16, 2001. The shocking revelation on May 10 that the FBI had failed to turn over 4,400 documents of evidence to the McVeigh defense team, as they were required to do by law, threatened to derail McVeigh's timely execution. However, Attorney General John Ashcroft granted only a one-month reprieve, which kept McVeigh just in front of Garza, absorbing the full media spotlight as the "first" prisoner executed by federal government in 38 years. In this sense, McVeigh's high profile execution was a perverse form of whiteface minstrelsy, a whiteout of the glaring racial inequities in the way capital punishment is meted out in America. Juan Raul Garza, a Mexican American who came to this country as an impoverished migrant laborer, was far more representative of death row inmates than Timothy McVeigh, especially the federal death row, which is 84 percent minorities. A similar whiteface staging occurred in 1979 when there was much maneuvering around who would be the historic "first" person executed since the Supreme Court reinstated the death penalty with the 1976 Gregg decision. John Spenkelink, a working-class white man, was cast in that leading role. Despite his lawyer's argument that his execution was speeded up for purely political reasons, that as a white man Spenkelink's execution "would inoculate Florida from 150 years of racial discrimination in capital cases," Spenkelink was carried, terrified, to Florida's electric chair on

Table 6. U.S. Military Death Row		
	Total	*7*
Minority	6	86%
Black	5	71%
Asian	1	14%
White	1	14%
Reinstated in 1984 by executive order of Pres. Ronald Reagan		
Last military execution in 1963 (hanging)		

Table 7. Federal Death Row		
	Total	*19*
Minority	16	84%
Black	14	74%
Latino	2	10%
White	3	16%
(Four cases pending: 3 Black, 1 Asian)		
January, 2002		

Table 8. Race of Prosecutors Responsible for Death Penalty Cases

95% White, 2% Black, 3% Latino

State	*White*	*Black*	*Latino*
Texas	137	0	11
Virginia	113	8	0
Missouri	115	0	0
Florida	19	1	0
Oklahoma	26	0	0

1998

May 25, 1979, to become the first person executed involuntarily since the 1976 restitution of capital punishment (McFeely 2000, 69).[23]

Race refracts and distorts other parts of the death penalty system as well. 95 percent of all the prosecutors responsible for death penalty cases are white. Because only a tiny fraction of all homicides are prosecuted as capital cases it is very disturbing to see such systemic racial asymmetry with an overwhelmingly white group of people holding the power and responsibility to decide which cases are prosecuted for death and at the other end a staggeringly disproportionate number of people of color sentenced to death (Table 8). Race registers its greatest impact when we look at the race of victims in capital cases (U.S. General Accounting Office 1997, 327). Even though only 50 percent of all murder victims are white, 81 percent of murder victims in capital cases are white. And interracial murders compound the effects of race: "African Americans who murder whites are 19 times as likely to be executed as whites who kill blacks" (Jackson et al. 2001, 75).

And in America, race articulates with class. Middle and upper class people who can afford to hire skilled lawyers do not end up on death row. Mumia Abu-Jamal, currently on Pennsylvania's death row, observed: "Them's that got the capital don't get capital punishment" (quoted in Jackson et al. 2001, 35).[24] All of the whites on death row are working class and poor. According to Stephen Bright, a seasoned death penalty lawyer, defendants get the death sentence "not for the worst crime but for the worst lawyer" (Bright 1997). Even though statistics on the class status of people sentenced to death and executed are not systematically collected or as accessible as those on race and gender, there are other ways of ascertaining class status. Anyone who doubts that people sentenced to death in this country are overwhelmingly impoverished and working class should go to the web site of the Texas Department of Criminal Justice. For some bizarre reason, it posts the last meal requests of all the people it has put to death.[25] Because food preferences are shaped and bounded by class "tastes," it is a very revealing and poignant experience to read through the last meals requested by the Texas condemned (Douglas 1982; Bourdieu 1984).

There is also some evidence of the role that homophobia plays in creating execution effigies. Because of the fluidity of sexualities, as well as the difficulty of collecting data on sexual orientation—prison is not a safe place to be "out," notwithstanding the non-normative sexual activity that is encouraged by these enforced homosocial environments—it is difficult to know exactly how many queers are on death row. However, one 1992 article in *Advocate* estimated that 40 percent of the women on death row are lesbians (Brownworth 1992).[26]

The death penalty is a potent political symbol, a sign and litmus test for tough-on-crime politicians. The symbolic center of the "war" on crime, it is a gendered symbol, a mantle of "political macho" that female politicians, like Dianne Feinstein and Jeanne Shaheen, the first woman governor of New Hampshire who vetoed the legislation to abolish that state's death penalty, can wear to masculinize themselves in the public sphere. Male Democratic politicians can use their vigorous support of the death penalty to counter charges of "soft" liberalism (Lifton and Mitchell 2000, 135). Bill Clinton masterminded this New Democrat centrist strategy. He infamously left the presidential campaign trail in 1992 to return to Arkansas to oversee the execution of Rickey Ray Rector, a young African American man so mentally impaired that at his last meal he asked the guards if he could save the piece of pecan pie for later (Lifton and Mitchell 2000, 101). During the year 2000, when he campaigned for the presidency, George W. Bush presided over 40 Texas executions, which broke the record for the largest number of annual executions ever performed by a state in the history of the nation.

In 1984, Velma Barfield, a North Carolina grandmother, probably became the first woman executed since 1962 because a trial judge set her clemency hearing four days before the general election. Her execution became a political issue because Democratic Governor James Hunt was locked in a tight race for the United States Senate against ultraconservative Jesse Helms. It had been twenty-two years since a woman had been put to death in this country, and there was strong support and pressure for Governor Hunt to grant clemency to this sweet-natured grandmother who had become a model prisoner. But fearing a political backlash in his closely contested senate race with Helms, Hunt allowed the execution of Barfield to proceed. The prison personnel responsible for killing Barfield, who was affectionately called "Granny," as well as the entire prison staff who had come to know and like her were absolutely devastated by her execution (Bessler 1997, 142).[27] It took fourteen years before another state had the stomach to execute a woman. In 1998 Karla Faye Tucker became the first woman put to death in Texas since before the Civil War. Her execution, which attracted widespread media coverage, seemed to break the execution chamber glass ceiling for women. In 2001, three women were executed, all in Oklahoma. The last time three women were executed was 1953, when the Federal government electrocuted Ethel Rosenberg in New York, gassed Bonnie Headley in Missouri, and electrocuted Earle Dennison in Alabama. Wanda Jean Allen, one of the three women executed in 2001, became the first black woman put to death in 47 years. The prosecution highlighted her lesbianism in arguing for the death penalty (McClary 2002).

Federal Judge Robert Bork provides insight into the expressive and performative politics of the death penalty. In a brief he filed in support of the 1976 Supreme Court decision that reinstated the death penalty—the Gregg Decision—he argued that capital punishment "serves a vital social function as society's expression of moral outrage" (quoted in Sarat 2001,

33). This thinking releases capital punishment from accountability as a crime-fighting tool, a deterrent, and reframes it as a theatre of retribution and revenge. It becomes a form of "poetic justice," a "revenge tragedy" that operates on the principle of mimetic magic: the belief that only violence can cross out violence. Timothy McVeigh was caught at both ends of this contagious chain of mimetic violence. He bombed the Murrah Federal Building in Oklahoma City to express his moral outrage and mimetically respond to the FBI's botched raid and burning of the Branch Davidian Compound in Waco, Texas. He chose April 19, 1995 as the date for blowing up the federal building because it was the second year anniversary of the Waco conflagration and the 220th anniversary of the Battle of Lexington and Concord (Michel and Herbeck 2001, 226). In his warped imagination and twisted aesthetics, the violence he perpetrated in Oklahoma City was the performative reparation for the violence that the federal government wreaked on the Branch Davidian Compound. He, in turn, paid with his life when the federal government responded in kind by killing him. At McVeigh's execution, anti-death penalty activists exposed the circular absurdity of mimetic violence with this question carried on placards and emblazoned on T-shirts: "Why Do We Kill People, Who Kill People, To Show that Killing People Is Wrong?"

The persistence of the death penalty defies logic and exceeds rational explanation. There are at least four troubling problems with capital punishment. (1) It is not a deterrent to crime. Even conservative criminologists no longer justify it as a deterrent to crime. (2) It is meted out in an inconsistent and capricious way. There are glaring racial and geographic disparities in its application. (3) The system sometimes executes the wrong person: one scholar estimates an error rate of one innocent person out of every seven executed (Sarat 2001, 258). (4) It is extremely expensive. Each execution (from trial to death chamber) costs on the average 1.5 million dollars, far more expensive than a life sentence (Jackson 2001, 110). Why then does it persist? When logic cannot uphold it, when it does not work, and when it is not cost-effective? It is adhered to for emotional and expressive purposes that can be exploited for political gain. Like other rituals of sacrifice, executions tap the generative power of violence and harness the volatile energies surrounding death for political purposes. Newt Gingrich once explained that the two cornerstones for building a conservative majority in the United States are (1) tax cuts, and (2) the Death Penalty (Sarat 2001, 17–18). A close reading of the dramaturgy of contemporary execution rituals reveals the deep and terribly fraught contradictions, conundra, tensions, and anxieties that are never fully reconciled.

The Dramaturgy of Contemporary Executions

The central performance challenge of execution rituals is to differentiate between judicial killing and murder.[28] This distinction is dramatized through the careful and elaborate staging of props, participants, and players: the entire scenography and choreography of the event signal order, control, propriety, and inevitability. The real violence of state killing is veiled behind protocols of civility and the pretense of courtesy toward the condemned—hence the hollow gestures of permitting the condemned to order his or her last meal and to speak his or her last words. Some guards and wardens even eat with the condemned to give them some company during the ceremony of the last meal. The prison staff show an unusual attentiveness and air of concern for the condemned during the final countdown hours of the death-watch (Johnson 1998).

But all this consideration is as much about controlling the performance, making sure that it proceeds smoothly without a glitch, as it is about compassion or empathy for the condemned. Inasmuch as possible, spontaneity and improvisation are foreclosed in the execution scenario. Everything is carefully scripted, choreographed, rehearsed, and directed—micro-managed right down to the tiniest of details, nothing left to chance. The condemned must order his or her last meal seven days in advance. Ritual theatre intersects with management science to produce the bizarre contemporary form of modern executions (McKenzie 2001). Much of the debate surrounding the death penalty since the 1890 invention of the electric chair has focused on the performance technology of executions.

Officials are anxious to control the performance because condemned prisoners, although acutely vulnerable, are not without agency. They can fight back and force the guards to drag them kicking and screaming to their death. In June 2000, Gary Graham, also called Sankofa, refused to cooperate and go quietly to the execution chamber. A helmeted "extraction team" maced and forcibly removed him from his holding cell. Protesting his innocence he resisted every step of the way, and even as the poison was dripping into his veins, he loudly protested, "They're killing me tonight, they're murdering me tonight."[29] On the other hand, prisoners sometimes panic and collapse in terror at the moment of the final walk to their premeditated death. Either response—defiant resistance or terrified hysteria—rips off the mask of civility, the illusion of order, inevitability, procedure, due process, the fiction that what is taking place is "natural," "clean," "solemn," "dignified," and "humane," an acceptable performance of Justice in a modern democracy.[30]

Table 9. All Nations Have Abolished the Juvenile Death Penalty Except Five:
Iran, Pakistan, Nigeria, Saudi Arabia, and the United States
The U.S. has executed seven juvenile offenders since 1998 (three in 2000)

Sometimes executions are botched simply because of the performance anxiety or ineptitude of the executioners. Each one of the methods for putting people to death requires a mastery of technique, and none guarantees a death that is quick, painless, and clean. Hanging involves an intricate calculus between the length of the rope and the weight of the prisoner. If the drop is too short, the neck is not broken, and the condemned kicks and writhes in the agony of slow strangulation. If the drop is too long, the head is ripped off. The electric chair requires skillful application of electrodes to the shaved head and leg to ensure a good connection, and the careful measurement of voltage and timing of the jolts. With too powerful a charge, the condemned catches on fire, which happened twice in Florida's electric chair in 1990 and 1997. But even when electrocutions go smoothly they are messy affairs. The eyes bulge, sometimes popping out of their sockets, and the condemned urinate and defecate in the chair. The gas chamber was supposed to be a technological improvement over the rope and the chair, but it proved no more efficient or humane than the other technologies. Prisoners had different reactions to the poison gas. Some convulsed violently, thrashed and foamed at the mouth, and bashed their head against the back metal pole. Even lethal injections, the most antiseptic and clinical of all the modes, are sometimes botched. Sometimes the technicians cannot find a good vein; there are documented cases of them searching and pricking both arms, ankle, and finally going to the neck, taking 45 minutes to insert the needle. Sometimes the needle pops out under the pressure of execution, spewing the toxic drugs and spraying the witnesses. Some prisoners heave and violently choke. Botched executions knock down the ritual frame and expose the gruesome reality of actually putting a human being to death. The illusion of nonviolent decency is torn away. Botched executions also are the stuff of sensational news stories and political embarrassments. Graphic images and grisly reports of botched executions erode the public faith in the "ultimate oxymoron: a humane killing" (Lifton and Mitchell 2000, 44).[31] To prevent embarrassing glitches and disruptions, modern executions have become ever more controlled, engineered, and bureaucratized performances.[32]

The regular rehearsals, precise stage directions, and obsessive planning and detail reveal the fragile and volatile nature of these modern rituals of state killing. *The Execution Protocol,* a 56-page manual issued by the Federal Bureau of Prisons, outlines the procedures (Table 10).[33] Leaving no detail to the imagination, the last page of the execution manual instructs that the execution chamber should be cleaned by staff "trained in hygiene and infectious disease control."

And the condemned prisoner is enlisted as a cooperative player within this grisly script. The condemned face a devil's bargain. When all hope for reprieve is gone, the only option left is in common phraseology "getting through this," with as much dignity and as little pain as possible. Perhaps one of the most perverse cruelties is the way the prisoner is coerced into a pact of complicity with his or her executioners. This is perversely apparent with the gas chamber, with the customary final admonition to the condemned as some form of: "Breathe deeply, it'll go easier for you that way." But the life-force is so strong that few comply, and that's why the gas chamber was soon dubbed a chamber of horrors. Norms of masculinity are deployed when wardens exhort prisoners in clichéd fashion to "go to your death like a man, take your medicine like a man." My interview with the warden at the Terre Haute Federal Prison revealed a new innovation in the casting of execution scenarios. With federal executions, the administrators now bring in staff from other institutions, just for the executions. As explained by the warden: "It's too traumatic for the local staff who know the prisoner and in some cases have formed a relationship with him or her over the years on death row." And I hasten to add that I interviewed the new warden, David Olson, who is now in charge of the Federal "execution facility," as it is called in the bureaucratic manuals. His immediate predecessor, Harley Lappin, scored high marks for directing the June, 2001 executions of McVeigh and Garza, again the first federal executions since 1963. By the time I was able to return to Terre Haute in September, 2001 to tour the prison and talk with staff, Lappin already had been rewarded with a promotion and transfer. He is now the Director of the Mid-Atlantic Region, with twenty prisons under his supervision.

Even the demonstrators who come to protest the executions are carefully monitored and controlled. No one is permitted onto the prison grounds with his or her own transportation. At both the McVeigh and Garza executions, we had to meet at a designated park, walk down a fenced corridor, and get searched before being permitted to board the Bureau of Prisons busses. We were required to take a "Pledge of Nonviolence," which included: "we will not swear or use insulting language. We will not run in public or otherwise make threatening motions. We will

Table 10.
Section V. "THE FINAL THIRTY MINUTES PRIOR TO THE EXECUTION"

A. Final Sequence of Events: Preparation

1. Bringing the Condemned Individual to the Execution Room: At a time determined by the warden, the condemned individual will be:
   a. removed from the Inmate Holding Cell by the Restraint Team
   b. strip-searched by the Restraint Team and then dressed in khaki pants, shirt, and slip-on shoes
   c. secured with restraints, if deemed appropriate by the Warden;
   d. escorted to the Execution Room by the Restraint Team
2. *Restraint Team Procedures*

   In the execution room the ambulatory restraints, if any, will be removed, and the condemned individual will be restrained to the Execution Table. . . .

VI: FINAL SEQUENCE OF EVENTS: EXECUTION

A. Staff Witnesses

1. Staff participating in the preparation for the execution will exit the Execution Room but stand by in an adjacent area
2. Staff members remaining to participate in and observe the execution will include the:
   a. Designated United States Marshal
   b. Warden
   c. Executioner
   d. Other staff authorized by the Director of the Bureau of Prisons

B. Countdown

1. Once the condemned individual has been secured to the table, at the direction of the Warden, staff inside the execution room will open the drapes covering the windows of the witness room
2. The Warden will ask the condemned individual if he/she has any last words, or wishes to make a statement. The condemned individual will have been advised in advance by the warden that this statement should be reasonably brief. . . .
3. At the conclusion of the remarks, or when the Warden determines it is time to proceed, the Warden will read documentation deemed necessary to the execution process. The Warden will then advise the Designated United States Marshal that, quote,"We are ready." Close quote. A prearranged signal will then be given by the Designated United States Marshal to the Warden, who will direct the executioner to administer the lethal injectionj.
4. If the execution is ordered delayed, the Designated United States Marshal will instruct the Executioner to step away from the execution equipment and will notify the condemned individual and all present that the execution has been stayed or delayed. the Warden will direct stand down procedures and return the institution to normal operations after the condemned individual has been returned to appropriate living quarters.

C. Execution

After receiving the signal from the Designated United States Marshal, the Warden will direct the executioner to administer the lethal injection.

honor the directions of the designated coordinators. In the event of serious disagreement, we will remove ourselves from the Vigil Action." Once on the bus, two guards with rifles accompanied us, one riding up front, the other in the back. Each bus was escorted to the prison by two police cars with flashing lights, one car in front, one in the rear.

"What is at stake," Sarat asks, "when the state imagines itself killing painlessly, humanely?" (Sarat 2001, 69) When it invents new and improved technologies for putting people to death with "decency" and "dignity"? What do the shifting modes and methods of execution say about public standards of taste and thresholds of squeamishness? The quest for quick, efficient, and clean modes of execution that do not disfigure the corpse is for the sake of spectators more than the condemned. When Ronald Reagan was governor of California, he was one of the first government officials to imagine lethal injection. He observed, "as a former rancher and horse raiser, I know what it's like to eliminate an injured horse by shooting him," recommending instead, "a simple shot or tranquilizer" (quoted in Jackson et al. 2001, 113).[34] Reagan's point was not to spare the defendant pain, but to shield the executioners—and by extension, civil society—from the horror and anguish of exterminating a human being.

In 1977 Oklahoma reinvented capital punishment for the modern age by developing the new performance technology of "lethal injection." In 1982 in Texas, Charles Brooks became the first prisoner executed by lethal injection. Outside the United States, China first used lethal injection in 1997, which it deemed more scientific than shooting a kneeling prisoner in the back of the head at close range. When lethal injection was first discussed in the Oklahoma legislature, advocates argued the merits of: "No pain, no spasms, no smells or sounds—just sleep, then death." Governor David Boren pointed out that it provided "a nice clean exit plan" (Wiseman 2001). Susan Blaustein, a media witness to a lethal injection in Texas, described the experience in a *Harper's Magazine* article titled "Witness to Another Execution in Texas: Death Walks an Assembly Line." She wrote: "The lethal injection method has turned dying into a *still life,* thereby enabling the state to kill without anyone involved feeling anything at all . . . . We have perfected the art of institutional killing to the degree that it has deadened our natural, quintessentially human response to death" (Blaustein 1997).

Tulsa Republican representative William Wiseman, Jr., was the principal architect of Oklahoma's lethal injection bill. He argued that the needle would "make the death penalty more humane by eliminating the brutality and violence of electrocution"—Oklahoma's then current method for executing criminals. In June 2001, Wiseman published an apologia in the *Christian Century*. He admitted: "The dramatic irony of my action as a legislator is that what purported to be a means of reducing violence became instead a means of increasing it. The moral burden I carry is that, if it were not for my *palatable technique* of death, many who have now been executed would likely have been spared by squeamish juries." He left politics and is now pursuing a Master's of Divinity degree at a theological seminary in Tulsa (Wiseman 2001).[35]

Lethal injection, the favored method of modern capital punishment, borrows props from the medical profession and eerily mimics a therapeutic intervention. Missouri's lethal injection chamber at Potosi Correctional Center is right in the center of the prison hospital ward (Lifton and Mitchell 2000, 97). One of the uncanny consequences of this slippage between curing and killing is that there is a new emergent justification for executions: executions are justified so that the families of victims can heal and achieve "closure." This is a new development in the history of justifications for capital punishment. We have moved from support of capital punishment as a deterrent, as retribution, and now as an extension and necessary part of the grieving process and form of group therapy. This link between capital punishment and mourning is aligned with the politics of the powerful victims rights movement: "By transforming courts into sites for the rituals of grieving, that movement seeks to make private experiences part of public discourse" (Sarat 2001, 35).[36] Appellate Judge Alex Kosinski says that when he reviews and signs off on executions, he "hear[s] the tortured voices of the victims calling out to [him] . . . for vindication" (quoted in Lifton and Mitchell 2000, 162).

The execution of McVeigh demonstrates the political efficacy of mourning. The same group of mourning survivors and family and friends of victims who planned the Oklahoma City National Memorial also campaigned for passage of the 1996 Antiterrorism and Effective Death Penalty Act, legislation that restricts the right of appeal and habeas corpus in order to streamline and speed up the execution process. They also successfully lobbied Attorney General Ashcroft to telecast McVeigh's execution to an invited group of designated mourners in Oklahoma. In an unprecedented move, Attorney General Ashcroft authorized the closed circuit telecast of McVeigh's execution to an arena filled with relatives of victims and survivors of the Murrah building bombing. He infamously said that survivors and families of victims need to be able to see McVeigh executed "to help them meet their need to close this chapter in their lives" (Doming 2001). Over one thousand people were invited to the live telecast of McVeigh's execution, more than half declined, and on the

McVeigh Dies for Oklahoma City Blast

Figure 1: *New York Times,* 12 June 2001.

morning of June 19, 2001, 232 showed up at the telecast site, a federal prison.[37]

Several of the invited people went directly from watching the telecast of McVeigh's execution to the Oklahoma City National Memorial Center, thus collapsing the execution into personal rituals of bereavement. One of them, Tom Kight, placed the blue federal badge identifying him as "Witness 223" at the execution telecast on the commemorative chair for his stepdaughter killed in the blast (Anderson 2001, 14).[38] Several newspapers reinforced this conflation of capital punishment with rites of mourning by running full color photographs of the Oklahoma City National Memorial Center underneath banner headlines announcing

Chicago Tribune

NORTH SPORTS FINAL

TUESDAY, JUNE 12, 2001

U.S. executes its worst terrorist

Figure 2: *Chicago Tribune,* 12 June 2001.

McVeigh's execution. On June 12, the *New York Times* ran "McVeigh Dies for Oklahoma City Blast" headline above a photograph of family members kneeling and grieving by the chair commemorating their mother at the Oklahoma City National Memorial Center (Fig. 1). The caption explained that the family members had just come from watching the execution on closed-circuit TV (Bragg 2001). The same day the *Chicago Tribune* ran "U.S. Executes Its Worst Terrorist" banner headline above a panoramic photograph of the Oklahoma City National Memorial Center likewise showing grieving family members just arrived from viewing the execution, kneeling at memorial chairs (Fig. 2). On an inside page, there was another photograph of a woman holding a radio and listening intently while kneeling in front of one of the memorial chairs. The caption read: "Renee Pendley listens to a radio report on the execution as she kneels near the memorial chair for her friend Teresa Lauderdale."[39]

Two of the relatives of Oklahoma City bombing victims, who won the lottery to witness the McVeigh execution live in Terre Haute, pressed photographs of deceased loved ones against the window as they watched

McVeigh die. What does it mean when the rituals of state killing are conflated and enfolded within rituals of mourning and bereavement? In the wake of September 11, 2001, with its massive trauma to the national psyche, we can expect to see the death penalty figure prominently in the politics of grief as executions are argued for and justified as necessary therapies of collective healing and closure.

NOTES

1. These are the last words of Napoleon Beazley, a young African American man, who was executed in Huntsville, Texas, May 28, 2002. His last words are posted on the web site of the Texas Department of Criminal Justice.

2. John Whitley, the warden responsible for directing executions at Louisiana's Angola State Prison, quoted in Ivan Solotaroff, *The Last Face You'll Ever See: The Private Life of the American Death Penalty* (New York: HarperCollins, 2001), 34.

3. There are several excellent books that track this history: Stuart Banner, *The Death Penalty: An American History* (Cambridge: Harvard University Press, 2002); Hugo Bedau, ed., *The Death Penalty in America: Current Controversies* (New York: Oxford University Press, 1997); Jesse L. Jackson, Sr., Jesse Jackson, Jr., and Bruce Shapiro, *Legal Lynching: The Death Penalty and America's Future* (New York: New Press, 2001); Robert Jay Lifton and Greg Mitchell, *Who Owns Death?: Capital Punishment, the American Conscience, and the End of Executions* (New York: Morrow, 2000). See also Thomas Laqueur, "Festival of Punishment," *London Review of Books,* 5 October 2000: 17–24; Gary Wills, "The Dramaturgy of Death," *New York Review of Books,* 21 June 2001: 6–10.

4. The most authoritative source for updated data on the death penalty is the Death Penalty Information Center, Washington, D.C. Their excellent web site address is http://www.deathpenaltyinfo.org/.

5. See especially Banner, *The Death Penalty.*

6. See Mary Douglas, *Purity and Danger* (London: Routledge & Kegan Paul, 1966); Clifford Geertz, *The Interpretation of Cultures* (New York: Basic, 1973); Victor Turner, *The Ritual Process: Structure and Anti-Structure* (Ithaca: Cornell University Press, 1969) and *From Ritual to Theatre: The Human Seriousness of Play* (New York: Performing Arts Journal Publications, 1982); Roy Rappaport, *Ritual and Religion in the Making of Humanity* (Cambridge: Cambridge University Press, 1999). See also Catherine Bell, *Ritual Theory, Ritual Practice* (New York: Oxford University Press, 1992), and *Ritual: Perspectives and Dimensions* (New York: Oxford University Press, 1997). For important studies of political rituals, see Katherine A. Bowie, *Rituals of National Unity: An Anthropology of the State and the Village Scout Movement in Thailand* (New York: Columbia University Press, 1997); David I. Kertzer, *Ritual, Politics, and Power* (New Haven: Yale University Press, 1988); Richard J. Evans, *Rituals of Retribution: Capital Punishment in Germany, 1600–1987* (New York: Oxford University Press, 1996). For a historical case study of execution rituals, see Mark Fearnow, "Theatre for an Angry God: Public Burnings and Hangings in Colonial New York, 1741," *Drama Review* 40, T150 (1996): 15–36.

7. Richard Schechner, *Between Theater and Anthropology* (Philadelphia: University of Pennsylvania Press, 1985), 36–37. See also Schechner's *The Future of Ritual: Writings on Culture and Performance* (New York: Routledge, 1993).

8. For pathfinding analyses of the processual and improvisatory dynamics of ritual see Nicholas B. Dirks, "Ritual and Resistance: Subversion as a Social Fact," in *Culture/Power/History: A Reader in Contemporary Social Theory,* ed. Nicholas B. Dirks, Geoff Eley, and Sherry B. Ortner (Princeton: Princeton University Press, 1994), 483–503; Margaret Thompson Drewal, *Yoruba Ritual: Performers, Play, and Agency* (Bloomington: Indiana University Press, 1992).

9. See also Norbert Elias, *The Civilizing Process: The History of Manners,* trans. Edmund Jephcott (New York: Urizen Books, 1978); John R. Kasson, *Rudeness and Civility: Manners in Nineteenth-Century Urban America* (New York: Hill & Wang, 1990); Lawrence W. Levine, *Highbrow/Lowbrow: The Emergence of Cultural Hierarchy in America* (Cambridge: Harvard University Press, 1988).

10. Theatre historian Peter G. Buckley concurs: "Of all colonial ritual, executions drew the largest crowds." See Peter G. Buckley, "Paratheatricals and Popular Stage Entertainments," in *The Cambridge History of American Theatre* I, ed. Don B. Wilmeth and Christopher Bigsby (Cambridge: Cambridge University Press, 1998), 428.

11. See "Hanging Day" in Banner, *The Death Penalty,* 24–52 and "The Design of Public Executions in the Early American Republic" in Masur, *Rites of Execution,* 25–49. See also Ronald A. Bosco, "Lectures at the Pillory: The Early American Execution Sermon," *American Quarterly* 30 (1978): 156–76; Daniel E. Williams, "'Behold a Tragic Scene Strangely Changed into a Theater of Mercy': The Structure and Significance of Criminal Conversion Narratives in Early New England," *American Quarterly* 38 (1986): 827–47.

12. For important historical studies of Puritan culture, see Daniel A. Cohen, *Pillars of Salt, Monuments of Grace: New England Crime Literature and the Origins of American Popular Culture, 1674–1860* (New York: Oxford University Press, 1993); David D. Hall, *Worlds of Wonder, Days of Judgment: Popular Religious Belief in Early New England* (New York: Knopf, 1989).

13. On "performative metaphors," see James Fernandez, *Persuasions and Performances: The Play of Tropes in Culture* (Bloomington: Indiana University Press, 1986).

14. On "interpretive communities," see Stanley Fish, *Is There a Text in this Class?: The Authority of Interpretive Communities* (Cambridge: Harvard University Press, 1980).

15. For important works on spectatorship see Jill Dolan, *The Feminist Spectator as Critic* (Ann Arbor: University of Michigan Press, 1988); Lisa Merrill, *When Romeo Was a Woman: Charlotte Cushman and Her Circle of Female Spectators* (Ann Arbor: University of Michigan Press, 1999).

16. See Thomas W. Laqueur, "Crowds, Carnival, and the State in Early English Executions, 1604–1868," in *The First Modern Society: Essays in English History in Honour of Lawrence Stone,* ed. A. L. Beier, David Carmadine, James M. Rosenheim (Cambridge: Cambridge University Press, 1989), 305–55.

17. See Karen Halttunen, *Murder Most Foul: The Killer and the American Gothic Imagination* (Cambridge: Harvard University Press, 1998); Leigh B. Bienen, "A Good Murder," in *The Death Penalty in America,* ed. Hugo Bedau (New York: Oxford University Press, 1997), 319–32.

18. Peck opens with an extended "essay on manners" and does not even mention capital punishment until page 292, ten pages into the essay. Peck is much more interested in the everyday performativity of class—manners, deportment, refinement, cultivation of speech and gesture—than he is in the cultural performance of executions. His essay resonates with other elocutionary texts of the period. For a discussion of the class and racial exclusions upon which the elocutionary movement was based, see my "Rethinking Elocution: The Trope of the Talking Book and Other Figures of Speech," *Text and Performance Quarterly* 20 (2000): 325–41.

19. On the massive incarceration campaign and prison building boom, see Elliott Currie, *Crime and Punishment in America* (New York: Metropolitan Books, 1998); Joseph T. Hallinan, *Going Up the River: Travels in a Prison Nation* (New York: Random House, 2001); Marc Mauer and The Sentencing Project, *Race to Incarcerate* (New York: Free Press, 1999); Christian Parenti, *Lockdown America: Police and Prisons in the Age of Crisis* (New York: Verso, 1999).

20. See the Center On Wrongful Convictions web site: http://www.law.north westentedu/depts /clinic /wrongful/ index.htm.

21. Joseph Roach, *Cities of the Dead: Circum-Atlantic Performance* (New York: Columbia University Press, 1996), 36–41; Michael Taussig, *Mimesis and Alterity: A Particular History of the Senses* (New York: Routledge, 1993).

22. The Death Penalty Information Center is a reliable source for demographic data on the death penalty. See also Deborah Fins, *Death Row USA*, Quarterly Report, NAACP Legal Defense and Educational Fund, 2002.

23. Gary Gilmore was executed by a firing squad in Utah in 1977, making his the first post-Furman execution. But because he refused all appeals, he was considered a "volunteer."

24. For an astute historical analysis of the codependent connection between capitalism and capital punishment, see Peter Linebaugh, *The London Hanged: Crime and Civil Society in the Eighteenth Century* (Cambridge: Cambridge University Press, 1992).

25. See http://www.tdcj.state.tx.us/stat/finalmeal.htm

26. See also Victor Streib, "Death Penalty for Lesbians," *National Journal of Sexual Orientation Law* 1(1995): 105–26; Richard Goldstein, "Queer on Death Row," *Village Voice*, March 2001.

27. For studies of the stress and trauma that executions wreak on the prison staff whose job it is to actually carry out this grisly work, see Donald A. Cabana, *Death at Midnight: The Confession of an Executioner* (Boston: Northeastern University Press, 1996); Johnson, *Death Work*, 109–16; Ivan Solotaroff, *The Last Face You'll Ever See: The Private Life of the American Death Penalty* (New York: HarperCollins, 2001).

28. Timothy McVeigh's death certificate listed the cause of death as "Homicide." See "Coroner Prepares to Sign Death Certificate," *Terre Haute Tribune-Star*, 11 June 2001, A6.

29. See Frank Bruni and Jim Yardley, "Inmate is Executed in Texas as 11th-Hour Appeals Fail," *New York Times*, 23 June 2000, A18. See also Amy Dorsett, "Execution Day," *San Antonio Express-News*, 22 June 2000,1A, 8A.

30. For scathing critiques of the hypocrisy of sanitized lethal injection as a modern and humane method, see Lifton and Mitchell, *Who Owns Death?*, 43–69; Sarat, *When the State Kills*, 60–84.

31. For examples of botched lethal injections, see ibid., 65–66. Bungled executions are so commonplace that the Death Pnealty Information Center documents them under the special topic, "Botched Executions." See http://www.deathpenaltyinfo.org /botched .html.

32. Modern executions conflate the three performance paradigms that Jon McKenzie identifies as "the efficacy of cultural performance," "the efficiency of organizational performance," and "the effectiveness of technological performance." See McKenzie, *Perform Or Else,* 27–135.

33. A redacted version of the *Execution Protocol* is posted on the internet at http://www .thesmokingun.com/archive/bopprotocolLshtml.

34. In 1984, Reagan issued an executive order that reinstated the Military Death Penalty.

35. See also James Welsh, "The Medicine that Kills: Lethal Injection for Execution," *Lancet,* 7 February 1998, 441.

36. On victims' rights movement, see Wendy Kaminer, *It's All the Rage: Crime and Culture* (New York: Addison-Wesley, 1995); for critique of the privatization of public discourse, especially the way victims are cast in the role of exemplary citizen, see Lauren Berlant, *The Queen of America Goes to Washington City: Essays on Sex and Citizenship* (Durham: Duke University Press, 1997).

37. See Rick Bragg, "McVeigh Dies for Oklahoma City Blast," *New York Times,* 12 June 2001, Al, A19; Lisa Anderson, "In Oklahoma City, Some Feel Cheated by 'Easy' Death," *Chicago Tribune,* 12 June 2001, 1, 14.

38. For an excellent study of the politics of memory and how this played out in the contested process of planning, designing, and building the Oklahoma City National Memorial Center, see Edward T. Linenthal, *The Unfinished Bombing: Oklahoma City in American Memory* (New York: Oxford University Press, 2001).

39. "The McVeigh Execution," *Chicago Tribune,* 12 June 2001, 14.

REFERENCES

The American Heritage Dictionary of the English Language, 4th ed. 2000. Boston: Houghton Mifflin.

Anderson, Lisa. 2001. "In Oklahoma City, Some Feel Cheated by 'Easy' Death." *Chicago Tribune,* 12 June, 1, 14.

Banner, Stuart. 2002. *The Death Penalty: An American History.* Cambridge: Harvard University Press.

Barish, Jonas. 1981. The *Antitheatrical Prejudice.* Berkeley: University of California Press.

Bedau, Hugo, ed. 1997. *The Death Penalty in America: Current Controversies.* New York: Oxford University Press.

Bell, Catherine. 1997. *Ritual: Perspectives and Dimensions.* New York: Oxford University Press.

Bell, Catherine. 1992. *Ritual Theory, Ritual Practice.* New York: Oxford University Press.

Berlant, Lauren. 1997. *The Queen of America Goes to Washington City: Essays on Sex and Citizenship.* Durham: Duke University Press.

Bessler, John D. 1997. *Death in the Dark: Midnight Executions in America.* Boston: Northeastern University Press.

Bienen, Leigh B. 1997. "A Good Murder." In *The Death Penalty in America,* edited by Hugo Bedau, 319–32. New York: Oxford University Press.

Blaustein, Susan. 1997. "Witness to Another Execution." In *Death Penalty in America,* edited by Hugo Bedau, 387–400. New York: Oxford University Press.

Bosco, Ronald A. 1978. "Lectures at the Pillory: The Early American Execution Sermon." *American Quarterly* 30: 156–76.

Bourdieu, Pierre. 1984. *Distinction: A Social Critique of the Judgment of Taste.* Translated by Richard Nice. Cambridge: Harvard University Press.

Bowie, Katherine A. 1997. *Rituals of National Unity: An Anthropology of the State and the Village Scout Movement in Thailand.* New York: Columbia University Press.

Bragg, Ric. 2001. "McVeigh Dies for Oklahoma City Blast." *New York Times,* 12 June, Al, A19.

Bright, Stephen. 1997. "Counsel for the Poor: The Death Sentence Not for the Worst Crime But for the Worst Lawyer." In *The Death Penalty in America,* edited by Hugo Bedau, 275–309. Oxford and New York: Oxford University Press.

Brownworth, Victoria. 1992. "Dykes on Death Row." *The Advocate,* June, 62–64.

Bruni, Frank and Jim Yardley. 2000. "Inmate is Executed in Texas as 11th-Hour Appeals Fail." *New York Times,* 23 June, A18.

Buckley, Peter G. 1998. "Paratheatricals and Popular Stage Entertainments." In *The Cambridge History of American Theatre,* edited by Don B. Wilmeth and Christopher Bigsby, 424–82. Cambridge: Cambridge University Press.

Cabana, Donald A. 1996. *Death at Midnight: The Confession of an Executioner.* Boston: Northeastern University Press.

Camus, Albert. 1995. *Resistance, Rebellion, and Death.* New York: Vintage.

The Center On Wrongful Convictions. http://www.law.northwestentedu/depts/clinic /wrongful/index.htm.

Cohen, Daniel A. 1993. *Pillars of Salt, Monuments of Grace: New England Crime Literature and the Origins of American Popular Culture, 1674–1860.* New York: Oxford University Press.

Conquergood, Dwight. 2000. "Rethinking Elocution: The Trope of the Talking Book and Other Figures of Speech." *Text and Performance Quarterly* 20: 325–41.

"Coroner Prepares to Sign Death Certificate." 2001. *Terre Haute Tribune-Star,* 11 June, A6.

Currie, Elliott. 1998. *Crime and Punishment in America.* New York: Metropolitan Books.

Danforth, Samuel. 1674. *The Cry of Sodom Enquired Into: Upon Occasion of the Arraignment and Condemnation of Benjamin Goad, For his Prodigious Villany. Together with a Solemn Exhortation to Tremble at Gods Judgements, and to Abandon Youthful Lusts.* Cambridge: printed by Marmaduke Johnson.

Death Penalty Information Center. http://www.deathpenaltyinfo.org.

Dirks, Nicholas B. 1994. "Ritual and Resistance: Subversion as a Social Fact." In *Culture/Power/History: A Reader in Contemporary Social Theory,* edited by Nicholas B. Dirks, Geoff Eley, and Sherry B. Ortner, 483–503. Princeton: Princeton University Press.

Dolan, Jill. 1988. *The Feminist Spectator as Critic.* Ann Arbor: University of Michigan Press.

Doming, Mike. 2001. "Hundreds Will Watch McVeigh Die." *Chicago Tribune,* 13 April, 1, 20.

Dorsett, Amy. 2000. "Execution Day." *San Antonio Express-News,* 22 June, 1A, 8A.

Douglas, Mary. 1982. *In The Active Voice.* London: Routledge & Kegan Paul.

Douglas, Mary. 1966. *Purity and Danger.* London: Routledge & Kegan Paul.

Drewal, Margaret Thompson. 1992. *Yoruba Ritual: Performers, Play, and Agency.* Bloomington: Indiana University Press.

Elias, Norbert. 1978. *The Civilizing Process: The History of Manners.* Translated by Edmund Jephcott. New York: Urizen Books.

Execution Protocol. 1996. http://www.thesmokingun.com/archive/bopprotocolLshtml.

Evans, Richard J. *Rituals of Retribution: Capital Punishment in Germany, 1600–1987.* New York: Oxford University Press.

Fearnow, Mark. 1996. "Theatre for an Angry God: Public Burnings and Hangings in Colonial New York, 1741." *Drama Review* 40: 15–36.

Fernandez, James. 1986. *Persuasions and Performances: The Play of Tropes in Culture.* Bloomington: Indiana University Press.

Fins, Deborah. 2002. *Death Row USA Quarterly Report.* NAACP Legal Defense and Educational Fund.

Fish, Stanley. 1980. *Is There a Text in this Class?: The Authority of Interpretive Communities.* Cambridge: Harvard University Press.

Foucault, Michel. 1979. *Discipline and Punish: The Birth of the Prison.* Translated by Alan Sheridan. New York: Vintage.

Foucault, Michael. 1994. *Power.* Edited by James D. Faubion. New York: New Press.

Godbeer, Richard. 2002. *Sexual Revolution in Early America.* Baltimore: Johns Hopkins University Press.

Geertz, Clifford. 1973. *The Interpretation of Cultures.* New York: Basic, 1973.

Goldstein, Richard. 2001. "Queer on Death Row." *Village Voice,* March.

Hall, David D. 1989. *Worlds of Wonder, Days of Judgment: Popular Religious Belief in Early New England.* New York: Knopf.

Hallinan, Joseph T. 2001. *Going Up the River: Travels in a Prison Nation* (New York: Random House.

Halttunen, Karen. 1998. *Murder Most Foul: The Killer and the American Gothic Imagination.* Cambridge: Harvard University Press.

Jackson, Sr., Jesse L., Jesse Jackson, Jr., and Bruce Shapiro. 2001. *Legal Lynching: The Death Penalty and America's Future.* New York: New Press.

Johnson, Robert. 1998. *Death Work: A Study of the Modern Execution Process,* 2nd ed. Belmont: Wadsworth.

Johnston, David. 2001. "Ashcroft Delays Death of McVeigh Over FBI's Lapse." *New York Times,* 12 May, Al.

Kaminer, Wendy. 1995. *It's All the Rage: Crime and Culture.* New York: Addison-Wesley.

Kasson, John R. 1990. *Rudeness and Civility: Manners in Nineteenth-Century Urban America.* New York: Hill & Wang.

Kertzer, David I. 1988. *Ritual, Politics, and Power.* New Haven: Yale University Press.

Laqueur, Thomas. 1989. "Crowds, Carnival, and the State in Early English Executions, 1604–1868." In *The First Modern Society: Essays in English History in*

Honour of Lawrence Stone, edited by A. L. Beier, David Carmadine and James M. Rosenheim, 305–55. Cambridge: Cambridge University Press.

Laqueur, Thomas. 2000. "Festival of Punishment." *London Review of Books* 5: 17–24.

Levine, Lawrence W. 1988. *Highbrow/Lowbrow: The Emergence of Cultural Hierarchy in America.* Cambridge: Harvard University Press.

Lifton, Robert Jay and Greg Mitchell. 2000. *Who Owns Death?: Capital Punishment, the American Conscience, and the End of Executions.* New York: Morrow.

Linebaugh, Peter. 1992. *The London Hanged: Crime and Civil Society in the Eighteenth Century.* Cambridge: Cambridge University Press.

Linenthal, Edward T. 2001. *The Unfinished Bombing: Oklahoma City in American Memory.* New York: Oxford University Press.

Masur, Louis P. 1989. *Rites of Execution: Capital Punishment and the Transformation of American Culture, 1776–1865.* New York: Oxford University Press.

Mather, Cotton. 1704. *Faithful Warnings to Prevent Fearful Judgments. Uttered in a Brief Discourse, Occasioned, by a Tragical Spectacle, In a Number of Miserables Under a Sentence of Death for Piracy.* Boston: printed and sold by Timothy Green.

Mather, Cotton. 1715. *A Sorrowful Spectacle. In Two Sermons, Occasioned by a Just Sentence of Death, on a Miserable Woman, for the Murder of a Spurious Offspring. The One Declaring, The Evil of an Heart Hardened, under and against all Means of Good. The Other Describing, The Fearful Case of Such as in a Suffering Time, and much more such as in a Dying Hour, are found without the Fear of God.* Boston: printed by T. Fleet & T. Crump.

Mauer, Marc and The Sentencing Project. 1999. *Race to Incarcerate.* New York: Free Press.

McClary, Tonya. 2002. "Sexuality and Capital Punishment: The Execution of Wanda Jean Allen." *Outfront: Amnesty International's Program for Lesbian, Gay, Bisexual, and Transgender Human Rights,* Winter, 1, 4, 6.

McFeely, William S. 2000. *Proximity to Death.* New York: Norton.

McKenzie, Jon. 2001. *Perform Or Else: From Discipline to Performance.* New York: Routledge.

"The McVeigh Execution." 2001. *Chicago Tribune,* 12 June, 14.

Merrill, Lisa. 1999. *When Romeo Was a Woman: Charlotte Cushman and Her Circle of Female Spectators.* Ann Arbor: University of Michigan Press.

Michel, Lou and Dan Herbeck. 2001. *American Terrorist: Timothy McVeigh and the Oklahoma City Bombing.* New York: HarperCollins.

Minnick, Wayne. 1968. "The New England Execution Sermon, 1639–1800." *Speech Monographs* 35: 77–89.

Parenti, Christian. 1999. *Lockdown America: Police and Prisons in the Age of Crisis.* New York: Verso.

Peck, G. W. 1848. "On the Use of Chloroform in Hanging." *American Whig Review* 8: 283–97.

Phelan, Peggy. 1993. *Unmarked: The Politics of Performance.* New York: Routledge.

Powers, Edwin. 1966. *Crime and Punishment in Early Massachusetts, 1620–1692: A Documentary History.* Boston: Beacon.

Rappaport, Roy. 1999. *Ritual and Religion in the Making of Humanity.* Cambridge: Cambridge University Press.

Roach, Joseph. 1996. *Cities of the Dead: Circum-Atlantic Performance.* New York: Columbia University Press.

Rogers, John. 1701. *Death the Certain Wages of Sin to the Impenitent: Life the Sure Reward of Grace to the Penitent: Together with the only Way for Youth To avoid the former, and attain the latter. Delivered in Three Lecture Sermons; Occasioned by the Imprisonment, condemnation and Execution, of a Young Woman, who was guilty of Murdering her infant begotten in Whoredom.* Boston: Printed by B. Green and T. Allen.

Sarat, Austin. 2001. *When the State Kills: Capital Punishment and the American Condition.* Princeton: Princeton University Press.

Schechner, Richard. 1985. *Between Theater and Anthropology.* Philadelphia: University of Pennsylvania Press.

Schechner, Richard. 1993. *The Future of Ritual: Writings on Culture and Performance.* New York: Routledge.

Solotaroff, Ivan. 2001. *The Last Face You'll Ever See: The Private Life of the American Death Penalty.* New York: HarperCollins.

Streib, Victor. 1995. "Death Penalty for Lesbians." *National Journal of Sexual Orientation Law* 1: 105–26.

Taussig, Michael. 1997. *The Magic of the State.* New York: Routledge.

Taussig, Michael. 1993. *Mimesis and Alterity: A Particular History of the Senses.* New York: Routledge.

Texas Department of Criminal Justice. http://www.tdcj.state.tx.us /stat/finalmeal.htm.

Turner, Victor. 1986. *The Anthropology of Performance.* New York: Performing Arts Journal Publications.

Turner, Victor. 1982. *From Ritual to Theatre: The Human Seriousness of Play.* New York: Performing Arts Journal Publications.

Turner, Victor. 1969. *The Ritual Process: Structure and Anti-Structure.* Ithaca: Cornell University Press.

U.S. General Accounting Office. 1997. "Death Penalty Sentencing: Research Indicates Pattern of Racial Disparities." In *The Death Penalty in America,* edited by Hugo Bedau, 268–74. Oxford and New York: Oxford University Press.

Welsh, James. 1998. "The Medicine that Kills: Lethal Injection for Execution." *Lancet* 7: 441.

The White House, Office of the Press Secretary. 2001. *Military Order: Detention, Treatment, and Trial of Certain Non-Citizens in the War Against Terrorism.* 13 November.

Williams, Daniel E. 1986. "'Behold a Tragic Scene Strangely Changed into a Theater of Mercy': The Structure and Significance of Criminal Conversion Narratives in Early New England." *American Quarterly* 38: 827–47.

Williams, John. 1699. *Warnings to the Unclean: In a Discourse from Rev. XXX/. 8. Preacht at Springfield Lecture, August 25th. 1698. At the Execution of Sarah Smith.* Boston: Printed by B. Green and J. Allen.

Wills, Gary. 2001. "The Dramaturgy of Death," *New York Review of Books,* 21 June: 6–10.

Wiseman, Jr., William J. 2001. "Inventing Lethal Injection." *Christian Century,* 20 June, 6.

IV
Critical Responses

Micaela di Leonardo

Dwight Conquergood and Performative Political Economy

Dwight Conquergood has received and will continue to receive wild encomia for his extraordinary contributions—as writer, filmmaker, and teacher—to performance theory and practice. But it is the particularly political-economic nature of his work that I most appreciated, as his colleague and friend, and that I continue to treasure. Dwight's work, I would say, offered us a vision of how to do and how to understand performative political economy.

What do I mean by this phrase? First let's consider the term *political economy,* the eighteenth-century term used to describe the whole-society but economically based analytic writings of Adam Smith, David Ricardo, James Mill, and others. Marx so used the label, and famously envisioned his work turning political economy on its head. He meant that in the sense that the classic political economists assumed a priori that capital preexisted labor—that societies sprung into being whole, with some owning land and/or other wealth, while others owned only their ability to work. Instead, Marx and other socialists assumed that over the course of human history, innately social humans cooperating with one another and acting on the environment in order to maintain and reproduce themselves had created various kinds of economies, with varying levels of private property and wealth, of power and powerlessness.

Nowadays the term *political economy* refers, ironically, to a broad modern-day Marxist analysis that includes the consideration of shifting economies, politics, and states and other institutions. Many scholars add adjectives to indicate the development of interdisciplinary Marxist thought beyond the midcentury ahistorical economic reductionism with which many identify it—"historical political economy" or "culture and political economy" (di Leonardo 1991, 1998; Lancaster and di Leonardo 1997). The late anthropologist William Roseberry articulated the "culture and political economy" vision well: it attempts to "place culture in time, to see a constant interplay between experience and meaning in a context in which both experience and meaning are shaped by inequality and domination," and to understand "the emergence of particular peoples at the conjunction of local and global histories, to place local populations in the larger currents of world history" (49).

This difficult, many-balls-in-the-air kind of cultural and economic analysis is precisely what Dwight's magnificent work—his articles, his films, his teaching—so well instantiated, with the organic addition of the performative lens. Dwight's justly famous article "Life in Big Red," for example, simultaneously analyzes the global, national, and local political-economic forces that brought impoverished people from elsewhere in Chicago and from the global South to one down-at-the-heels neighborhood, how they made ends meet, how they related to one another and inhabited space, and how they and others in Albany Park apprehended their presence and its meanings. Dwight moved seamlessly between the precise demographic, labor, and property history of Albany Park and Chicago (replete with statistics), and deep ethnographic narrative.

These narratives, more often than not, gave us windows onto the contingent, bricolage performances of the urban poor—turning an alley into a *bracero* party site, indoor hallways into sociability havens, an outside courtyard into a safe children's playground, policed ironically by gang members. When the city turned off the building's water because of the absentee landlord's nonpayment, in the midst of a major summer heat wave, Dwight, a participant in the subsequent events, gives us the precise accounting of neighbors'—including adjacent home-owners'—cooperation first to provide some water for households, but finally to dig into the water department's equipment, fashion appropriate tools, and then illegally turn the water back on. In all of these vignettes, we see "the interplay between experience and meaning in a context in which both experience and meaning are shaped by inequality and domination"—and we see that interplay as bodies moving in space, making meaning, and being observed to do so.

Heart Broken in Half, Dwight's ethnographic film on Albany Park, also gives the viewer an excellent sense of contrasting senses of neighborhood, illuminating in particular what he labeled the local "rhetoric of transgression and redevelopment"—the ways in which those whose interests lay with urban growth politics, of which gentrification is the most obvious contemporary example, discursively framed their realities. But in this film he also delves deeply into the life-worlds of kids who are or were members of the local Latin Kings gang. Dwight became so "tight," in their parlance, with these kids that we see them taking him (a heartbreakingly young, healthy Dwight) to their primary graffiti sites, many of them memorializing murdered comrades, and explaining to him exactly the meanings of each symbol and their arrangements together. Dwight's 1997 essay "Street Literacy" simultaneously analyzes the semiotics of the practice and its political-economic context: "This outlawed literacy grotesquely mirrors and mocks the literate bureaucracy that administers licenses, receipts, badges, diplomas, ordinances, arrest warrants, green cards, and other deeds of power and possession" (355).

Dwight leaves us, then, a magnificent legacy—a model for the doing of interdisciplinary performative political economy—for not only its specific skills and methods, but also for its deep, highly political, openhearted engagement with human beings globally who are caught on the losing ends of neoliberal globalization, and who act collectively against their fates. Continuing Dwight's engagement will involve his level of hard work, of commitment. But it especially involves his consistent and fearless ability to see human lives broadly, their connections through the webs of political economy to one another. As E. M. Forster reminded us, Only Connect.

REFERENCES

Conquergood, Dwight. "Life in Big Red: Struggles and Accommodations in a Chicago Polyethnic Tenement." In Louise Lamphere, ed., *Structuring Diversity,* 95–144. Chicago: University of Chicago Press, 1992.

Conquergood, Dwight, and Taggart Siegel. *Heart Broken in Half.* Evanston: Siegel Productions, 1990.

Conquergood, Dwight. "Street Literacy." In James Flood et al., eds., *Handbook of Research on Teaching Literacy Through Communicative and Visual Arts,* 354–75. New York: Simon and Schuster Macmillan, 1997.

di Leonardo, Micaela. "Introduction: Gender, Culture and Political Economy: Feminist Anthropology in Historical Perspective." In Micaela di Leonardo, ed., *Gender at the Crossroads of Knowledge: Feminist Anthropology in the Postmodern Era,* 1–50. Berkeley: University of California Press, 1991.

di Leonardo, Micaela. *Exotics at Home: Anthropologies, Others, American Modernity.* Chicago: University of Chicago Press, 1998.

di Leonardo, Micaela, and Roger Lancaster. "Introduction: Embodied Meanings, Carnal Practices." In Roger Lancaster and Micaela di Leonardo, eds., *The Gender/Sexuality Reader: Culture, History, Political Economy,* 1–12. New York: Routledge, 1997.

Roseberry, William. *Anthropologies and Histories.* New Brunswick: Rutgers University Press, 1990.

Judith Hamera

Response-ability, Vulnerability, and Other(s') Bodies

I am responsible for the other insofar as he is mortal.

—JACQUES DERRIDA, *THE WORK OF MOURNING*

In a tribute to his friend, the late Emmanuel Levinas, Jacques Derrida observed: "Death: not, first of all, annihilation, nonbeing or nothingness, but a certain experience for the survivor of the 'without-response.'"[1] Dwight Conquergood was so articulate, brilliant and bitingly funny, and intellectually and socially generous that even now, years after his death, I am not yet fully resigned to the reality of his nonresponse.

I suspect this arises in part from teaching Dwight's work again and again in course after course. My students seem to actively elicit his responses to their methodological dilemmas, or demand my imagining of his response, or perform their own, or produce some other performative ventriloquism that comfortingly if temporarily defers the finality of postmortem silence. Simply put: Dwight always *seems* to answer back, reminding me that the stages of grief are very like those in the birth of a critical performance ethnographer. Both processes move one from denial-as-fictive-innocence to confrontation with radical vulnerability, radical contingency, and radical alterity.

The persistence of Dwight's (non)response is also intimately tied to the presence/absence oscillations that characterize ethnographic inquiry and performance itself. Whether on stage or in print, performance ethnography demands that we evoke, translate, and hold ourselves accountable to others' bodies: bodies, in all their precious, impossible specificity, that challenge us to analyze the forms of their persistence even as we reckon with their inevitable disappearances. Richard Schechner uses the "not-not" formulation to describe this double consciousness of presence/absence: not simply my body present onstage but also not the absent other's. Not the field on the page but not-not it either. Despite its obvious utility, I'm uncomfortable with this double negative construction, perhaps because syntactically it seems less an assertion of possibility than a double interdiction: no and more no. I prefer the admittedly more cumbersome metaphor of the asymptote, the line a curve approaches but does not cross, in Elizabeth Bishop's words "closing and closing in, but never quite."[2] We can never "fully capture" the field, "accurately" perform the other, "hear" from the dead. Alterity is our absolute limit. But alongside such inevitable "nots" is the imperative to approach, even as we continually identify the material and representational gaps separating us from one another into infinity.

As Dwight so ably demonstrated, negotiating these gaps means avoiding the enthusiast's infatuated insistence that they don't exist and the cynic's refusal to even approach. Negotiating the approach means resisting exhibitionist and entrepreneurial motives. Dwight grounded these ethical obligations in an epistemology privileging the body as a site of knowing: "The same bodily participation is at play whether one moves into the center of a village or inside a text through performance—one is attempting to understand a form of life by learning 'on the pulses,' dwelling within it."[3] "Bodily participation," "life," and "pulses" animated his work, but so did corporeal absences, deaths, and silences. Herbert Blau famously observed that a universal of live performance is watching someone die on stage. This recognition of mortality—*shared* mortality—is no less true of fieldwork: another reason why performance-ethnography is such a potent partnership.

The tribute essay is the paradigmatic genre for wrestling with the messy, painful vexations of presence and absence, alterity and responsibility. Dwight wrote a number of them. What comes through very powerfully in these pieces is the idea that vulnerability—irreducible corporeal vulnerability—is ethical and methodological prerequisite to performance ethnography. Perhaps the reflections on mortality these essays require bring vulnerability to the fore with special clarity. In a tribute to Victor Turner, Dwight writes:

> Performers . . . submit themselves to the gaze of multiple onlookers, offering themselves to the variable apprehensions of audiences. It is a kind of *sparagmos,* dismembering of the body. . . . For performing researchers the body becomes the porous boundary of exchange, the interface.[4]

The image of dismemberment recurs in Dwight's tribute to Wallace Bacon:

> Sacrifice, rending, wounding—opening up the self and turning it outward, inside-out, is, paradoxically, as Bacon understands, a rebirth, a remaking, a coming into being for the self. . . . This breaking and remaking of the self through performative exposure to Others is echoed in Richard Schechner's idea of performance as moving between identities, the Not-Me and Not-Not-Me.[5]

In a *Festschrift* for Hellmut Geissner, he states: "There is an interdependence between Self and Other in the performative view [of ethnography]; both are vulnerable."[6] "Vulnerability," Dwight argues, is "a key to performance hermeneutics."[7]

In Dwight's ethics, the vulnerability of the performance ethnographer impels her to respond to the vulnerability of the other, to structures of marginalization that dismember and wound physically and psychically. These vulnerabilities are often asymmetrical, but corporeality is the interface through which they are communicable, if never fully so. "What I'm writing here," Ghetto Boy told Dwight, "is the heart broken in half."[8] The absent body haunts the tribute and the fieldnote; the writings of a departed friend address exigencies of the moment. The gaps separating our representational efforts, our ears straining to listen and recall, from there/then materialities now gone seem both tantalizingly minuscule and hopelessly insurmountable.

Mourners and performance ethnographers approach others' bodies, present and absent, knowing they can never be fully reached, captured, captioned. We approach these asymptotic dilemmas more precisely and insistently, with more wisdom, bravery, vulnerability, and self-awareness than we otherwise would, because we respond to Dwight. That his work continues to answer back, as if from across the gap that divides us, is both a gift and no surprise.

NOTES

1. Jacques Derrida, *The Work of Mourning,* ed. P. A. Brault and M. Naas (Chicago: University of Chicago Press, 2001), 203.
2. Elizabeth Bishop, "Crusoe in England," *The Complete Poems, 1927–1979* (New York: Farrar, Straus, Giroux, 1984), 162.
3. Dwight Conquergood, "Victor Turner: Experience, Performance, Vulnerability," unpublished manuscript (n.d.), 4.
4. Ibid., 5.

5. Dwight Conquergood. "'A Sense of the Other': Interpreting Texts and Performing Others," unpublished conference paper, Speech Communication Association (Atlanta, GA, 1991), 4.

6. Dwight Conquergood, "Performing Cultures: Ethnography, Epistemology, and Ethics," in *Miteinander sprechen und handeln,*ed. Edith Slembeck (Frankfurt: Scriptor, 1986), 61.

7. "Victor Turner," 5.

8. Dwight Conquergood, "Street Literacy," in *Handbook of Research on Teaching Literacy through the Communicative and Visual Arts,* ed. J. Flood et al. (New York: Macmillan, 1997), 354.

Shannon Jackson

Caravans Continued

In Memory of Dwight Conquergood

At the premature January memorial of Dwight Conquergood—teacher, scholar, activist, performer, foster parent, foster grandparent, godfather, neighbor, and professor of performance studies at Northwestern University—former students and colleagues from around the world gathered to pay tribute. The gathering drew academics of all varieties; it drew theatre directors and actors, community organizers and legal activists. And it drew members of both Dwight's family of origin—his biological siblings—and his adopted Hmong family. The memorial's performance was also eclectic, including gospel singing, poetry recitation, and oratorical tributes that ranged from the staid to the incantatory. It included performances of Zora Neale Hurston, theatrical performances about gang violence, performances of an African funereal lament, and performances of personal memories of Conquergood's exchanges of food, ideas, inspiration, and gossip.

Coming to terms with the disciplinary legacies of what is sometimes erroneously called the "Northwestern" strain of Performance Studies in the United States is, to some degree, about contending with the heterogeneity of that memorial gathering. It indexed a wider network of scholars and practitioners engaged culturally and aesthetically in the communicative dimension of performance. To be so engaged is to take particular interest in performance's oral, embodied, and narrative dimensions, especially as those conceptual concerns have been developed and refracted in the interdisciplinary humanities. To bear witness to his passing was thus also to wonder whether our field could possibly be ready to let go of a person and symbol who so epitomized a disciplinary future. It was to worry, and for many of us to resist, the dumb temporality that would allow his death to push progressive hope into the recent past.

This collection resists that push by remembering the political, intellectual, international, interdisciplinary, and aesthetic combinations that

Dwight Conquergood pursued in his scholarship and in his classroom. I want briefly to touch on a few themes that seem to me to recur again and again in Dwight's work. By the end, you will find me reflecting more broadly upon the significance of his work ethic, particularly as it manifested itself in a daily political practice of human attachment.

1. Instituting Performance Studies: Members of other fields do not always have to do the intense institutional work that those of us in performance studies have to do in order to create a place for our work. Dwight's commitment to that act was visible in almost every essay he wrote and every keynote he gave. At all times, one had the feeling that he was never only speaking for himself but constantly reaching for a meta-language within which all of us could place our efforts and gauge our contributions. Dwight's commitment to that act also took place in the less visible domains of institution-building; in memos written, in curricula defined, in meetings planned and agendas set. To commit institutionally to the discipline of performance studies meant also having to be present, centered, and rhetorically expedient at some difficult moments of growth and transformation. Dwight was there when canons had to be expanded and methods had to be re-thought. And he was also there to argue for a continuity between these curricular shifts and the larger preoccupations of the arts and humanities.

2. Theory and Practice: That sense of continuity manifested itself also in Dwight's commitment to the creation of curricular, artistic, political, and scholarly spheres that unsettled assumed oppositions between theory and practice. This strain of PS began with a tradition of "making a piece" rather than the tradition of "casting a show"; to break with—and I mean with—such a tradition thus propels a slightly different course. In a variety of sites—medical theatres, immigrant parades, Ghanaian storytelling, queer autobiography, and so many more—the interest in the propulsion of embodied narrative animated our practice. The interest in cultivating a centered and indexical mode as a performer, the interest in performances that would allow the voice of another to be heard but never claimed—that pursuit of "speaking with"—animated what we did on our feet as often as it animated what we did in print.

3. Poetics and Politics of the Disenfranchised: To the pursuit of embodied narrative, Dwight incorporated a political imagination: whose narratives were heard, under what conditions, and through what vehicles? It is no secret that Dwight strongly identified with the strain of social science and humanistic thought that did its "history from below." To work with marginal, under-represented, and often undocumented populations was to politicize one's scholarship, but it was also to cultivate

humility and other-directedness. He worried about the danger of cross-cultural theft as much as he argued for the importance of cross-cultural knowledge. He was as adamantly against scholarly appropriation as he was against scholarly cynicism. The impossibility of a fully symmetrical cross-cultural exchange was never an excuse to stop trying.

4. Cultural and Political Economic Analysis: Dwight's commitment to the incorporation of cultural and political economic analysis is probably one of the most rare elements of his profile in performance studies. He called the bluff of PS's interdisciplinarity by incorporating methods from quantitative social sciences. As he rounded up statistics on immigration patterns, on household incomes, on attrition rates in public housing, you could almost feel all the experimental humanities scholars cringing. In a field that liked to measure agency through embodied gesture and that wanted to keep its anthropology "cultural," Dwight's integration of political economic analysis was pathbreaking and sobering. If this former medievalist-turned-ethnographer could use numbers, then we could do it, too.

With qualitative or quantitative, Dwight required of himself and his students a hyper-rigorous work ethic. He was, he constantly told us, "a Calvinist." Doing interdisciplinary work meant doing more work; it was not an excuse for doing less. Doing fieldwork or archival work meant reckoning, unconditionally, with the alteration in one's own habitus as a scholar. It meant sitting all day at a site, waiting for someone to talk to you; it meant slogging through dusty bins in library basements. It did not mean using one example found in one conversation as synecdoche for an entire culture. To experiment in the domain of performative writing meant intensive labor with the arrangement of words and arguments; it did not mean turning in the "meditation," the "notes toward," or—that much abused term—the "riff" to disguise the fact that one hadn't done any work.

The collection of essays in this book represents his wide-ranging research and his particular orientation toward the world. While many of us claim political commitments in our scholarship, his writing is also that of a scholar who gave his rhetorical skills over to the causes of others, to Latin King members, to Hmong refugees, and to death row inmates. In courtrooms, in family gatherings, in civic meetings, in national protests, Dwight served as cultural translator, therapist, booster, and defensive lawyer. Coming to terms with the legacies of Dwight Conquergood is finally to return to that memorial gathering and his network of extended kin. That kinship network is not simply a warm fuzzy sign that Dwight was well-loved but also the result of a self-conscious personal politics.

To become a foster parent, cousin, uncle, or grandparent (legally or unofficially) with the many friends he made, was part and parcel of what it meant for him to live in the world as a progressive activist. Dwight's extension of unconditional love beyond the biological nuclear family derived from the same impulse that extended his unconditional political commitments beyond the university. In recalling his lectures on immigration politics, a story from his adopted family always emerged. In his courses on cultural performance and in his scholarship on border politics, Dwight's critical insights derived from lessons learned in his practices of extended kin-building. Indeed, his participatory fieldwork and his practices of kinship were quite often one and the same. The radicality of that coincidence, the rarity of that coincidence, and the necessity of that coincidence is celebrated by this collection. In this place, in Dwight's place, a queer politics of attachment and kinship coalesced with a transcultural ethic of political engagement; the fusion was unheralded in his scholarship, but it was evidenced in every aspect of his daily life. He worked harder, in more varied ways, on more varied fronts, for more hours of the day than any scholar/teacher/activist/parent/neighbor/artist I know. And it will be the true test of performance studies if, as much as we remember Dwight's commitment to print, we decide to remember Dwight's commitment to action, to embodied practice, to the transformative effects of undocumented acts, and to the affective ties that bind human beings in varied ways, on varied fronts, at all hours of the day.

D. Soyini Madison

"Is Dwight, White?!"
or Black Transgressions and the Preeminent Performance of Whiteness

At one of the many memorial services for Dwight, a beloved African American female student of his, Professor Renee Alexander-Craft,[1] stepped up to the podium and told the story of how she shared with her dearest friends or "sisterhood" a visit with Dwight in the hospital, during his last days. Renee softly and graciously told the audience how she described to her friends (who had never met him) the way cancer had transformed Dwight's body. She then slowly looked up, with a gentle smile, and said one of them suddenly cried out: "You've talked about Dwight all these years—is Dwight, white?!"

I retell Renee's story in this essay because it is both emblematic and ironic as it reflects how Dwight taught, researched, and lived a racial politics that refused placid notions of looking past racial difference but, instead, was always strategically marking difference in the service of racial justice inside the academy, across fieldwork in Asia, the Middle East, and the streets of Chicago as well as prisons and death penalty sites across this nation. For Dwight, the realities of racial identity in all these domains were a serious matter. In the tradition of African American struggle, and as an antiracist activist, Dwight would be considered a "race-man" putting his body on the line in perilous territories at home and abroad and in the vortices of ideological struggles inside and outside the academy. It is ironic that those of us who are racially and often defiantly black, who "when and where we enter our race enters with us,"[2] and who talked about Dwight "all the time," often forgot he was white. While Dwight was always aware of his own white privilege and his status as a white male, it ironically made his racial phenotype rescind under the mighty weight of his racial principles.

In the late 1980s at the University of North Carolina in Chapel Hill, after a riveting presentation of his ethnographic research with Chicago street gangs, an audience member gravely raised his hand: "Please be careful, Dwight. You are very brave, but please be very careful." Other members of the audience nodded their heads in solemn agreement. Later that evening, Dwight and I were walking along my neighborhood in Durham. He remarked on the impenetrably quiet road and the stark blackness of the Carolina night sky, and then he paused and said, "Everyone is so worried about the white man. What about the children, the families, the old and the young people living there every day? Everyone is worried about the white man."

Textual Imperialism and Black Bodies of Meaning

In this brief meditation, I want to reflect upon Dwight's legacy as it pertains to race, specifically the eighteenth- and nineteenth-century elocutionary movement, in the way he employed enslaved black literacies to radically unravel what he called "textual imperialism" (1995, 3). These are instances where black people through risk, threat, and tactics seized a written text, learned and deciphered its words, and then used it against dominating forces for the purposes of liberation. Dwight embraced "theories of the Flesh,"[3] subaltern practices, and contested bodies in motion that unsettled hegemony and elocution's valorized textual paradigms that absented bodies of color. It is through Dwight's critique of textuality or text-centered ways of knowing, that both his contributions and transgressions on race theory and racial justice are arguably most compelling. This was a provocative call to break open the racial hegemony of text-based elocution and its "preeminent performances of whiteness" (2000, 326) by illuminating the liberating impulses of black bodies where words were lifted from writing and performatively set loose in countercultural publics. This was elocution from "below," a subaltern override of normative whiteness that upset certain disciplinary histories by disturbing the racial privileging and the pedagogical relevance of their taken-for-granted foundations. This is provocatively illustrated in Dwight's "resuturing of elocution and oral interpretation into the intertwining disciplinary genealogies of English, speech, theatre, and performance studies" (325). In his classic and controversial essay "Rethinking Elocution: The Trope of the Talking Book and Other Figures of Speech," Dwight states his purpose is "to relocate elocution within a wider sociohistorical context of racial tension and class struggle" (326). He goes on to state that his approach to the elocutionary movement is "from the angle of working-class and enslaved people who were excluded from this bourgeois tradition, disciplined by it, but who nonetheless raided and redeployed it for their own subversive ends" (326).

Dwight's intervention in recasting the history of elocution, in this instance within the frame of black literacy and enslaved performativities, was beautifully set forth in his strategic association of elocution's "superiority of the voice" with that of industrial capitalism's "political economy of the voice" (326). He was ever mindful that elocution was operating under the backdrop of industrial capitalism and chattel slavery whose disciplining characteristics created both the effect and affect of separating "black savagery" from "white civility," as well as the refined, highbred, and ruling cultures of the bourgeoisie elite from the "vulgar," "lowbred," and ruled cultures of the masses (328). What does it mean for Dwight to make the case that the influencing power animating the rules, regulations, and rituals of slavery and capitalism tamed and disciplined the "uncouth" speech of the illiterate poor, the rural, the enslaved, and the working class into the "proper decorum" of elocution? It means that his critique has rejoined class and race back to its more true, troubled, and complicated political history (too often dismissed and ignored) where rules of conduct, the aesthetics of public speech, and the materiality of voice become inseparable from the social-political milieu of industrial capitalism's affective grip in the distribution and disciplining of labor and race in America—slave wages and enslaved persons. For Dwight, human expression, action, and value are always already constituted by history, work, race, and materiality. What does it mean for Dwight to make the case that as elocutionary readings seized the spoken word and the "performative excess" (330) of subaltern speech—written and fenced off by "studied rules, regulations and refinements"—that these same subaltern identities, through their own urgencies and strategies of belonging, reclaimed and rerouted these readings for their own "subversive ends" (326)? It means that Dwight was most interested in small spectacles of subversion. He was interested in how vulnerable spaces and contested locations that were under siege prevailed in grand yet quotidian gestures to rebuild and reinhabit the local and the familial through alternative visions of futurity. He was interested in those spectacular moments when power's ruling hand and death wish were disguised behind the natural order of things only to be exposed—that is, for the curtain of power's violent secrets and cruel hiding places to be lifted by the very victims who were silenced no more.

This is illustrated in Dwight's rethinking of "The Talking Book" and in the black voices of Mary E. Webb, Sella Martin, and Bartley Townsley Extending Henry Louis Gates's notion of the "Talking Book," by moving the black voice from metaphor to "a concrete material practice" (330), Dwight brings Ngũgĩ wa Thiong'o's concept of "orature" forth in breaking through the history of elocution where the "Talking Book" is positioned to "talk back" at the preeminent performance of whiteness and its blank pages. Mary Webb was formally trained in elocution, born of a wealthy Spanish father and escaped enslaved mother. She read from Harriet Beecher Stowe's adaptation of *Uncle Tom's Cabin*, rendered especially for her, and performed in twenty-seven voices before enthusiastic crowds. Dwight demonstrates how Webb broke the rules of white elocutionary expectation as one sole colored woman's body and voice became the voice and body of all those in the audience—white man, woman, and child—as well as the black workers in their fields and the wealthy, landed classes from above. This is significant because blackness is witnessed by white people, in a not-not-me replay, as "acting white," and as being ironically and enthusiastically accepted as white for the sake of performance, in a time of black terror. Dwight shows us how cross-casting is high-stakes and deepened by one lone black woman becoming every white person and then transcending back and forth to every black person in a heteroglossia of racial tension, terror, and fantasy. Dwight suggests the paradox of this virtuosic performance: a black female body showing white people to their racial selves, about their racial selves, within a racial system where they sit in active appreciation, not always knowing what she's thinking or the "signifying codes" that underlie quieter acts of resistance.

Sella Martin, according to Dwight, represents the black counterpublic to Webb's white patronage and protocols of elocution. Sold from his mother at the age of ten, Martin "made up his mind that he would" learn to read and "set about cajoling and tricking the white boys to teach him the alphabet" (333). One day the other slaves tricked him into the woods and demanded that he read about abolitionists, but never having read a newspaper before and out of fear of angering his companions, he began to "fake it." But in the midst of faking it, "to his surprise and delight he began to actually read words." If Webb represented the virtuosic performer before an admiring white audience, Martin represents her contrast. Martin is taken hostage to garner information from the very community to which he belongs. In this example, Dwight has opened the question of racial belonging as it is constituted by performance. Martin's community of companions *made* him read, invoking fakery. If there was a virtuosic performance it must be those black folks, who *made a way out of no way* to set the counter-stage for their own elocutionary purpose. Meaning hides from them inside writing, and their life-blood economies are closed to them; and they know it. Dwight showed us how bringing Martin into the woods to read became a counterpublic elocutionary moment, rich in the history of African American struggle, illuminating the clandestine power of determined black bodies and the purposeful force to know what must be known. Martin formed words because he discovered it was possible, but only through the communal power to hold him accountable, to read aloud for freedom.

Bartley Townsley enacts, according to Dwight, "how enslaved people raided, short-circuited, and rerouted white texts, re-citing them for their own subversive ends" (326). He presents the story of how Townsley recounts a dream of being in a large white room where someone taught him the alphabet on the stark white walls. After the dream, Townsley tried to teach himself how to read and spell, but he came upon a word he did not know. One night, he secretly went through the yard in search of Uncle Jesse who could help him with the word. When he found Uncle Jesse, Townsley said: "I want to know what 'i-n-k' spells." The old man said, "ink." As the story goes, in 1852 he began to learn how to write well enough to write his own passes to steal away (333; E. R. Carter, 112–13). Dwight honors this obscure story by not only highlighting its subversive elements but by also pointing to its metaphorical elegance. He demonstrates the literary brilliance of Townsley's story as a testament to the pervasiveness of whiteness as a looming presence of race and writing that is always under threat of exposure or intrusion by its opposite that is "black as ink." Ink is there, writ large, on the white page as black marks transcend to the voice that writing unleashes.

I will close this essay with Dwight's words to serve as a punctuation point against the tensive histories of preeminent performances of whiteness and innovations of black transgressions: "A strong black voice calling out 'Ink!' to him in the dark of night revealed the blackness that was inside texts all the time, and that he had not been able to recognize in the blinding whiteness of the enclosed room . . . 'Ink!' became the signifyin(g) password that liberated literacy from the 'all white room'" (335).

NOTES

1. Renee Alexander is now an assistant professor of Communication Studies at the University of North Carolina at Chapel Hill. Dwight served as a mentor and adviser. Alexander received her PhD from Northwestern in 2005.

2. Taken from Paul Giddings, *When and Where I Enter: The Impact of Black Women on Race and Sex in America* (New York: Harper, 1996) which she quoted from the black feminist writer Anna Julia Cooper (1858–1964).

3. See Cherríe Moraga and Gloria Anzaldúa, eds., *This Bridge Called My Back: Writings by Radical Women of Color.* New York: Kitchen Table, Women of Color Press, 1983.

BIBLIOGRAPHY

Carter, E. R. 1969. *Our Pulpit Illustrated: Biographical Sketches 1888.* Chicago: African America Press. Quoted in Conquergood, "Rethinking Elocution."

Conquergood, Dwight. 1995. "Beyond the Text: Toward a Performative Cultural Politics." Paper presented at the "Future of the Field" Performance Studies Conference, New York University, March 25.

Conquergood, Dwight. 2000. "Rethinking Elocution: The Trope of the Talking Book and Other Figures of Speech." *Text and Performance Quarterly* (October) 20:325–41.

Lisa Merrill

"Soundscapes of Power"
Attending to Orality, Communicating Class, and Hearing the Humor in Dwight Conquergood's "Voice"

"Voice" is often used as a metaphor for individuality, agency, and point of view. Readers of this collection are fortunate to be introduced to Dwight Conquergood's work through his unique voice that resonates in his writing. Engaging, powerful, and replete with wry wit, Dwight's voice compels readers to consider the ethical dimensions of performance in formal and informal cultural, social, juridical, and academic settings, and, in so doing, to take responsibility for redressing the power imbalances in our world.

Transcending traditional disciplinary boundaries (which Dwight Conquergood identified in racialized and power-inflected terms as "an apartheid of knowledges"), Dwight's work often highlighted the importance of the oral and aural dimensions of performative encounters, particularly the ways oral performances "register and radiate dynamic 'structures of feeling' and pull us into alternate ways of knowing that exceed cognitive control" valorized by dominant and dominating groups.[1] Therefore, in this brief essay, I have chosen to examine the power of Dwight Conquergood's voice by briefly looking at the power of "voice" in his work.

Few embodied behaviors are as indicative of in-group solidarity as the spoken word. In his article "Rethinking Elocution: The Trope of the Talking Book and Other Figures of Speech," Dwight described this as "the common currency" to which poor, illiterate, and enslaved persons had access. Dwight explored the classed and racialized dimensions of "the power of popular speech . . . its unruly embodiments . . . its coarse and uncouth features" in this work.[2] Drawing on the slave narratives of Frederick Douglass, Olaudah Equiano, and James Ukawsaw Gronniosaw, among others, Dwight examined the ways formerly enslaved persons narrated their experiences with the dialogic power and strategic value of reading *aloud* as a specific material practice within racialized contexts; as such, "giving voice" was predicated on gaining access to the literacy originally denied them. In other work, Dwight explored Frederick Douglass's injunction to readers who wanted to understand the horrors of slavery that, instead of reading about it, they listen, in silence, to the grief and sorrow in slaves' songs, so as to "analyze the sounds that shall pass through the chambers of [the listener's] heart."[3]

Whether in his research with Cambodian refugees, inner-city street gang members, or incarcerated persons on death row, Dwight honored oppressed persons' voices. Respecting his own working-class heritage—an identification that he and I shared—Dwight was particularly attuned to and committed to subverting "the soundscapes of power within which the ruling classes typically are listened to while the subordinate classes listen in silence."[4] But Dwight was also committed to examining (and, for those fortunate enough to have known him personally, to exhibiting) what Adriana Caverero has described as the "sonorous materiality"[5] of *actual* embodied voices, particularly in their classed, raced, and gendered dimensions.

In *Orality and Literacy*, Walter J. Ong asserted that "because in its physical constitution as sound, the spoken word proceeds from the human interior" permeating the bodies of listeners "and manifests human beings to one another as conscious interiors, as persons, the spoken word forms human beings into close-knit groups."[6] Passing from one person's body to another's, sounds emanating from what Roland Barthes described as "the grain of one's voice" simultaneously express a speaker's insider status as a member of a given group and animate and create a sense of community among those who listen. Dwight's work highlights such embodied community-building by oppressed persons as well as acknowledges the performative and strategic oral code-switching oppressed persons are often enjoined to perform.

Actual, material voices are ephemeral. Necessarily missing from this collection of Dwight Conquergood's essays is Dwight's *actual* voice; its cadences, timbre, and resonance; his deft performances of irony, communicated through precise and subtle shifts in intonation, and his trickster's pleasure in mimicry; all of which he deployed so masterfully in person. It is that I miss the most. Those privileged to have met Dwight and heard him speak encountered those dimensions of his work. But readers of this text *can* recognize, along with the powerful arguments in Dwight Conquergood's essays, what Walter J. Ong has identified as "the heavy oral residue" of voice present in literary texts in the forms of formulary structures, antithesis, balance, and alliteration, and so readers may experience those aspects of Dwight's voice in this medium as well.[7]

Dwight's love of alliteration and pleasure in puns is evident in much of his written work. Valuing orality over the visual, in his definitional essay on the field of Performance Studies Dwight forces us to question "the ocular politics that links the power to see, to search, and to seize." Rather than privileging formal "textocentric" models of knowing (that disadvantage subaltern persons) over embodied modes of expression, Dwight encourages readers to struggle to "live betwixt and between theory and theatricality, paradigms and practices, critical reflection and creative accomplishment." And perhaps most famously, in the same essay, Dwight provides readers with such alliterative tools with which to engage in the politics of performance studies research as *both* the "three *a*'s" of "artistry, analysis, activism" and the "three *c*'s" of "creativity, critique, citizenship (civic struggles for social justice)."[8]

Furthermore, in the earlier essay "Street Literacy," Dwight explicates the use of puns and visual-verbal play by street gangs. Dwight notes, "the pleasure of punning is its rough-house creativity . . . a play between written and verbal forms of language" that "trick" or "startle . . . the reader or audience into participatory play with meanings."[9] Dwight Conquergood loved to play; trickster-like, he artfully startled others into seeing the need to participate in changing the world along with him, from the bottom up. His humility, generosity of spirit, and gripping commitment to redress inequality are features in all of his written work. But his wicked, raucous, winking sense of humor and animated pleasure of engagement with others also shine through his writing, if you listen.

NOTES

1. Dwight Conquergood, "Performance Studies: Interventions and Radical Research," *Drama Review* 46, no. 2 (Summer 2002): 149.
2. Dwight Conquergood, "Rethinking Elocution: The Trope of the Talking Book and Other Figures of Speech," *Text and Performance Quarterly* 20, no. 4 (October 2000): 327.
3. Dwight Conquergood, "Performance Studies: Interventions and Radical Research," *Drama Review* 46, no. 2 (Summer 2002): 149.
4. Dwight Conquergood, "Performance Studies: Interventions and Radical Research," *Drama Review* 46, no. 2 (Summer 2002): 149.
5. Adriana Caverero, *For More Than One Voice: Toward a Philosophy of Vocal Expression,* trans. Paul A. Kottman (Stanford: Stanford University Press, 2005), 1. Cited in Liz Mills, "When the Voice Itself Is Image," *Modern Drama* 52, no. 2 (Winter 2009): 393.
6. Walter J. Ong, *Orality and Literacy* (London: Routledge, 1982), 74.

7. Ong, *Orality and Literacy* (London: Routledge, 1982), 115.

8. Dwight Conquergood, "Performance Studies: Interventions and Radical Research," *Drama Review* 46, no. 2 (Summer 2002): 151–52.

9. Dwight Conquergood, "Street Literacy," in *Handbook of Research on Teaching Literacy through Communicative and Visual Arts*, ed. J. Flood et al. (New York: Simon and Schuster Macmillan, 1997), 371.

Della Pollock

Performance into Policy

Dwight gained some renown for being out of place. To turn one of his preferred phrases: he *mattered* out of place.[1] He moved into Big Red, one of the Chicago tenements where many of the gang members with whom he worked for many subsequent years as an ethnographic co-subject lived. He'd giddily relay slipping the Thai refugee camp cops by hiding out with the lepers after 5—the hour at which his daily research permit expired.[2] During the mid-eighties, he allied with Palestinian settlers on the Gaza Strip when it was still under Israeli military occupation. Dwight had a way of *being there;* the borders he crossed and the locations out of which he made uncanny homes are the stuff of legend. But what seems to fall off the map that was, as he always reminded us, following de Certeau, "cut across" by stories, were the many performative doings embodied in negative space:[3] the legal advocacy he performed for Hmong refugees; the respect he paid in grief and consolation for so many gang-related deaths; the coaching and cheering and care he offered kids affiliated with the Albany Park youth theatre project; the weekends spent standing in protest of the death penalty; even his own shamanistic encounters and final, hospital ethnographics.

I was often beguiled by the apparent thereness of Dwight's disappearances and reappearances (the perverse magic of which was enhanced by lack of a car, much less a license to drive one). Now I wonder whether many of us weren't caught out by this sleight of hand. Trickster ever, Dwight seemed to cover his tracks by the textuality of location—even as, as Zora Neale Hurston observed (by Dwight's own reckoning),[4] the subaltern tricked out the white man by placing an enticing artifact at the gate: something solid and mysterious to be removed for textual decoding. And while those at the curtain's edge watch the scholar steal away with his precious *thing,* they cannot help but laugh at how easily distracted he is. He has missed the boat by looking too hard at the sign on the shore.

And so, in the cartography-cum-hagiography of Big Red/Gaza Strip/ refugee camp, we may also have participated in a self-deluding reification of place at the expense of the tactical maneuvers, practices of co-witness, and kinetic re-fashioning of social relation in/as space that defined Dwight's relationship to place and so completely displaced anything like a foundational thereness on which the ocularcentrism of eyewitness depends. *I was there and so it is true.* I came, *I saw,* I conquered. What Dwight embodied in differential time and space was *doing* beyond the I/eye—often thus slipping the gaze of even his most devoted readers. For many of his students, Dwight's most important words were in margins, on a frontispiece, or held in suspense over the threshold of his office door. Here the stage whisper of truly artful gossip, the surging words of a conversation that just won't end, the final press of encouragement to do more and better *happened.* Nothing finished, everything as if in advent: this crossing-place was a kind of no-where of partiality. From it flowed a political performative imaginary in which everything was intriguing, possible, and incomplete. Everything was in the doing; nothing was ever done. Thrilling in the moment, the utopic drive Dwight exemplified and encouraged pushed physical and material limits, sometimes to the point of exhaustion, sometimes exceeding itself in unimaginable material outcomes.

One of the latter occurred the night of June 20, 2011, when the Town Council in my university town issued a temporary moratorium on new construction in a loose group of neighborhoods in which I have been working since the mid-2000s. This may seem a minor accomplishment except that: (1) For many of the people whose families had lived in these neighborhoods under and since Jim Crow, this was the first or second time any had attended a council meeting (the first being when the initial petition was presented); by attending, they lifted the veil on Town Hall and fundamentally changed its contours of witness. (2) In the last three to five years, gentrification has threatened to decimate not just this place but the much broader communities of work, worship, and play that make it a tightly networked space of African-American affiliation. And (3) until it saw a ten-story gold-LEED certified, mixed-use, high density/low impact—or what should have been the liberal vision of urban renewal perfectly materialized—start to sputter and spit, the council had dismissed most claims for sustenance of "the Northside" as at best nostalgic (apparently looking back to the glory days of segregation). As the numbers of black residents rapidly decreased, so did their literal staying power. The story is common across the United States: emplacement by white economic supremacy becomes displacement by white economic supremacy becomes disappearance of the cog in the wheel of "progress." In the end, the council expedited passage of the moratorium because, while they deliberated, a bill banning bans on development was sitting expectantly on the state's ("liberal") governor's desk. It could have been signed into law at any moment—and was, only a matter of hours later.

I watched the video recording of the town hearing in Nairobi. I was in Kenya as part of a collaborative fieldwork team intent on listening to oral histories of land loss and so-called resettlement in the Coast Province, where government support for development of a Canadian titanium mining company had exiled hundreds of people from ancestral lands. I was in awe.[5] The fact of digital access brought the doubled locales—the Kenyan Coast Province and the Northside of Chapel Hill, North Carolina—into resonance and radical dissonance. By just about any measure of poverty and infrastructural support, the two places (and places and spaces within places) couldn't be more different. Their overlay in virtual space, however, confused historical and cultural specificities, for the moment bringing into hyper-focus the irredeemable promise of modern development bedeviling both. Far away, watching back: I could see the global drama of capital reproduction playing itself out on the backs of poor folks one more time—this time, however, with a comic twist.

I thought of Dwight, of course. Or, more accurately, he claimed my thoughts. Five years of various, persistent, and consistently unpredictable performativities in Chapel Hill—including festival, worship, fellowship, rites, co-labor, co-witness, coalition, protest, organization and listening, listening again, then listening again and listening out loud[6]—had suddenly spun out into a domino-relay of "aye" "aye" "aye" to a short (six-month) halt to local bulldozing. The strange complementarity of centripetal and centrifugal performance energy flows Dwight repeatedly emphasized had, for a startling moment, whipped place, no-place, and dissed place into an at least temporarily open space of reflexivity and re-vision. With this transformative moment—its story-in-the-making already not only cutting across a map that conventionally divides "developed" and "developing" worlds but also cutting up the macro-narrative of faux-liberal progress that contains both—the harder work of creating new, secure, and somehow equitable policy began. Will there be more stories? Absolutely. To what place *out of place* (that of "outside agitators," naïveté, nostalgia, special interest, righteousness?) will they be consigned? Who knows. Will it ever be done? Not likely. Should or could it be? Ask Dwight.

NOTES

1. From Mary Douglas, *Purity and Danger* (Routledge and Kegan Paul, 1978).

2. See Conquergood, "Health Theatre in a Hmong Refugee Camp: Performance, Communication, Culture," *TDR* 32, no. 3 (1988): 174–208.

3. Michel de Certeau, *The Practice of Everyday Life,* trans. Steven Rendell (Berkeley: University of California Press, 1984), 129.

4. See Conquergood reflecting on Zora Neale Hurston, *Mules and Men* (New York: Harper, 1935/1990), 3, in "Performance Studies: Interventions and Radical Research," *TDR* 46, no. 2 (2002): 145–56.

5. I was as overwhelmed by the proceedings and the mineral trace of sublimity they seemed to manifest as by the eloquent leadership of associates at the Marian Cheek Jackson Center for Saving and Making History, Hudson Vaughan, Aleck Stephens, C. J. Suitt, Chelsea Alston, and Rob Stephens. See www.jacksoncenter.info.

6. See Pollock, "Memory, Remembering, and Histories of Change: A Performance Praxis," *Sage Handbook of Performance Studies,* ed. Judith Hamera and Soyini Madison (Thousand Oaks, CA: Sage, 2005), 87–105.

Joseph Roach

Eloquence and Vocation

Dwight's Calling

Dwight Conquergood's career-long commitment to people with hyphenated identities began with Anglo-Saxons. He wrote his dissertation as a medievalist, exploring the literary remains of a primordial speech act—the boast. He submitted "The Anglo-Saxon Boast: Structure and Function" to the School of Speech at Northwestern in August 1977 after accepting his first job, in the English department at the State University of New York at Binghamton. His scholarship on *Beowulf,* the Old English poem about the epic deeds of a Norse warrior-hero, and *The Battle of Maldon,* the verse record of a Saxon defeat by the Vikings in 991 CE during the unfortunate reign of Aethelred the Unready, qualified him as a respectable exegete of Old English, a West Germanic language closely related to Old Frisian. Fully inflected, with five grammatical cases—nominative, accusative, genitive, dative, and instrumental—Old English is a foreign language to readers of modern English or even Middle English. Many of the translations in the dissertation are Dwight's own,[1] and the oral-formulaic *gilpwide,* or "boast speech," gave him expansive opportunities to demonstrate his linguistic mastery, philological learning, and trans-cultural imagination.

"The Anglo-Saxon Boast" is Dwight's only completed book-length work of scholarship until now. Like many scholars trained as medievalists, he made his reputation by publishing a series of influential articles, a number of which are collected here. He consolidated his reputation by publishing an edition with learned commentary, namely, *I Am a Shaman: A Hmong Life Story with Ethnographic Commentary* (1989). Like many scholars trained as medievalists, he was an ethnolinguist or ethnographer at heart, attuned to language as the culturally expressive behavior of other peoples, made strange by time or intercultural distance, then increasingly familiar by sustained close reading or deep listening. By returning to his 221-page dissertation, in which he had the scope to follow an unbroken arc of thinking about culture and performance, I intend to reflect on his vocation. By *vocation* I mean something like his *voice*, in several meanings of that word. As distinctively particular to each of us as our eyes, the physical voice is the capacity to produce sound by action of the lungs, larynx, and resonators that is shared by all vertebrates. But voice is also what lucky poets find when they become most unlike other poets. That latter voice is cognate to *invocation, evocation,* and most urgently, *vocation.* Voice is thus a call, drawing people together, and a calling, drawing them individually along their chosen or fated paths. In a certain sense, vocation is the life that chooses them, not the life they choose. "Shamanism," Dwight writes, in a passage I believe to be in some measure autobiographical, "is a *vocation* in the true sense of 'calling.' An individual does not decide to become a shaman as a career choice."[2] Dwight was called to the study of promissory speech acts (of which the Anglo-Saxon boast is a particularly vivid example), and in those acts, I believe, he found his voice—as a scholar, thinker, and compassionate activist—even as his vocation found him.

The Oral Interpretation of Literature, as Performance Studies at Northwestern University was once known, was the founding department of the School of Oratory, circa 1868, which later became the School of Speech, now Communication. Under any of those names, it ought to have been (and ought to be) a good place to go to find a voice, and so it proved for Dwight. The ties between literature and speech were still close when Dwight arrived in Evanston in 1974. Dwight's dissertation adviser was Wallace Bacon, long-time chair of Oral Interpretation, who wrote his own dissertation ("Shakespeare's Dramatic Romances") in English literature at the University of Michigan. Dwight's committee included Catharine Regan, an Anglo-Saxonist in Northwestern's English department. Rather than publishing their interpretations of poems and other literary works in the form of books and articles, however, the Northwestern Interpretation faculty performed them out loud—*viva voce,* as it were, or with "the living voice"—in their office-studios, fitted with lecterns for that purpose, and on auditorium stages, for the better edification of interdisciplinary listeners. While their colleagues in English literature located across the courtyard in University Hall performed on the pages of *PMLA* and *Tri-Quarterly,* the oral interpreters gave recitals.[3] In an unpublished address to the Speech Association of America in 1949, Wallace Bacon boldly projected the nascent field of Oral Interpretation as a future nodal point among the arts and human sciences, claiming parity with their learning and hermeneutical rigor: "Interpretation is allied as closely to areas outside of speech as it is to areas within the confines of a speech department: to English, to foreign languages, to philosophy, to aesthetics, to psychology, and even to such apparently remote fields as history and anthropology."[4] Here Dwight, looking back, assessing the progress of the department as it built upon interdisciplinary strength to become performance studies, might have said of his self-assertive mentor what the poetic speaker says of Hrothgar in the early going of *Beowulf*: "He beot ne alek," or "He did not fail to fulfill his boast" ("The Anglo-Saxon Boast," 2): for the *beot* or *gilp* is a promise to be kept, or as Dwight defined it, "the narrative assertion of identity as a pledge to future action" (19). The speaker says, "I am" as the guarantor of "I will."

In Chapter Two, "Toward a Theory of the Boast," Dwight, having defined what the boast *is* (structure), goes on to explain what it *does* (function). The boast functions: "1) to constitute the self-hood of the speaker; 2) to commit and bind the speaker to a course of action, way of life; 3) to help the speaker cope with uncertainty and the terror of failure; and 4) to reinforce and perpetuate community values in a rhetorically compelling manner" (36). In the words of this apparently prosaic passage, I hear the heart of Dwight's lifelong philosophy, as well as the thrilling strength of his speaking voice. I also hear the iteration of a promise that commits the speaker to a course of action, "a way of life," that begins with self-knowledge and culminates in the assertion of a community summoned together by eloquence. His citation of modern examples, updating the Anglo-Saxon boast, brings home the power of his ideas: Helen Reddy's "I am Woman [hear me roar]" and Dr. Martin Luther King Jr.'s "We Shall Overcome" (42, 45). Dwight cautions that the boast is a promise for action in the future that can still retain its truth even if its fulfillment in the present remains incomplete. As of this writing, not all of us have overcome. "So it is," Dwight sums up, "that the *truth* of a boast must be understood in the sense of *troth*" (44), which means, despite "uncertainty" and "the terror of failure," despite the disappointment of shifting allegiances and the pain of conflicting values (not to speak of the caprice of mortality), one is troth-plighted to do one's level best.

He beot ne alek.

NOTES

1. Lorne Dwight Conquergood, "The Anglo-Saxon Boast: Structure and Function," PhD diss., Northwestern University, 1977, 2 note 1. Subsequent references parenthetical.

2. Dwight Conquergood, Paja Tao, and Xa Thao, *I Am a Shaman: A Hmong Life Story with Ethnographic Commentary* (Minneapolis: Southeast Asian Refugee Studies Project, Center for Urban and Regional Affairs, 1989), 47.

3. Joseph Roach, "Viva Voce: The Efficacy of Oral Interpretation," *Yale Review* 99, no. 4 (2011): 108–18.

4. "Graduate Studies in Interpretation," Wallace Bacon Papers, Northwestern University Archives, Box 22, Folder 7.

Contributors

E. Patrick Johnson is the Carlos Montezuma Professor of Performance Studies and African-American Studies at Northwestern University. He is also an Artistic Fellow at the Ellen Stone Belic Institute for the Study of Women and Gender in the Arts and Media at Columbia College, Chicago. A scholar, artist, and activist, Johnson has performed nationally and internationally and has published widely in the area of race, gender, sexuality, and performance. He is the author of *Appropriating Blackness: Performance and the Politics of Authenticity* (2003) and *Sweet Tea: Black Gay Men of the South—An Oral History* (2008). He is the co-editor with Mae G. Henderson of *Black Queer Studies: A Critical Anthology* (2005), and with Ramón H. Rivera Servera of *solo/black/woman: scripts, interviews, and essays* (2013).

Micaela di Leonardo is Professor of Anthropology and Performance Studies at Northwestern University. She has written *The Varieties of Ethnic Experience* (Cornell, 1984), and *Exotics at Home: Anthropologies, Others, American Modernity* (Chicago, 1998), edited *Gender at the Crossroads of Knowledge: Feminist Anthropology in the Postmodern Era* (California, 1991), and co-edited *The Gender/Sexuality Reader* (Routledge, 1997) and *New Landscapes of Inequality: Neoliberalism and the Erosion of American Democracy* (SAR, 2008). She misses Dwight terribly.

Shannon Jackson is the Richard and Rhoda Goldman Distinguished Professor in the Arts and Humanities at the University of California at Berkeley. Her areas of research include performance theory; contemporary visual and performance art; American studies; sex/gender/race studies; history of disciplines; solo performance; new media theatre. She is the author of *Lines of Activity: Performance, Historiography, Hull-House Domesticity* (2000), *Professing Performance: Theatre in the Academy from Philology to Performativity* (2004), and *Social Works: Performing Art, Supporting Publics* (2011).

Judith Hamera is Professor of Performance Studies at Texas A&M University. Her scholarship contributes to American, communication, and cultural studies, as well as performance, theatre, and dance studies. Her books include *Parlor Ponds: The Cultural Lives of the American Home Aquarium, 1870–1970* (2012); *The Cambridge Companion to American Travel Writing* (2009), with Alfred Bendixen; *Dancing Communities: Performance, Difference and Connection in the Global City* (Studies in International Performance: Palgrave Macmillan, 2007/2011); *Opening Acts: Performance In/As Communication and Cultural Studies* (Sage, 2006); and the *Sage Handbook of Performance Studies*, co-edited with D. Soyini Madison (2006). Her essays have appeared in *Com-*

munication and Critical/Cultural Studies, Cultural Studies, TDR: The Drama Review, Modern Drama, Text and Performance Quarterly, Theatre Topics, and *Women and Language.*

D. Soyini Madison is Professor and Chair in the Department of Performance Studies and Professor of Anthropology, African American Studies, and the Program of African Studies at Northwestern University. She is the author of *Acts of Activism: Human Rights as Radical Performance* (2010) and *Critical Ethnography: Methods, Ethics, and Performance* (2005); editor of *The Woman That I Am: The Literature and Culture of Contemporary Women of Color* (1995); and co-editor with Judith Hamera of *The Sage Handbook of Performance Studies* (2006) and with Karen Hansen of *African Dress: Fashion, Agency, Performance* (2013).

Lisa Merrill is Professor of Communication, Rhetoric & Performance Studies, at Hofstra University. Professor Merrill's ongoing research and publications are in the fields of performance studies, American studies, critical race and cultural studies, and women's and gay and lesbian history. She has published widely on the performance of gender, race, and sexuality in historical and contemporary cultural settings. Professor Merrill's critical biography of nineteenth-century actress Charlotte Cushman, *When Romeo was a Woman: Charlotte Cushman and Her Circle of Female Spectators* (University of Michigan Press), received the 2000 Joe A. Callaway Prize for Best Book in Theatre or Drama.

Della Pollock is Professor in Communication Studies at the University of North Carolina at Chapel Hill and Executive Director of the Jackson Center for Saving and Making History. She is the author of *Telling Bodies Performing Birth,* editor of *Remembering: Oral History Performance* and *Exceptional Spaces: Essays in Performance and History,* and co-editor of the journal *Cultural Studies.*

Joseph Roach is the Sterling Professor of Theatre and English at Yale University. He is the author of *The Player's Passion: Studies in the Science of Acting* (1985), *Cities of the Dead: Circum-Atlantic Performance* (1996), and *It* (2007). He is the editor (with Janelle Reinelt) of *Critical Theory and Performance* (2nd edition, revised 2007) and *Changing the Subject: Marvin Carlson and Theatre Studies, 1959–2009* (2009). He is the recipient of a Lifetime Distinguished Scholar Award from the American Society for Theatre Research and a Distinguished Achievement Award from the Andrew W. Mellon Foundation, which funds the World Performance Project at Yale. In 2009, he was awarded an honorary Doctor of Letters from the University of Warwick (UK) and the Fletcher Jones Distinguished Fellowship from the Huntington Library.

Index